I0792750

O'Neil Ford Monograph 4: Banco de Londres y América del Sud

Buenos Aires 1959–1966

SEPRA and Clorindo Testa

The O'Neil Ford Monograph Series, Volume 4
– Banco de Londres y América del Sud
SEPRA and Clorindo Testa
THE UNIVERSITY OF TEXAS AT AUSTIN
Center for American Architecture and Design
O'Neil Ford Chair in Architecture

Editors
Manuel Cuadra and Wilfried Wang

Essays
Jorge Francisco Liernur
Manuel Cuadra
Wilfried Wang

Translations
Louise Mereles
Jorge Villota Peña
Ilan Vit

Series Editors
Kevin Alter
Michael Benedikt
Barbara Hoidn
Wilfried Wang

Associate Editors
Barbara Terrell
Tyler Collins

Production Editors
Susan McNally
Leora Visotzky

Typographic Design
Tyler Collins

Cover Photograph
Wilfried Wang

Printed and bound in Canada

Sole Distributor in Europe:
Ernst Wasmuth Verlag GmbH & Co.
D-72072 Tübingen, Germany
www.wasmuth-verlag.de
info@wasmuth-verlag.de

ISBN 978-3-8030-0740-7

Sole Distributor in the United States of America and Canada:
D.A.P. / Distributed Art Publishers
155 Sixth Avenue, 2nd Floor
New York, New York 10013, U.S.A.
Tel. (212) 627-1999, Fax. (212) 67-9484

Contents

4	Acknowledgments	
6	Autonomy and Engagement	Wilfried Wang
14	Polysemy: Rereading the Readings of BLAS	Jorge Francisco Liernur
28	Fictions and Realities in Clorindo Testa's Work	Manuel Cuadra
40	Sketches	
46	Competition and Executive Drawings	
182	Historic and Contemporary Photographs	
230	50 years later: a conversation with Clorindo Testa	
240	Selected Bibliography	
247	Project Credits and Chronology	
248	Biographies	
251	Photo Credits	

Acknowledgments

The research for this publication was extensive both in terms of time and space. Thanks to contemporary communication systems, it was possible to coordinate a team that was at times spread from Argentina, the USA, Spain and Germany.

This Monograph has its origin in Manuel Cuadra's book, *Clorindo Testa Architect*, of 2000, the first comprehensive study of the varied work of the painter and architect Clorindo Testa. It led to the fruitful collaboration between Manuel Cuadra and the editors of the O'Neil Ford Monograph Series, the result of which is a double-sized Monograph on this one building of the Bank.

We would like to thank our collaborators in Argentina, at the head Prof. Jorge Francisco Liernur, whose unrivalled knowledge not only of the architecture of Argentina, but of the history of modern architecture altogether, resulted in memorable meetings in Buenos Aires and a fruitful seminar on the significance of the Banco de Londres y América del Sud in 2010 at the Universidad Torcuato Di Tella.

Through our Spanish connection at the Universidad de Navarra, Pamplona, it was Federico Pastorino (contributor to O'NFD_3: Argentina) who introduced us to Carolina Kogan, PhD candidate at the Universidad Torcuato Di Tella, whose patient persistence was crowned by the trove of documents that could be found in numerous archives for this Monograph. Together with the help of colleagues at the archives, at the Banco Hipotecario, the successor offices of SEPRA and the office of Clorindo Testa, we were able to gather all the documents to cover the different design phases. A large selection of the key documents is included in this publication.

We would like to thank the directors of the Banco Hipotecario for granting us access to their archives and for permitting us to reproduce the selected documents, as well as the architects at the Bank, Carolina Garmendia and Verónica Luzarreta, for making available the original set of construction drawings. Equally, we are thankful to the office of Sánchez Elía – SEPRA, and there especially to Gregorio de Laferrere, for making available the original set of construction drawings for the Banco and for allowing us to publish these. We are deeply indebted to Clorindo Testa, whose calm generosity and warm welcome made us feel part of the creative team. Our thanks also go to Juan Fontana, office partner of Clorindo Testa and also painter, who impressed us by his knowledge of where all the various documents were and who gave us the key to finding the rest of the extant drawings.

Finally, we are grateful to Gustavo Sosa Pinilla, who took a set of new photographs, our translators Louise Mereles, Jorge Villota Peña and Ilan Vit for undertaking the arduous tasks of rendering the essays readable in English and for our colleagues at the School of Architecture, particularly Leora Visotzky, whose quick immersion in the complex tasks went smoothly. Tyler Collins deserves our deepest gratitude for his patience and precision in co-editing and designing not only this Monograph, but also the parallel publication of the Duograph on México.

Essays

Autonomy and Engagement

Wilfried Wang

Great Expectations

"Architecture arouses sentiments in people. Therefore the architect's task is to make these sentiments more precise. The room has to be comfortable; the house has to look habitable. The law courts must appear as a threatening gesture towards secret vice. The bank has to say: here your money is secure and well looked after by honest people."

Adolf Loos, "Architecture" (1910), in *Trotzdem 1900-1930*, Vienna 1931, p. 109 (transl. by author)

The public expectations of a bank, both in its professional behavior and in its appearance, from its physical presence to the way its employees carry themselves, could be said to form a corset that guarantees the institution an air of conservatism. Banks seek to affirm solidity and tradition. In the realm of architecture, this corset of public expectations, or cultural discipline, vis-à-vis banks has secured Neo-Classical syntax and semantics a widely accepted place. The bank with a pediment and stone portico on the outside and a tall hall for transactions on the inside has the key architectural elements of such a tradition. In financial districts all over the world, established banks that have survived to this day are not surprisingly fashioned in this manner.

For the large number of banks founded in the 19th century in Argentina, this affirmation in the Neo-Classical syntax and semantics was de rigueur, an affirmation that simultaneously connected public expectations with the Spanish and Italian roots of the Porteños (the natives of Buenos Aires). Thus in Buenos Aires' financial district there is one representative bank headquarters next to another. Giant orders, whether merely applied as pilasters or rendered fully three dimensional, abound. In the largest realization of this kind, the Banco de la Nación Argentina (the largest bank in Argentina, owned by the state, but not Argentina's Central Bank, which is the Banco Central de la República Argentina, located just north of the Banco de Londres y América del Sud), occupies an entire urban block and is wrapped in a subtle articulation of Ionic pilasters and a stone clad wall with framed openings. It is situated diagonally across from the Governor's Palace. Besides tall windows and doorways, there are arched niches, all of which help to articulate the building's large perimeter and hence surfaces of walls enshrouding the institution. Like Sir John Soane's Bank of England in London (1788-1833, Britain's central bank), the impenetrable nature of a central bank was counterpoised by the inventive application of articulating elements: rusticated bases, recessed bays, giant orders both as semi-engaged columns or even as colonnades, projecting corner bays, porticoes.

Beyond the protective envelope of the Banco de la Nación Argentina, a vast hall covered with a steel and glass cupola can be found at the core of the block. Here, the bank is a defensive pallazzo, shrouding the assets from marauding assailants, a true phenomenon seen in the immediate aftermath of Argentina's catastrophic financial crisis of 2001. The assaults on the banks with bare hands, pots and pans, left their permanent marks. Ad hoc protective structures were erected, some of which have been retained just in case there is another crisis. The banks' once assertive and affirmative poise has thus been put into question by the real attitude of the nation's financial institutions, including the banks' own mismanagement: short-termism, loose lending regimes and rampant speculation disguised by complex "products".

Changing Clients and Owners' Interests

The precursor of the Banco de Londres y América del Sud was the "London, Buenos Ayres and River Plate Bank" (sic) of London, founded there in 1862. The first branch was opened in Buenos Aires in 1863 on the corner of Piedad and Florida. Three years later a site was bought on the corner of Reconquista and Bartolomé Mitre, on which a new building was completed in 1869 to the design of Hunt y Schroeder, encompassing a grand steel and glass banking hall at its center. The bank was merged with the Banco de Londres y Brasil in 1923 and renamed Banco de Londres y América del Sud.

In 1918 the then Lloyds Bank (since 2009 the Lloyds Banking Group) bought a controlling share in the Banco de Londres y América del Sud, not however, assuming a majority stake until 1971. In 1959 then, the client of the new headquarters on the corner site of Bartolomé Mitre and Reconquista was the Argentinian subsidiary of Lloyds Bank. It occupied the building from the date of completion to 1997, when it was sold to the Banco Hipotecario, a leading mortgage bank in which the Argentinian government maintains a majority share. The Banco Hipotecario has since used the building for its own functions as its headquarters. However, between the original client and the subsequent owner and user, there are significant differences in use patterns, all of which have resulted from gradual as well as precipitous change in the finance industry.

Argentina in particular and South America in general were territories of service expansion for Lloyds Bank. For many London banks, overseas business during much of the 20th century was full of potential, risks and rewards. South America had, up to that time, been first and foremost a source of raw materials and agricultural products, real products, so to speak. However, thanks to the neo-liberal inspired "Big Bang" enacted for Britain's financial industry in 1986 (a form of market deregulation that removed restrictions in services and product lines), there was a growth in alternative and "innovative" services and products. Thus, during the last decade of the 20th century, parallel to the mushrooming of these new services and products, numerous take-overs within the banking, mortgage and insurance branches took place, creating both an increasingly non-transparent network of ownerships, funds and hedge funds and almost incomprehensible packaged financial products. The focus of the financial industry was less on the real economy with its real products than on the virtual economy with such things as derivatives, trading in futures and credit default swaps.

Particularly in London up to the "Big Bang", the old banks were largely headed by cultured individuals. Their sensitivity for questions of design may not have been of the most courageous kind; nevertheless, when seen in comparison with other financial districts around the world, London's financial district was the place for ambitious clients and architects, albeit working in the majority of cases in a Neo-Classical, Beaux-Arts language, that is to say, principally satisfying the great expectations placed in their institutions. Following the Second World War, and with particular vehemence following the "Big Bang", well over two thirds of the fabric of London's financial district, that is the City of London, was either replaced entirely or had its substance changed behind the historic facades. What Adolf Loos stated as a truth no longer applies in reality. Financial institutions worldwide need nothing other than a laptop and the internet. Space, form and architecture are optional extras.

Over the course of five decades, banks' patterns of use have thus changed markedly. These changes in the patterns of use apply equally to the building of the former Banco de Londres y América del Sud. Though still functioning much as a regular banking headquarters, the original division of public access and interface from the more discrete office spaces for personal exchanges was a means by which to separate the thousands of daily routine transactions on the lower floors from the more intensive negotiations above. The grand entertaining, usual amongst banks of the pre-crisis years, is less common these days. However, the generous employee spaces, including the new gym facility, are being used with increased intensity. Today, there are only a few hundred members of the public entering off the street each day and even fewer personal negotiations. In fact, the upper office levels are essentially used for regular back office functions. This main difference in the number of visits by the public and the resultant increased demand on private office spaces with sound insulation as opposed to the open plan offices of the 1960s, has given rise to serious alterations to the internal fabric (partitions and internal glazing), including changes in the individualized needs of air conditioning. For the state mortgage bank, the spatial concept behind the Banco de Londres y América del Sud is no longer ideally suited, but the bank's management is committed to preserving what is generally acknowledged to be at least a monument of national, if not international importance.

Affirmation, Innovation

The Banco de Londres y América del Sud is one of the most impressive and innovative modern buildings of the 20th century. Its sense of space and form expresses an altogether distinct Lebensgefühl, a view of life, distinct from that of its neighbours or fellow Porteño banks, certainly also distinct from what else was being built at the time not only for this building type, but in architecture altogether, including on an international level. However, besides this distinctiveness, its uniqueness, the Banco de Londres y América del Sud engages with its context, indeed resonates with its Neo-Classical neighbors.

This apparent paradox of being both distinct as well as resonant is itself an unusual occurrence in orthodox modern architecture. Orthodox modern architecture, even its late, contemporary counterparts, seeks to set itself completely apart from its neighbors, its immediate context and its larger culture. Orthodox modern architecture wants to be completely autonomous. It wants to trailblaze originality. Orthodox modern architecture propagandizes the myth of uncompromising innovation, a propaganda campaign undertaken by self-advertising architects and their critics-in-tow. Subsequently, many orthodox architectural historians, lacking the critical distance, have bought into this value system and neglected to show the continuity in much that claims to be the creation of an individual's genius. It does not come as a surprise then, when seen from the global perspective, that there are few buildings simultaneously embracing a relatively independent architectural language and yet also communicating with the neighboring buildings in a highly sensitive and abstract manner. It is this simultaneous embrace of an attitude of autonomy as well as engagement that makes the Banco de Londres y América del Sud an exceptional and exemplary piece of modern architecture, overcoming the autism besetting orthodox modernism, the cause of its alienation from contemporary culture.

The notion of autonomy, not merely a highly desirable characteristic that was once cultivated by avant-garde modernism, but very much an underlying force in the entire civilizing process, can be understood per se as a force for innovation, of asserting an inherent logic distinct from tradition. Autonomous phenomena, however, also risk the atomization of networks, of the dissolution of once integrated cultures. Thus increased autonomization, not only within architecture and urbanism, severs relationships while at the same time seemingly liberating the object, and by extension human life form, from external constraints. The mobility of the individual as idealized in the motor vehicle, the ubiquity of civilization as manifested by dwellings even in the remotest of the world's regions, and the constant availability of data as enabled by the internet even in its virtual realism, each of these cases is a paradigm of the human strife for ever greater autonomy. However, translating these paradigms into the vast quotidian dimension, we merely see freeways, suburbia and forlorn people, the latter acting in an autistic manner thanks to earphones, data pods or laptops.

The individual architectural instantiation of autonomy, by the way it seeks to appear unique, even solitary in its idealized object-like isolation, by the way that it is rendered by client and architect as a golden calf waiting for adulation, is but a link in the contemporary chain of means of cultural representation. Within this chain, each component seeks to maximize attention to itself. The genotypical homogeneity of each link does not have an outward manifestation.

On the other hand, the notion of engagement can be understood as an integrating force, the means by which complex organisms cohere by encouraging communication, fostering mutual respect and appreciation and thereby enabling a complex organism to balance potentially diverging interests. In its authentic form, engagement is self-willed and pro-active. Engagement is a form of participation in a wider context that acknowledges the prerogatives of the pre-existing phenomena while also seeking to contribute to this greater whole.

The simultaneity of a phenomenon being true unto itself, and only in this sense autonomous, while also able to relate to a given context, and in this sense being engaged without appearing to be servile, can be found, for example, in Adolf Loos' Michaelerhaus in Vienna (1909-1910); Erik G. Asplund's Extension of the Law Courts in Gothenburg (1912-1938); Erich Mendelsohn's Schocken Department Store in Stuttgart (1926-1928); Alvar Aalto's National Pensions Institute in Helsinki (1952-1956); Alison and Peter Smithson's Economist Building in London (1959-64); Peter Celsing's urban complex of Kulturhuset, Teatret and Riksbanken in Stockholm (1965-76); and a number of designs by Venturi Scott-Brown, Alvaro Siza, Hermann Czech and Diener & Diener.

The Modernist Idea of Essence

Given the modernist belief in the irreducible essence, and that this essence is defined by primary geometric forms (beginning with the so-called Phileban Solids and ending with the cylinder, pyramid, cube, rectangular parallelepiped and sphere) and coupled with Jean-Nicolas-Louis Durand's mechanistic composition techniques (as published in Nouveau Précis de Leçons d'Architecture, Paris 1813), the superficially logical, if crude, conclusion to the modernist idea of essence was the dematerialized abstraction of all architectural elements, including the resultant three-dimensional appearance. In this reductive view, architecture is subsumed to a figureless embodiment of abstract typologies. The stalwart representatives of this "functionalist" essentialization were Hannes Meyer and Jacobus Johannes Pieter Oud. On a larger urban scale the advocates were Ludwig Hilberseimer and Le Corbusier; subsequently the disasters of modernist "enlightenment" manifested themselves in the social housing schemes of the late modernist and post-Second World War years along the reductive rationalist lines.

Against this crude simplification by hard-line modernists, a few architects showed ambitions to overcome the poverty of spatial and formal expression in architecture. In hindsight, such ambitions could be regarded as either being particularly courageous given the peer pressure exerted on avant-garde designers at the height of the establishment of modernism, or, depending on the direction in which the figuration of elements was taken, exhibiting attitudes ranging from nostalgic to innovative.

Both pre-Second World War examples cited above, the Michaelerhaus by Loos and the Law Courts Extension by Asplund, used Neo-Classical orders, literally in the former, abstracted in the latter case. However, in spatial terms, the

George Grosz: Ohne Titel (Untitled), 1923, Kunstsammlung NRW Düsseldorf, © VG Bildkunst

interior typologies were unprecedented: Loos' almost labyrinthine Raumplan or spatial plan on the one hand, and Asplund's amalgam of the constant Nordic dream of a Mediterranean public square, in Asplund's case by necessity internalized. Both buildings employed structural dares, albeit timid compared to the Banco de Londres y América del Sud: (invisible) suspended construction elements such as the mezzanine gallery in the Michaelerhaus or the grand stair and galleries in the Law Courts Extension.

But perhaps of greatest significance is Asplund's departure from either a figurative classicizing or a metaphoric organicism. At the Law Courts Extension, we can see a more life-assertive, Nordic fusion of the spatial vastness of de Chirico with Asplund's own reinterpretation of Ragnar Östberg's Stockholm Town Hall (on which Asplund also worked), itself a reinterpretation of Venice's Doge Palace. The curtain glazing between the exterior and interior courts ideally does not want to be there. From the interior, the more sturdy I-sectioned supports to the galleries are seen in front of the curtain glazing, allowing the latter's frame to appear less present.

The marble clad floor of the interior court matches in color and level that of the outside: a spatial continuity is implied. Asplund's Law Courts Extension is to be read as a refreshing, more Mediterranean, less historicizing environment than Stockholm's Town Hall. Here, the large courtrooms are encased with curvilinear walls; the elemental staircase rising from the piano nobile to the office level has minimally externally bulging balustrades, thus defining the space of movement as if it were a vessel; the uplights and the suspended trefoiled lamps are not simple cones or cylinders but expressed as part vegetal, part historic (Roman torches); the glass drinking fountain at the entrance to the central space greets the visitor and can be understood as representing the building in a "nut shell" — transparency, clarity, lightness, all borne in a spatially unifying organic vessel.

On the Law Courts Extension's main façade, a design challenge on which Asplund worked for a long time[1], the abstracted giant order with its vestigial bases and the proportional diminution of the upper most pilasters with their equivalent vestigial capitals, the integration of reliefs in the fenestration of the piano nobile, the extension's modern character is clearly expressed as an autonomous as well as engaged response to the Neo-Classical language of the pre-existing building.

The Both/And of Autonomy and Engagement

The Banco de Londres y América del Sud exhibits similar design integrity as the Law Courts Extension. The structural logic of the two central cores, centrally supporting the deep roof structure, being assisted by the perimeter "bundled" and outwardly curved piers (a related, vessel-like gesture as Asplund's balustrade to the lateral public staircase in the Law Courts Extension), creates a grand spatial cage. While this concept might recall Paul Nelson's "Maison Suspendue" (1936-1938)[2], the latter's proposal emphasized the spider-like notion of the perimeter leg-like supports with the undercroft of the roof slab gathering different volumes as if they were luggage strapped under the belly of an animal. Such thoughts, stylized as metallic armadillos, were to be seen again three decades later in London in the images of "Walking Cities" (1964), predated by John Wyndham's Day of the Triffids (1951), in which plants created by the oil industry prove to be able to walk around and thus terrorize humans. Cedric Price's quite opposite, unbuilt "Fun Palace" (1961), together with Peter Celsing's Kulturhuset in Stockholm (1965-1974) as conceptual precedents for the Centre Georges Pompidou (Piano & Rogers, 1969-1977), foresaw a large structural frame, in which different volumes were placed or suspended. Its ludic and flexible character naturally incorporates the picturesqueness that is understood by most architects as a necessary counterpoint to an otherwise bland rationalism.

Seen against these two foils, the modern reductive versus the organic one, the Banco de Londres y América del Sud might be understood as either a flamboyant sculpture or a sanctuary of formal rectitude. Actually, when all the elements are viewed, whether in their composition or on their own, the underlying will to a formal honing of what otherwise might as well have been conventionally mute right-angled shapes can be seen everywhere[3]. Most noticeably on the outside, the deep framed, bundled curvilinear piers create unprecedented structural frames. The interior cores are that much more conventional, though they too are highly wrought in their three-dimensional appearance: they face the central void as if they were spines or kouroi, standing in proud silence as if ready to flex their muscles.

Down to the sinews: the interrelation between the structural components that speak partly of their performance in bearing loads, partly of their honorific address, and services such as the air conditioning ducts; and the interrelation between the coffered voids in the floor slabs and the integrated lamps (as seen in the staff entrance foyer) reveal an integrated thought process in which architectural design is comprehensive—that is, every detail counts — and resolved. The team effort required to realize such coordination is taken to an exemplary level in the case of the Banco de Londres y América del Sud. It is rarely seen today.

The external and internal balusters, encountered when entering the building on the corner of the two streets, are paradigmatic for this baroque flexure. Oversized for their immediate task, they are scaled to the size of the building and commensurate with the honorific task of welcoming the customer. They also stand as intermediaries between the human figure and the larger structural elements of the bundled, curvilinear piers. At the point of entry, standing on the raised landing, the reverberation between the integral language of the Banco de Londres y América del Sud and its much larger neighbor, the Banco de la Nación Argentina, are most distinctly felt. A scalar, rhythmic and formal match exists between the conventional Neo-Classical envelope of the Banco de la Nación Argentina and the porous, spatial, sculpturally bundled, curvilinear piers of the Banco de Londres y América del Sud.

In these bundled, curvilinear piers, the architects have created a modern equivalent to the peristyle temple, of equal weight to the omnipresent Neo-Classical structures of Buenos Aires' financial district. The Banco de Londres y América del Sud is to be regarded from this point as much an independent marker of the reinterpretation of the Doric temple as, say Peter Behrens' AEG Turbine Factory (Berlin, 1909), distinct from the more literal reinterpretation as, say, seen in the hypertrophic Boston City Hall (Kallmann McKinnell & Wood, 1963-1969).

Avoiding the repetitive and systematized dullness of pure rationalism, the Banco de Londres y América del Sud engages the different inflections of the context. At a smaller detailed level, the cornice of the northern neighbor is integrated in the Banco's roof edge; similarly, the Banco responds to the diagonals of the three street junction neighbors with the suspended wall panel, which is not angled at 45°, but less, however, still sufficiently indicative to be understood as a response to the diagonal. While many of the non-regular design decisions can be attributed to such an

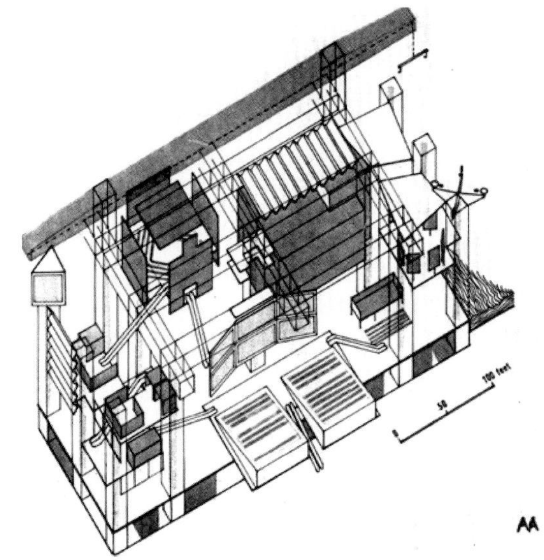

Cedric Price: Project for Fun Palace (unbuilt), London 1961

interest in avoiding orthodoxy, or, put in another way, as discussed in relation to Price's "Fun Palace", to a positive interest in the picturesque, the irregular context with a range of edge conditions and skewed geometries had its impact too on the final realization.

As much the principle of autonomy and engagement can be read in the Banco de Londres y América del Sud's configuration and its tectonic elements, so this principle is visible on the interior. For example, the relation between what is primary structure and what is infill or cladding is clearly expressed. Here, in the

SEPRA, Banco de Londres y América del Sud, Rosario 1973

rendering of the unadorned, in-situ reinforced concrete structure, literally the brut (French for "raw") frame, the architects' inspiration from European models is evident, if once again autonomously developed. If Le Corbusier's Brutalism had been in part a tactic to deal with poor craftsmanship, thereby ennobling the coarseness of irregular formwork as seen at the Unité d'habitation in Marseille (1947-1952), then the Brutalism of the Banco de Londres y América del Sud is of an intended kind. The junctions between the reinforced concrete and the applied elements express this, whether it is the red terrazzo cladding panels in the main staff staircase or the in-situ terrazzo skirting and massive wooden handrail to the circular staircase; every single detail is designed and realized in the manner of a tailor-made suit. The raw and the "cooked"— in other words, the primary and the refined secondary — stand in a dialectic relation that is readable, touchable and understandable.

Autonomy and Engagement at the Urban Level

In some instances in the post — Second World War years, architects made an attempt to engage the context in their new buildings by taking up building lines, cornice levels, similar materials or colors, opening dimensions, rhythms and proportions. It was the age of finally asserting modernism's coming of age after academic architecture, the Beaux-Arts style, had finally been buried with the end of the war. To the degree that the new did not attempt to mimic its neighbors with formal references (a strategy that was to be used during the Post-Modernist era), the new buildings by necessity had to demonstrate their self-sufficiency, that is, their ability to establish an integral, autonomous language.

The differences between the Banco de Londres y América del Sud are still so clear today for most observers, including lay people, that this autonomy in its language is understood. However, for those oblivious individuals, who have never stopped for a second to reflect upon this difference in language, perhaps it has not occurred to them that there is anything particularly unusual about the building, given the fact that the reinforced concrete has almost the same sandy color as its neighbors.

Adolf Loos' Michaelerhaus, when seen today in its context that is largely unchanged since the days of its completion, does not cause any controversy amongst observers, including architects. It looks as if it had been there since the end of the 19th century. The controversy that surrounded it during the construction phase cannot be understood any longer, even by architects. Unless the plain nature of the upper floors is pointed out, the fact that there are no mouldings, most observers do not begin to realize Loos' revolutionary approach.

In the middle position could be said to lie Alison and Peter Smithson's Economist Building. Seen in its context today, a lay person might walk past it without noticing the difference from the neighbors, given the banking hall and bay window addition to Boodle's Club appearing to read like a typical stone clad palazzo on the one hand and a cozy English bay window on the other. The banking hall and its offices above relate in terms of configurational geometry, height, proportions of floors and window openings, materials, implied giant orders and so forth, to its immediate neighbor on the opposite side of the street.

As a complex too, the Economist Building is straddled between Mies van der Rohe's truly autonomous podium with high rise towers as seen at the Toronto Dominion Centre (first phase 1964-1971) and Peter Celsing's attempt at creating a new tight urban scale based on a variety of building units as seen at the cluster between the two squares of Sergels Torg and Brunkebergstorg in Stockholm for Kulturhuset–Teatret–Riksbanken (various phases from 1965-1976).

The Banco de Londres y América del Sud is an urban fabric at a smaller, intensive scale; here the recessed main entrance establishes a smaller external piazza in order to prepare the visitor for the large breath of air on the interior, as an internal piazza. Asplund's concept of enlarging the old Law Court's inner courtyard by the new interior courtyard in the Extension is paralleled by the Banco's telescopic extension of the external piazza into the Banco's public atrium. It is true to say that a lighter curtain glazing would, in both the Law Courts Extension and the Banco de Londres y América del Sud, create a more credible continuity between inside and out.

Conclusion

While the world appears to be full of images and possibilities, it is only on very rare occasions in architecture that there is a fusion of necessity and idea; the necessity being embodied by a client organization and the idea being provided by a correctly selected design team. The examples cited here, besides the Banco de Londres y América del Sud, are each exceptional realizations, albeit marking different possibilities and expressing distinct views of the world.

The Banco de Londres y América del Sud marks a position in time and a particular way in which banking business was conducted. Much of this has been swept away by developments in the financial world. The building is no longer used in the way for which it was conceived. However, the impressive qualities of the Banco de Londres y América del Sud have been such that its owners have been touched by its value, convinced by its exceptional character, and thus have always made an effort to respect it. That may be the building's lasting legacy: the manner in which it expresses its presence through each flexure of form, well beyond the rationalist convention. And in this way, it still shows us paths into the future.

[1]Claes Caldenby et al, *Asplunds Rådhus i Göteborg*, Arkitekturmuseet Stockholm 2010.

[2]See Jorge Francisco Liernur's essay in this book, "Polysemy: rereading the Reading of BLAS", p. 14.

[3]Significantly, SEPRA's subsequent Banco de Londres y América del Sud, now Banco Patagonia, in Rosario, completed in 1973, consists of orthogonal boxes, all lifted in place by a large exo-skeletal truss: structural daring in a more compact and more conventional language.

Polysemy: Rereading the Readings of BLAS [1]

Jorge Francisco Liernur
Translated by Jorge Villota Peña

Clorindo Testa is one of the few contemporary Argentinian architects who have received international acknowledgment; this recognition is largely due to his participation in the design of the Banco del Londres y América del Sud in Buenos Aires. Vice versa, the building is immediately associated with his name.

Critics have widely contributed to consolidate this association. Not so long ago, in an article eloquently titled "Clorindo Testa´s Bank of London and South America, Buenos Aires"[2] Peter Cook regarded the building as the most influential of his own career. He considered the Banco as the extraordinary creation of a genius and described it with adjective appropriate to that condition, such as "funny," "fresh," or "non-reasonable." The idea of the Banco as a brilliant work, closer to the ineffable art world than to the mundane field of building industry, was not new. One of the first to have such an approach was the critic Damián Bayón in *Panorámica de la Arquitectura Latinoamericana*, a book with photographs of Paolo Gasparini published in 1977.[3] Here again, Testa is presented as the only author of the work, in which, additionally, some traces of his particular artistic procedures might be identified. During the interview published in that book, Bayón asked him:

> Two years ago, when you were explaining to me the Banco del Londres, I remembered I made a bloody joke, since I saw reinforced concrete walls, and at that time your painting looked much like that. And I remembered having told you that that wall seemed like a painting of Clorindo Testa,' but much better, because it can be used; it was a stairs' wall, it was the Banco's center, it was the structural heart of the work. There is a problem: how does Clorindo Testa, as a painter, face Clorindo Testa as an architect? Are both of them the same? I have a feeling that in your paintings you made the projects of what you are going to do later in architecture, or vice versa. Can you explain this?

Typical of his well-known laconism, Testa's answer ("Well, I don't know, because I never asked that question myself") as expected, left the conclusion open.

Although less definitive on the architect's authorship, Ramón Gutiérrez (alluding to "the work of Clorindo Testa for the Banco de Londres y América del Sud [with SEPRA, 1965]") considered the building again in the same way in his book on architecture and urbanism in Latin America.[4] Here, the building appeared to form a part of a set of "works with intrinsic quality, capable of being on any site; because of their conception as 'work of art,' they are also elements of rupture and deformation of the urban environment."

In an article published in *Arquitecturas BIS*, in 1981, Oriol Bohigas expressed the surprise of European architects vis-à-vis the work.[5] Like the cases we have been analyzing, on this occasion the building was also regarded as the work of one unique creator. Thus, Bohigas asked:

> From here, and examined through the publications, the building would be easily classified as Corbusian, even Brutalist, with some influences of Le Corbusier's British disciples. Do you agree this way of judging it? At the time of designing it, how did you see those relations to international architecture? (...) Which architects did you then consider as your masters?

The interviewee just mentioned Le Corbusier in his answer, and Bohigas acknowledged that

> actually, the Banco del Londres might be included in certain trends just to fulfill classification requirements, but what really surprised me is that it represented a personal contribution, with a very *sui generis* expressive language.

To the increased attribution of the building to Clorindo Testa as a sole author (or at least, to the gradual ignorance of the role that SEPRA played) contributed the death of his partners and the dissolution of theirs office as a unity[6]: Testa has remained as the only alive referent of a collective process.

Moreover, some Testa's sketches are usually mistaken for the project's preliminary outline, so much so that someone assured that "even the earliest sketches for the design suggested the idea of the building as a void, as an absence, and not as an object."[7] However it is evident that those drawings are *a posteriori* production (probably prepared ad hoc for the publication of the building in the special issue of *Summa*, in 1967), a procedure very frequent in Clorindo Testa: it is noticeable in those sketches that both the pendant panels of reinforced concrete over the vestibule (the so called "elephant ears") are separated from the porticos on both the streets, whereas this separation was not in the early stages of the project.[8]

We are paying special attention to the authorship because, just as the prominence given to Testa leads us to interpret the bank in artistic, unique terms, by the same token the rescue of SEPRA's role forces us to read it from a technical and professional point of view.

Indeed, Testa's creativity and his crucial participation in the project is beyond any doubt, but it is necessary to rethink the building as the result of a team work, with an uncommon balance. According to different testimonies[9], in spite of their main focus on the relations with the clients and on administrative aspects, Santiago Sánchez Elia and Federico Peralta Ramos played an important role providing many design suggestions, such as the proposal of trying even to achieve the mobility and exchange of the mezzanines. Moreover, all the testimonies coincide in underlining the leading role of Alfredo Agostini — an austere personality, but a decisive figure in the wonderful previous production of SEPRA — in the design of the Banco, from the general ideas to the apparently most insignificant details.

Contrasting the oversimplification of the authorship in the figure of Testa, some publications even considered that the building should be attributed to five professionals, rescuing Gerald W. Wakeham (named by the Banco's board to supervise the whole process) because his equally significant role. As we are going to see, it would be probably more accurate to even consider seven authors, including among them the engineers Hilario Fernández Long and Horacio Reggini.

Reduced to the topic of "artistic creation of a genius", the building usually has been presented as floating in an utter non-place, non-time space. Therefore it is not surprising that some critics like Ramon Gutiérrez conclude that it could have being built "in any place." Furthermore, in this way it was possible to declare not just the ubiquitous condition of the work, but also to propose its impertinence, or even its ability to exist beyond its physical and cultural concrete reality. This was the reading of Alberto Petrina in a *Summa* magazine's monograph issue on Testa:

> I always thought that the art of Clorindo Testa (spanning architecture, painting, drawing and sculpture) would be easier to be explained in another context, different from that of Argentina: Brazil or Mexico, for instance. Any of these countries, with the lack of moderation that characterizes them, would induce a lesser violent insertion than it is actually verified in our cultural environment, since it is almost evident that his work would be more "digestible" if accompanied either by the Teotihuacan pyramids or the tropical exuberance of the Tijuca Forest than in the monotonous grey of Buenos Aires. Here, this exotic work (from the point of view of the country's ethical-aesthetic canons) is not totally accepted.[9]

It is important to note that, in this case, the "exoticism" of the work was not seen as weakness, but as strength. In the interpretation of Petrina, Testa's work is presented as a sort of act of resistance against what is considered as a dull, generic cosmopolitanism presumably characteristic of Buenos Aires' culture. Following a picture of the bank as a "tarantula in the middle of a dish with cream" proposed by another colleague regarding the work of Testa, Petrina considered:

> that this represents exactly the work (the Banco) in the middle of such an old-fashioned, hypocritical, and conventional city as Buenos Aires. In a city in which all its women deserve to have a Chanel costume, and all its men an English suit, and where even the "new wave" teenagers wear colors as a uniform, he would not be able to have his art incorporated without having faced a traumatic situation.

Strikingly, this interpretation of the Banco as a "challenging", "resistant" monument was an inversion of the comments that the criticism from the left constructed at the moment of the building's inauguration. Although perhaps this reversal was not so strange. As a consequence of the tragic experience that Argentinian society lived during the 1970s, the strong slogans of those days turned into the "weak thoughts" of the next decade. In this sense, the conception of the "popular forces" as agents of radical change turned into the belief in the "popular culture" as a reservoir of values. Consequently, if in the "revolutionary" 1970s the Banco was considered a "bourgeois excess" contrasting with the urgent need to solve the housing problem, seen against the background of the domesticated political climate of the 1980s (as in Petrina's comment) the building could be recovered as an expression of anti-systemic individuality.

In the special issue on the building published by *Summa* magazine shortly after its opening in 1966 Horacio Pando's opinion represented the agitated state of the debates of that moment in the best way:

> The truth is that we would have appreciated it, if our most serious architectural problems (specially the low cost housing) would have being solved first, instead of creating these exponents of "luxury consumerism" and waste of our efforts and our so limited resources. The fact that these islands of excessive wealth rise in the middle of too much spatial poverty is almost insulting.

Pando expressed the relatively moderate critical positions of a Social Christian, in a tone. One year later, in the same issue of Architectural Design that presented the building, the section for letters published a kind of manifesto[12] signed by seven Argentinian architects of Marxist persuasion.[13] For them the Banco was "architecturally an advanced building," but maintained "the rites of

View of entrance area from first gallery

the banking tradition, solidity, security, closed-in space." They wrote that, as happened in the old institutions, here it was possible to notice the "symbolism of authority over the simple city-dweller, (the) symbolism of authority over the client". Those reasons explained why in the building "nothing is standard; everything is exclusive. Should great architecture be exclusive?" Furthermore, according to the authors, the bank was a collection of

Staff staircase with terrazzo panel cladding

odd, novel forms apparently modern but expressed in artistic terms far removed from the industrial repetitive concepts of the Masters. The building has not reinterpreted the program of a bank, it has redesigned it formally, decoratively, rhetorically, a great architectural gesture that pretends to miss out stages, but merely invents new forms, while leaving the rest unaltered (...)

The signatories of the manifesto also considered that the building would not be able to absorb future changes: "no technical solution which could be regarded as an experiment for a large scale approach to our social and architectural problems; no urban sense." According to them, the building was only a monument (in a pejorative sense, as used at that time) that did not contribute to the solution of the social problems they denounced. Moreover, they also rejected "the pretentious visions of those who believe they can alter the world by a mere change in architectural forms," while proclaiming that "if we want our countries to emerge from their state of dependence and under-development, we architects should come down to earth and assume the true role of committed intellectuals instead of medieval knights, pencil in scabbard."

As we can see, this critique and, to a lesser extent, the one of Horacio Pando, were aimed at the morphological aspects of the design despising its technological achievements. Therefore (independently of the obvious acknowledgement of Clorindo Testa's creative talent) neither one needed to recognize the role played by the rest of the design team. Nonetheless, taking into account the explicitly political content of their positions, they were not interested in detaching the building from the context. On the contrary: it was essential for them to consider it as an expression of the dominant social sectors of the Argentinian society, the same society that the letter's authors wanted to criticize. In this case the building was considered as perfectly coherent with Buenos Aires, but representing the party of the "enemy".

Following the same line, the Banco would be eventually mentioned by two other Marxist critics, Ramón Vargas Salgueiro and Rafael López Rangel,[14] who inscribed the building in the specific Argentinian context, according to them characterized by "the aestheticist tradition, the private character of a large number of significant constructions (such as the Banco de Londres y América del Sud in Buenos Aires, the work of Santiago Sánchez Elía, Federico Peralta Ramos, Alfredo Agostini and Clorindo Testa), the monumental works (...) and the urgency of social solutions that just the State can face."

The diffusion of the ideas of Aldo Rossi, who visited Buenos Aires on different occasions since 1978, contributed to the reversal of this position, i.e. the understanding of the work as a unique and brilliant one, above or even opposed to society. So, while Pando had seen the building as a dissonant "island of excessive wealth" inserted in the urban tissue, in a Rossian manner Petrina, and previously Gutiérrez, described it in the opposite way. Actually, Guttierrez noticed "its purpose of urban integration, respectful of its urban environment," whereas Petrina went beyond, nominating it as a precursor of the Milanese architect's ideas. According to

Petrina, "seven years before the publication of *L'Architettura della Cittá*, Clorindo Testa teaches, through the Banco de Londres, a master class on the assimilation of the architectural object into the surrounding urban tissue."

In postmodern terms, in a context characterized by the demystification of "modernist unique narratives" and the diffusion of the cultural relativism, the Banco would be eventually reinterpreted not only as a "Rossian" piece, but also as a dialectic expression of "the same" vs. "the other." Although Kenneth Frampton just mentioned it briefly in the original publication on "critical regionalism,"[15] this is sufficiently eloquent to support our argument: here, the criticism of the 1970s was turned upside down, and through the pen of the British critic the same building, once co-responsible for the social backwardness of the country, and an exponent of the "dominant classes", was transformed into one of the signs of resistance to globalization. According to Frampton, "regionalism manifested itself (...) recently perhaps in Clorindo Testa's Banco of London and South America, built in Buenos Aires in 1959."

But: in what way might the Banco constitute an entrenched episode of resistance to globalization? This presumption most probably is based on a conceptual mistake, due to both the attribution of the project to the supposed outsider role of Testa (ignoring the highly professional and pro-establishment SEPRA office)[16] and the consolidated consideration of the building as a clear example of Brutalist architecture. Taking into account that Brutalism is based on the use of available building materials ("as found"), it would be understandable to read the Banco's presumably Brutalism as a "resistance" to the docile acceptance of building criteria imposed by the International Style.

Federico Ortiz was one of the first critics who linked the Banco to Brutalism. In his small book on SEPRA, he pointed out that during the early 1970s the work of the group had turned into "the plastic and structural experimentalism, in a Brutalist, Corbusian way." Regarding the Banco, as Ortiz observed in *Casabella No. 285*, "people have said this is a Brutalist work, but we can't think this way." In his opinion, the building should be identified with a "more markedly expressionist line (...) that we dare to classify it as structural 'para-expressionist' (...), more markedly plastic, in a quasi-verbal sense, and in which Brutalism is left as an epidermal topic."

In his book on Latin American Architecture (1969), Francisco Bullrich also linked the Banco to Brutalism, although with certain caution. Actually, regarding previous works of Testa and SEPRA, among other things, he considered that "in many works executed between 1958 and 1962 it was the use of reinforced concrete, as well as raw and direct solutions, that produced a kind of Neo-Brutalism."[17] Bullrich was very clear about the meaning that the term should have in the conditions of Argentina. He recognized

> the renunciation of using the most modern technology (regarded at that time as a prerequisite of all new architecture), (as) something that was considered necessary in order to tailor the technical proposal to the reality of the country. This renunciation (...) although temporary, made possible a reconsideration of the attitudes vis-à-vis the technology.

As Testa's partner in the National Library project, Bullrich was perfectly aware of the complex issues involved in the building of the Banco, which meant that "the created image did not rest on the pseudo-Roman gravitas, but on a fascinating environment of technology." Because of this, the relation of the Banco with brutalism was carefully formulated, and when Bullrich mentioned the building, he pointed out that "from the Brutalist raw expression of the early 1960s, obviously it has been turning into a more elaborated expression."

Despite these moderate, early approaches to the presumably Brutalist character of the building, many subsequent comments kept feeding this identification, regardless of the contradiction between this adjective and the "fascinating technology world" that Bullrich mentioned.

Reducing Brutalism to the "use of reinforced concrete in huge masses and volumes," and without realizing the contradiction within the terms utilized in their statement, Gutierrez and Viñules considered the building as an example of Brutalism maintaining that, in this movement,

> formalism predominated in this diffusion of a 'strong' and technologically 'advanced' language, which was spread under the sponsorship of Le Corbusier's seed (...) Later Testa made sculptural proposals for both the Banco de Londres and the National Library (...). In the first case, the structural capabilities of the reinforced concrete made possible an interesting suspending structure, which allowed it to become an enormous, high quality open space.[18]

The association between the building and Brutalism still stands until the present day.[19] A recent work by Ingrid Rojas is a clear expression of the misunderstandings on this issue. According to her

> New Brutalism, an architectural tendency that originated in Europe, triggered some significant developments in Argentina's architecture during the 1950s until the 1970s. Emphasizing the search of poetic elements in the use of light, the creation of large volumes, and the application of technologies as well as materials available, it was both innovative and appropriate in the historical and cultural context of Argentina at that time.[20]

In this interpretation the identification of the building as an inappropriate technological *tour de force* has turned into the opposite. Moreover, Rojas even thinks that

> concrete — then the most readily available material — was used as principal building material, formed with striking repetitive angular geometries. Buildings of concrete can be characterized by its rough, blocky forms and forthright exposure of the buildings' functions ranging from structure and services to their human use.[21]

As an example of the partial authorship attribution that we mentioned at the beginning of this paper, she also holds that the

> Banco de Londres y América del Sud, built by Clorindo Testa between 1959 and 1966 at the center of Buenos Aires, is considered the most representative building for this new way of making use of the available building material in Argentina and for its novel technological and stylistic characteristics.

Neither has Jantje Engels been able to avoid the temptation to ignore SEPRA. He pointed out that "Testa wanted to create distinctive and meaningful pieces of architecture. His work shows the same concrete roughness as the work of the Smithson's and other Brutalist architects (...)."[22]

Enrique Browne presented a new inflection on the Banco's reading in his work entitled *Otra Arquitectura en América Latina* (The Other Architecture in Latin America), published in 1983. Following the relativist trend of that time and searching for opposition against the supposedly monolithic Euro-American "modern movement," in his book Browne attempted to construct a critical system that makes it possible to give a common identity to regional works. It was a paradoxical position, not so different from the one headed by Kenneth Frampton in the Anglo-Saxon (central) world, which countered the supposedly "central" architecture of the Modern Movement with the notion of "Critical Regionalism." The Chilean essayist appealed to a binary paradigm, made up of what he called "spirit of the times" and "spirit of the place." He wrote that to get away from the former implied an anachronism, while to get away from the latter implied uprooting.

As an expression of the second attitude, and coinciding with a widespread interpretation, Browne defined "International Style" as a "civilizational-imported" architecture, brought from Europe in a Universalist attitude, still in use. Nevertheless, his most hazardous critical invention was the idea of a "developmentalist architecture" (arquitectura del desarrollo), to which he dedicated three chapters of his book.

Applying a sociopolitical– based concept to architectural history, Browne could bypass contextual, cultural, and aesthetic differences, subsuming under that homogenizing mantle examples ranging from the Church of Saint Francis of Assisi by Oscar Niemeyer to the State Television Building in Buenos Aires, by Justo Solsona's group; from the House Over the Brook by Amancio Williams[23] to the UNAM's Central Library by Juan O'Gorman; from the church of the Miraculous Virgin by Félix Candela to the Banco de Londres y América del Sud by SEPRA + Testa. In his opinion, the "developmentalist architecture" was a consequence of a forced attempt to move societies forward, regardless of "the history and the culture of each region."

Since this architecture "was not the result of pre-existing material conditions, but the promoter of its progress," Browne judged it as inappropriate. Also, according to him, it was equally inconvenient that "the architects, vis-à-vis their social reality, looking at themselves as development injectors, fostering the use of reinforced concrete and other technologies, and promoting the structural engineering and other sciences as well."

According to Browne this impulse was gradually weaken during the crisis of the 1970s (fortunately, in his opinion), starting a new attitude that he identified as the "other architecture" (otra arquitectura). In the opposite direction to the "other architecture," Browne established the main defining features of that "developmentalist architecture" as follows: 1) acontextuality; 2) structural expressionism; 3) predominant use of expressive reinforced concrete; 4) synthesis of the arts, and 5) governmental commission. Inexplicably, in spite of the fact that the Banco does not fulfill three of the five premises that he had established (1, 4 and 5) for Browne, it must be considered "a prime work of the developmentalist architecture".

If, instead of focusing its authorship on Testa, insisting on its Brutalist character, or considering it could be built "in any place," we take into account both the whole creative team of the building and its most important and specific characteristics in relation to the place and the time it was built the conclusions may be very different.

First of all, it must be noticed that the link of the Banco with its urban environment was not an original gesture of the authors: other entries of the contest organized by the committee,[24] also proposed the construction of a block with homogeneous height, following the contextual height lines on both streets. Moreover, the concern with the context was usual at that time. In the same special issue that Summa dedicated to the Banco, a further two office buildings were published, each with different approaches on this topic. The first one was the FIAT Building, which attempted to respond to the Teatro Colón by means of its façade panels; the second one was the "Brunetta" Tower, located at the corner of Suipacha and Santa Fé, a complex housing block which was carefully adapted to the neighboring buildings, in the manner of the Smithson's "Economist" in London.

If in this sense, the proposal was not innovating, what is undoubtedly outstanding in the building is its character of a *boîte à miracles*: the program was sheltered within an extraordinary rich envelope, obtained by means of an apparent absence of supporting structure. It is obvious that there was no such absence: the structure disappeared into the *sui generis* exterior screens, adopted the form of elevators, camouflaged itself with the air conditioning ducts in the lateral mezzanines, and became imperceptible through the tie rods from which three office levels were hung.

However, here it is evident that the predominant association of the building with the Corbusian precedents turns out too reductive. The idea of a big box containing planes and architectonic "objects," placed and suspended, was not new. It was already present in the photo collage that

Mies van der Rohe made for his Concert Hall Project in 1942 (based on the interior open space of the Martin Bomber Plant, by Albert Kahn), and later in the Convention Hall that Mies van der Rohe designed in the collaboration with a group of IIT students in 1952. In short, this idea was known at the time of the Banco competition. Like in the project, the structure of the Convention Hall consists of some perimeter "trees" that support the large roof, from which other components of the program can be hung. The "Maison Suspendue" had to be equally known. Paul Nelson, its author, was related to the Austral group, some of whose members had graduated with SEPRA's partners at the same time.[25]

It is true that in most known modern international buildings the use of tie rods and tensile rods was not usual. Moreover, we have no idea whether the constructivist projects of 1920s, such as the pendant restaurant of Simbirchev or the Petersschule of Hannes Meyer, were known during the 1950s in Buenos Aires. Some interest in the architecture of Paul Rudolph can be recognized by judging from the coincidence in the expressionist use of the reinforce concrete. Furthermore, this interest is noticeable in the similarities that can be observed between the Banco and Rudolph's perimeter tree-like locations, as in the Blue Cross offices (1957); or with its emphasis on the plastic quality of the ribbed stilts, as in the Greeley Memorial Laboratory (1957); or his modeling of frames and parapets, as in New Haven's parking garages (1959), and finally with his frequent use of pendant structures.

It is hard to imagine that the authors did not know about the Museum of Modern Art in Rio de Janeiro, which Affonso Eduardo Reidy designed in 1954 based also on a powerful external structure, where its interior mezzanines were suspended from its roof. This example was too close to be ignored. Moreover, another work, even closer, should not be disregarded: El Pilar building, located in the Pocitos neighborhood of Montevideo. Designed by Luis García Pardo and Sommer Smith in 1958 (with structural project by Leonel Viera), this small tower consists of built-in brackets, located at the top of a strong cylindrical reinforced concrete core, from which the apartments are hung.

In addition, the ideas of the Banco had significant precedents within Argentina, where a significant amount of experiences with international recognition was being developed during and after the post-Second World War. Actually, we should consider the Banco as an expression of this heritage. Although both the scale and the quality of big open interior spaces were a valuable heritage from the academic teaching (such as the magnificent interior of the Central Post Office or the Palace of Justice), which the students of 1937 had learned to admire in Buenos Aires, there were equally significant examples of new structural solutions. The hanging slabs that Alberto Prebisch had already used in the impressive hall of the Gran Rex Theater and that Mario Roberto Álvarez employed in the lateral mezzanines of the General San Martin Municipal Theater's hall (inaugurated in 1960), are good examples of this. Furthermore, as Docampo and Dieguez had pointed out,[26] Amancio Williams had already proposed and published in 1946 the idea of a whole office building made of slabs suspended from an upper structure, supported by strong pillars on the perimeter.

This heritage was present in the Banco as a clear contribution of SEPRA. Although Testa would eventually use hanging structures in parts of the National Library project (which he presented several months after the Banco competition, jointly with Francisco Bullrich and Alicia Cazzaniga), his previous works were carried out using a traditional tectonic. But SEPRA had had at least two previous experiences of built spaces using suspended elements. One of them was the Perdriel workshop in Buenos Aires, designed by Maria Carmen Agostini de Dellepiane in 1956, a structure from which the metallic bridge cranes were hung. The second one, closer to the Banco project, was the Cordoba Municipality building (1954). Its entrance hall, characterized by the presence of huge porticos that support the upper slabs (and between them a suspended mezzanine "slides"), is a prelude of what would be the space of the Banco.

Moreover, one should not forget the Church of Notre Dame du Raincy by Auguste Perret, an interior structure of reinforced concrete, contrasting with its light perimeter. In fact, Perret had visited Buenos Aires in 1936, producing a strong impression on the members of SEPRA, who were students at that time. It is important to note that the use of reinforced concrete as an architectural theme was not introduced into Argentina by Le Corbusier, but by Perret, and that it happened many years before the appearance of "Neo-Brutalism."

Besides some examples of exceptional value, such as the large soccer stadiums of River Plate (Aslan & Ezcurra, 1936-38) and Boca Juniors (Delpini-Sulcic, 1937-40) and the enormous building for the city purveyance market (mercado de abasto) (Delpini-Sulcic, 1933-36), SEPRA office *per se* had already used brick and expressive reinforced concrete in its Educational Center for Workers (Centro Obrero de Intrucción, 1942). Lastly, since its construction in the early forties everybody admired The Casa del Arroyo (Bridge House, 1943-45) by Amancio Williams, an emblematic architectural piece in the use of expressive reinforced concrete.

Despite all these previous experiences, the complexity of the Banco's project demanded a technological *tour de force*, which was possible just because it was developed within a context that provided material, managerial and intellectual conditions to do it successfully. Although this effort reached different aspects of the construction, we will focus on the structural engineering and on the air conditioning system. In this sense we are going to see that the architecture of the Banco should be considered diametrically opposed to Brutalism. In order to do so we must introduce now the two other co-protagonists also responsible for the building, without whom it would have never attained the level of a masterpiece: engineers Hilario Fernández Long and Horacio Reggini. Unlike the antecedents previously mentioned, the Banco demanded the suspension of three office stories (relatively irregular in form), hung from a reticular structure. The latter, for its parts, was supported by pillars; they each had different characteristics (vertical circulation core, perimeter portal frames, vertical ribs, perimeter walls, and supplementary portal frames) and were partially symmetric.

What is more, the reticular structure had to be projected both over the entrance in order to hang the "elephant ears" (those two banner-like concrete screens, seen from the street, which supported the manager's office), and above the lateral courtyard, in order to sustain the tie rods from which a metallic roof at the first floor was suspended. Other partial problems must be mentioned, such as the complex two-dimensional torsion of the perimeter portal frames (those pierced pillars that supported the lower mezzanines) proposed in the project from the beginning or the horizontal tension rods that were needed because of the expansion of the upper slab. In this sense, we must take into account that the latter attained a length of 75 meters and a width of almost 50 meters, and weighed 4,500 ton, and there was no possibility to use expansion joints.

The engineers were efficiently supported by Crivelli & Cuenya Construction Company, the third stalwart of the technical team, which made possible a high level of refinement for all building components and procedures. For the portal frames, a high-strength reinforced concrete type B 350[27] with a non-vibrated high water-cement ratio[28] was used. The three suspended mezzanines, covering an area of 4,000 m^2, were made of prefabricated slabs of 1.5 x 6.00 m and 1,800 kg each; the assembly was made in 40 days using a monorail that ran through the upper slab.[29] Even apparently insignificant details, such as the formwork separators, were specially designed using rivets and elastic pieces to guarantee a perfect finish.

At the moment of his initial introduction to the project, Hilario Fernández Long was already one of the most famous academic figures of the Engineering School at the University of Buenos Aires. Here, besides being a member of faculty, he headed the Department of Applied Mechanics, and was appointed Dean in 1962. He even became President of the University of Buenos

Aires in 1965 (some months before the military intervention to the universities in 1966). When he started working on the project, he already had twenty years' professional experience behind him, counting significant works. He had never undertaken, however, a challenge of such magnitude. Fernández Long was one of the first professionals to be interested in the use of computers; as a result, in 1960 he counted on the new contributions that Horacio Reggini, a young colleague, introduced in this field.

Having graduated in 1958, and being a disciple of Delpini,[30] later on Reggini had been as visiting scholar at Columbia University, where the ideas of Buckminster Fuller seduced him too. During that time he also contacted Seymour Papert and Malvin Minsky at MIT, well-known as the fathers of Artificial Intelligence, and participated in the MAC project (Machine Aided Cognition or Multiple Access Computer). Reggini's interest in this field was not isolated. Although with certain backwardness vis-à-vis the most developed countries, Argentina was making huge steps in that direction at the end of the 1950s: thanks to the actions that Dr. Manuel Sadovsky took in 1958, the National Council of Scientific and Technical Research (Consejo Nacional de Investigaciones Científicas y Técnicas) approved the purchase of a sophisticated computer in England, which will work as a base for the Institute of Calculus at the Exact Sciences School (Instituto de Cálculo, Facultad de Ciencias Exactas) at the University of Buenos Aires.[31]

Immediately after his return, Reggini created the GEAC (Grupo de Aplicaciones de Computadora (Applied Computing Group)) at the Engineering School; he was convinced of the need and the potential in using those new means and methods, not just for abstract functions in mathematical calculus, but also for solving specific problems in structural engineering. The presence of both Fernández Long and Reggini was not just limited to solving calculus problems; they played an important role in the design of the structure, especially in the exterior portal frame. As seen in the drawings submitted to the competition those pieces had been conceived initially as a thick wall of reinforced concrete, with two types of perforation: circular holes throughout the surface and big open porticos along the lower half of the wall. Working jointly, engineers were turning the oculus into those round-corner squares, so characteristic in the building,[32] and later the massive wall into the magnificent, surprising portal frames. Originally showing a curved section, the portal frames eventually were shaped using a variable section along their pillars. Finally, pieces that absorb horizontal tensile loads were incorporated into subsequent proposals.

As is well known, the solution of the air conditioning system turned into a sculptural theme in the hands of the architects. The matter

View through skylight into main hall

was not just to show the installations "as found," in the way that was being popularized by the Smithsons. On the contrary, although less complex than the structural engineering, the design solution for the air conditioning was equally sophisticated. It had to take into account that the Banco building had a surface of 3,000 m^2 in plan, with 26 m in height (a total volume of 80,000 m^3). All rooms had to be provided with the same level of comfort, although the weather conditions are very different either along the glass panels in both façades or in the remote corners.

This topic was developed in collaboration with

a society constituted by a North American and a local firm: Carrier and Lix Klett respectively. The professional interaction between them had been a long-term one. As a matter of fact, the founders of both companies, engineer Ernesto Lix Klett, and Willis Haviland Carrier, had graduated from Cornell University (in 1908 and 1901). Both of them were interested in new systems for regulating interior temperatures. Carrier had created in the United States his first air conditioning company during the First World War, something that Lix Klett did in Argentina few years later; they joined forces in 1933. This early partnership made possible several great steps forward in the consolidation of this field in Argentina: in 1933 the world's first collective housing with "exact weather", in 1936 the Kavanagh building, the world's first skyscraper using centralized air conditioning system with centrifugal compressors, and Weathermaster units started being used in Buenos Aires in 1946 at the Plaza Hotel.

The distribution, gauge, and expression of this system in the Banco were carefully studied, applying different criteria. In order to counteract the heat loss through the perimeter building envelopes, air injection equipment was installed, which formed a thermal curtain along the facades. The system was divided in two. Some of the equipment was located on the third basement; from here conditioned air was introduced through the central space of the building up to the second floor. The rest of the equipment was placed on the sixth level to serve the suspended offices.

Two types of equipment were used: a conventional one was installed to supply the large area of public use, while the offices were air-conditioned by Weathermaster units, in order to regulate temperature individually. In some cases, pipes were hidden and outlets were barely seen. For other situations, some "colored trees" were designed; these emerged autonomously, providing different areas and levels and especially the areas for public access.

The air conditioning installation even attained a monumental expression, helping to determine the section of the piers that support the lower slabs. The separation between an expressionist structure and the curtain wall had been already used at the Banco de la República (Bank of the Republic) in Montevideo (1957). However, this is not the most striking aspect in the Banco de Londres y América del Sud. Here, the piers function by way of ducts, carrying the air from the basement to the central space, and at the same time crossing and shaping the brackets that support the slabs.

This solution was not applied for the first time in Buenos Aires. Marco Sanuzo had already experimented with the fusion between structure and the system of air conditioning in his Olivetti factory project in Buenos Aires (1956-62). There Sanuzo created mighty hollow beams, at the ends of which was located the cooling equipment. It is possible to verify in the earliest drawings of the Banco that this idea was not part of the original project, and therefore it is not surprising that its inclusion could be suggested by the diffusion of the mentioned work.

As we can see, the project did not just depend exclusively on the artistic imagination of Clorindo Testa. It also counted on the knowledge and previous experience of SEPRA and the creativity of Alfredo Agostini; the talent and advanced theoretical, practical formation of two engineers, with a refined architectural sensitivity, and finally on the most sophisticated technical ideas and means that were disposable in the world at that time. Taking this into account, the building was so far from being a Brutalist exercise, that it could be even considered one of the first high-tech buildings instead (and not by chance closely related to the British culture of that time). Although it is true that high-tech is usually identified with the use of metallic elements and large glass surfaces, this criterion is debatable (unless it is understood just as a stylistic definition). Strictly speaking, the idea of high-tech is not related to architecture, but to engineering, and originally it was linked to the use of computers. So, it would not be inappropriate to regard the building as a high-tech one.

It could be argued that, although the knowledge and the procedures used in the building might be considered high-tech, its construction was made possible by means of a traditional method. However, regarding the structure, this argument can be disputed. In this case, the high quality finish of the reinforced concrete was due to different factors. Both the use of advanced methods in its composition and cast system (as already mentioned) and the application of transparent and opaque paints, developed ad hoc by Alba (one of the largest Argentinian firms in this field), are some of them.

Nevertheless, the wonderful quality of the concrete and its texture are due to the use of furniture-like formwork, the components of which were mostly made and assembled in a carpenter's workshop, instead of being made by unskilled workers on site. Therefore – taking into account its refined finishes – it could be argued that if the building certainly cannot be considered to be Brutalist, it should also not be regarded as being high-tech either because of its "old" construction system. This understanding of high-tech architecture, however, is based on a mistaken idea, since it is, first of all, a myth.

Due to its condition of unique pieces, buildings can barely be identified with the serial objects that constitute the contemporary "high-technology" universe,[33] especially if we include on it the countless paraphernalia of electronic devices created during the latest decade. In most of the cases, the pieces identified with the so-called high-tech architecture are, as well as the Banco, a peculiar combination of different means and techniques. In any case, instead of being identified by means of building processes, the high-tech architecture should be defined in terms of its intention of being recognized as the synthesis of technological breakthroughs (hence its fast obsolescence). In this sense, in order to achieve that appearance and fulfill that intention, in many cases the procedures require old techniques.

It is not surprising that the Banco had caught the attention of the young Peter Cook, or even that Nikolaus Pevsner had associated it with the new brood of British architects of the early 1960s (probably thinking of either the technological delirium of the factory that Michael Webb designed or the Fun Palace by Cedric Price).[34] But the Banco was not a delirium; it was real construction, highly noticeable.

Actually, after its opening, the building was given significant international diffusion. We have already mentioned some cases, but it is important to remember the way several journals emphasized precisely that avant-garde character (in a certain way perplexed, vis-à-vis this unusual artifact built on the edge of the exotic Pampas, in the south end of Latin America). One of them was the magazine *Design*, which published information on the building in two occasions.[35] In the first instance, the magazine said, "solid and impressive as befits a bank, but with none of the conservatism which is the other side of the banking image, the new central office of the Banco de Londres y América del Sud was opened recently in Buenos Aires." As a matter of fact, the board of directors of the Banco had to deal with the British community in Buenos Aires, among others, whose more eminent members would have preferred an image more in keeping with the old representative traditions of these institutions in the United Kingdom, instead of that extremely advanced character of the building. Two years later, the magazine published a comment by Michael Manser, who stated that

> the winning design (...) can only be described as a riveting piece of streetscape and a structural pyrotechnic (...). The exuberance of the architectural expression externally and the daring, dramatic structure produce an interior of cathedral-nave proportions.[36]

Manser was impressed by the interior space, which he regarded as "a baroque voluptuousness." But the most remarkable is that, according to him, the Banco as an institution

> deserves to be as well rewarded by its new building. It has patronized *a piece of architecture that is stridently and genuinely*

modern and would have been technically unconstructible even a few years before.[37] Rightly, this British bank has earned itself an image of modernity and progress in South America.

Even more emphatic, concerning the advanced technology of the building, was the observation of Pierre Dufau, published in *Technique & Architecture* in 1966.[38] In this case, the critic spared no effort to present the Banco de Londres y América del Sud as conceived for "tackling the hardest conditions:"[39] complicated landscape, "conservative" bank. According to Dufau, it was a "joint work of five architects, one English, three Argentines, and one Italian become Argentine."[40] Notably, the construction was presented here as an example of how to overcome the state of uncertainty and paralysis in architecture at that time. In order to update the architecture, Dufau thought that it

> "can take several paths. There is the path of Brasilia, the grand gesture that hits the crowd, but at the same time the formalism and the contempt of the intrinsic quality of the construction. The difficult route of austere heresy may be preferred, and from my point of view I preferred it, but for this reason being even more admirable, a route chosen by the architects of the Banco de Londres. With a humble frame of mind but with stubborn courage, *implying in the battle all the technical possibilities of the time,*[41] but also all the resources of imagination, not bullied but exalted by the difficulties encountered, they sought not the glory but a more intense satisfaction, that of having themselves grappled with a difficult architectural problem and having solved it with a superior quality.[42]

The value of the Banco lay precisely in the fact that it did not constitute an escape of the increasingly dominant technological world (as proposed by Le Corbusier in Ronchamp or India), but an attempt of a complete immersion in that world, basing its control on an exercise of sensitivity. According to Dufau, "if the architects want to master the scientific and technological world, which has a strong tendency to deny the architectural values, I think this the way to follow, instead of the other."[43]

In the light of what happened during the subsequent decades, the critique published in *Techniques & Architecture* helps us to recover the magnitude of the Banco de Londres y América del Sud and what it represented within the international debate at the time. Moreover, people certainly remember the near-dissolution of Argentina at the beginning of the 21st century, when it was possible to watch on TV thousands of its citizens waiting in front of the European consulates for their documents to flee the country. In this context, the enthusiastic conclusion of Dufau turns out to be a surprise not only in terms of architectural culture. According to him, the construction of the Banco had been possible because of the conjunction of three protagonists: a third of the merit went to the Banco's board of directors, the second third to the architects. "To whom will the last third go?" ("A qui le dernir tiers?"), he asked himself. And answered:

> To the city of Buenos Aires. Despite my regret to close that panegyric on a melancholy note, I must say that *such a building would be difficult to construct in most capital cities, and unthinkable to build in Paris.*[44] In Buenos Aires it was possible. The freshness of spirit and the vitality, required on the part of the local administration, are evident here. Do we have to take the plane to Buenos Aires?[45]

[1]The acronym "BLAS" in the original title ("Polisemia: releyendo las lecturas de BLAS"), refers to *Banco de Londres y America del Sur* (Bank of London and South America) (Note of the translator.)

[2]Peter Cook, "Clorindo Testa´s Bank of London and South America, Buenos Aires," *Architectural Design*, no. 74 (Sept. 10, 2001).

[3]Damián Bayón and Paolo Gasparini (photography), *Panorámica de la arquitectura latinoamericana* (Barcelona, 1977).

[4]Ramón Gutiérrez, *Arquitectura y Urbanismo en Iberoamérica* (Madrid, 1983).

[5]Oriol Bohigas, "Un profesional sin angustia: entrevista a Clorindo Testa," ("A non-anxiety profesional: interview with Clorindo Testa"), published in *Arquitecturas Bis*, no.35 (Jan.-March, 1981).

[6]In 1986 SEPRA split up into two offices: Sánchez Elia-SEPRA and Peralta Ramos-SEPRA.

[7]Jorge Glusberg, "Banco de Londres y América del Sud, casa central," *GA*, no.65, 1983.

[8]In those sketches the interior space of the bank is presented as integrated with its environment, formulating an idea that has remained as a determinant of the project. Nevertheless, comparing those sketches with the original drawings of the façade, it is possible to see that this idea was also a subsequent verification, since the initial perimeter wall's compactness could hardly make possible the relation expressed in the famous section sketch.

[9] Author's interviews with Eng. Horacio Reggini (Nov. 4, 2010) and architects Santiago Sánchez Elía and Gregorio de la Ferrere (Nov. 25, 1996).

[10]Alberto Petrina, "El imperio de los sentidos" (In the empire of the senses), Summa, no.183/184 (Jan.-Feb., 1983). In this sense, Petrina repeated an observation that Jorge Glusberg had made in 1977 — *Hacia una Arquitectura Topológica* (*Toward an Topological Architecture*), Buenos Aires: "The BOLSA, erected in the middle of Buenos Aires City, from the rhetorical viewpoint, is a transgression of the context in which it is placed."

[11]Horacio Pando, "Opiniones," Summa 6/7 (Dec. 1966).

[12]"Bank of London and South America. Open letter from 7 Argentinian architects" (Eduardo Charosky, Gerardo Clusellas, José Kuperszmit, Martha Levisman, Ignacio Lopatin, Jorge Moreo [sic], and Leonardo Zylberberg).

[13]*Architectural Design*, 37 (Jan. 1967). The publication of this letter in parallel with the presentation of the Bank, in the same issue, can be explained through the close relationships of Monica Pidgeon, the editor of *Architectural Design*, with the South American progressive circles. Resident in the United Kingdom, but born in Chile, Pidgeon had revisited South America in 1962 and had known about John Turner's work in the slums of Peru. On this topic, she had published "Dwelling Resources in South America" in volume 33 (Aug. 1963), written by Turner and William Mangin. Also Kenneth Frampton, technical editor of the magazine, had the same kind of relationships at that time.

[14]Ramón Vargas Salguero and Rafael López Rangel, "La crisis actual de la arquitectura latinoamericana" (The present crisis of the Latin American architecture), in Roberto Segre (editor), *America Latina en su Arquitectura* (México D.F.: Unesco, 1975).

[15]Kenneth Frampton, "Prospects for a Critical Regionalism," *Perspecta* 20 (1983).

[16]Federico Peralta Ramos and Santiago Sánchez belong to some of the most characteristic families of this establishment; to cap it all SEPRA had acquired the office of Lyman O. Dudley, born and graduated in the United States, who had distinguished clients.

[17]Francisco Bullrich, *Arquitectura Latinoamericana. 1930-1970* (Buenos Aires: Sudamericana, 1969).

[18]R. Gutiérrez and G. Viñuales, "Grandes voces" (Big voices), en R. Gutierrez (ed.), *Architettura e Societá. L'America Latina nel XX secolo*, 1996. The authors just repeated the numerous previous statements along the same line. Roberto Segre, for instance, had lent credence to this interpretation already, emphasizing in the Bank "the formal and constructive Brutalism, which allows us to perceive its image as detached from the context" (R. Segre, *Las Estructuras Ambientales de America Latina* [Havana, 1977]).

[19]The author of this paper was also seduced by this association some years ago. Cf. Jorge F. Liernur, "The Bank of London and South America Head Office, Buenos Aires, 1960-1966; Architects (1966): SEPRA with Clorindo Testa," *AA files* 34, 1997.

[20] "Banco de Londres. Clorindo Testa", in *Appropiate Technologies. Technological Culture in Modern Latin American Architecture*; Prof. Renato D'Alençonm, Habitat Unit, TU Berlin, 2009.

[21]Idem

[22]Jantje Engels, "Rejecting the international style. Search for identity through an integrated structure. Search for identity through tectonic as seen in the competition for the Bank of London and South America, Buenos Aires, Argentina, in 1959," *Appropriate Technologies...*, op.cit.

[23]The House over the Stream or "Casa sobre el Arroyo," name used by the author, is better known as Bridge House in the American and British literature (note of the translator).

[24]The following offices participated in the contest: A.L. Jacobs and A. J. Falomir; S.G Follet and Follett, associated with Dodds & Cattaneo; De la Maria Prins Olivera, and Clorindo Testa, Santiago Sanchez Elia, Diego Peralta Ramos and Alfredo Agostini (S.E.P.R.A.)

[25]Nelson was certainly known in Buenos Aires. In 1938, the young members of Austral had called him to design the hospital, on the occasion of the University City project that they planned together. See Jorge Ferrari Hardoy Archive, Special Collections, GSD, Harvard.

[26]Claudio Docampo and Gustavo Dieguez, "El sueño de la razón" (The dream of the reason), *Revista de Arquitectura*, 173/175, 1995.

[27]At that time "common" buildings used concrete with a resistance between 60 and 160 kg/m^2. The reinforced concrete utilized in the Bank, with a resistance of 350 kg/m^2, was recommended for bridge construction by DIN standard 4225, which should have a resistance between 160 and 600 kg/m^2.

[28]For a structural analysis see José Manuel Pedregal, "Sobre la concepción estructural del Banco de Londres" (On the structural conception of the Bank of London), Summa 6/7 (Buenos Aires, Dec. 1996). See also Horacio Reggini.

[29]4,000 m^2 are approximately 43,055 ft^2. 1.5 x 6 m is equivalent to 4.92 x 19.68 ft, while 1,800 kg are approximately 3,968 lb (note of the translator).

[30]During his stay in the United States, Reggini made a trip with Delpini to know the most important engineering works in that country. Interview with Horacio Reggini.

[31]As an indication of academic excellence, we must remember that the Nobel Prize in chemistry Cesar Milstein graduated from the Exact Sciences School at the University of Buenos Aires.

[32]Interviewed, Clorindo Testa mentioned that it was Wakeman who proposed to change them, since "it looks like a Gruyère cheese."

[33]Statement of Gregorio de la Ferrere, cit.

[34]Francisco Bullrich, "Opiniones" (Opinions), *Summa* 6/7, op. cit. In order to understand the statement it is important to take into account that Pevsner visited Buenos Aires in 1963, when the Bank was not finished yet. In that occasion, however, there was already a non-definitive version of the drawings, showing similar characteristics to the project of Webb, and the Fun Palace project of 1961 (after the Bank) was already known

[35]The first of them was the Editorial of *Design*, 214 (Jan. 10th, 1966).

[36]Michael Manser, "Building and image abroad," *Design*, 234 (Jan. 6th, 1968).

[37]emphasis added

[38]Pierre Dufau, "Buenos Aires (Argentine). Le Nouveau siège de la Bank of London and South America," *Techniques & Architecture*, serie 27th, 3 (Nov., 1966). Gerald Wakeham, architecte, conseil de la Banque, Sanchez Elya [sic], Peralta Ramos, Agostini, Clorindo Testa architectes. F.Long et Riggini [sic] ingénieurs de béton.

[39]Originally in French, as cited by the author: "dans les pires conditions de difficultes." (Note of the translator).

[40]Originally in French, as cited by the author: "oeuvre conjointe de cinc architectes, un Anglais, trois Argentins et un Italien devenu Argentin." (Note of the translator).

[41]emphasis added

[42]"peut prendre plusieurs chemins. Il y a la voie de Brasilia, le grand geste qui frappe les foules, mais en même temps le formalisme et le mépris de la qualité intrinsèque de la construction. On peut préférer, et pour mon compte se le préfére, la voie austère, hérisèe de difficultés, mais par cela même plus admirable, qu'ont choisie les architectes de la Bank of London; dans une disposition d'esprit modeste mais avec un courage entêté, jetant dans la bataille toutes les possibilités techniques de l'époque mais aussi toutes les ressources d'une imagination non pas brimée mais exaltée par les contraites rencontrées, ils ont cherché non la gloire mais une satisfaction beacoup plus intense: celle de s'être colleté avec un problème architectural ardu et de l'avoir supérieurement résolu"

[43]Originally in French, as cited by the author: "si les architectes veulent dominer ce monde scientifique et technique qui n'a que trop tendente à nier les valeurs architecturales, il me semble que la voie à suivre, c'est plutôt celle-là. La porte est étroite maisi le chemin mène plus loin." (Note of the translator).

[44]Emphasis added.

[45] Originally in French, as cited by the author: "A la ville de Buenos Aires. Malgré mon regret de clore ce dithyrambe par une note mélancolique, je dois dire qu'il serait probablemente difficile de construire un tel édifice dans la plupart des capitales et qu'il est impensable de le construire a Paris. A Buenos Aires , c'était possible. La fraîcheur d'esprit et la vitalité que cela súpose de la part de l'administration locale sont ici évidentes. Devons-nous prendre l'avion pour Buenos Aires?" (Note of the translator).

Fictions and realities in the work of Clorindo Testa

Manuel Cuadra
Translated by Louise Mereles

Clorindo Testa's capacity of conviction surprises even more as it pertains to a variety of works: on one hand we have Clorindo Testa the artist, on the other, the architect; from the artist we have drawings, paintings, objects, installations and from the architect a great variety of major and minor works, more and less complex, always answering to concrete moments in Argentinian social life.

There is a great variety over time as well, as great as the developments in the history of architecture in the world, in Latin America and Argentina over the last half century. Clorindo Testa's work has kept and keeps a notable relevance, in his artistic as well as architectonic endeavours.

All of this raises the question: from where does this capacity for conviction come? We will try to answer this question here, taking as a reference the Banco de Londres y América del Sud, carried out by Clorindo in partnership with studio SEPRA.

The Absolute Eye

In *Clorindo Testa Architect*[1] I outlined a thesis based on the contemplation of his biographical aspects. Having dealt with themes of pedagogy and preschool architectures in *Der Kindergarten*[2] I knew the work of María Montessori and the underlying concepts of the kindergartens inspired by her.

I discovered that, as a child, Clorindo had been a student of one of these kindergartens and I thought this was revealing: the faith in the precedence of perception that translated into the systematic cultivation of the senses as a starting point of everything that follows, seemed fitting for the understanding of the immediacy between lines, surfaces, forms or spaces as proposed by Clorindo and their effects on the spectator. In other words: I thought I understood that the capacity for conviction in Clorindo's designs is based on the direct contact that he establishes, as only a few know how, between the spectator and himself, with the line, the surface, the shape or the space proposed by him always being a direct road, leaving no room for misinterpretations.

I spoke at the time of an "absolute eye", a variation on the "absolute pitch" in music — which here refers to the capacity of identifying a sound infallibly by some people without the need of reference sounds, or, if you will, having these sounds recorded inside.

I related this concept to Clorindo endowed with the same security at the time he generates in the spectator the visual resonance meant for him. It is a beautiful talent. But is it enough to explain this fascinating capacity for conviction?

> *The consolation was found in the fact that around that time a Montessorian school was opened in Cataca; the teachers stimulated the five senses through practical exercises and taught singing. With the talent and beauty of the director, Rosa Elena Ferguson, studying was as wonderful as playing to be alive. I learned how to appreciate the sense of smell, whose power of nostalgic recollections is overwhelming. The palate, I refined it to the point of having tried beverages that taste like a window, old breads that taste like a trunk, and infusions that taste like a mass. In theory it is hard to understand those subjective pleasures, but those who have experienced them will understand immediately.*

The person who writes this is Gabriel García Márquez, in his autobiography *Vivir para contarla*[3]. When Gabo speaks of "beverages that taste like a window", he distinguishes the different aspects that make up perception.

To speak about perception making reference to the senses, trained according to María Montessori, suggests a sharpening of the senses like that which can be exercised on a seismograph, in a technical way. If that were so, the result of training taste in that way might produce, as a result, an accentuated capacity to distinguish very precisely, for instance, the different components which make up the flavour of a beverage.

In Gabo's case, he talks about the flavour of a window. The sharpening of perception to which he makes a reference is not a technical sharpening, or not primarily so, instead he is referring to a cultural sharpening, one in which the person is involved profoundly, with all their culture and knowledge and their memories and conditioning and all that which he has absorbed in the environment in which he has lived and lives. The beverage that Gabo tasted, through its flavour, unleashed in him an impression which, in a way, was unleashed as well by a window, surely not any window, but what Gabo at that point understood to be a window, what "window" meant for him at that time.

In a similar way, in Clorindo's case, for example, a line or a grey circle could simply be a line and a circle and at the same time have connotations, like the "flavor" of a determined thing, a "flavor" that for the drawing or the painting ended up being as decisive as the line and the circle themselves. And if Clorindo the artist painted and drew that way it is because he thought, sensed, and felt that way: shouldn't Clorindo Testa, the architect, act in an analogous manner?

In this case, more than metaphors we are facing associations that appear to be subjective and personal, but are rather perfectly understood by the inspired reader or spectator. Gabo as well as Clorindo show a great freedom to travel across the world of perceptions and the resonances that these awaken, likewise to formulate associations, connecting to the meanings that exist in a way in the collective conscience, meanings that are sometimes so tenuous and subtle, that instead of existing one could talk as well of discovered meanings and even further, invented meanings: fictions, if you will.

Subjectivities and Objectivities

This talent would seem to be a very solid basis for artistic and architectural production, but it would be likewise only a foundation. Architecture, as well as art, are and require more than this. Speaking of architecture you can find the functional aspects: without an adequate management of these, the end result would be fastidious or annoying, independently of other aesthetic qualities that the work might have. There are also the constructional aspects, related to the carrying structure of a building, the partition walls, the materials used, with the constructive methods, with the details, finally a fundamental part of what makes up the physical presence of a work, in the forms as well as the surfaces and their textures and colours. Again, with an inadequate handling of the construction, the result would be fastidious.

Enlarging the perspective, there are the urban planning design aspects, the consideration of the urban context if you will, the relationship proposed by the building towards the neighbourhood in which it is located, and particularly with the places, spaces and the constructions located in its vicinity. Likewise, at this level we are confronted with a series of questions and topics in general, which we can deal with in a more or less objective way. The objectivity would seem greater at the time of considering functional and constructive matters; at least that is what we are accustomed to think.

And the objectivity would seem lesser at the time of locating a work of architecture in an historical context, and above all bowing to historicism like downtown Buenos Aires, between the streets of Reconquista and Bartolomé Mitre, where the headquarters of the Bank is situated. History makes of a work of architecture a container of the cultural moment of its origin, and thence a world of functions and constructions in addition to the forms and spaces that have lost — from the point of view of the spectators above all of the moment that follows — their validity and meaning.

This occurrence precisely at that moment when architectures are full of historicism and at the same time as they are making reference to historical moments to which they do not belong, but that they quote and interpret, transforming themselves thus in containers of a second degree of complexity. How to establish a dialogue with an environment like this, such as it was intended by Clorindo Testa? Confronted by a multiplicity of conditions to be dealt with in an objective manner, and these to be dealt with through a primarily cultural sensitivity, Clorindo Testa demonstrated that he could move with great comfort and effectiveness in a situation like this, plagued with ambiguities, complexities and contradictions.

Authors and Authorships

Without a doubt, the Banco de Londres y América del Sud is simultaneously a very clear and a mysterious work; clear in its functional and constructive logic, and mysterious because it always is, more than logic, spirit. What or who is behind this? At first glance his authorship is an indisputable thing: as is known, this was a joint work by the SEPRA studio, formed by the architects Santiago Sánchez Elía, Federico Peralta Ramos and Alfredo Agostini and the architect and painter Clorindo Testa. It is, thus, the result of an uneven union of personalities. In 1959, when SEPRA was invited to participate in the architectural competition, the practice, founded in 1936, had more than 20 years of experience through many great achievements and an excellent professional reputation. Clorindo Testa, born in 1923, was 36 at the time, and being the youngest person on the team, he stood out because of his work as a painter and because

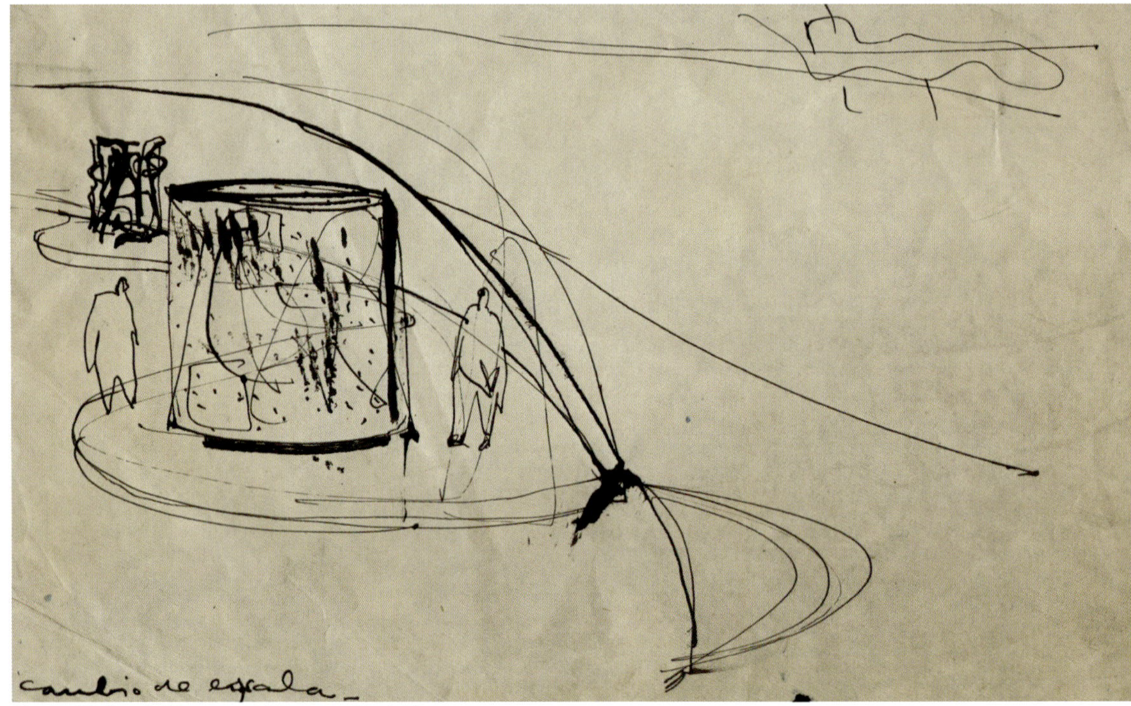

Sketch of Batlle y Ordóñez memorial for competition in Uruguay, Clorindo Testa

of his first major buildings carried out in the provinces as an artist-architect.

It must have been the understanding of their strengths and limits as well as those of Clorindo Testa that encouraged the experienced architects to involve Clorindo in joint contribution for the Memorial a Batlle y Ordóñez competition in Uruguay[4]. The result — a second place in the first round and a third in the second and definitive, the first place being void — must have convinced Sánchez Elia, Peralta Ramos and Agostini of the convenience of extending the collaboration to the contest for the Banco de Londres y América del Sud. The quality of the design must have convinced them as well, a design whose themes would come back in the project for the Bank.

Painting, Clorindo Testa

Behind this capacity for conviction are the architects. According to the convincing words of Clorindo Testa and in spite of the general assumption that the authorship resides mainly in him, the project for the Bank was an authentic team effort: a product of the dynamic of a very special group, in which all participants were able to collaborate and be more than they would be in other circumstances, previously and subsequently, individually and collectively. On SEPRA's side, Sánchez Elía and Agostini stood out, while Peralta Ramos was left in charge of the other numerous projects that were being developed at the same time by the office. Clorindo points out the great experience and creativity of Sánchez Elía in all that pertains to the construction and development of the plans, as well as Agostini's intelligence regarding the architectural design. On his own role, he does not waste any words.

Thus, it is public opinion that has assigned authorship to Clorindo Testa, although not in general but in the aspects which are considered exceptional. Actually, the Banco de Londres y América del Sud is exceptional in several ways: in the nature of its realization, in its artistic quality and in the correlation between both: in the poetic and the material. All of this, as Testa explains, is the result of an exceptional group dynamic, in which each player pitched in their contribution and the final result is greater than the sum of these contributions.

If public opinion insists on highlighting Clorindo, it is because it appreciates more the artistic value than the material one, and furthermore because it finds artistic value in previous and subsequent works by Clorindo, both in the fields of art and architecture. In other words: it is thought that the only one without whose contributions the project would have lacked quality, was Clorindo Testa.

For the proof of this thesis, his artistic production would be enough. From the 1950s, when the project of the Bank was conceived, and the 1960s, when the plans were laid out and the work executed, Clorindo produced two oil paintings that hang in the dining room at his home: both are untitled, both make do with white, black and the intermediate greys, and both are "abstract". As such, in this case they show lines and surfaces, individual figures and groups in different constellations, that are available to be read, figuratively, by those who would want to do so, but that in truth are not seeking this. In other words: the echo that they awaken in the spectator is not motivated by reasons taken from the material reality, or at least not primarily, but simply and directly by what this echo is, such as is evoked in the spectator and for the spectator.

Buenos Aires: the Contribution of the Place and Its Architectural Culture

The Banco de Londres y América del Sud stands out amongst the enormous architectural production of its time, not only in Argentina, but also in Latin America and beyond. For this it launches the question of its relationship to place: how was it possible that a work so architecturally advanced was conceived and realized in Buenos Aires, so far from the centres that are otherwise considered to be the leaders?

The exact circumstances have to do with the British presence in Argentina and its ambitious projections for the future; with a cultured and educated client who put the organization and scheduling of an architectural competition in the hands of an architect who specialized in such matters, namely Gerald Wakeham. A client who, in the face of Wakeham's evaluation of the submitted competition projects, accepted the results without question, transforming them into a decision; a relationship that would also later do without direct communication between the client and architects, channelling said communication always through Wakeham. These are truly exceptional conditions not only for Argentina, but for the respect that they show for the discipline of architecture and its complexities, as for the architects themselves.

The architectural quality that these conditions permitted is, however, something that they themselves could not generate, as positive and generous as they might have been. This quality can only arise from a medium where it already exists, or where it potentially exists, lacking only a small step to achieve a new level. In this case, that of the Bank. On a personal level, SEPRA — as well as other architectural practices in Buenos Aires — had a grasp on all the techniques required for the completion of a work of this nature and on — paraphrasing Auguste Perret — the language of architecture that was for him that of construction. And the poem to be written, continuing with Perret, was formulated by Clorindo Testa: it is he as an artist who uses the language to express and tell the story in an architecturally convincing way.

At the time of conceiving the Bank Clorindo Testa was a young architect. His special gift was a double talent as architect and painter; the most distant background sounds good, but it would not have suggested anything further: with others he had in common the architectural studies in Buenos Aires, his visits to Europe as well as his internship in Ernesto Rogers, Gian Luigi Banfi, Ludovico Belgiojoso and Enrico Peressutti's studio BBPR in Milan. The difference again falls in the personal talent and aptitudes that allowed Clorindo to transform that which he assimilated into something new and at the same time a synthesis of that which he had lived and knew.

For someone with a talent such as this to have spent his infancy in Buenos Aires constitutes a real starting point. Having arrived in this world in 1928, the Buenos Aires of Testa's childhood was in many respects that which fascinated Le Corbusier in his visit in 1929. Buenos Aires at that time represented the New World, concretely recognizable in the sheer size of the country, of its territories and its landscapes, which were the basis for the great scale of its economy. All of this was evident in the production structures that were concentrated in the ports: in the silos, the shipyards, the cranes and the railway facilities.

These structures, with which the young Clorindo grew up, were, for example, edifices made out of reinforced concrete, built with the most modern techniques, amongst them that of the slipform. Compared to the scale of the city and the architecture of the city, its scale was gigantic: it corresponded to the scale of the modern world and economy. And its language — developed from functions, from the materials and constructive techniques — ended up being new as well, and as convincing as all this was of a new world which, still young, always prevailed and displaced, with such naturalness and apparent ease, that which was known.

For the movable components or for those things that for other reasons needed to be light, steel was preferred. Amongst those that have been preserved until today we can highlight the portal cranes in the neighbourhood of La Boca: structures that were at once skilful and of large spans, suitable to assume large and dynamic loads, thus able to lift weights, transmitting the loads by cables and pulleys to the beams and the pillars that ultimately rest on metal wheels sliding on rails. For those who have the visual fantasy and sufficient structural comprehension, it is here that a very exciting performance unfolds.

At the same time as Buenos Aires concentrated in the port and industrial areas as built documents of industrialization, it made a strong case as an urban centre for the New World. This is expressed in its urbanism, of a distinct conceptual consistency following and reinterpreting the models of the 19th century and at the same time with its own sense of the optimum from a pragmatic point of view. The Mayo and 9 de Julio avenues in combination with the weave of blocks and streets are a convincing example of urban culture and above all a demonstration of the capacity for achievement by Porteños in a project of this complexity, involving the contribution of planners, investors, users, citizens in general and architects. There is no shortage of notable works of architecture of this period. These range from the Mercado de Abastos[5], to the Barolo and Kavanagh buildings, and many others, as outstanding as individual objects as they are representative of a building activity of a high level in matters of design and technology.

All of this was absorbed by Clorindo Testa: the proof is the architecture of the Banco de Londres y América del Sud, read as a creative synthesis of all that was produced in and by Buenos Aires until that point. This is not only generally the case, but more concretely at the time of considering the relationship between the Bank and its neighbors, especially that of the Banco de la Nación Argentina. A work of one of the great local architects of the time, Alejandro Bustillo, and taking up a whole city block, very well and prominently located, between the block on which the Banco de Londres y América del Sud sits and Plaza de Mayo, with a direct view of the Casa Rosada[6] it is clad with a conventional neoclassical façade. The building's highlight is the interior space, almost as large as the whole block and of an architecture that is at the same time part of the city and a city in itself.

Complexities

The Banco de Londres y América del Sud is on the one hand a very rational piece of architecture, very logical. Obviously the architects attached great importance to the functional organization of the Bank, — so much so that Clorindo thinks that Gerald Wakeham chose the project mainly because it corresponded in a very literal way to that which was stipulated in the competition rules and conditions.

Precisely. In order to understand the clarity and accuracy of the organization of the three dimensions, it is enough to visualize the horizontal organization that is contained in the floor plans and the way in which these, once they are superimposed, define the vertical organization: with the public access at the corner of the building and at the junction of Reconquista and Bartolomé Mitre streets, which is the most open and luminous place, the more urban and communicative, and at one end of the lot; with the access for employees towards the opposite end, in the shade; with the public area thus near the corresponding entrance, and the back offices on the opposing side; generating in this way a movement from the public to the internal and from the internal to the public. This is a purely functional consideration.

In a second step, the functional organization is translated exactly into the building's spatial organization. The resultant areas, spaces and volumes accompany and are at the disposal of these movements, thus corresponding to the encounters between users and bank employees.

In a third step, closely intertwined with the first two, but unlike what is generally carried out, at the same time displaying a very high degree of consequence and depth at the time of translating the determining factor in architecture, into spaces and forms, visual relations and experiences, the architects developed a spatial organization that corresponds and expresses the separation and the interaction between the various protagonists and their flows within the building: all the public zones rest directly on the floor; the two upper floors, also open to the public, are also connected to the ground by the columns, on which they rest and though which they transmit their load to the foundations.

This would not attract any attention were it not for the fact that on the other side, for the bank's internal operations, things are built in an inverted way: unlike the structural plates of the public areas those of the internal areas do not rest on the ground, but they are suspended — yes, suspended — from the megastructure, a megastructure that expresses itself at the same time in the great roof and the piers on the façade. The interaction between all the aspects and elements is fascinating: between the functional, the spatial and the structural, and between flagstone, beams, suspended columns, megastructure beam, the great waffle ceiling, pillar, foundation of the pillar... The lay person might not be able to understand completely all these relations, but he or she can perceive them, even if it is only at an instinctive level: the space vibrates with information such as a landscape does; the latter also communicates many aspects that are at the same time profoundly related to one another, in which each one is in turn the expression of the landscape and a shaping element without which it would not be what it is, or at least it would be incomplete.

And like in a landscape, there are many elements that converse and interact amongst themselves, maybe not an infinite number, but nevertheless all present, as they are in the Bank. In the landscape the weather and the vegetation are related as well as the vegetation and the ground, and both of them with the fauna; the fauna itself has a relationship to the weather... Even in their colour the animals denote and express the medium in which they live, besides their other characteristics like their scales, their nudity or their fur, more or less protective of the water and more or less hot according to the thousands of requirements of the place, and of life there, underground, above it or in the air or the water... Architecture is not, under any circumstances, as complex as nature. But our thirst for nature makes us smell it and enjoy it gratefully wherever it is evoked even though it happens in a very subtle way, as is the case of the Bank.

The dialogue between the public and the internal operations is also expressed in the scale of the different areas. Logically, it could be said, if logic were so strong and worked normally, the public area has a big scale: it is the scale of the building as a whole, it is also the scale of the city block in which the building is located, a scale that the building takes up and reinforces in a conscious manner. This big scale becomes clear specifically at the corner, in which the building opens to the city and access to the public is provided.

On the other hand, the scale of the internal zone is small, it is of a functionally necessary order, that which offers the indispensable heights, but not more: the Bank's employees show themselves before the clients as the servants that they are or ought to be; they have the necessary things to serve, but not more, thus they do not consider themselves more important than their clients.

In other words: the architecture ends up expressing much more than functional relationships. Rather, it expresses human relationships.

To speak of human relationships, involves speaking on the one hand about human beings and on the other about society as a whole, therefore treating human beings both as individuals and as a collective. This difference is necessary when contemplating the Banco de Londres y América del Sud.

What has been observed up until now has a lot to do with the collective aspects of human relations. The city is an expression of such relations, with its structure of city blocks and lots, with the streets and the intersections, with the buildings that occupy these lots and define the streets, fulfilling when they do so the corresponding rules and regulations, destined to generate a city where the organization and the spirit correspond to the wishes and needs of the urban society.

Architecture is at the same time an element of the city and a whole city — or a world — in itself. The individual is unavoidably one theme. As is the social aspect, to the extent that architecture assumes it as its own, which requires the social and the individual to become precisely its central theme. Thus architecture and the city are distinguished by place and the language: the void left by one is filled by the other, and it is done filling said void with the other's contents. At best, like in case of the Banco de Londres y América del Sud, the city, at the crossroads of Reconquista and Bartolomé Mitre, is more of a city thanks to the presence of the Bank, and the Bank is more of a work of architecture thanks to the city.

Archaisms

Surprisingly as well, no matter how many times one has seen it, the Banco de Londres y América del Sud feels once and again as something unknown: is this the result of the difficulty of recording in one's memory and experience something that is so alive with the essential? And what would the essential be? And why would that be experienced here?

The fascination that the Bank has aroused right from the beginning has to do in some way with its material constitution and what it evokes: the exposed concrete is not what is known as exposed concrete, but rock. And rock that is not in reality rock, at least not in the sense of that which is present in the contiguous buildings, supposedly made of stone. This rock has been liquid and has taken the shape of the construction that would become the Banco de Londres y América del Sud. This building is in itself a monolith, a stone monument in one piece, there is no doubt about it. But it is a habitable monolith, with big voids, almost a cave. Because it is a monolith, and because of its great dimension, it seems it has always been there, in Buenos Aires, on the corner of Reconquista and Bartolomé Mitre streets. It was even here before being here, before 1964, before the year in which it was discovered — so is its subcutaneous message.

Existing as an idea even before having been constructed, and yet not having been here all the time: material contradictions being unbound by the mere presence of a work of architecture that is alive. Contradictions that are typical also of other architectures, especially those that are as mute as this one: the architecture of the megalith, for example. Because they are prehistoric we know little about them, or better said: nothing concrete. Or more exactly: only that which we sense, because there are no explanatory documents. Mute only in terms of documented words, because these works are very rich in physical expressions: for starters, their location in the landscape tells stories, for those who want and can read them, of course. And the choice of not one stone, but several from different varieties; not a stone that is found in situ, but one that is frequently brought from afar; not a stone which is easy to work on, but the one that assures the communication of the desired message and promises to survive the passage of time so as to communicate once and again the message that it carries.

Yes, mute architectures which shake the spectator, just as the Banco de Londres y América del Sud does so well and with the same resources. What we know about the Bank is that which corresponds to our world, to the present, to the world of functions and the constructions in which we know how to move. But unlike many other architectures from our time, this is also a timeless architecture, and as such mute and at the same time, in its way, very eloquent: resorting to the innate understanding of all the human beings, in that common base which is all that is archaic, that substratum that unites us beyond time and place, culture and Zeitgeist.

The Artistic Construction of Architecture: the Urban and Architectonic Context

The elements with which Clorindo plays and which he integrates in his conception of the Banco de Londres y América del Sud, amongst them those that he finds in the location, correspond to the horizontal and vertical lines, as well as the circles and other figures of his drawings and paintings from this period.

In these can be found the urban structure, based on the city block with a square plan and octagonal corners, streets that are relatively narrow, sidewalks that are also narrow, and a closed building. Clorindo was determined to respect this structure. This affirmation is necessary, because at the time it constituted an exceptional gesture. Annoyed by the narrowness of the sidewalk, the Bank demanded a wider one in the requirements for the competition. Of the four projects presented, three of them translated this requirement as a recess of the entire building — which consequently led to a break from the urban grid. Only the scheme by SEPRA and Clorindo searched for a different solution to resolve the conflict generated by the rules of the competition in a positive manner — and it was found in the setback of the ground floors through the curving of the piers that at the higher floors cantilever into the street section until they take up again, at the highest level, the historical profile of the street and the contiguous buildings. A solution that could be taken as a purely formal gesture is therefore based on an urban strategy that is as simple as it is convincing.

The architectural structure of the contiguous buildings with their historic language can also be found here: with the socles, the colonnades and the cornices; with the more or less voluminous and detailed decorative elements; with the general character of stone and solidity. Clorindo takes up if not all these elements, then enough of them to understand that the new building joins in the conversation with its pre-existent neighbors . The Banco de Londres y América del Sud also has what can be called a socle, but instead of projecting to the outside takes on a negative form and sits back, leaving a recess between each pier. These piers are in turn the result of gathering the vertical supports at the ground floor so as to increase the permeability of the façade, allowing light to enter and generating views from the inside to the outside. In any case, these piers define a continuous rhythm just as the neoclassical columns do in the neighboring buildings; as in those instances, a vegetal origin is suggested, it has remains of the trunk of a tree at the bottom and a crown of a tree at the higher part.

The cornice of the Banco de Londres y América del Sud is a direct expression of the ledge that resumes the profile of the contiguous constructions. The stone-like character is translated directly into the exposed concrete, where concrete may be found, and into a giant curtain glazing screen made out of aluminium and glass: this explains the heavy profiling and above all the horizontal proportions of the window panes, that, besides being what they are, windows, make up a metaphor of the blocks of stone specially of the socles of the contiguous buildings — the ashlar, or dressed stone work, that stands out.

In its interior spaces, the Bank is organized in a precise manner with regard to the public and internal sectors: at least from the point of view that the Bank wished and sought to have with its clients. In other words: in spatial terms the Banco de Londres y América del Sud is a metaphor for the relationship between the Bank and the citizens of Buenos Aires, a relationship simultaneously based on the respect and on the wish to convince of and involve the public in the business that the Bank offers. In this light, the Bank constitutes a masterpiece: it is based closely on the understanding of what human relations are, something rather complex in itself. Human relations are complex in general, but even more so in the particular case of the situation generated and wished by the Bank.

This relationship is linked in an indissoluble manner to the place that the Bank occupies in Buenos Aires, in the first neighbourhood in which the city had expanded, only one block away from what used to be the fort of the city that would later be occupied by the presidential palace known as the Casa Rosada. The most politically prominent contiguous building is that of the Banco de la Nación, that occupies the block between the Casa Rosada and the Banco de Londres y América del Sud. The main entrance of the Bank is positioned toward the Plaza de Mayo, and it is located as near to it as possible, the Plaza being the centre of political life in Buenos Aires and in Argentina.

Clorindo Testa's project was able to transform the intersection of Reconquista and Bartolomé Mitre streets, where it is located, into something that was not expected in that place: a space that besides being a crossroads becomes something static, like a *plazuela* — a small square. This is achieved by putting the main access of the Bank in this spot; by giving this entrance an urban scale superior to the already generous scale of the contiguous buildings and that of its own piers; by generating a recess, that, when added to the space of the crossing of the streets, acquires the aspect of a small square; finally, by covering the space with ledges from the roof of the Bank, and closing the space with a flap, or "lapel", that hangs from these ledges in the same corner.

Clorindo Testa makes use of the methods of Baroque architecture: the interplay of projections and recesses, concave and convex elements, gestures that attract and others that repel, with all the ambivalence that this implicates. All of this was essential so that the difficult amalgamation of the public and the private would seem acceptable — politically acceptable, because it is above all that: a political gesture that is expressed through urban design and architecture. Specifically: the exterior layer of the Bank is made up of rows of piers, which define a plane interrupted exclusively and in a very demonstrative way by the small public space in front of the main entrance. These piers have a shape that besides their perfectly valid structural explanation, evoke trees, or for those who prefer it so, a heavy curtain tied every few feet to let the light in. This first level constitutes, in any case, more of a filter than an enclosure: taking a peek from the outside to the inside is similar to looking through a veil, a creeper or the crown of a tree.

The closed aspect is provided by the large aluminium and glass screen already mentioned, an envelope interrupted by dividing walls between Reconquista and Bartolomé Mitre. An envelope that is interrupted to allow the clients access: this passage is possible only through a great portal of exposed concrete, a great sculpture that evokes historical triumphal arches and that in this location makes a theme out of the transition from outside to inside, a transition that is dramatized in an extreme way. A possible precedent, although more delicate, is the portal of the Dr. Currutchet house by Le Corbusier in La Plata —a precedent that confirms the interest by Le Corbusier, shared by Clorindo, to find an anthropological foundation — instead of a historic one — in architecture. In contrast to that fragile solution, the one in the Bank could not be heavier.

In its heaviness it reminds us more of the ecclesiastic architecture of the Latin American Baroque, a Baroque of clay and thus very massive. And some of the details that can be found on entering the building are Baroque, like the oversized and heavy handrail on the stairs that lead from the entrance area to the first level of customer services, and that has to solve the difficult spatial task of a change in direction of ninety degrees as regards to both orientation and movement of the customer, refocusing both on the interior of the Bank. Typically for Clorindo, the gesture is presented just as is, for the one who wishes to understand: the handrail is made out of red polished granite and does not pretend to be a part of the structure; on the contrary it is clearly presented as covering added afterwards to the exposed concrete structure.

Those who enter the Bank look to their right and see, first through the "padded" effect of the screen and then through the foliage of a tree —

this time made up by one or two pillars located in this place —the façade of the Banco de la Nación on the opposing sidewalk of the Bank: it is this plane that closes visually the interior space of the Bank both towards Bartolomé Mitre and Reconquista. And this will be the view offered to those leaving the customer areas to step outside.

A person entering the Bank turns towards the left, being invited to take this turn at the lower landing of the wide staircase with its giant handrail and on a higher level by a passageway that opens up — in a Baroque welcoming gesture, by a concave space, one that embraces. The embracing arms are made up of structural slabs that extend towards the welcoming area in which the complementary functions to those at the access level of customer services are located. The straight path to these upper levels is offered to the public via the escalator, which is oriented in the direction of the visitor. The people who take up this welcoming offer and who allow themselves to slowly glide upwards do so by crossing a space that presents itself like a natural landscape with slopes, plateaus, gorges...

For those who are interested in it or who come with the necessary spare time, many beautiful views are offered on the inside of the building, some of them spectacular, as well as to the outside, always with the "trees" in view. Sometimes it is the architecture with its different levels that fascinates; but mostly it is the human and urban performance in the entry zone and outside on the street, in the atrium and at the junction of Reconquista and Bartolomé Mitre that is the protagonist.

The Artistic Construction of Architecture: the Interior Life

What is presented as a landscape, appealing to the sensitivity towards nature, topography, spaces, places and paths with which human beings have been gifted and blessed since time immemorial, is at the same time a refined technical device. It conjugates basically three macro elements — "macro" because each of them integrates many minor elements: there is the entrance area at ground level, that is the level of the city, where the city enters and floods the Bank; there is the customer service area, that starts a few steps above the access level and continues on the upper floors; there is also the internal restricted entrance area for the employees of the Bank. The technical refinement refers to the structural solution developed for each area. This technical solution is very distinctive of Clorindo Testa and it goes hand in hand with his game of associations and metaphors.

In structural terms, the entrance area supports itself on the ground in the same way as the pavement and sidewalks do on the outside. The indirect support of the customer service areas follows this very elemental solution: both the ground level and the floor slabs on the upper levels are supported by columns that in turn transmit the load to the foundation and these to the ground. This is an apparently conventional solution. It stops being apparent when it is contrasted with the back offices that are contained in a suspension structure. Instead of supporting these back offices on strong pillars, obviously working in compression and bending, and that in turn concentrate on beams and ledges, the floor slabs hang from long rows of thin steel rods that obviously — as is evidenced by their slenderness — work exclusively in tension. In the absence of a direct connection with the foundations, the impression — dramatic enough as it is — from the access and service areas is that the floor slabs are kept floating in space by all sorts of invisible forces, magnetic maybe, or, for those who look at them with the eyes of the muses, by magic.

To the attentive observer with an eye trained in the engineering field the matter is clear from the moment he enters the building: the view upward from the atrium shows the exposed concrete structure of the roof resting on the large pillars, all of them sufficiently strong to support in midair all the levels that one would want to suspend from them. And that is the case for all of the back offices.

Two elements articulate visually the public world of gravity and the back offices with its stratospheric air: the large tower made of exposed concrete that closes the public landscape and definitively separates it from the world beyond; and the relatively small cylinder that limits the access zone from the public area. This cylinder, as seen from the public access, is located behind the mechanical stairs and contains in it the public elevators, looking outwards, and a spiral staircase, positioned inwards. The combination of all these elements transforms the cylinder into a multifunctional object.

By comparison, the large concrete tower, instead of constituting an axis, wants to be and is a limit, a barrier, the end of a world: it is completely closed; its convex shape confirms the emphatic nature of its message. On the opposite side, towards the back offices, the tower gathers the elevators and stairs and in this way all the internal flows between the different levels of the Bank: therefore it is the centre of a giant ant hill that sprouts from the darkness and narrowness of the subsoil, moving upwards, increasing in size from floor to floor, and reaching its fullness and highest extension in the luminous and airy top floor that houses the social areas, the canteen and assembly rooms, besides the offices of the managers.

On the different levels bigger and smaller areas come together, where groups of equally varied dimensions work. Unlike the public landscapes with their heights, depths and forever changing perspectives, these areas are used for concentration on the job at hand, for work at a desk, are galleries with a height that is always adequate and constant, but never fascinating. The fascination begins only in areas that are in contact with public spaces, in places where the perspective opens up suddenly to the landscapes below. In work areas all is work: the floor, the walls, the ceiling, the lighting, and all sorts of details: everything has been developed and decided on with an objective criterion, therefore dispensing with subjectivities. In other words: the architecture here is a metaphor for the social and human fact that takes place at this spot to the extent that this social and human fact is reduced to a single dimension of work at the heart of the Bank.

However, there are still subtle references to the urban and architectural fact of which it is part: details such as the exposed concrete that is revealed here and there at the central core of elevators and stairways, or in the sporadic coating of the stairways with the same red granite of the handrail in the entrance area, and above all the view towards the outside through the treetops made out of piers, whose shape, varying from floor to floor, hints at the height where one finds oneself.

Seen as a whole, the Bank presents itself as a dialogue with the city, transforming itself into a public dialogue from the interior of the building to its exterior. Each dialoguing part is represented by an architectural part, each of a different shape, each in a different location, all of them entwined: the technical structure is a metaphor, the metaphor takes on a technical shape, neither of them makes sense without the other one. And above all, those who want to understand, can: intuition is enough, a complete and exact understanding is not possible and is likewise as unnecessary as it is in front of any other work of art.

Furthermore, the theme of this work of art is that the Banco de Londres y América del Sud, as it was conceived and developed by Clorindo Testa in collaboration with SEPRA, is a great metaphor for the social life in and around a Bank. The actors are the urban community, the clients of the Bank and the Bank itself, with its roots in that place and in distant London; the actors are represented by the city as a spatial and constructive fact, the public area of the Bank and the internal area. The stage, in which the play takes place, is given by the actors themselves and by a landscape of exact characteristics. That the whole is more than the sum of its parts is what makes it an architectural work of art.

[1]Manuel Cuadra, Clorindo Testa Architect. NAI Publishers, Rotterdam 2000.
[2]Manuel Cuadra, Der Kindergarten – Seine Architektur in Geschichte und Gegenwart; Anforderungen an den Kindergartenbau; Aktuelle Beispiele. Ernst & Sohn, Berlin 1997.
[3]Gabriel García Márquez, Vivir para contarla (Living to Tell the Tale), Norma, Bogotá 2002, page 117.
[4]Batlle y Ordóñez Memorial. Montevideo, Uruguay, 1959. International Competition in two rounds; Third Prize for SEPRA and Clorindo Testa architects.
[5]Supply Market
[6]Presidential Palace

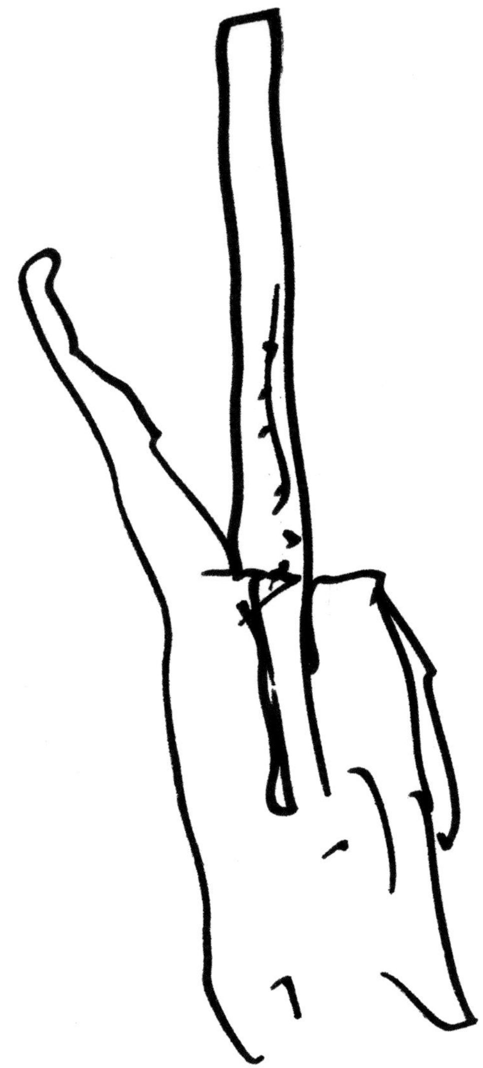

Sketches & Drawings

Opposite: Sketch, Global Architecture, 1984

Opposite: Organizational sketches
This page: Sketch of street view along Bartolomé Mitre

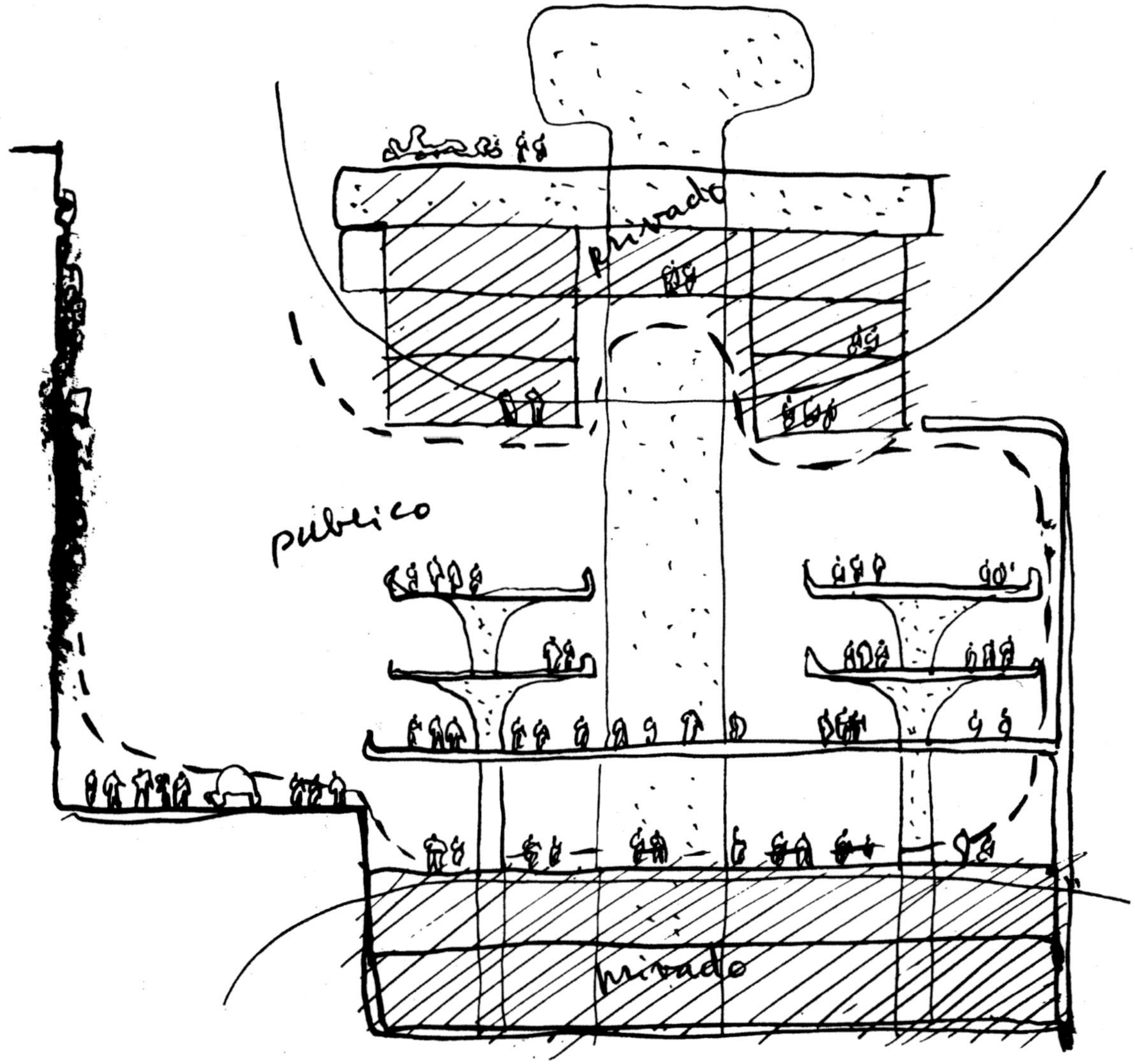

Opposite: Initial conceptual sketches, Global Architecture, 1984
This page: Interior organizational sketch

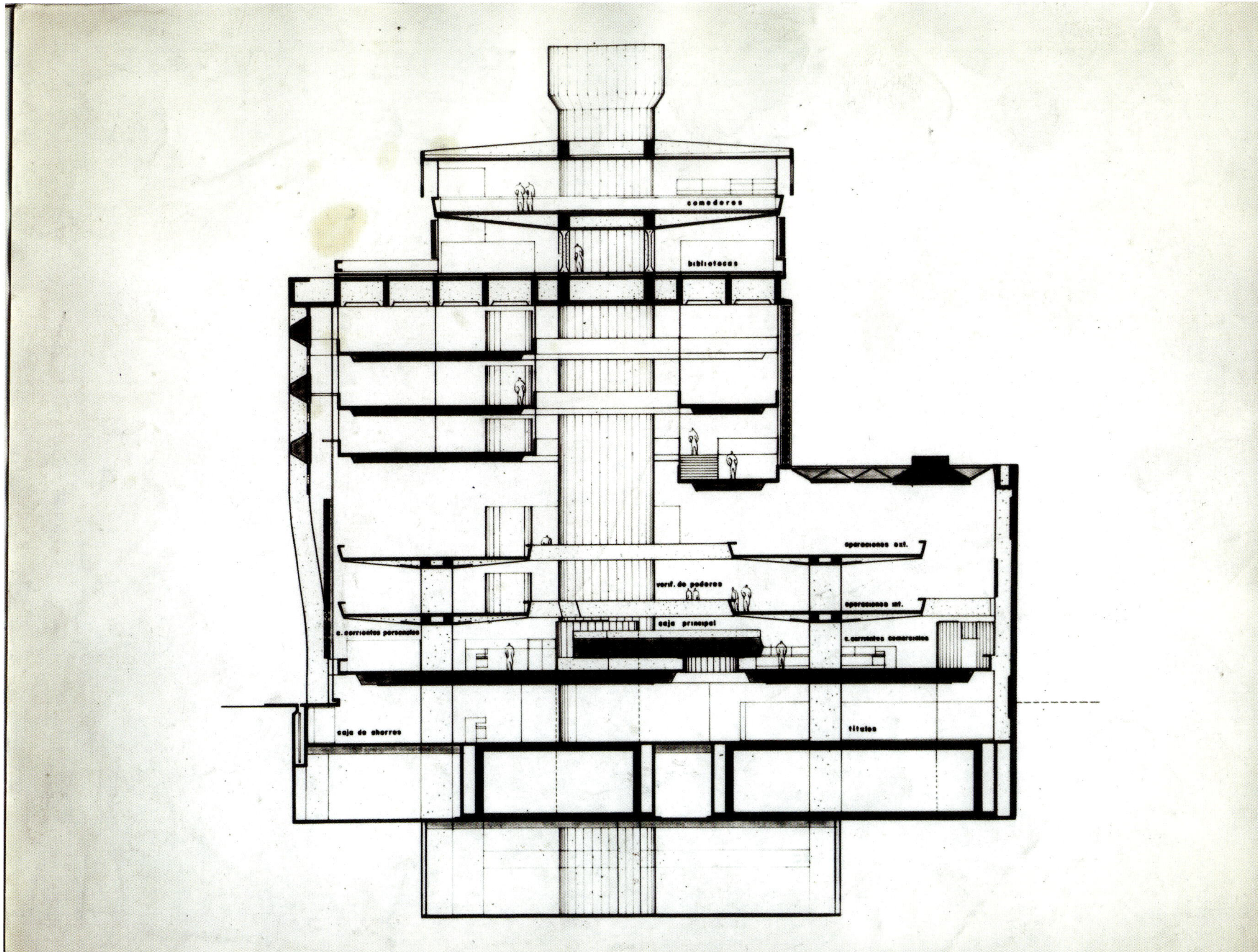

Opposite: Competition elevation (Reconquista Facade), Clorindo Testa estudio file.
This page: Competition section, Clorindo Testa estudio file.

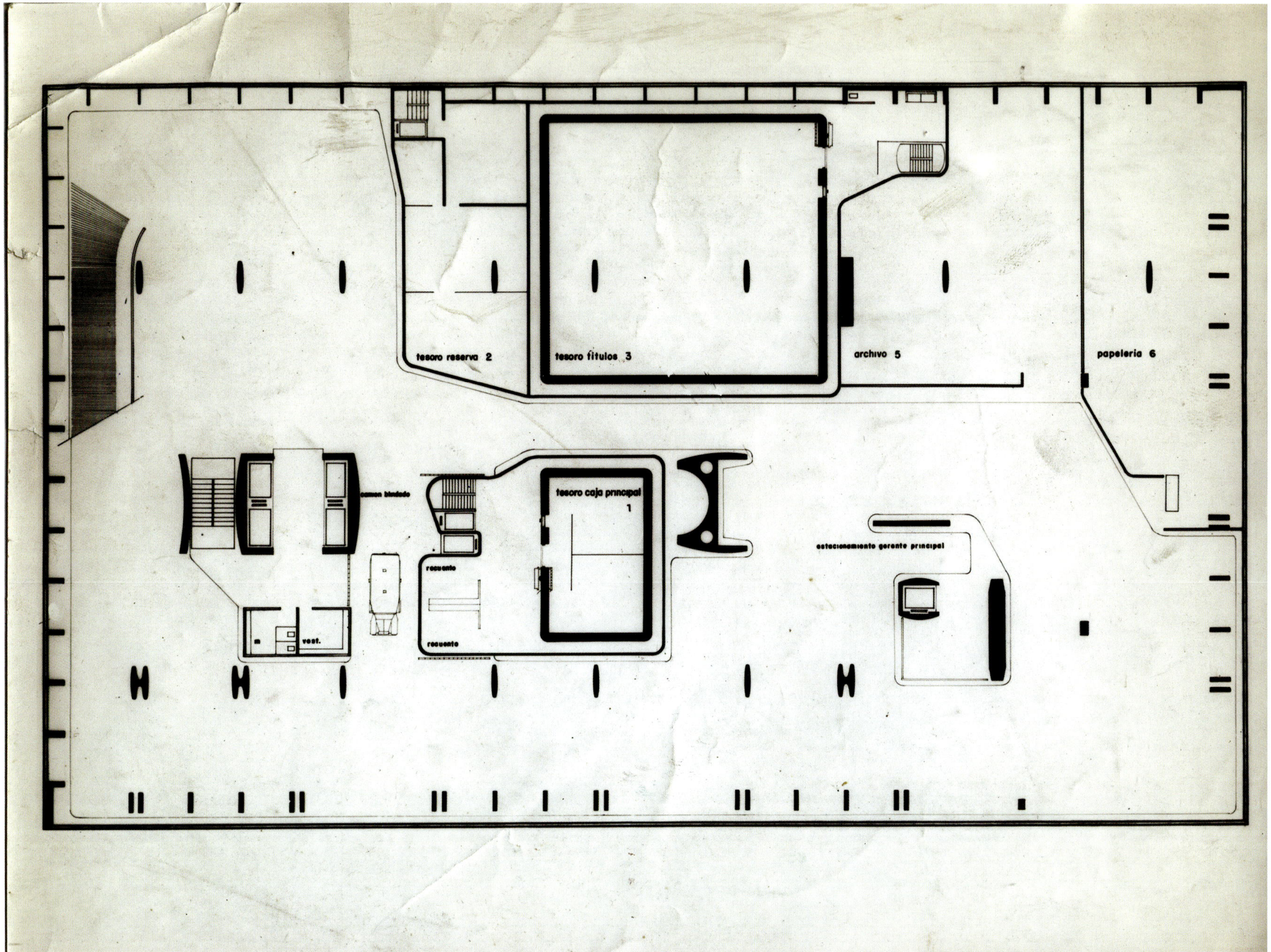
tesoro reserva 2
tesoro títulos 3
archivo 5
papelería 6
camion blindado
tesoro caja principal
1
recuento
recuento
vest.
estacionamiento gerente principal

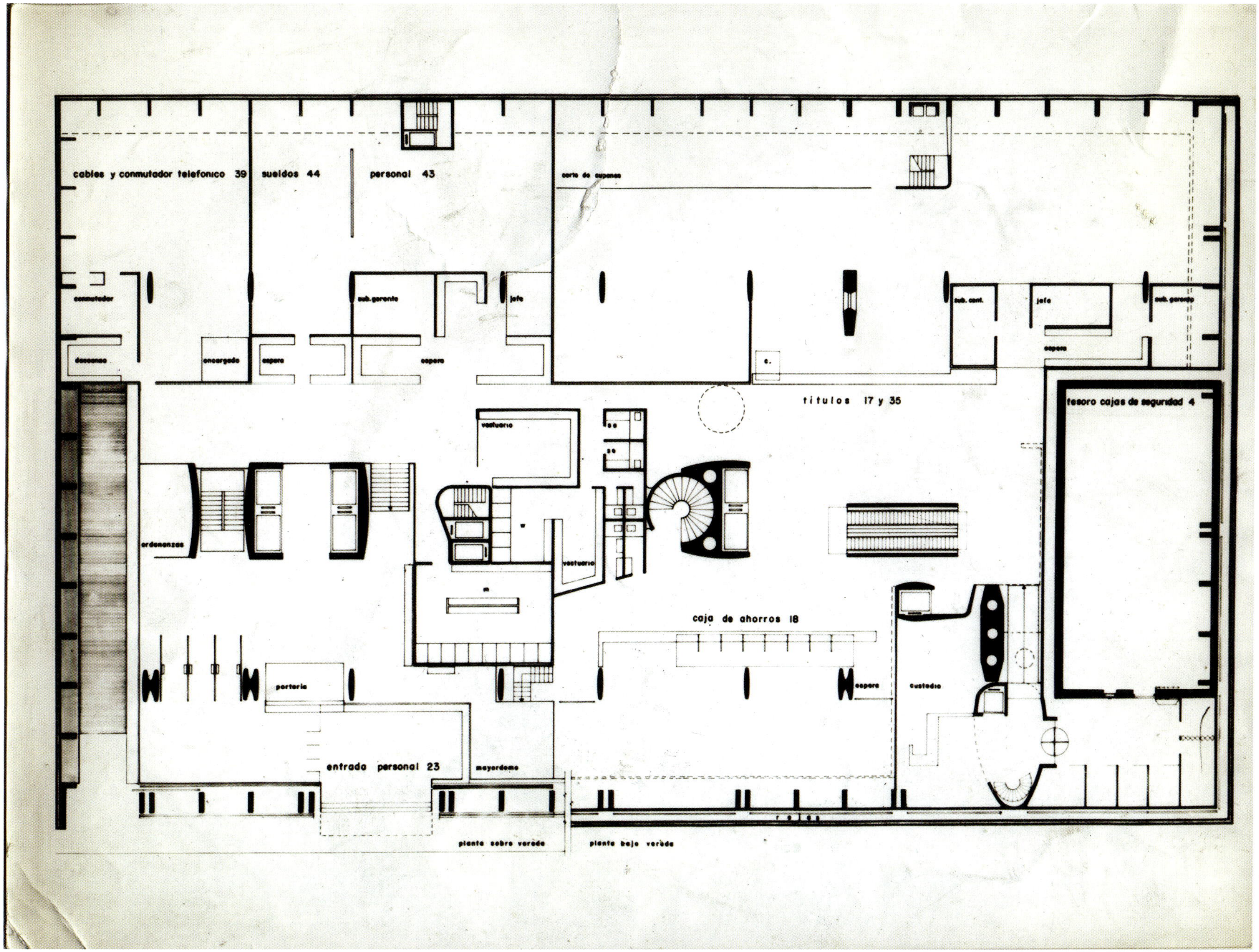

Opposite: Competition plan: Subsoil, Clorindo Testa file.
This page: Competition plan: Employee's entrance (street level), Clorindo Testa file.

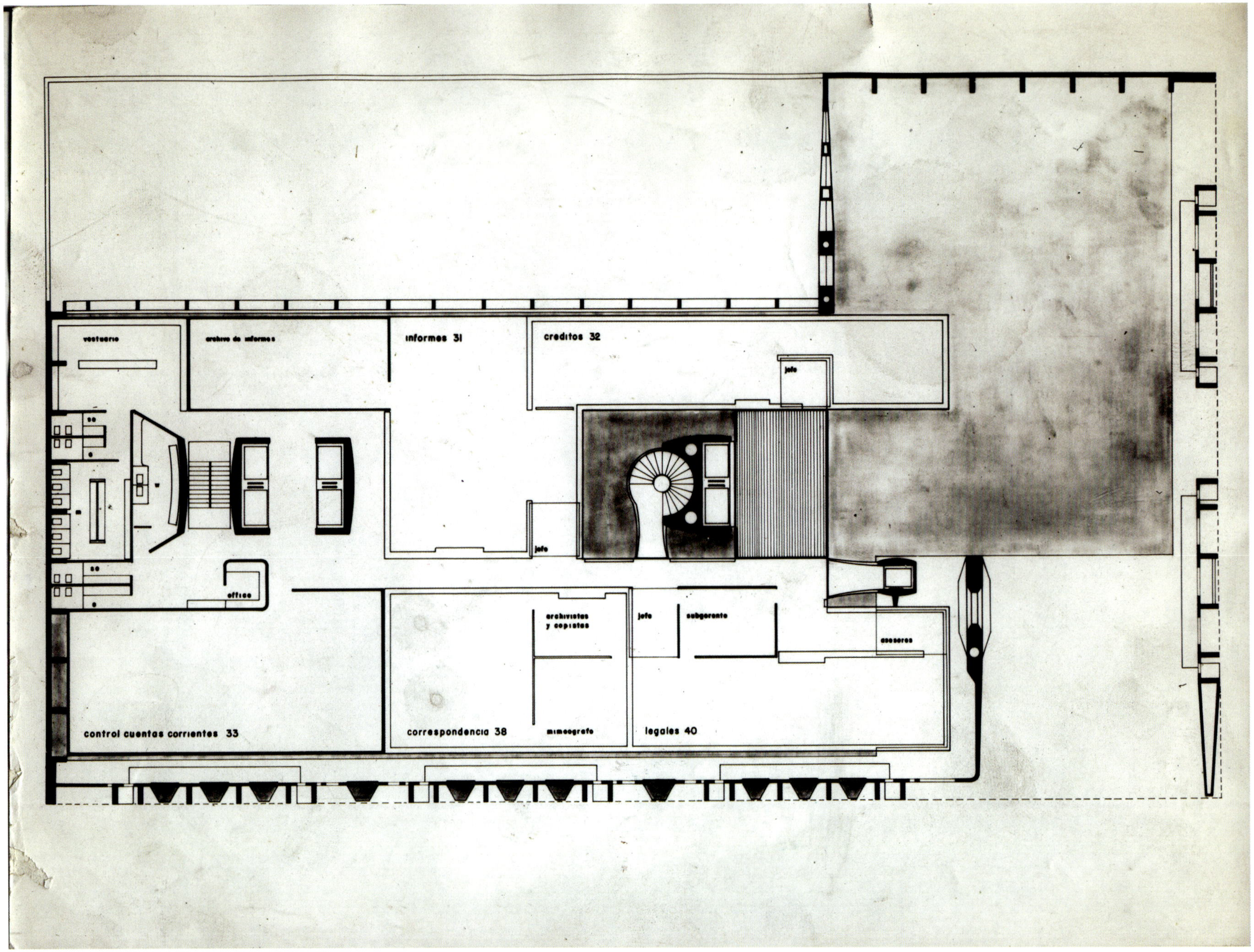
vestuario
archivo de informes
informes 31
creditos 32
jefe
jefe
office
archivistas
y copistas
jefe
subgerente
asesores
control cuentas corrientes 33
correspondencia 38
mimeografo
legales 40

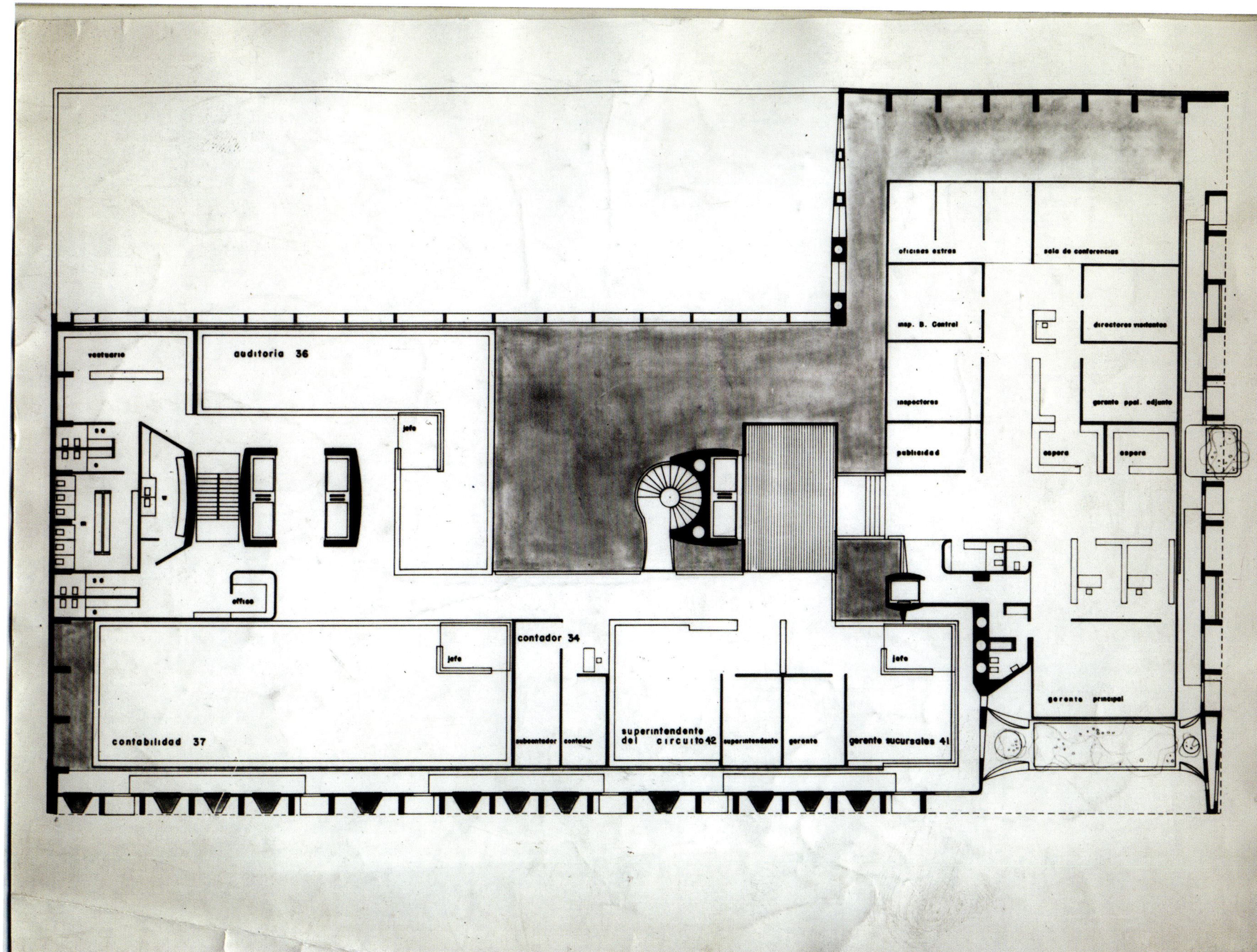

Opposite: Competition plan: Working level, Clorindo Testa file.
This page: Competition plan: Manager's level (6th floor), Clorindo Testa file.

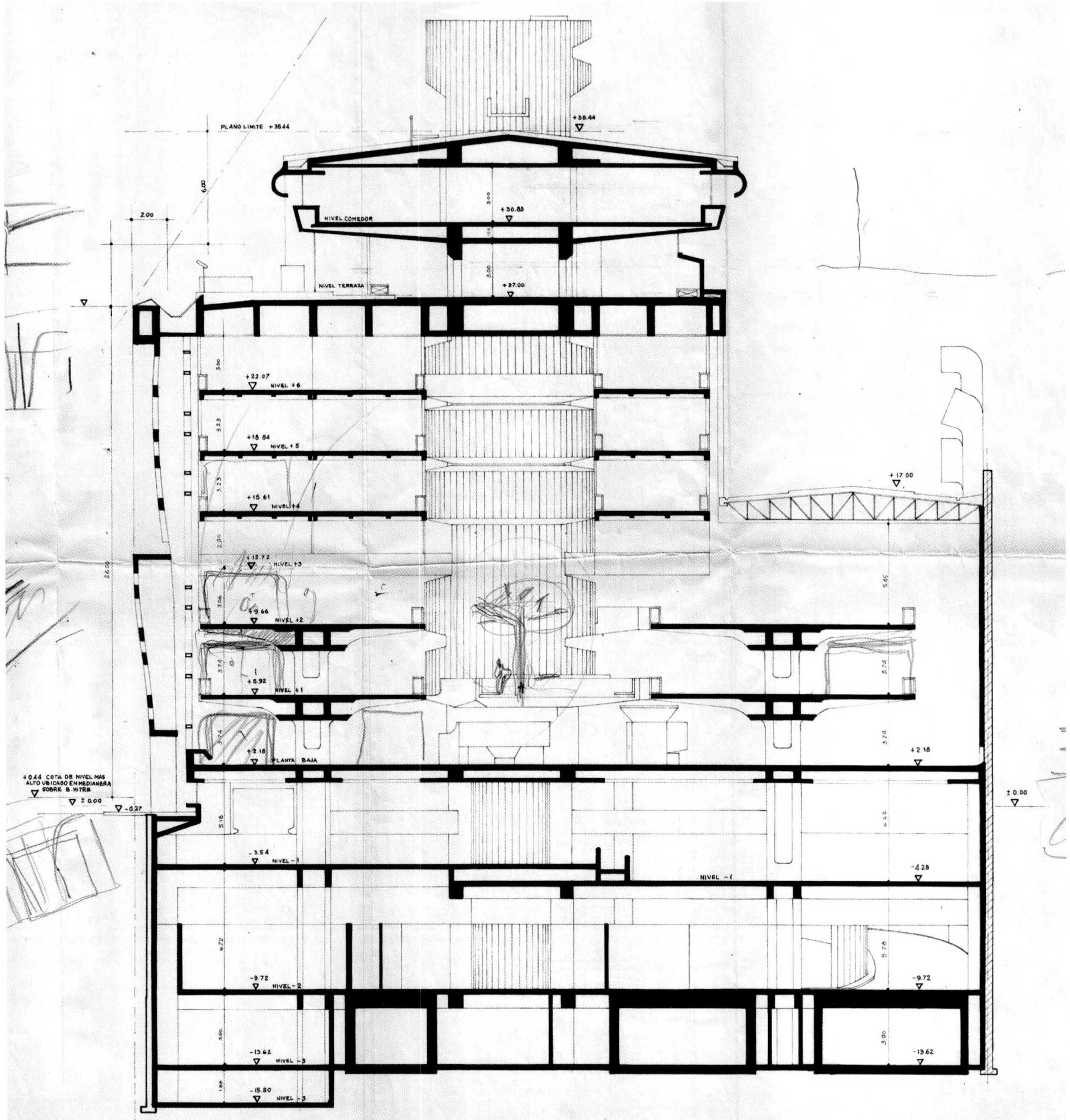

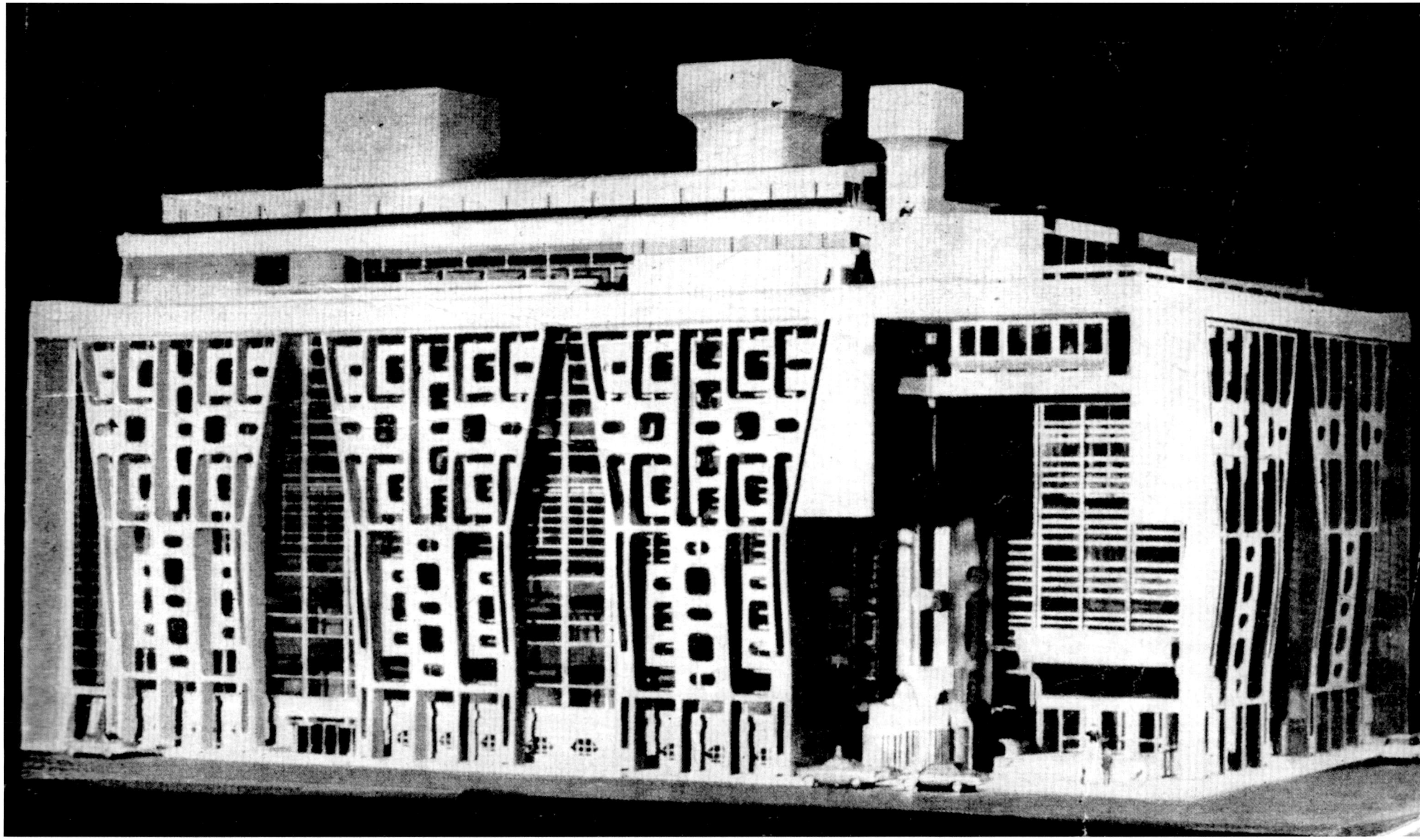

Opposite: Section, Authorization plan (plano de habilitación), Banco Hipotecario's file.
This page: Competition Model

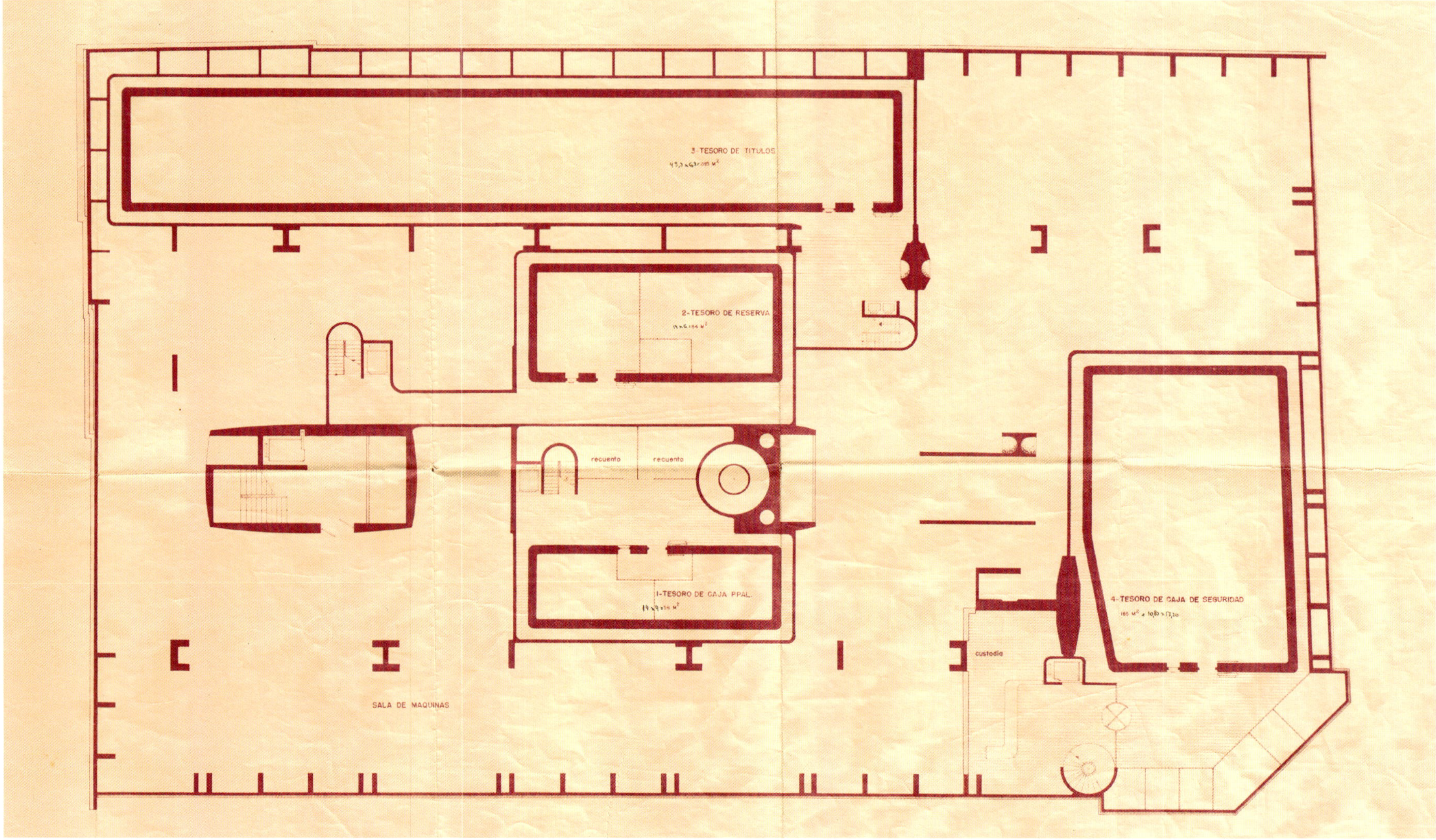
3-TESORO DE TITULOS
2-TESORO DE RESERVA
recuento
recuento
1-TESORO DE CAJA PPAL.
4-TESORO DE CAJA DE SEGURIDAD
custodia
SALA DE MAQUINAS

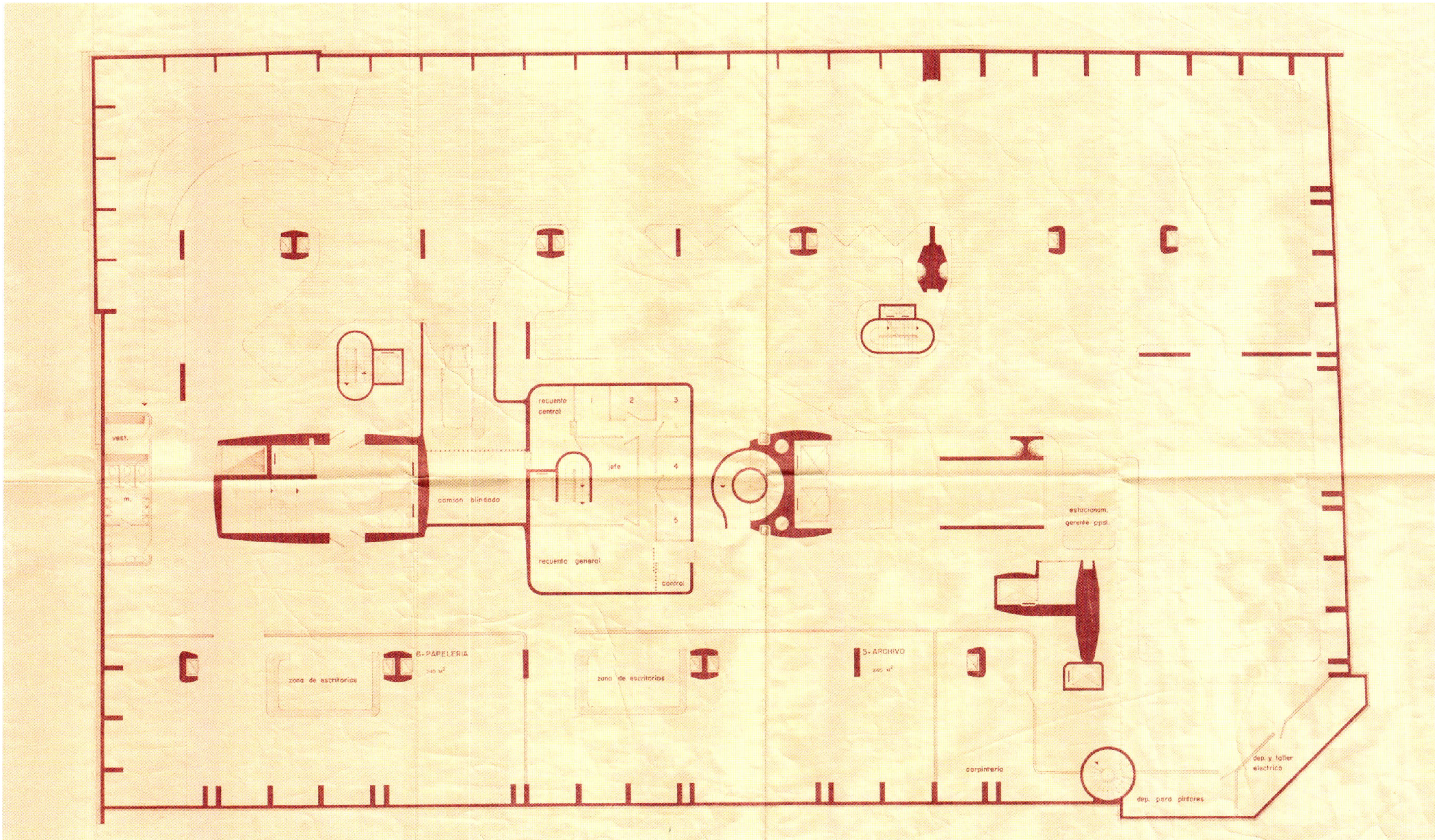

Opposite: Level -3, architecture plan, 1961, Banco Hipotecario's file (box 21, plan 1)
This page: Level -2, architecture plan, 1961, Banco Hipotecario's file (box 21, plan 2)

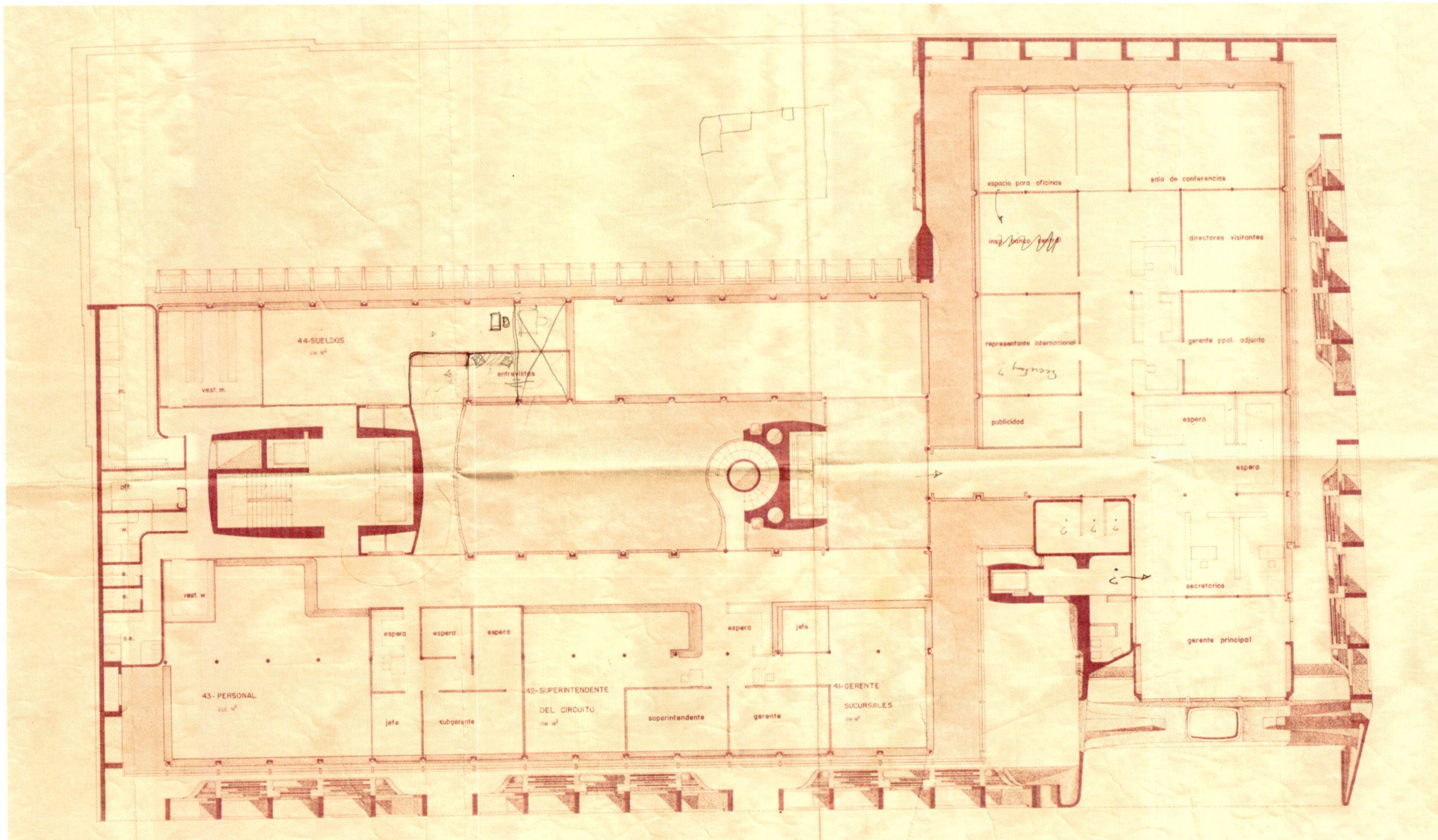
espacio para oficinas
sala de conferencias
directores visitantes
representante internacional
gerente ppal. adjunto
publicidad
espera
espera
secretarias
gerente principal
44-SUELDOS
vest. m.
entrevistas
off.
vest. w.
43- PERSONAL
espera
espera
espera
42-SUPERINTENDENTE DEL CIRCUITO
espera
jefe
41-GERENTE SUCURSALES
jefe
subgerente
superintendente
gerente

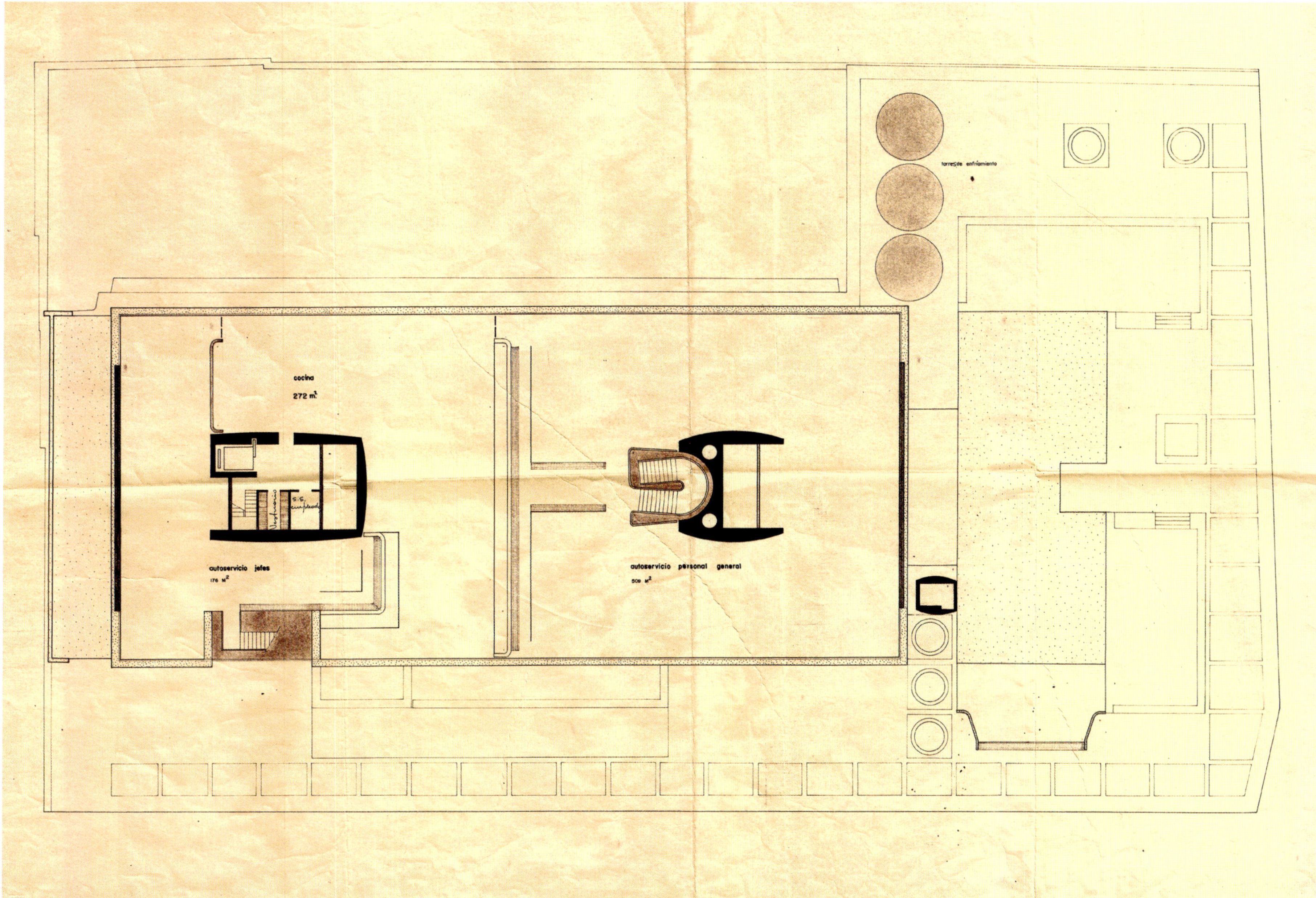

Opposite: Level +6, architecture plan, 1961, Banco Hipotecario's file (box 21, plan 10)
This page: Dining hall level, architecture plan, 1961, Banco Hipotecario's file (box 21, plan 12)

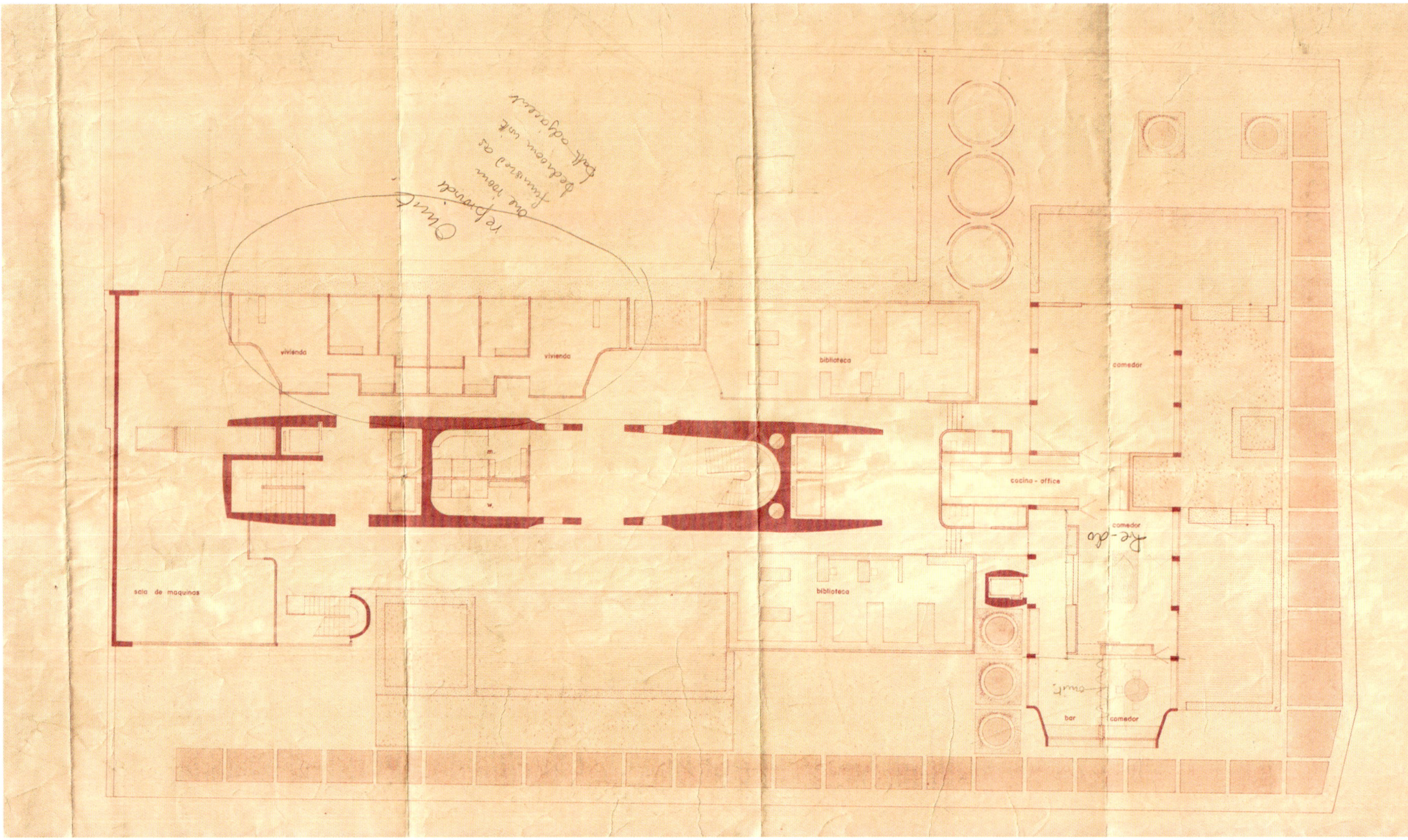
vivienda
vivienda
biblioteca
comedor
cocina - office
comedor
sala de maquinas
biblioteca
bar
comedor

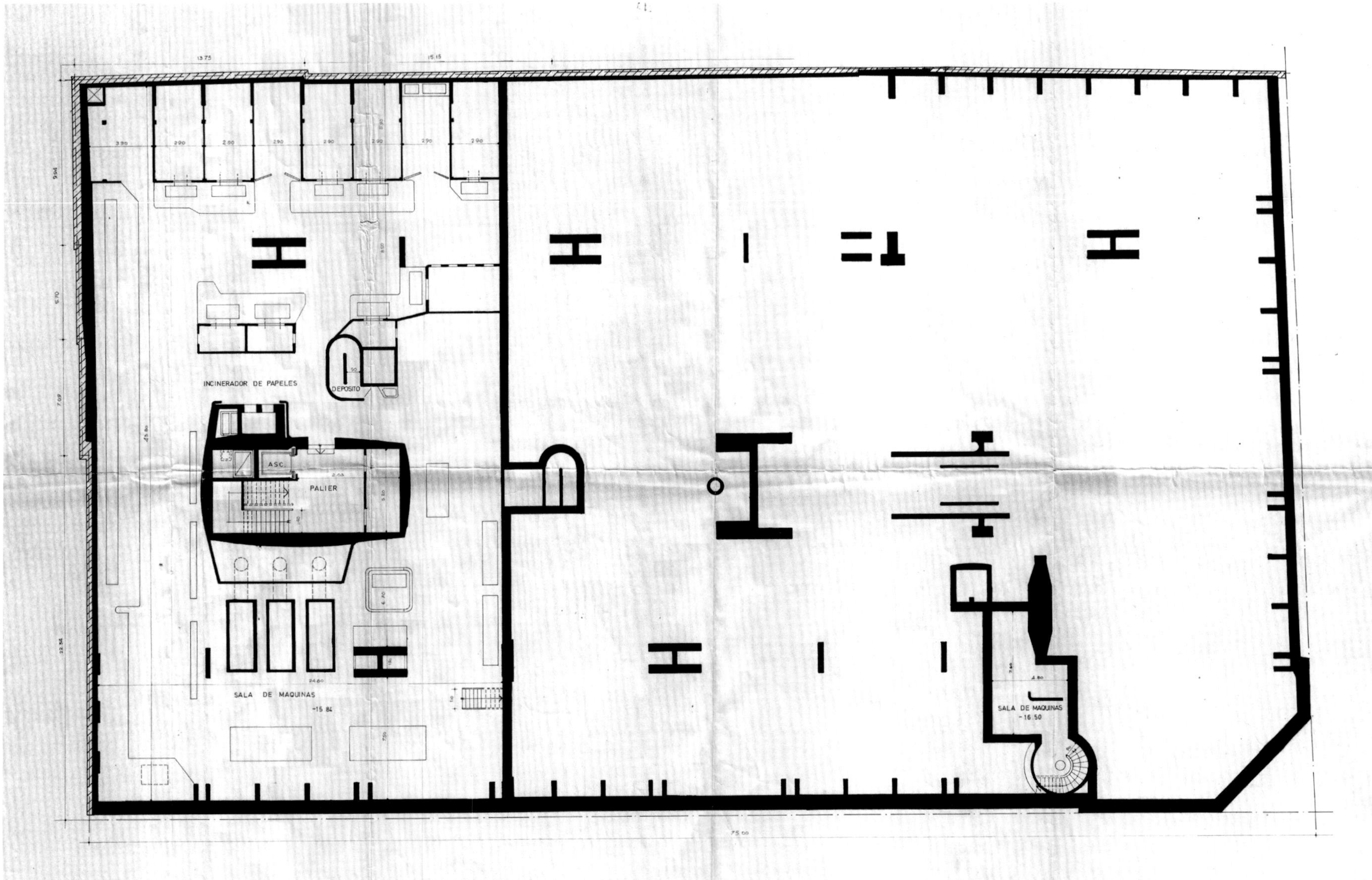

Opposite: Terrace level, architecture plan, 1961, Banco Hipotecario's file (box 21, plan 11)
This page: Level -3 (-15,84m), Machine room, authorization plan, Banco Hipotecario's file (box 7, plan 1)

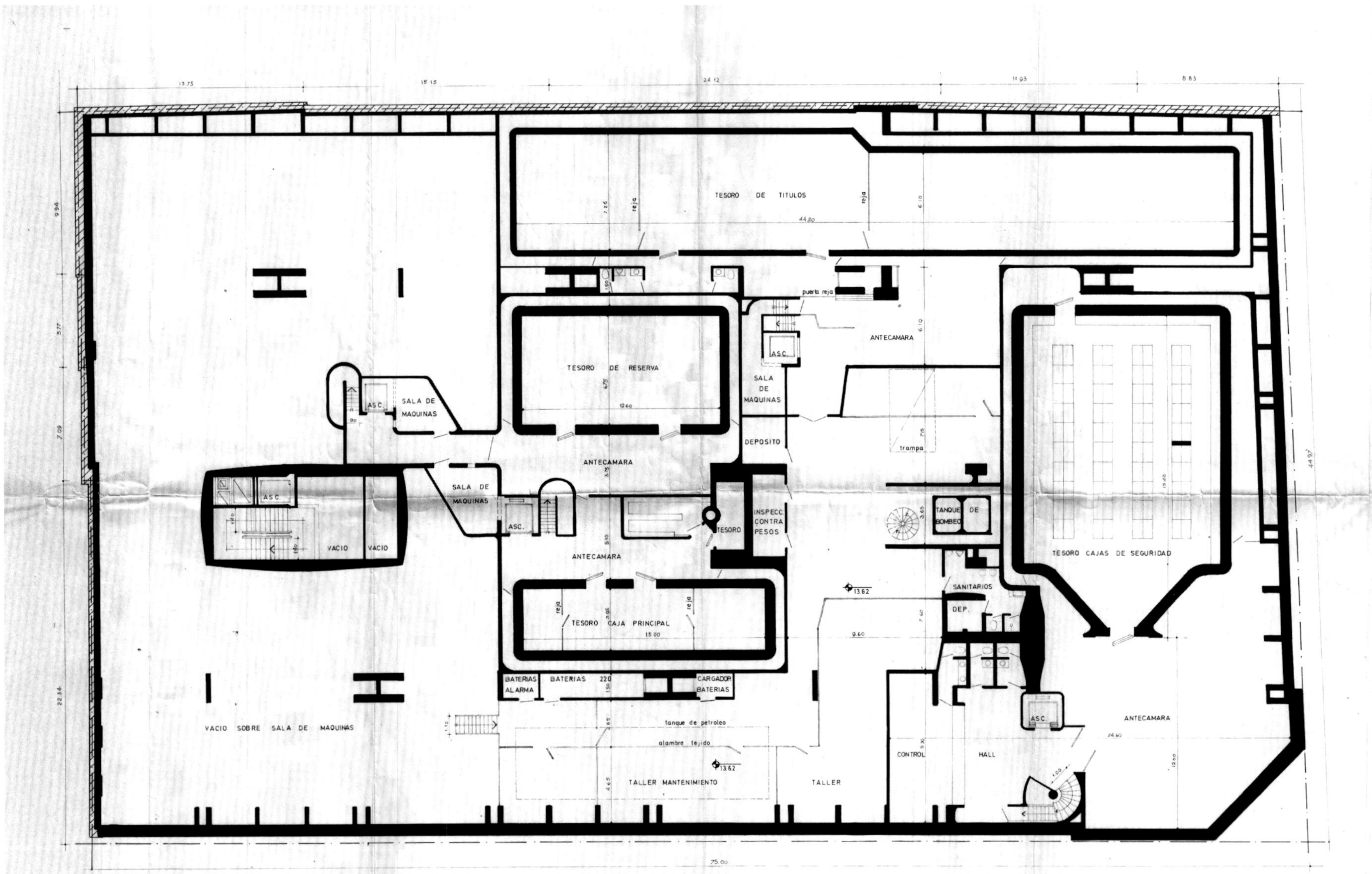
TESORO DE TITULOS
TESORO DE RESERVA
TESORO CAJA PRINCIPAL
TESORO CAJAS DE SEGURIDAD
ANTECAMARA
SALA DE MAQUINAS
ASC.
DEPOSITO
trampa
puerta reja
reja
INSPECC CONTRA PESOS
TESORO
TANQUE DE BOMBEO
SANITARIOS
DEP.
VACIO
VACIO SOBRE SALA DE MAQUINAS
BATERIAS ALARMA
BATERIAS 220
CARGADOR BATERIAS
tanque de petroleo
alambre tejido
TALLER MANTENIMIENTO
TALLER
CONTROL
HALL
75.00

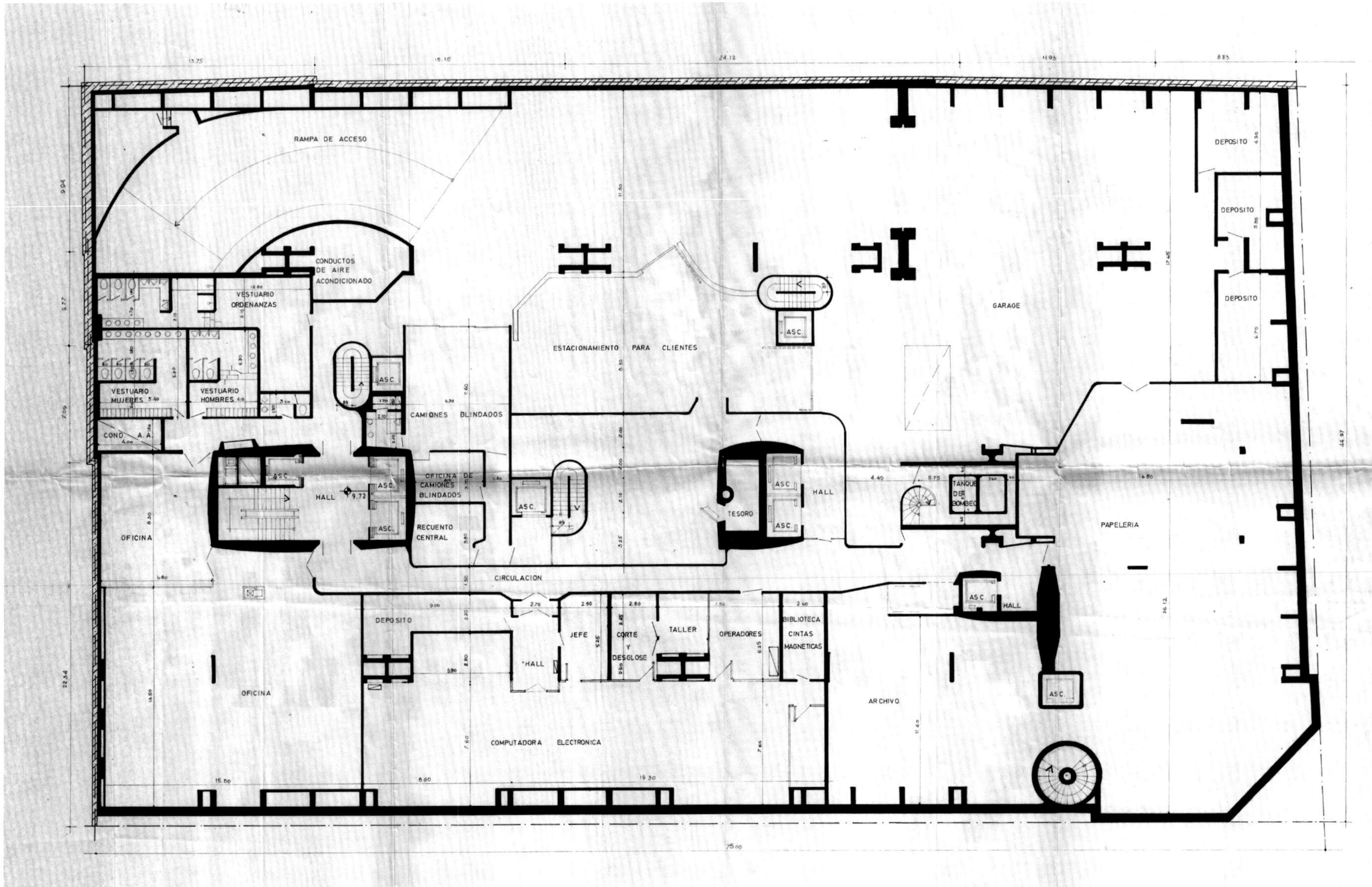

Opposite: Level -3 (-13,62m), Safe deposit vaults, authorization plan, Banco Hipotecario's file (box 7, plan 2)
This page: Level -2 (-9,72m), authorization plan, Banco Hipotecario's file (box 7, plan 3)

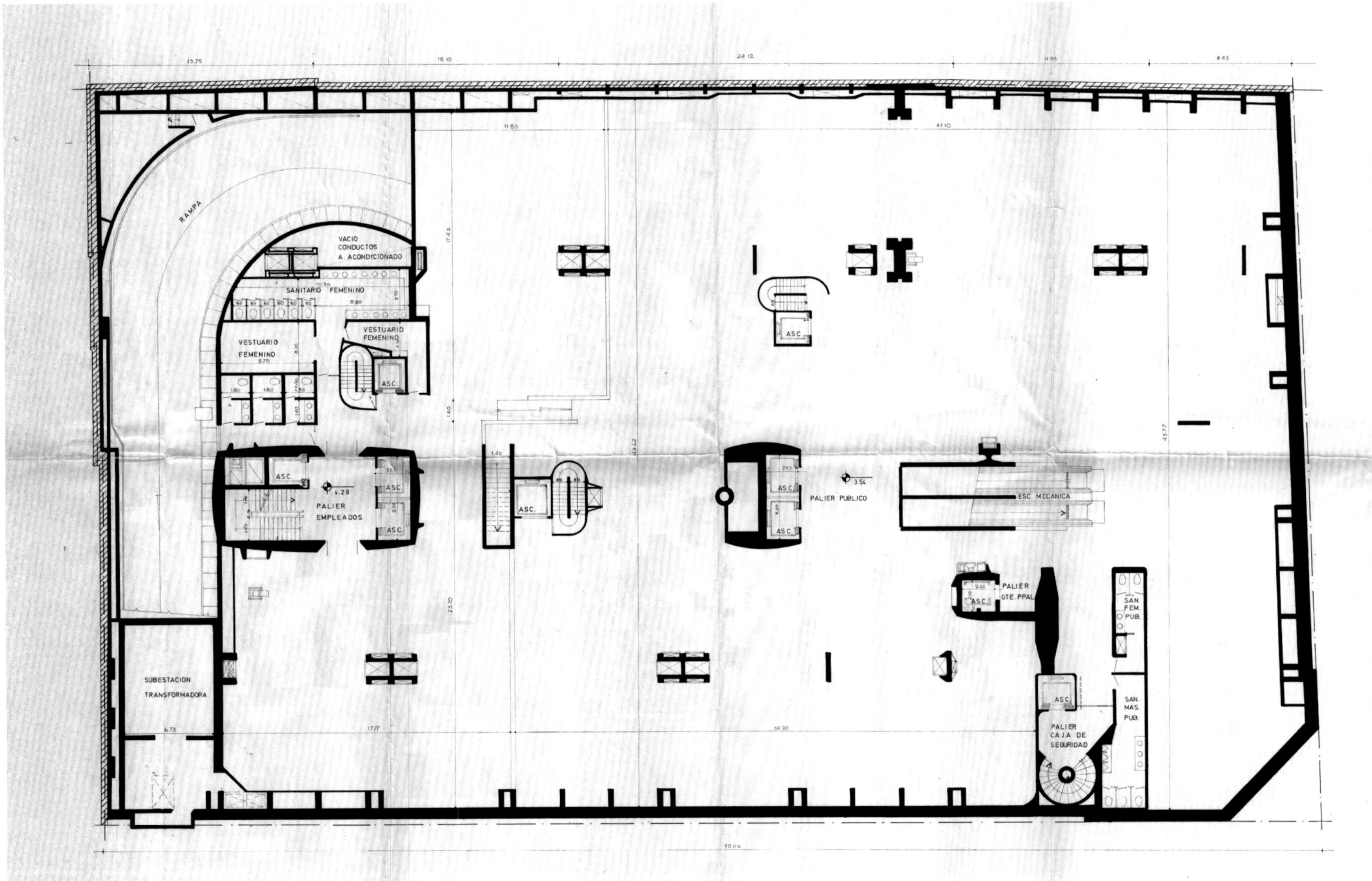
RAMPA
VACIO CONDUCTOS A. ACONDICIONADO
SANITARIO FEMENINO
VESTUARIO FEMENINO
VESTUARIO FEMENINO
ASC.
PALIER EMPLEADOS
ASC.
ASC.
ASC.
ASC.
ASC.
PALIER PUBLICO
ASC.
ASC.
ESC. MECANICA
PALIER GTE. PPAL.
ASC.
SAN. FEM. PUB.
SUBESTACION TRANSFORMADORA
ASC.
PALIER CAJA DE SEGURIDAD
SAN. MAS. PUB.

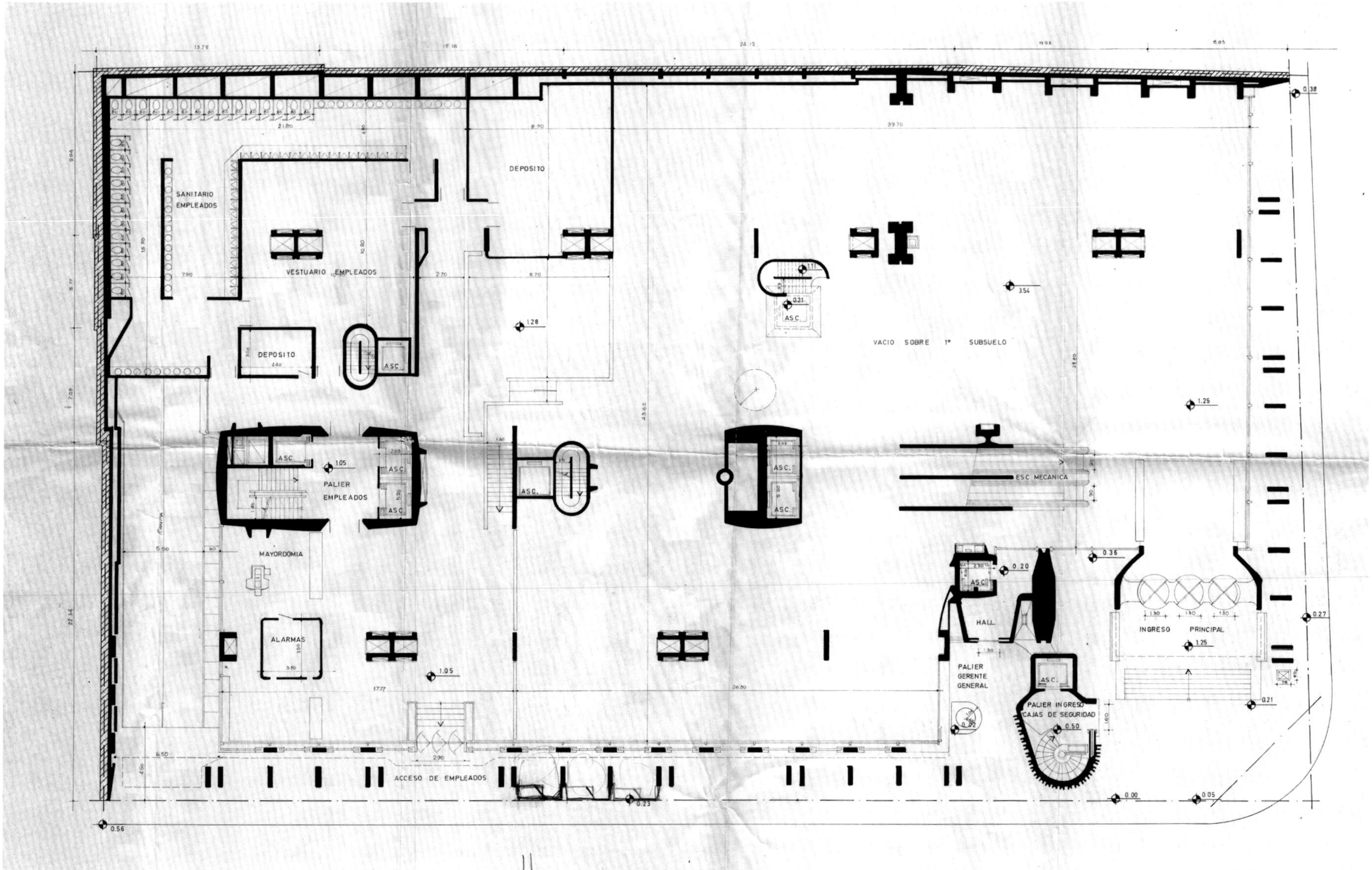

Opposite: Level -1 (-4,28 and -3,54m), authorization plan, Banco Hipotecario's file (box 7, plan 4)
This page: Street level (-1,05m), employee's entrance, authorization plan Banco Hipotecario's file (box 7, plan 5)

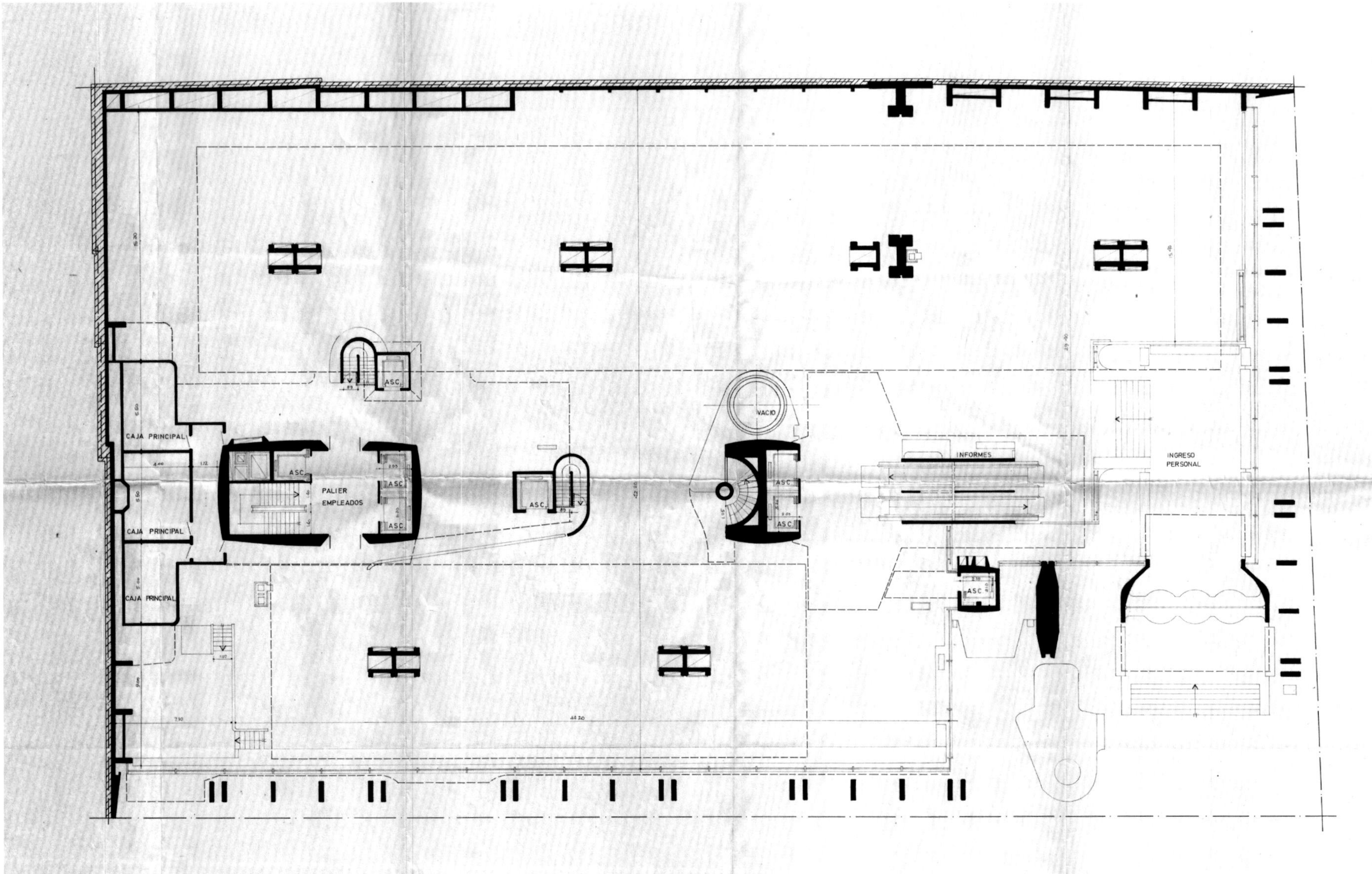
CAJA PRINCIPAL
CAJA PRINCIPAL
CAJA PRINCIPAL
PALIER
EMPLEADOS
ASC.
VACIO
INFORMES
INGRESO
PERSONAL

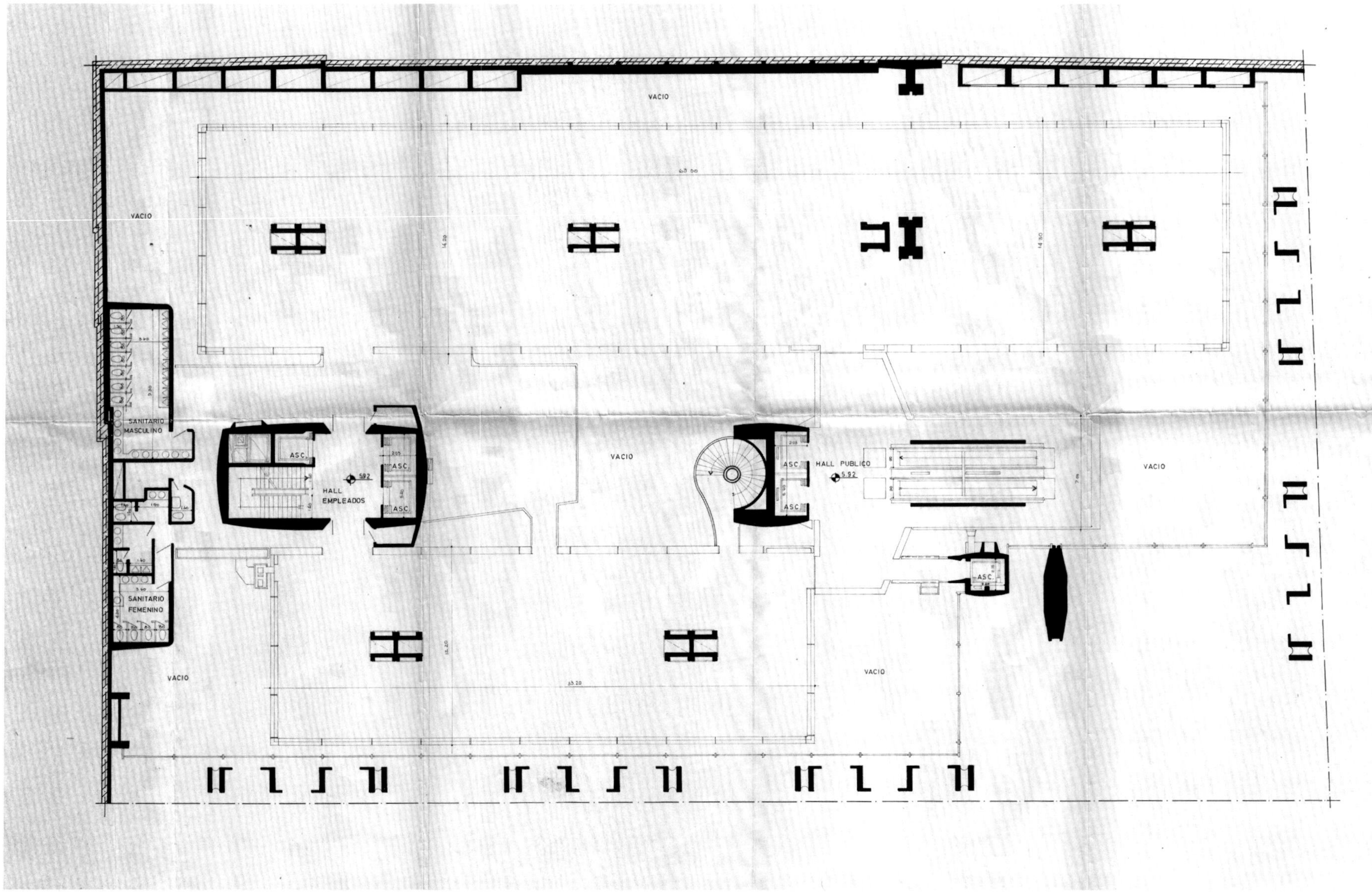

This page: Level +1 (+5,90m) authorization plan, Banco Hipotecario's file (box 7, plan 7)

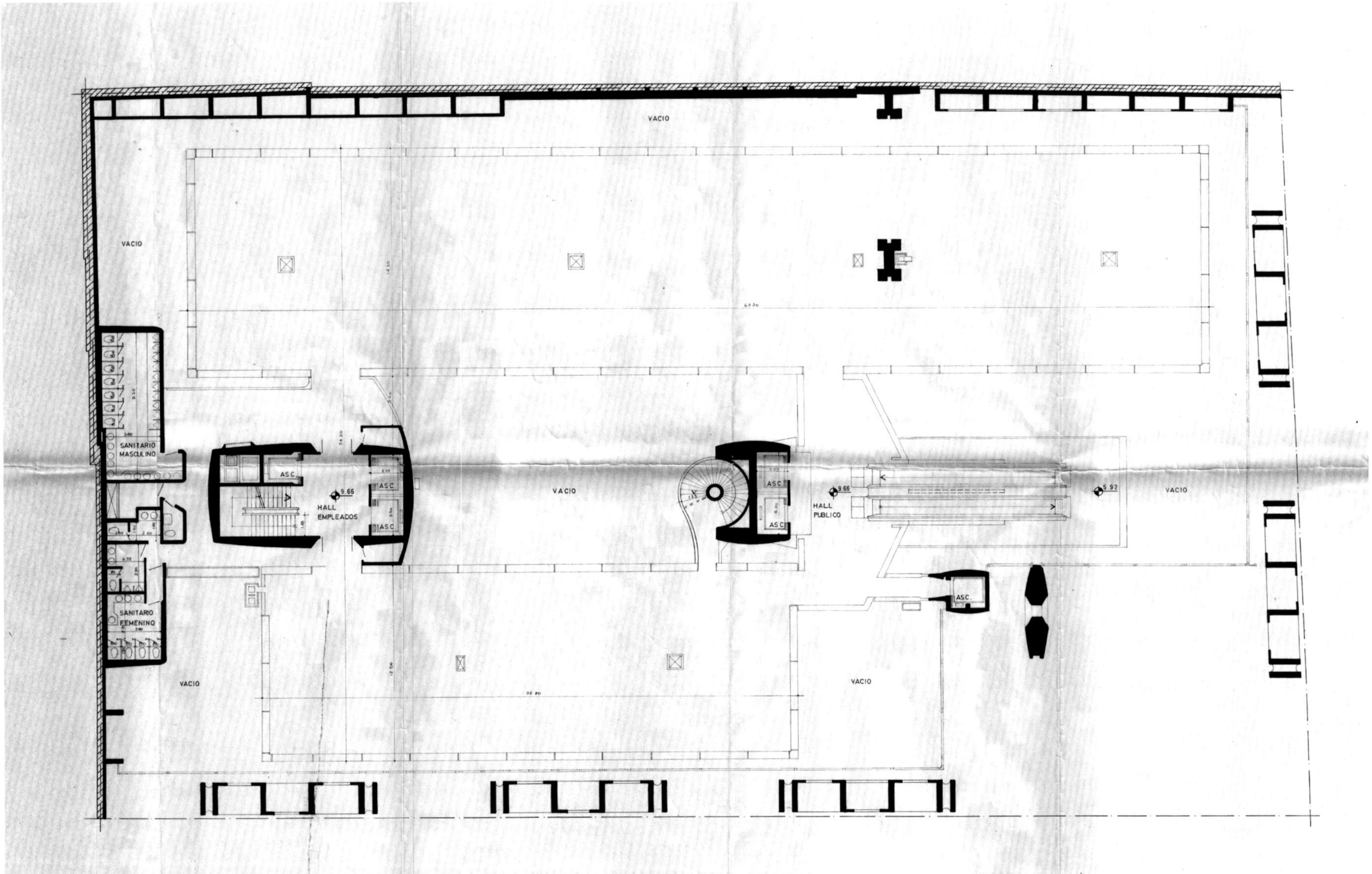
VACIO
VACIO
SANITARIO MASCULINO
SANITARIO FEMENINO
ASC
HALL EMPLEADOS
VACIO
ASC
HALL PUBLICO
VACIO
ASC.
VACIO
VACIO

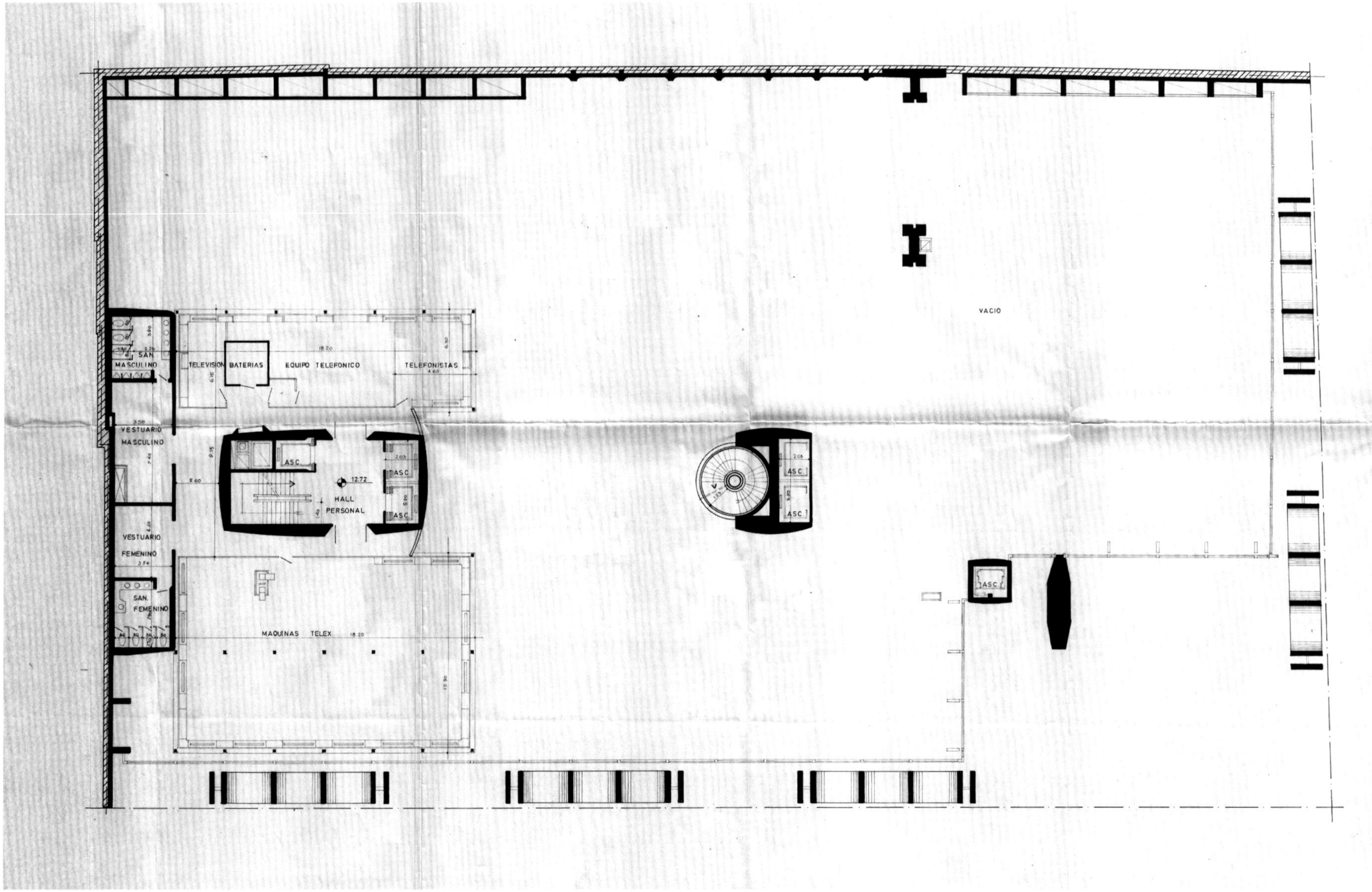

Opposite: Level +2 (+5,60m), authorization plan, Banco Hipotecario's file (box 7, plan 8)
This page: Level +3 (+12,72m), authorization plan, Banco Hipotecario's file (box 7, plan 9)

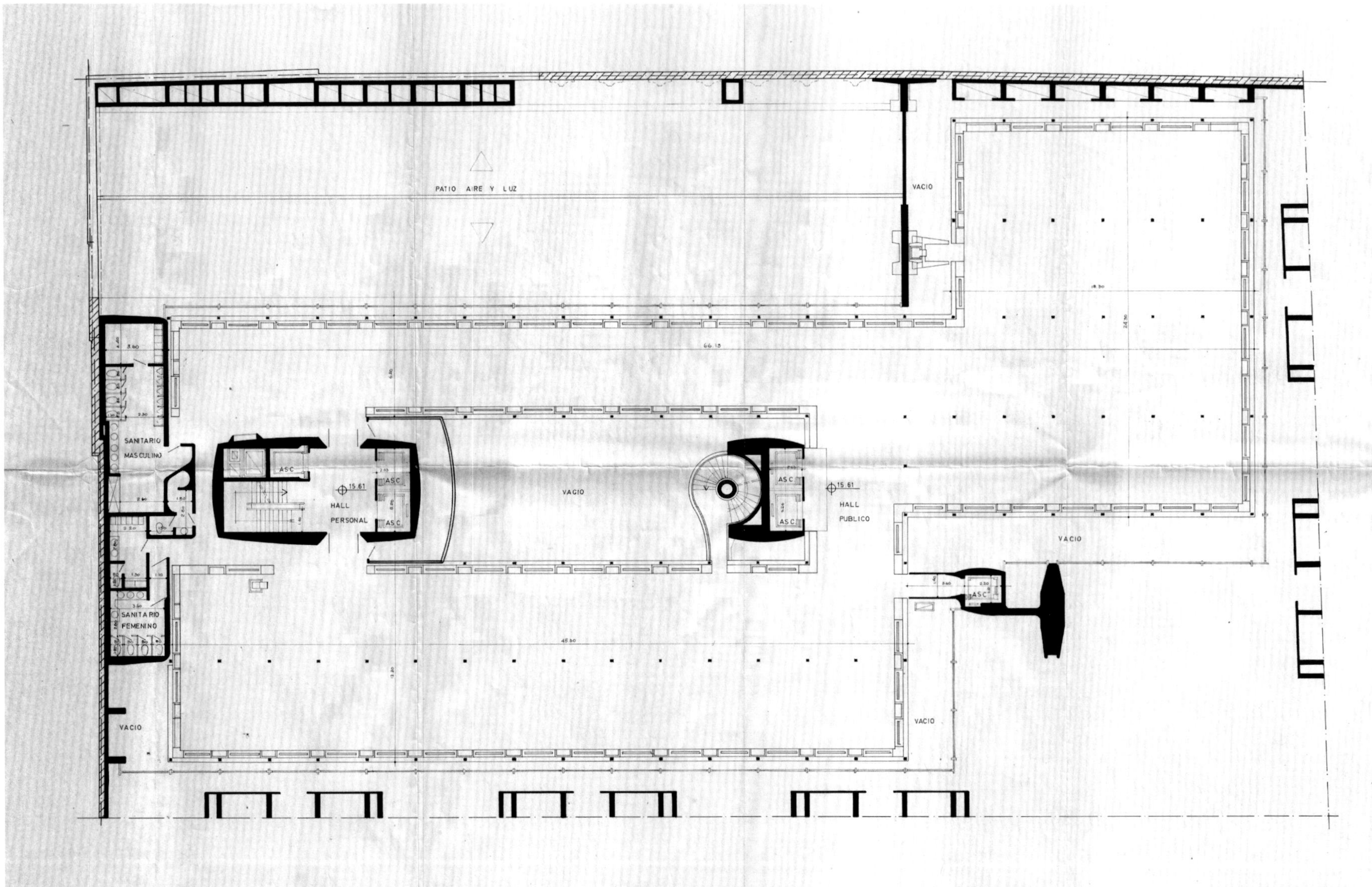
PATIO AIRE Y LUZ
VACIO
SANITARIO MASCULINO
ASC
HALL PERSONAL
VACIO
ASC
HALL PUBLICO
VACIO
ASC
SANITARIO FEMENINO
VACIO
VACIO

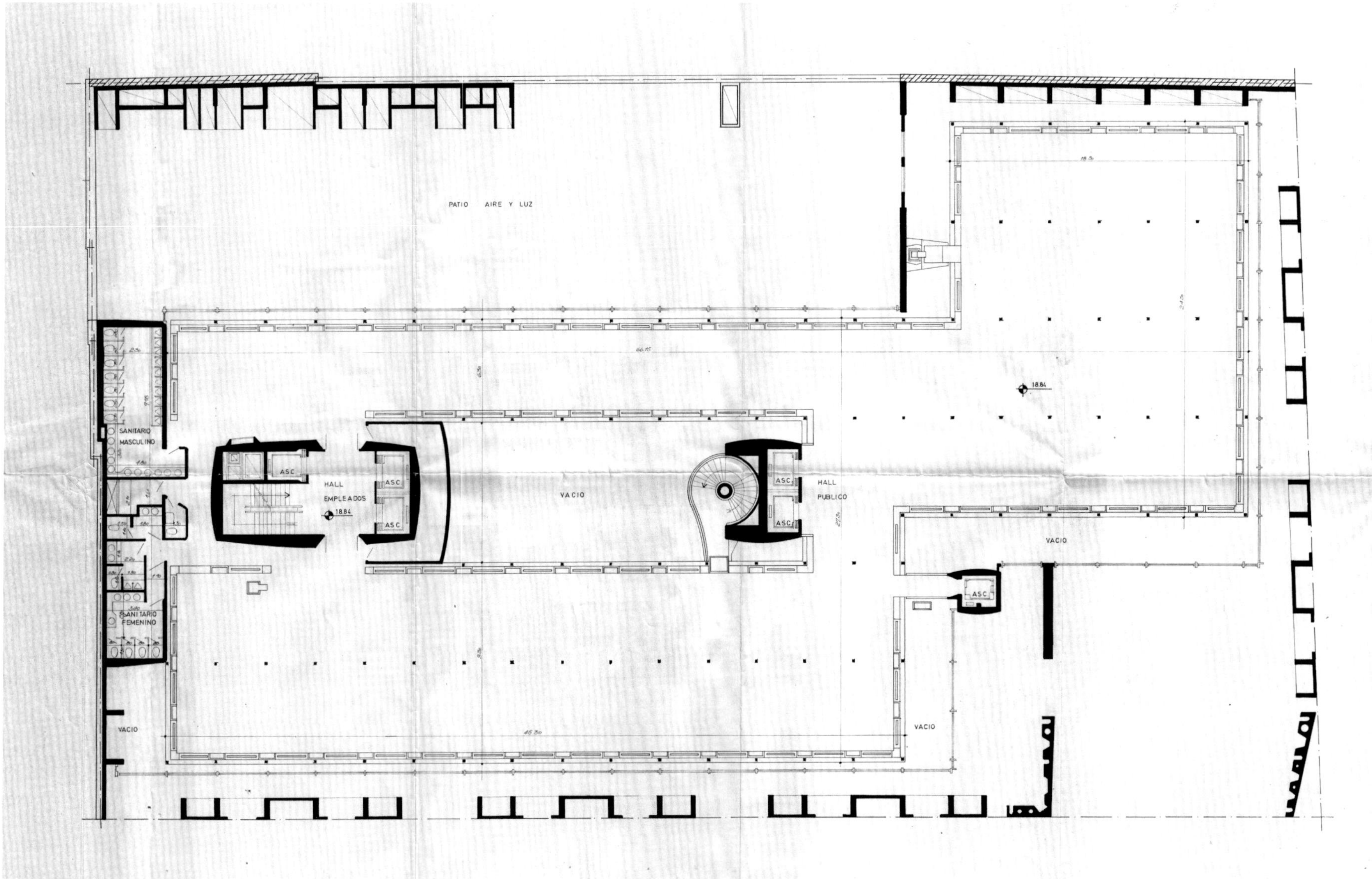

Opposite: Level +4 (+15,0[illegible]m), authorization plan, Banco Hipotecario's file (box 7, plan 10)
This page: Level +5 (+18,84m), authorization plan, Banco Hipotecario's file (box 7, plan 10)

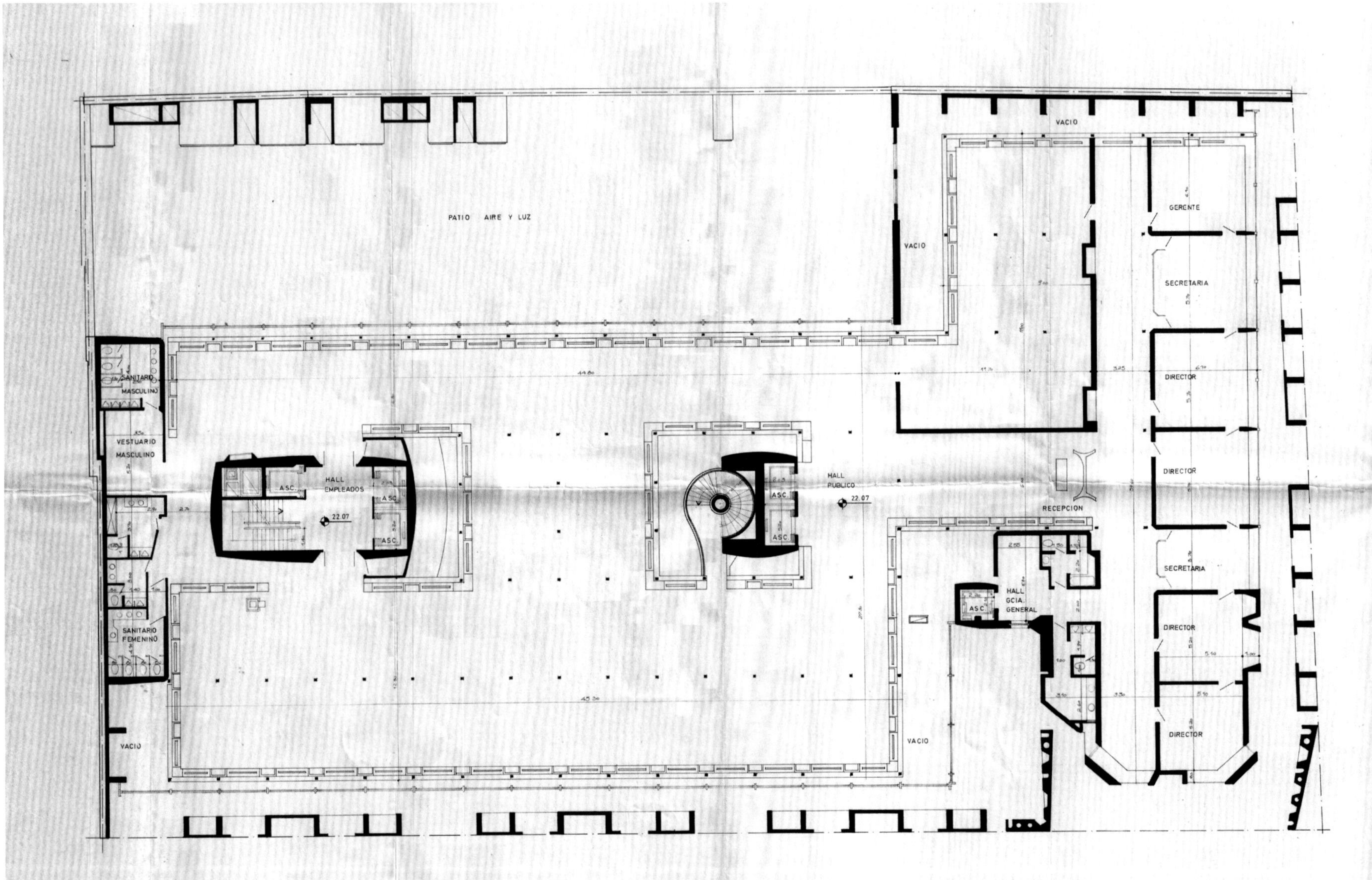
PATIO AIRE Y LUZ
VACIO
VACIO
GERENTE
SECRETARIA
DIRECTOR
DIRECTOR
SECRETARIA
DIRECTOR
DIRECTOR
SANITARIO MASCULINO
VESTUARIO MASCULINO
SANITARIO FEMENINO
HALL EMPLEADOS
ASC
HALL PUBLICO
RECEPCION
HALL GCIA GENERAL
VACIO
VACIO

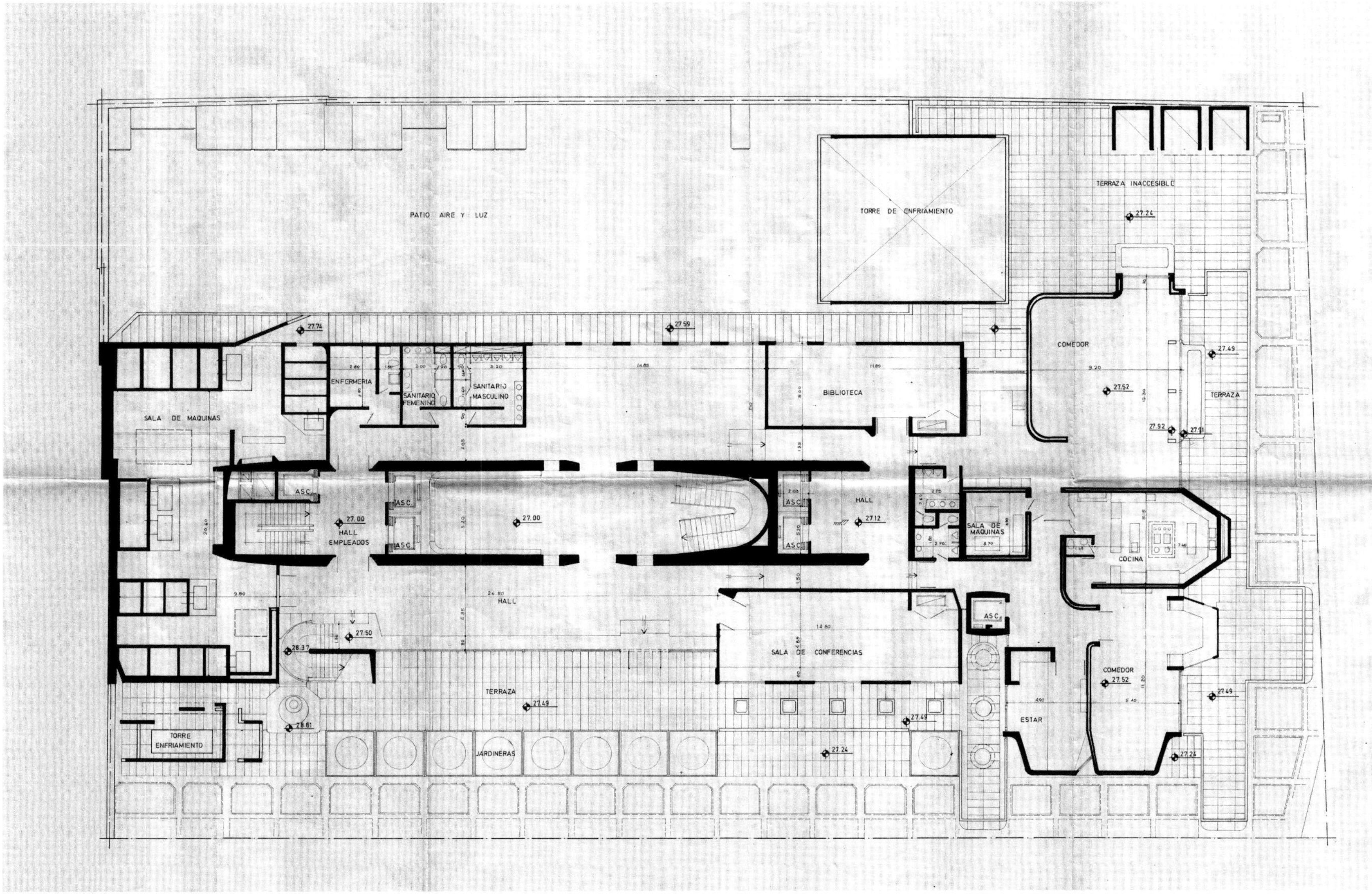

Opposite: Level +6 (+22,07m), manager's level, authorization plan, Banco Hipotecario's file (box 7, plan 11)
This page: Terrace level (+26.83m), authorization plan, Banco Hipotecario's file (box 7, plan 13)

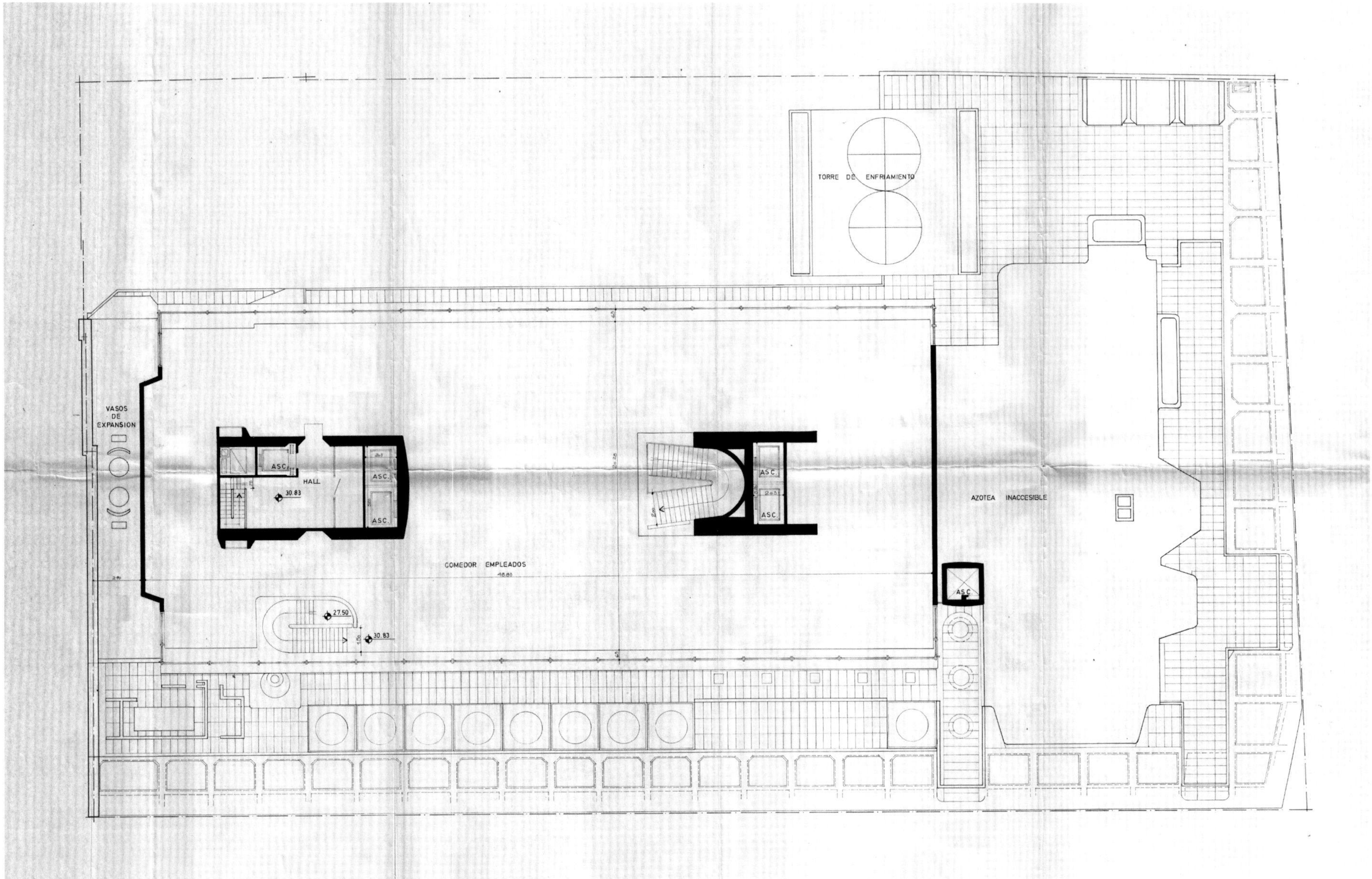
TORRE DE ENFRIAMIENTO
VASOS DE EXPANSION
HALL
ASC.
30.83
COMEDOR EMPLEADOS
27.50
AZOTEA INACCESIBLE

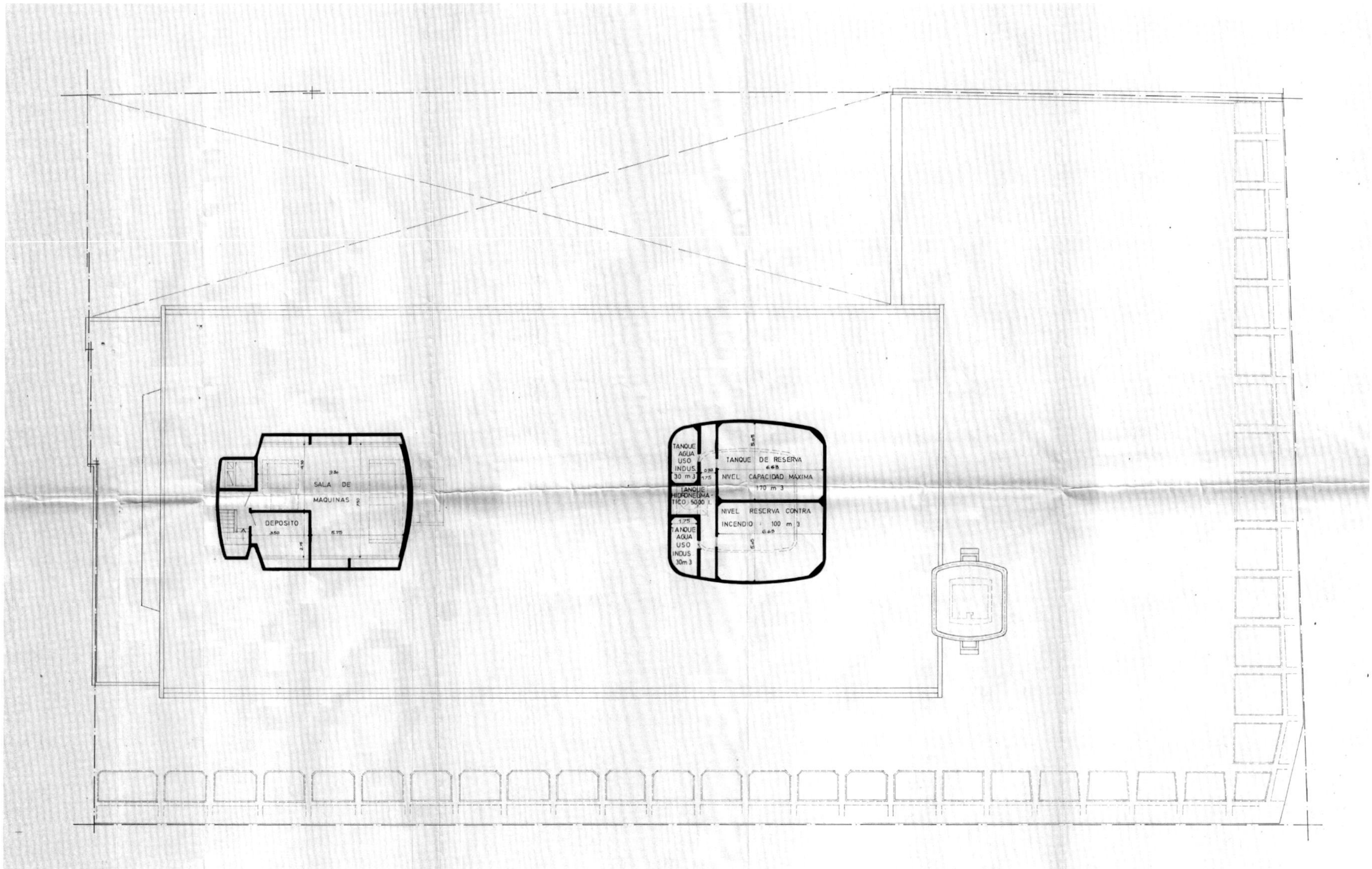

Opposite: Dining hall level (+30,83m), authorization plan, Banco Hipotecario's file (box 7, plan 14)
This page: Terrace roof (+53,79m), authorization plan, Banco Hipotecario's file (box 7, plan 15)

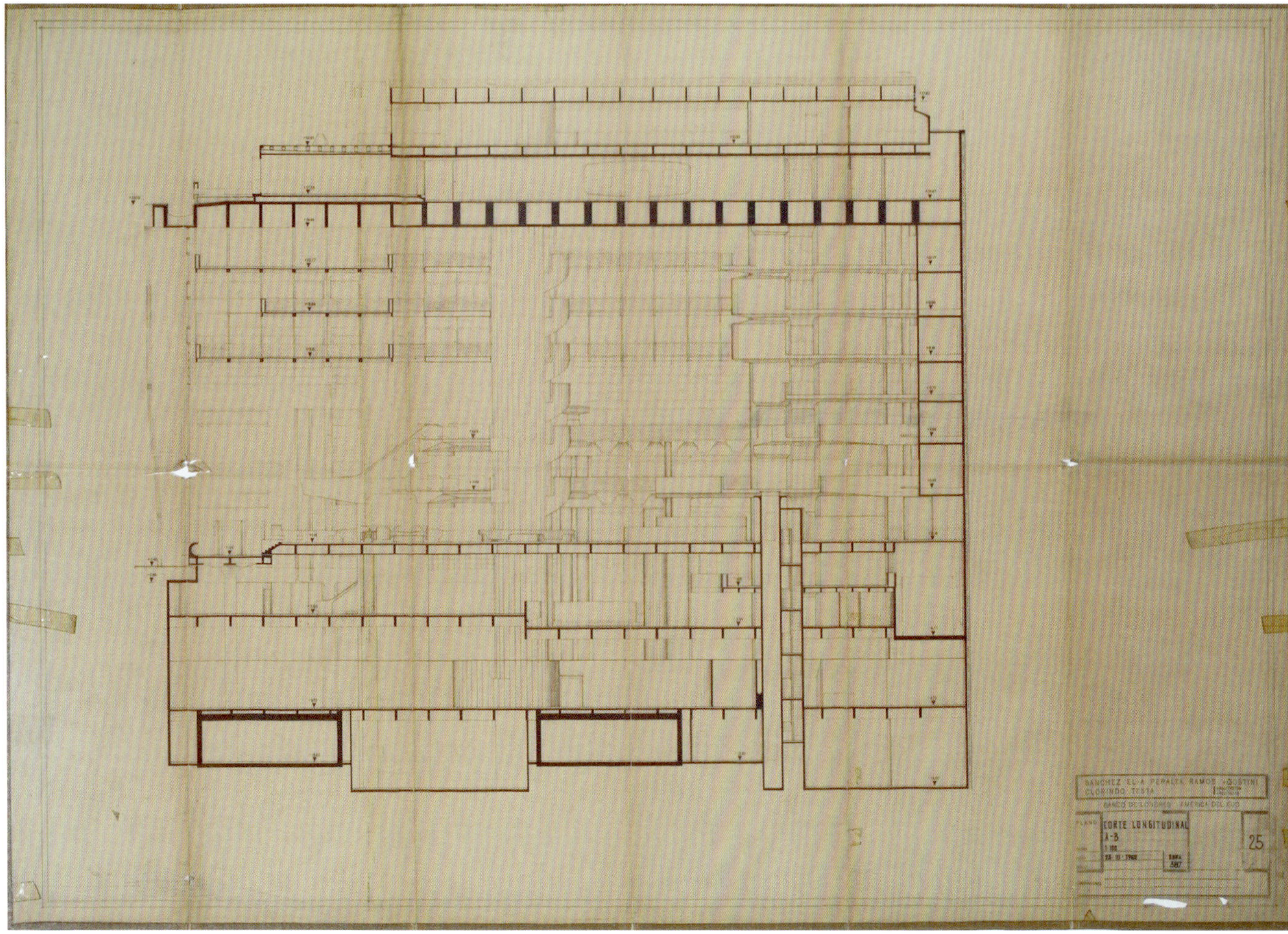
SANCHEZ ELIA PERALTA RAMOS AGOSTINI
CLORINDO TESTA
BANCO DE LONDRES AMERICA DEL SUD
CORTE LONGITUDINAL
A-B
25

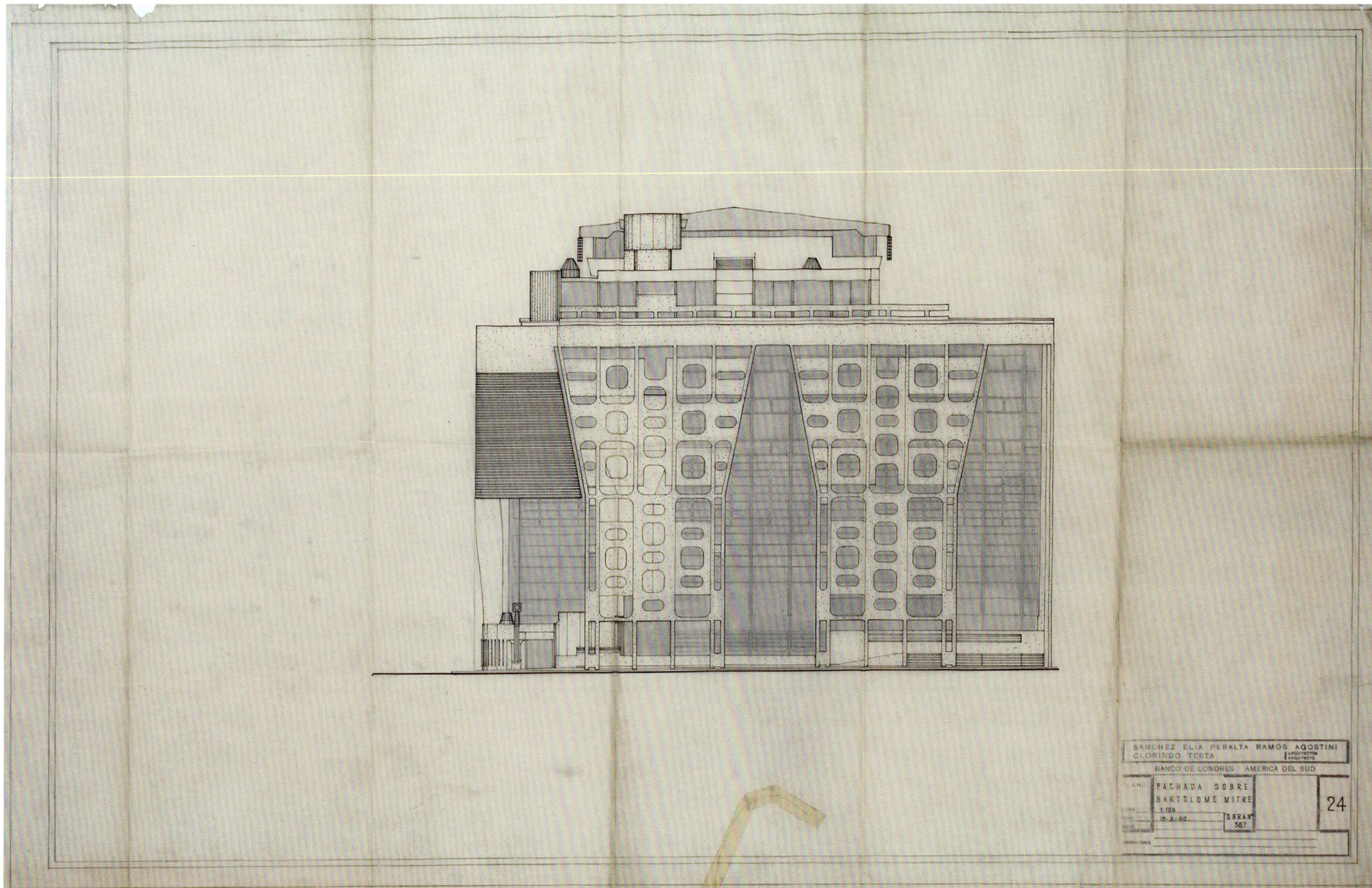

Opposite: Long section, 1962, SEPRA's studio file (plan 25). Scale 3:500
This page: Bartolome Mitre st. Facade, 1962, SEPRA's studio file (plan 24). Scale 3:500

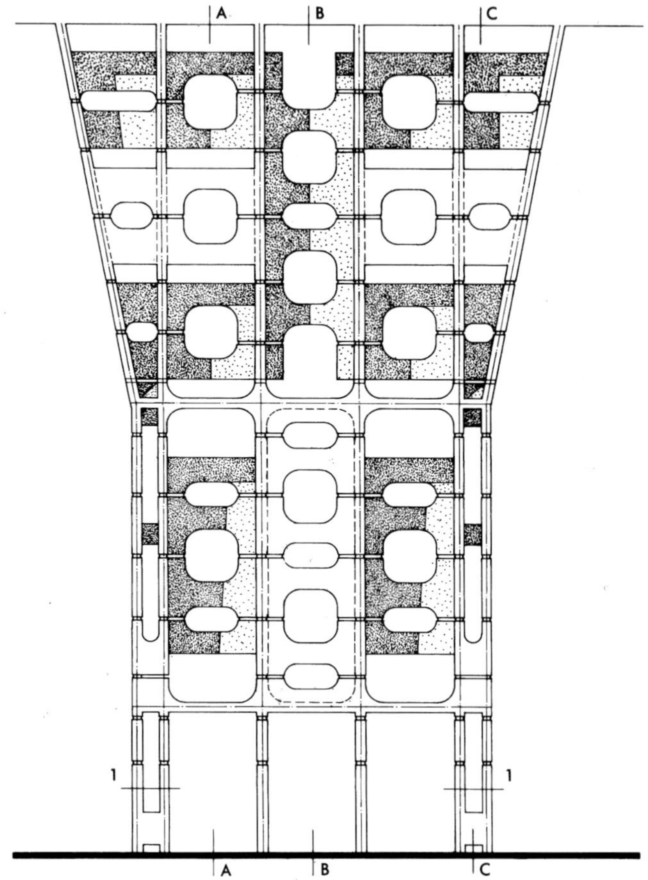

Front elevation

Section 1-1

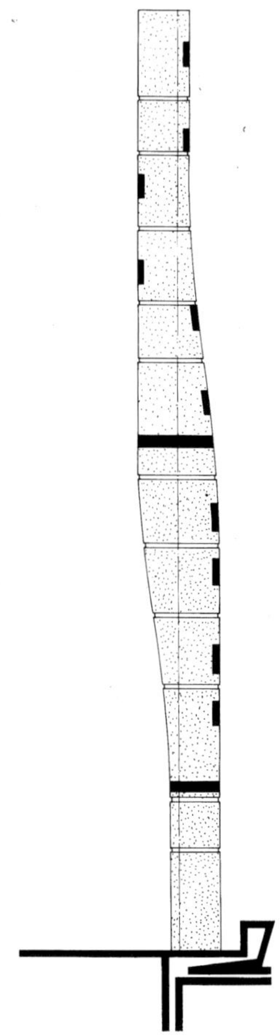

Section A-A

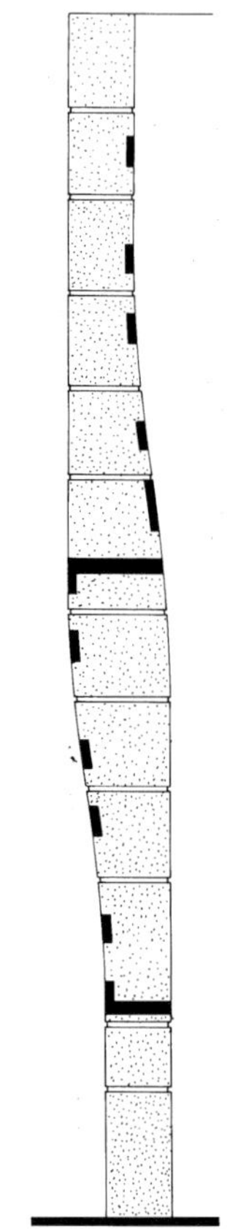

Section B-B

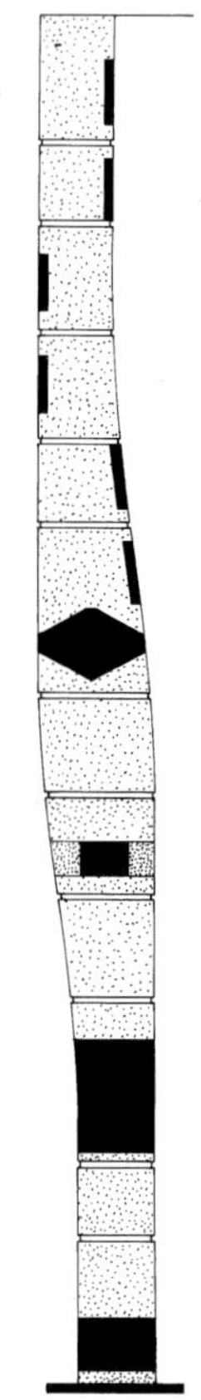

Section C-C

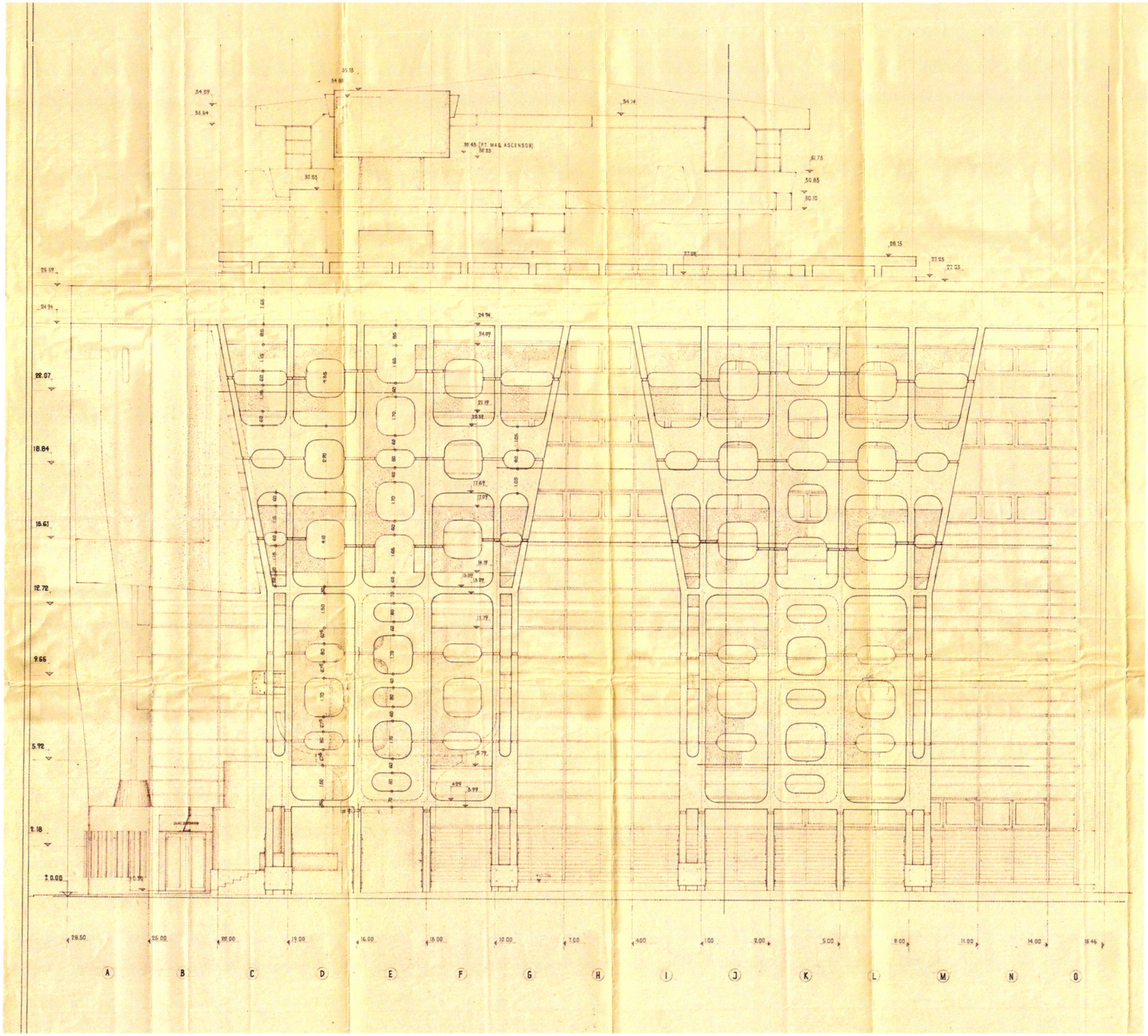

Opposite: Schematic elevation of façade element, *Global Architecture 1984*
This page: Façade, Bartolomé Mitre Street, 1963, Banco Hipotecarios's file (bos 21, plan 23)

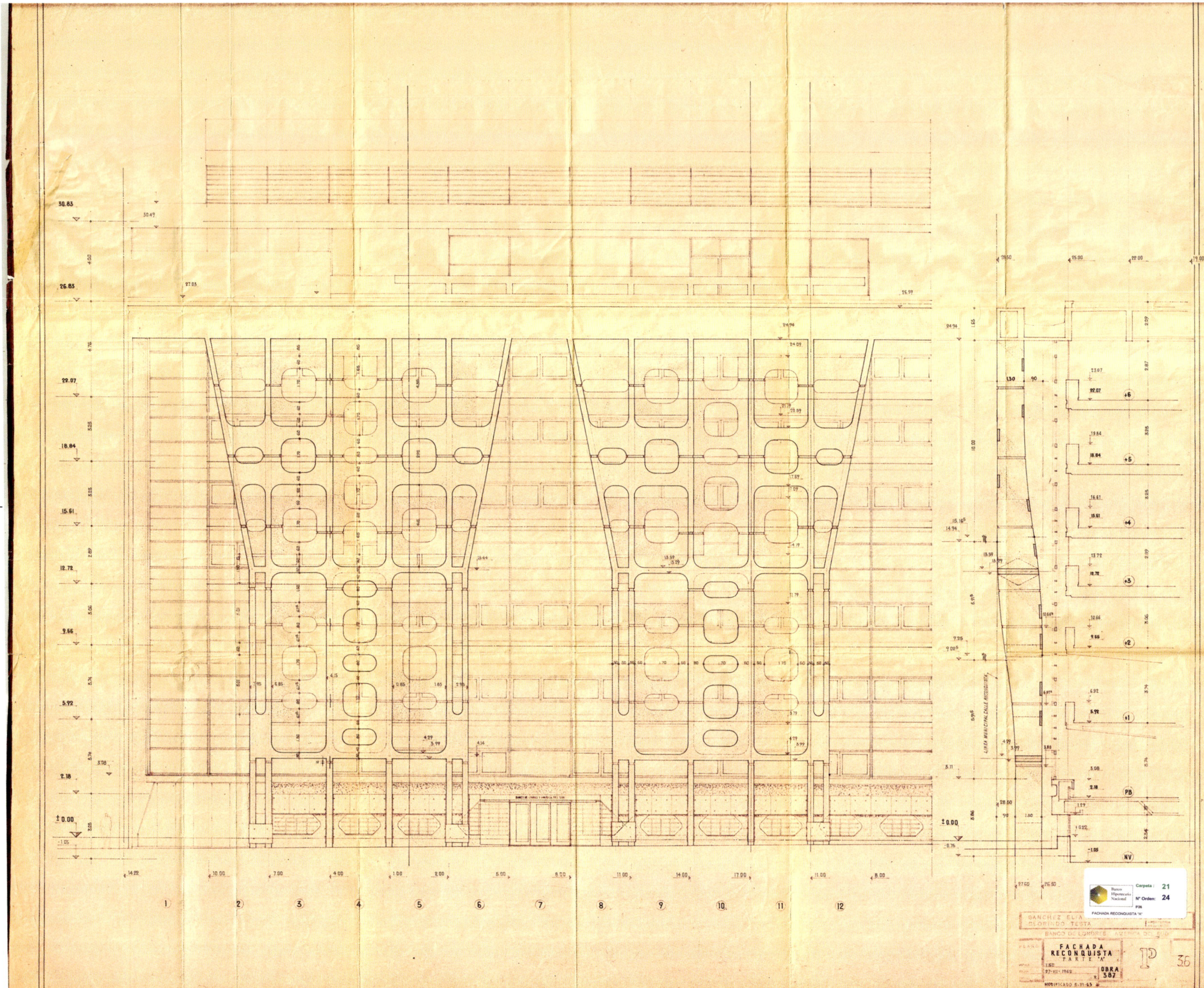
Banco Hipotecario Nacional
Carpeta : 21
Nº Orden: 24
P36
FACHADA RECONQUISTA "A"
SANCHEZ ELIA
CLORINDO TESTA
FACHADA
RECONQUISTA
PARTE 'A'
1:50
27-VII-1962
OBRA
387
MODIFICADO 5-VI-63
36

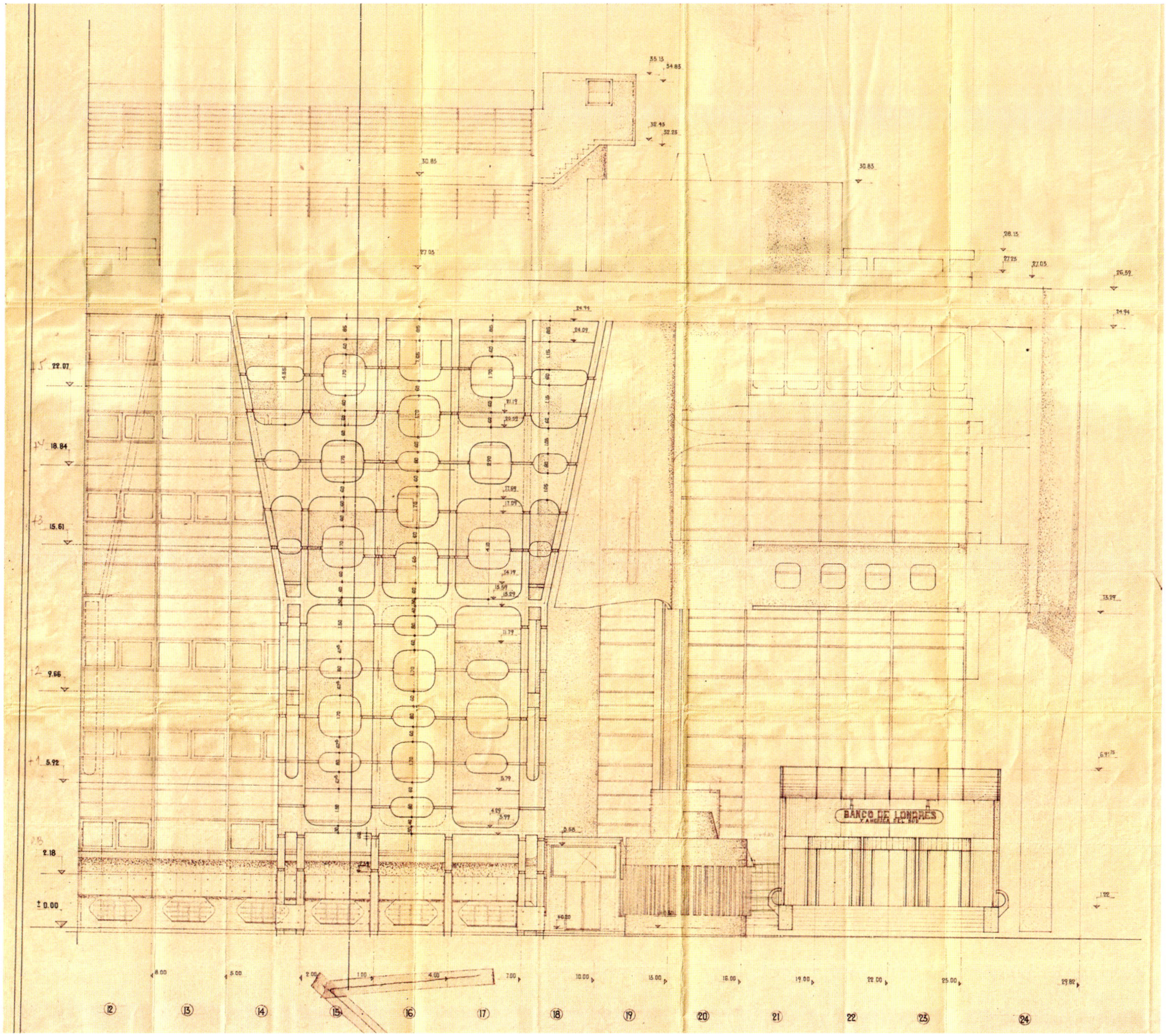

Opposite: Façade, Reconquista Street, Part A, 1963, Banco Hipotecario's file (box 21, plan 24). Scale 1:250
This page: Façade, Reconquista Street, Part B, 1963, Banco Hipotecario's file (box 21, plan 25)

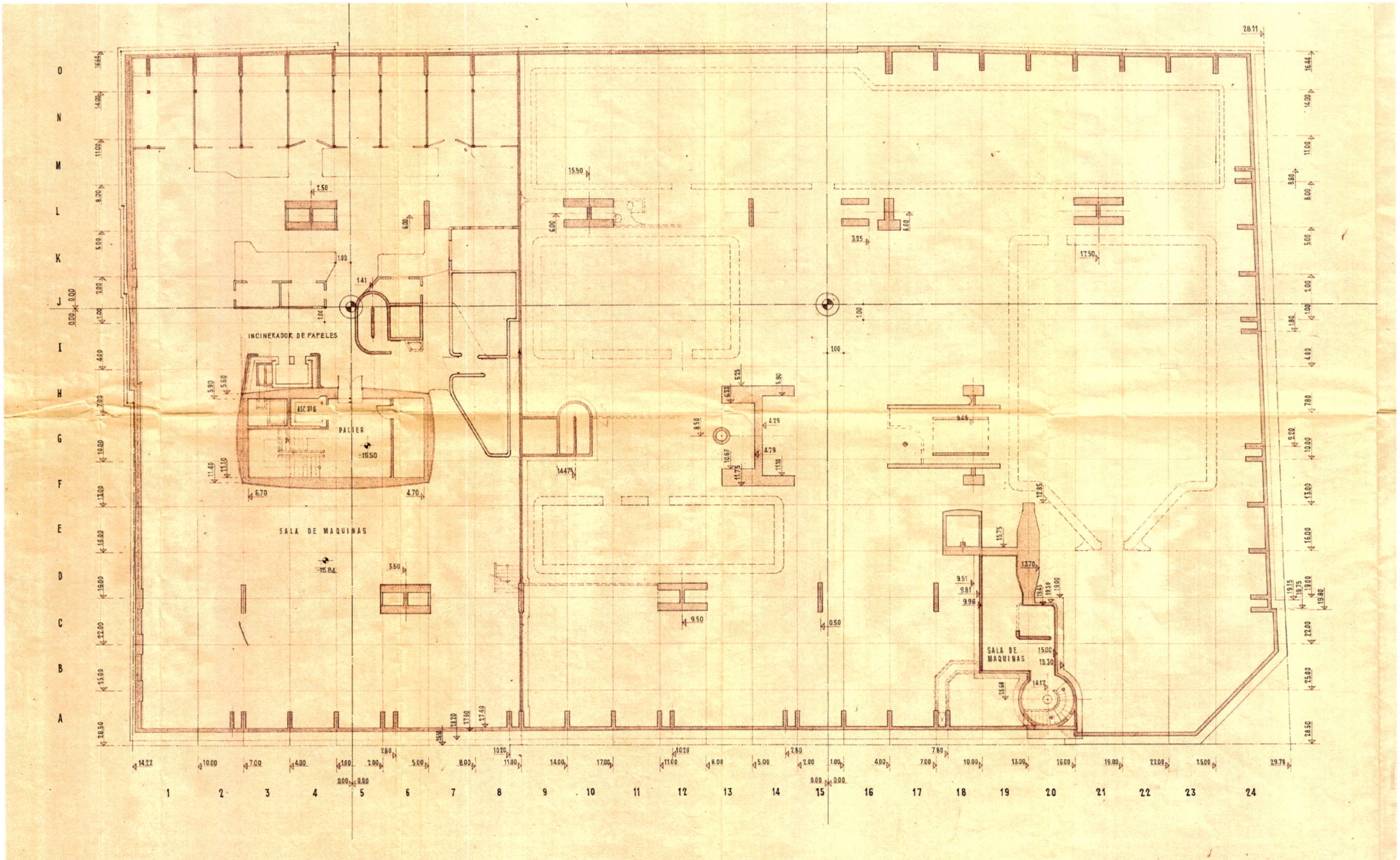
INCINERADOR DE PAPELES
PALIER
SALA DE MAQUINAS
SALA DE MAQUINAS

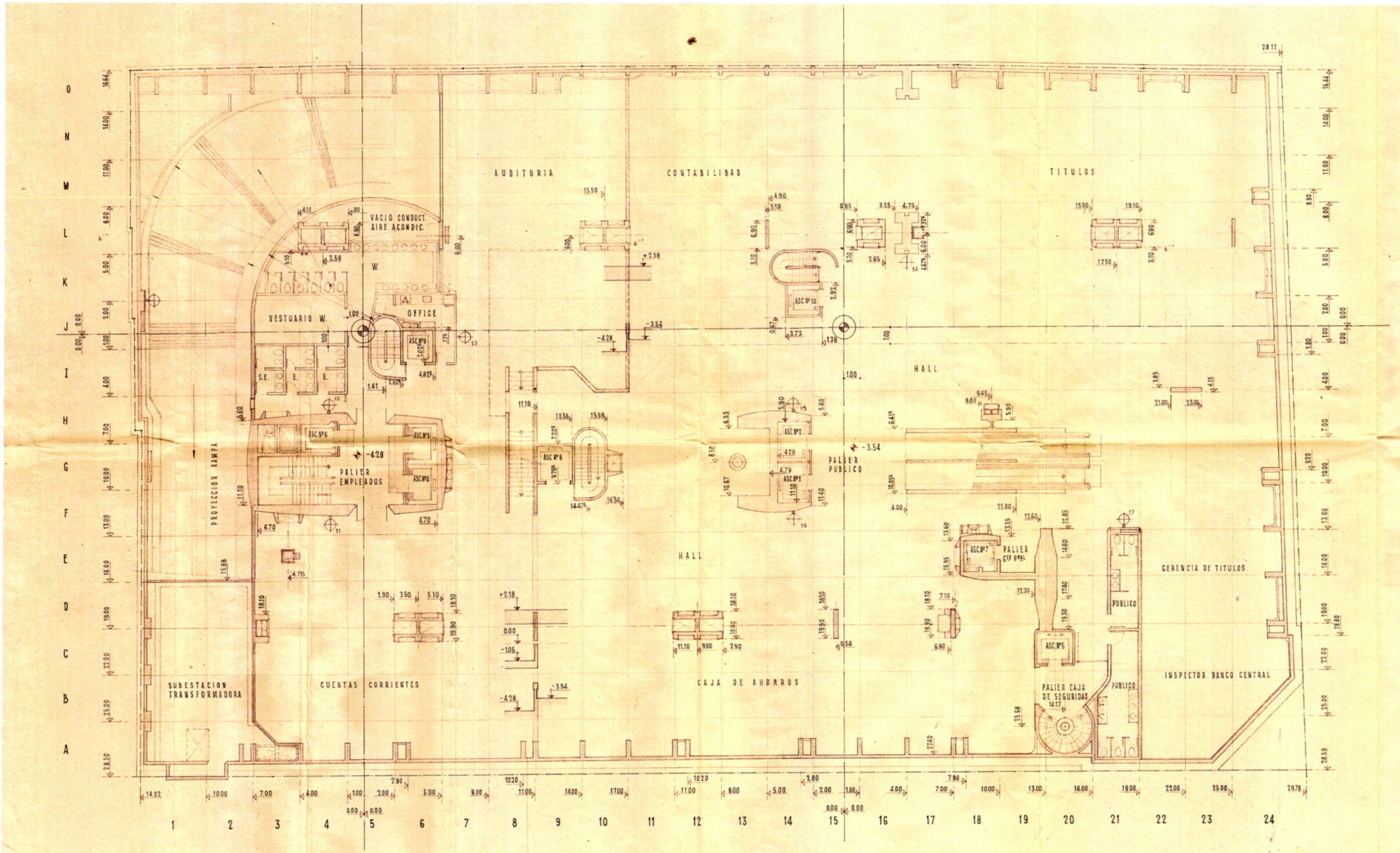

Opposite: Level -3, architecture plan, 1964, Banco Hipotecario's file (box 21, plan 13)
This page: Level -1, architecture plan, 1964, Banco Hipotecario's file (box 21, plan 15)

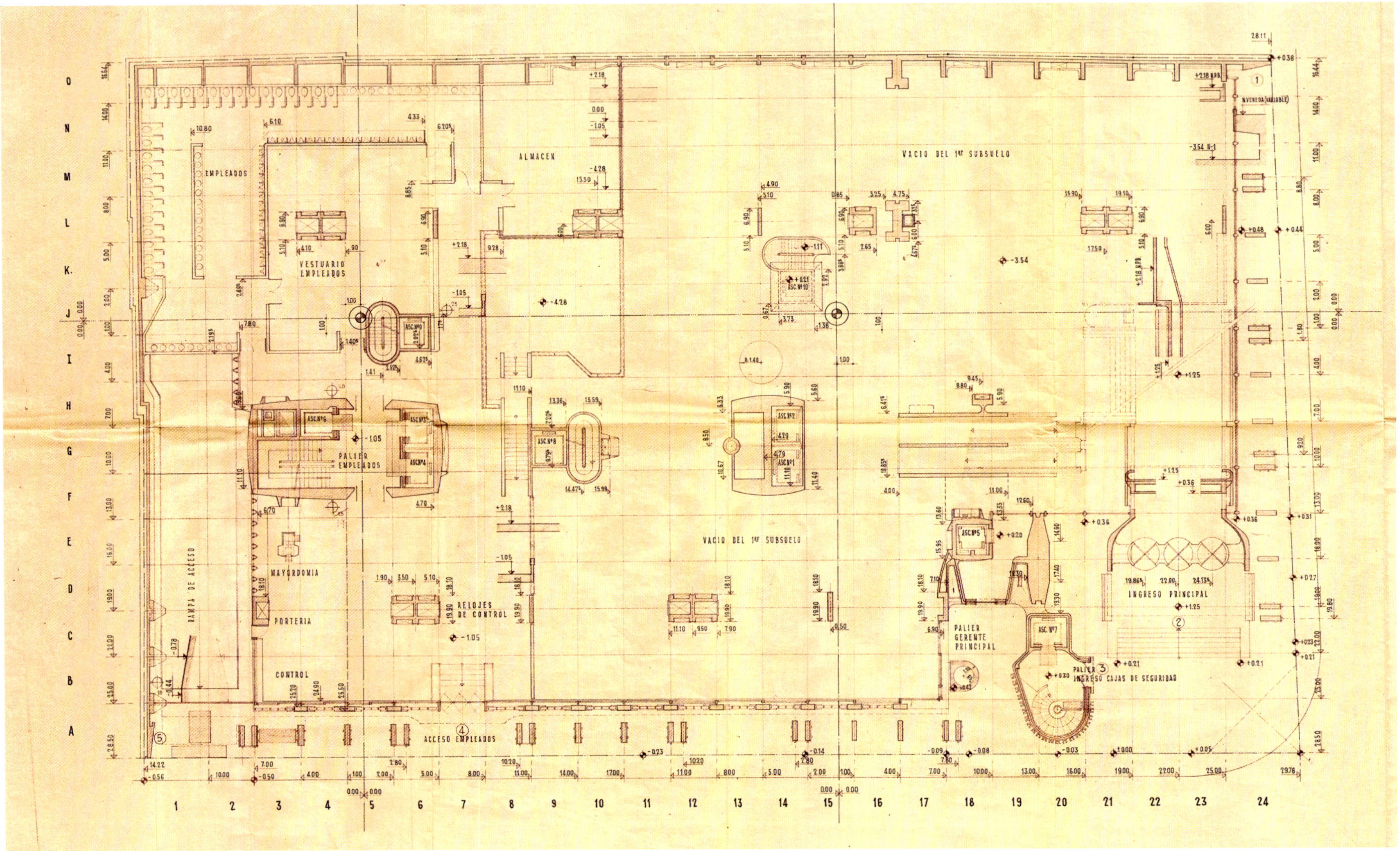
EMPLEADOS
VESTUARIO EMPLEADOS
ALMACEN
VACIO DEL 1er SUBSUELO
PALIER EMPLEADOS
MAYORDOMIA
PORTERIA
CONTROL
RELOJES DE CONTROL
RAMPA DE ACCESO
ACCESO EMPLEADOS
PALIER GERENTE PRINCIPAL
PALIER INGRESO CAJAS DE SEGURIDAD
INGRESO PRINCIPAL

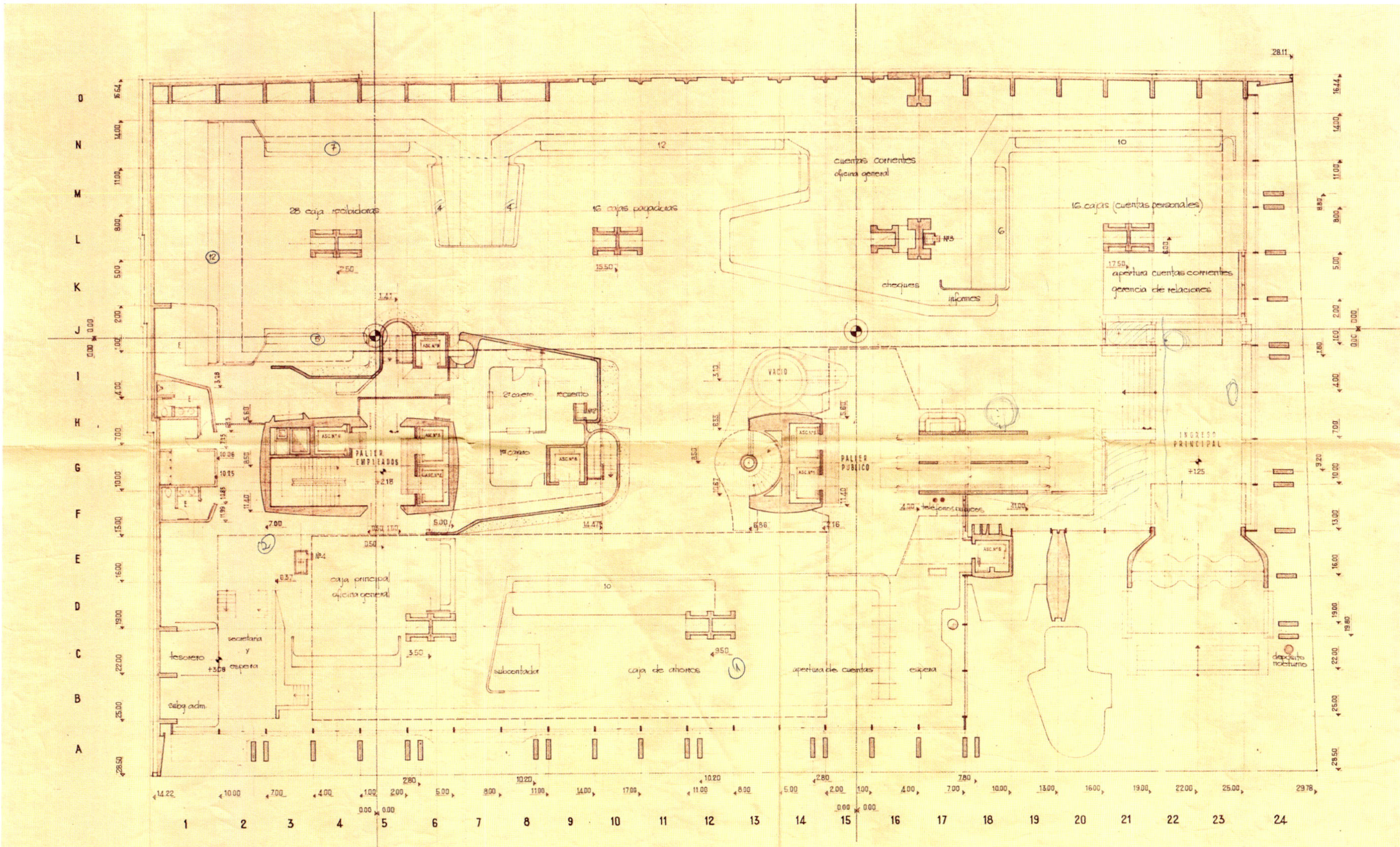

Opposite: Street level, architecture plan, 1964, Banco Hipotecario's file (box 21, plan 16)
This page: Ground floor, architecture plan, 30, sept,1964, Banco Hipotecario's file (box 21, plan 17)

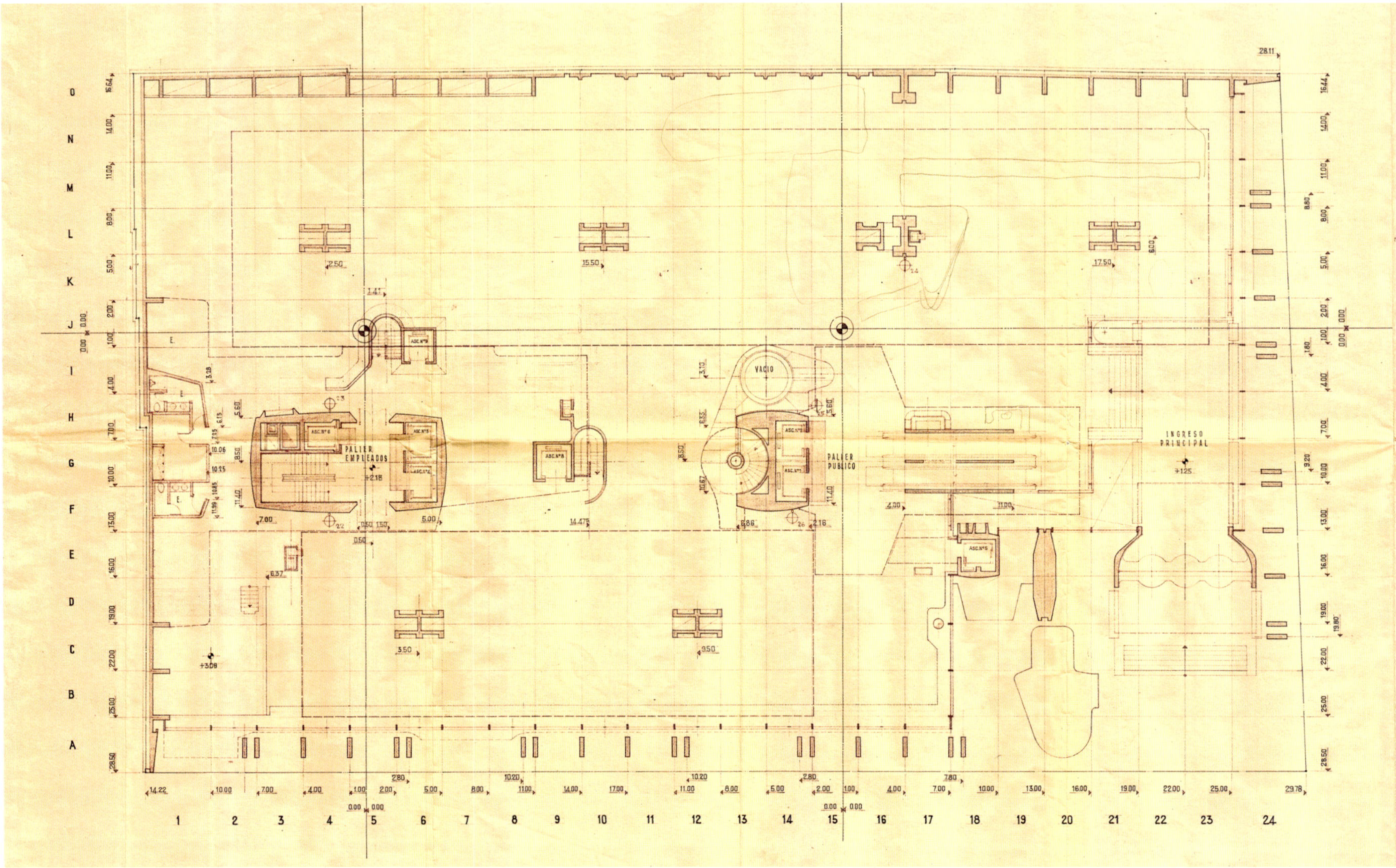
PALIER EMPLEADOS
PALIER PUBLICO
VACIO
INGRESO PRINCIPAL

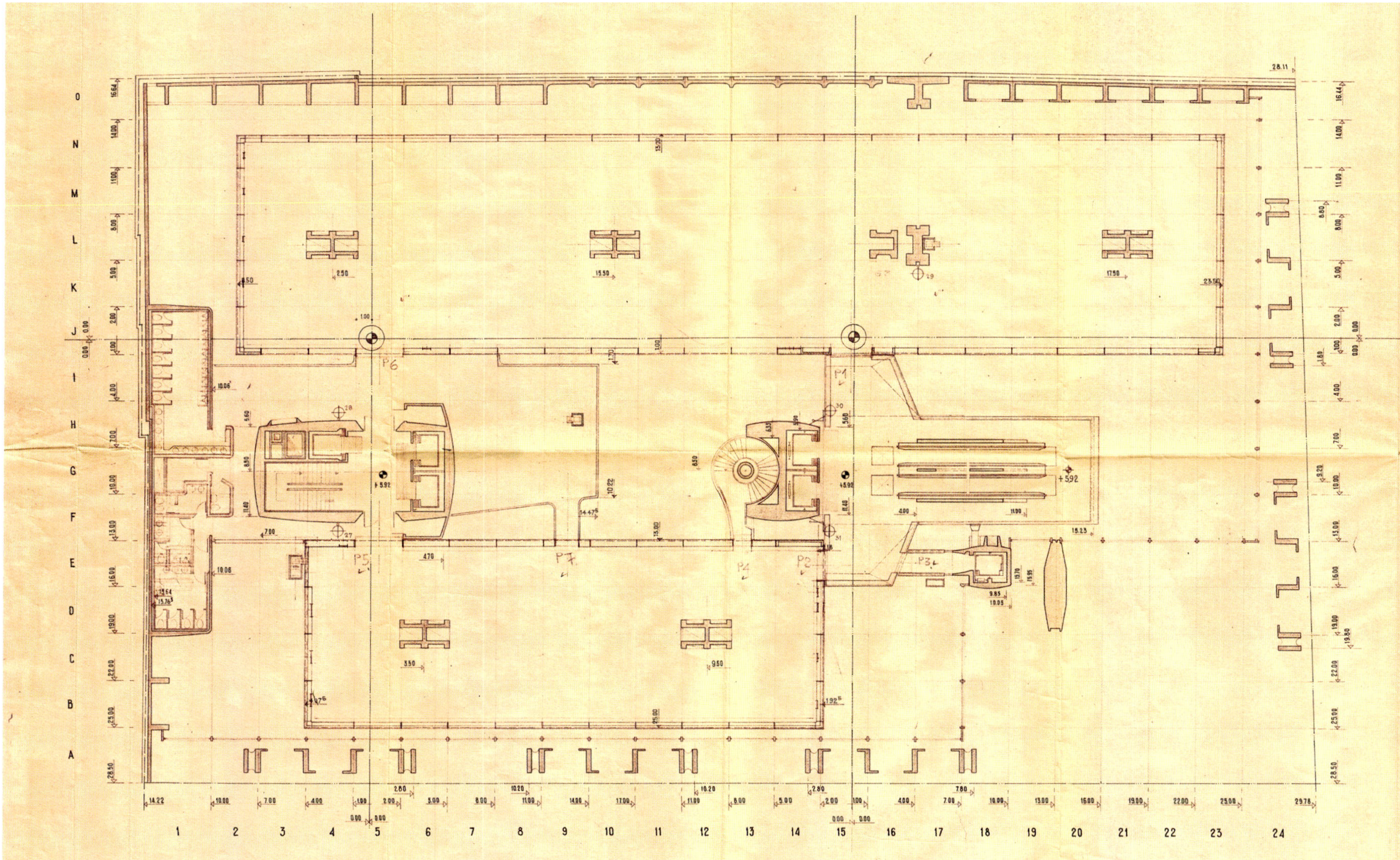

Opposite: Mezzanine, architecture plan, 4, sept, 1964, Banco Hipotecario's file (box 21, plan 18)
This page: Level +1, architecture plan, 1963, Banco Hipotecario's file (box 21, plan 19)

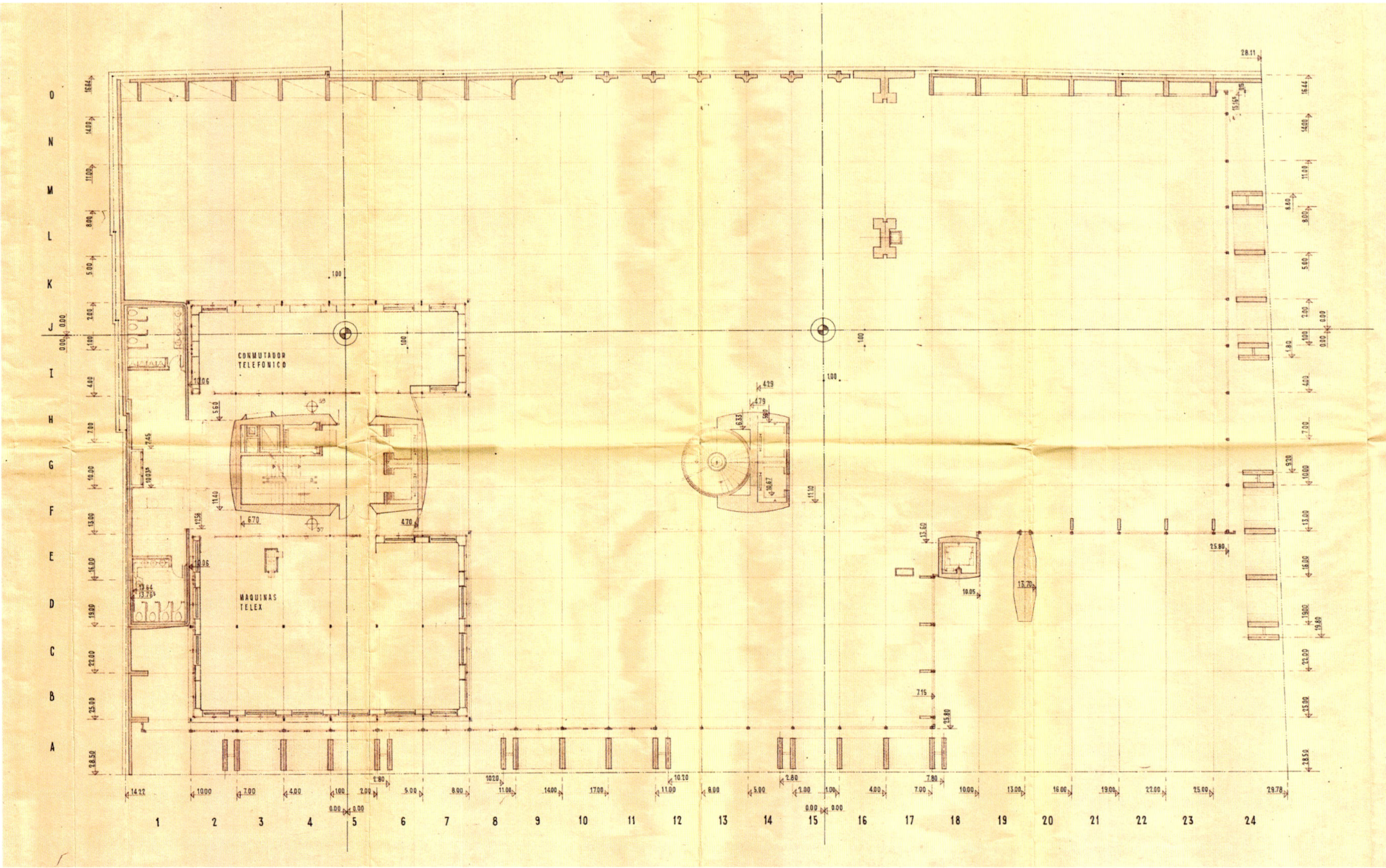
CONMUTADOR TELEFONICO
MAQUINAS TELEX
O N M L K J I H G F E D C B A
1 2 3 4 5 6 7 8 9 10 11 12 13 14 15 16 17 18 19 20 21 22 23 24

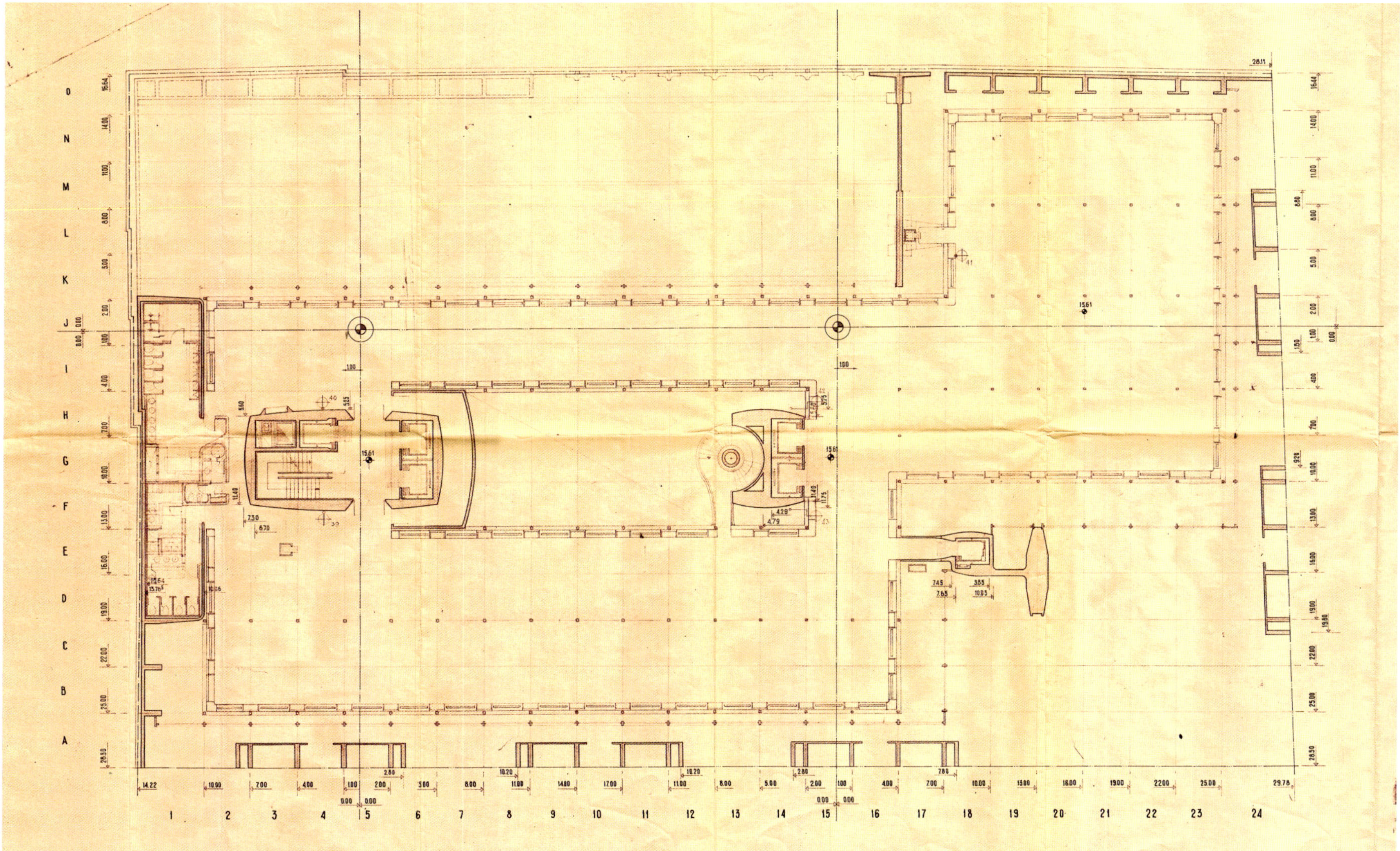

Opposite: Level +3, architecture plan, 1963, Banco Hipotecario's file (box 21, plan 20)
This page: Level +4, architecture plan, 1965, Banco Hipotecario's file (box 21, plan 21)

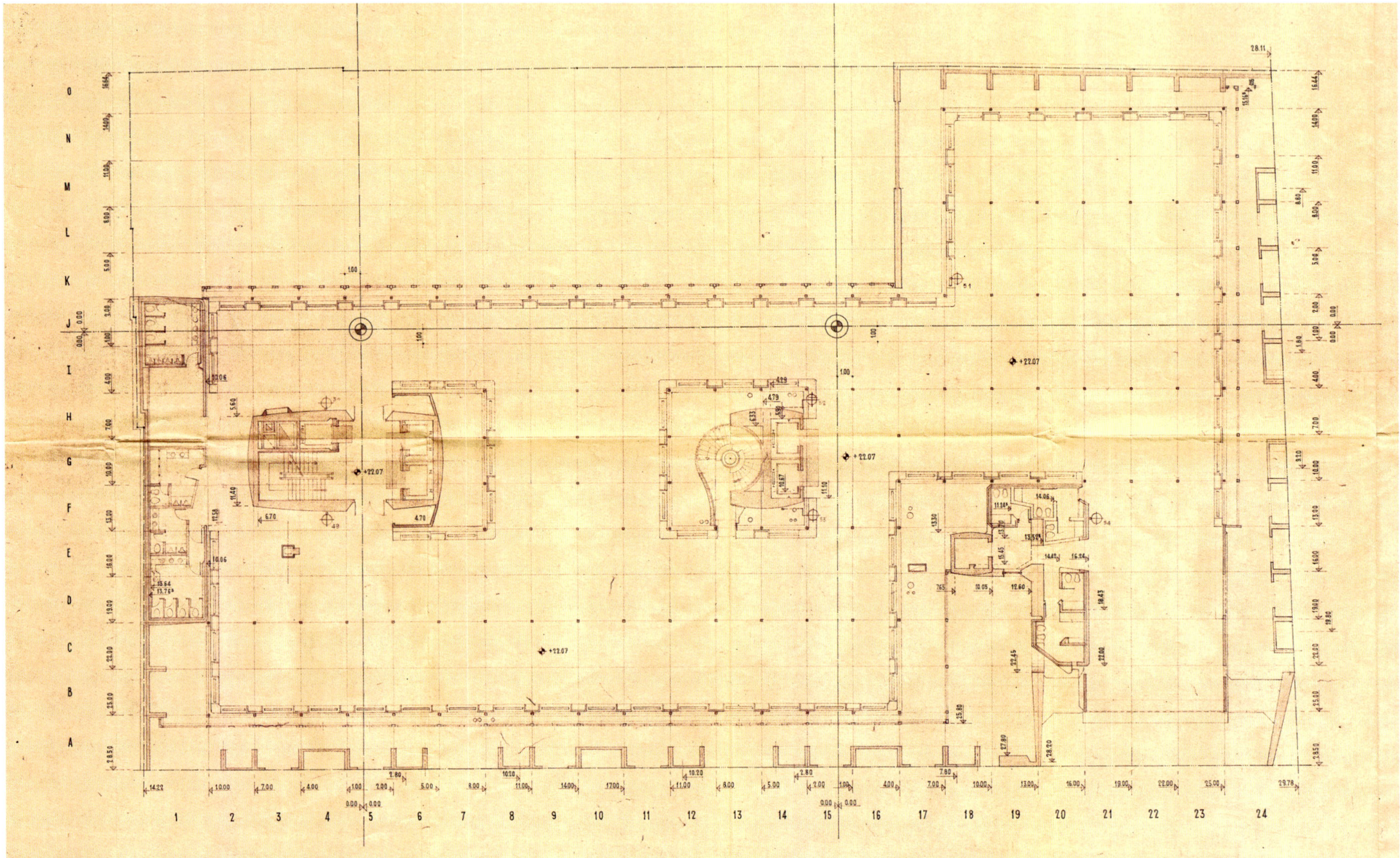

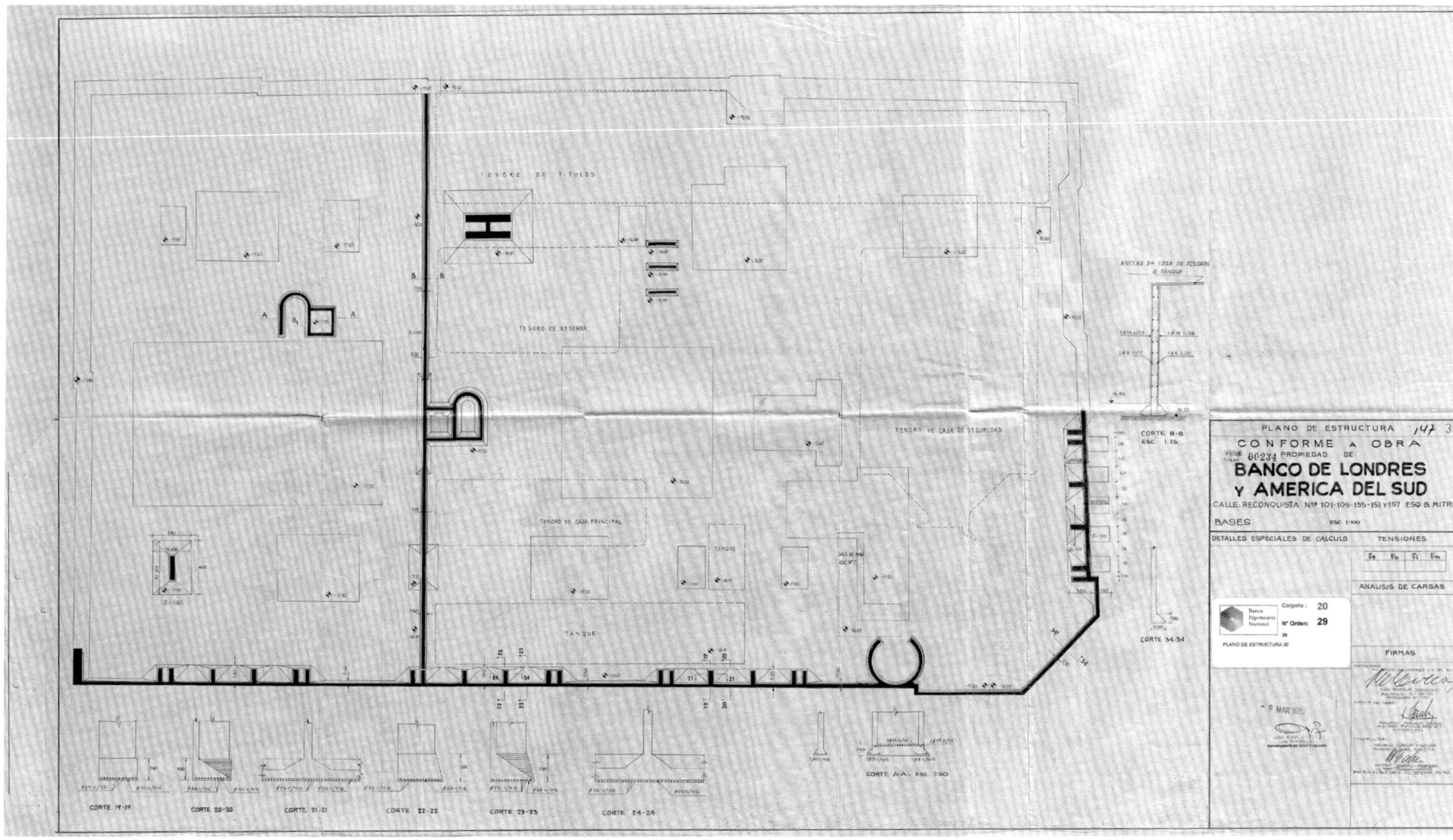

Opposite: Level +6, architecture plan, 1964, Banco Hipotecario's file (box 21, plan 22)
This page: Structural details of base, according to the built structure authorization plan, 1967, Banco Hipotecario's file (box 20, plan 29). Scale 1:250

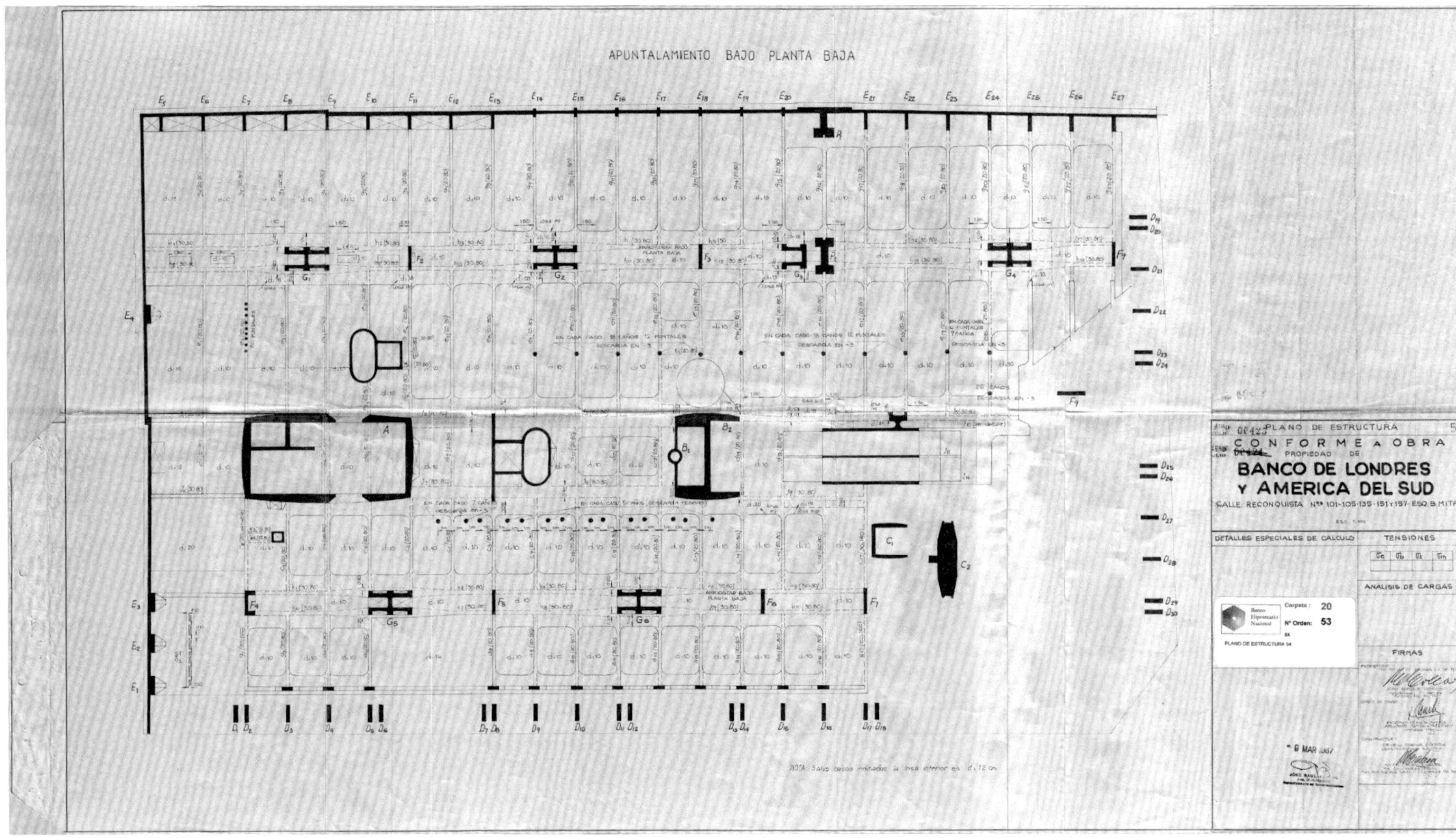
APUNTALAMIENTO BAJO PLANTA BAJA
PLANO DE ESTRUCTURA
54
CONFORME A OBRA
PROPIEDAD DE
BANCO DE LONDRES
Y AMERICA DEL SUD
CALLE RECONQUISTA Nº 101-105-135-151 Y 157 ESQ. B. MITRE
DETALLES ESPECIALES DE CALCULO
TENSIONES
ANALISIS DE CARGAS
FIRMAS
Carpeta: 20
Nº Orden: 53
PLANO DE ESTRUCTURA 54

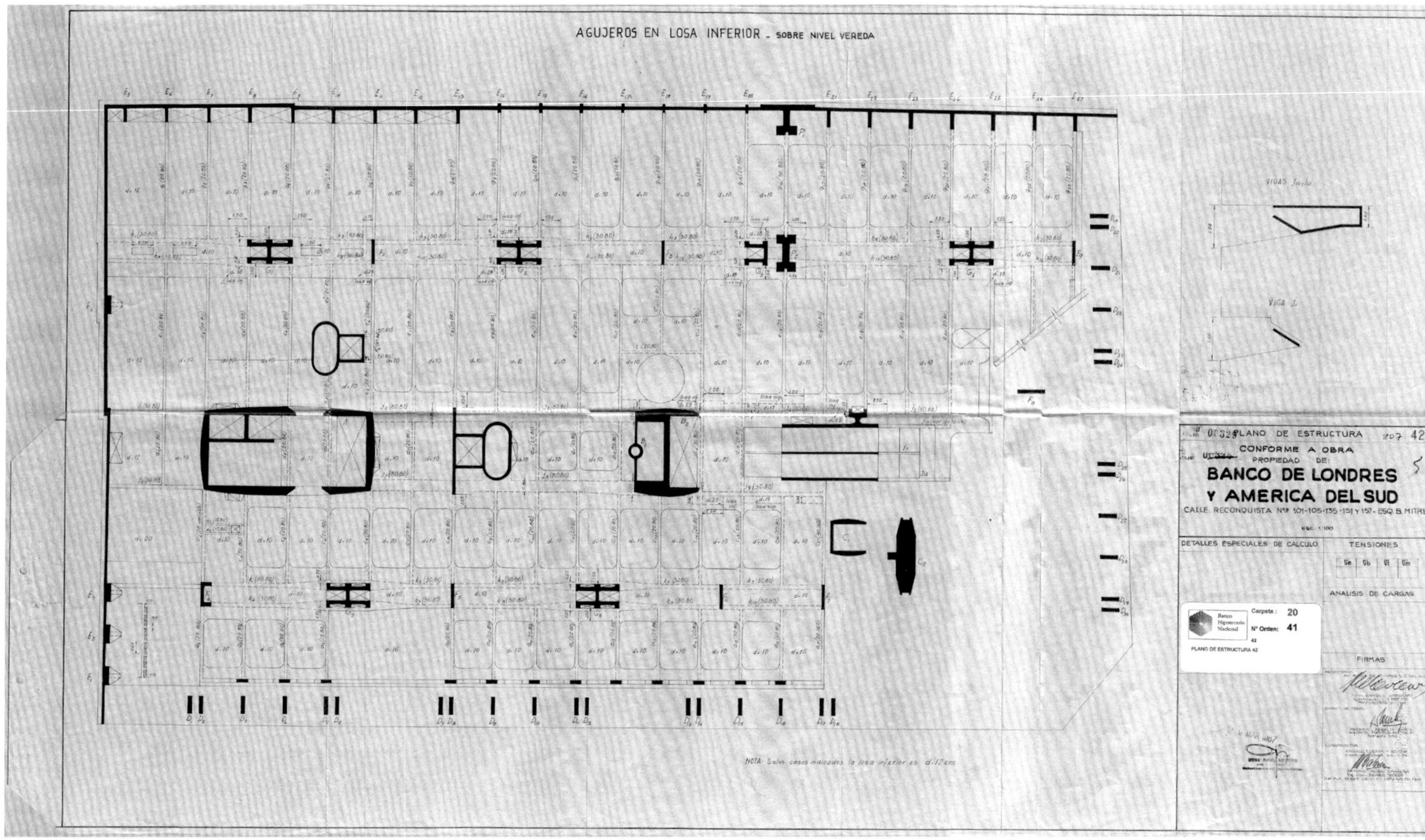

Opposite: Ground floor bracing, according to the built structure authorization plan, 1967, Banco Hipotecario's file (box 20, plan 53). Scale 1:250
This page: Structure over street level (holes), according to the built structure authorization plan, 1967, Banco Hipotecario's file (box 20, plan 41). Scale 1:250

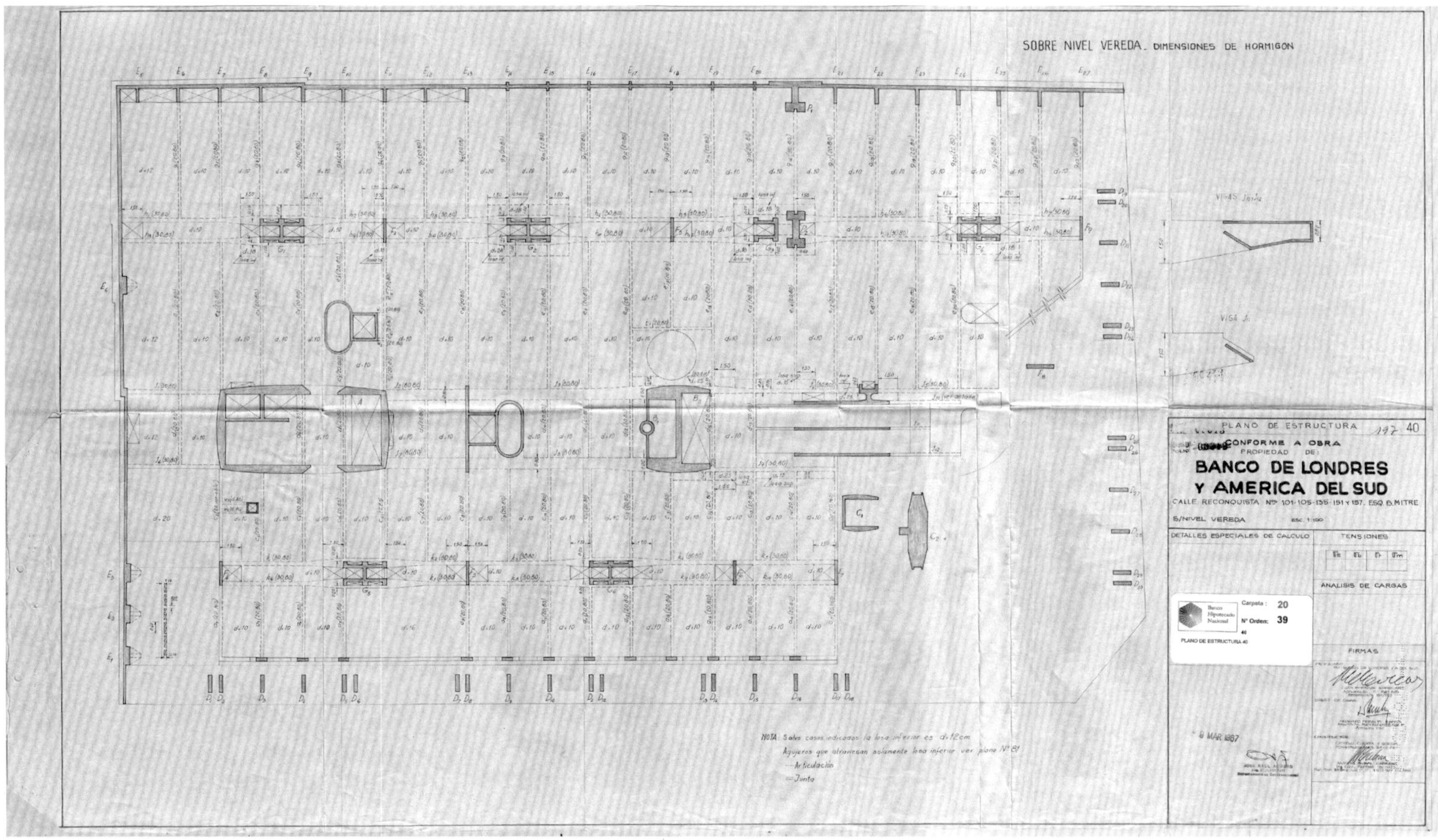
SOBRE NIVEL VEREDA. DIMENSIONES DE HORMIGON
PLANO DE ESTRUCTURA
40
CONFORME A OBRA
PROPIEDAD DE
BANCO DE LONDRES
Y AMERICA DEL SUD
S/NIVEL VEREDA
DETALLES ESPECIALES DE CALCULO
TENSIONES
ANALISIS DE CARGAS
Carpeta : 20
Nº Orden: 39
PLANO DE ESTRUCTURA 40
FIRMAS

Opposite: Structural details over street level, according to the built structure authorization plan, 1967, Banco Hipotecario's file (box 20, plan 39). Scale 1:250
This page: Structural reinforcement, according to the built structure authorization plan, 1967, Banco Hipotecario's file (box 20, plan 18). Scale 1:250

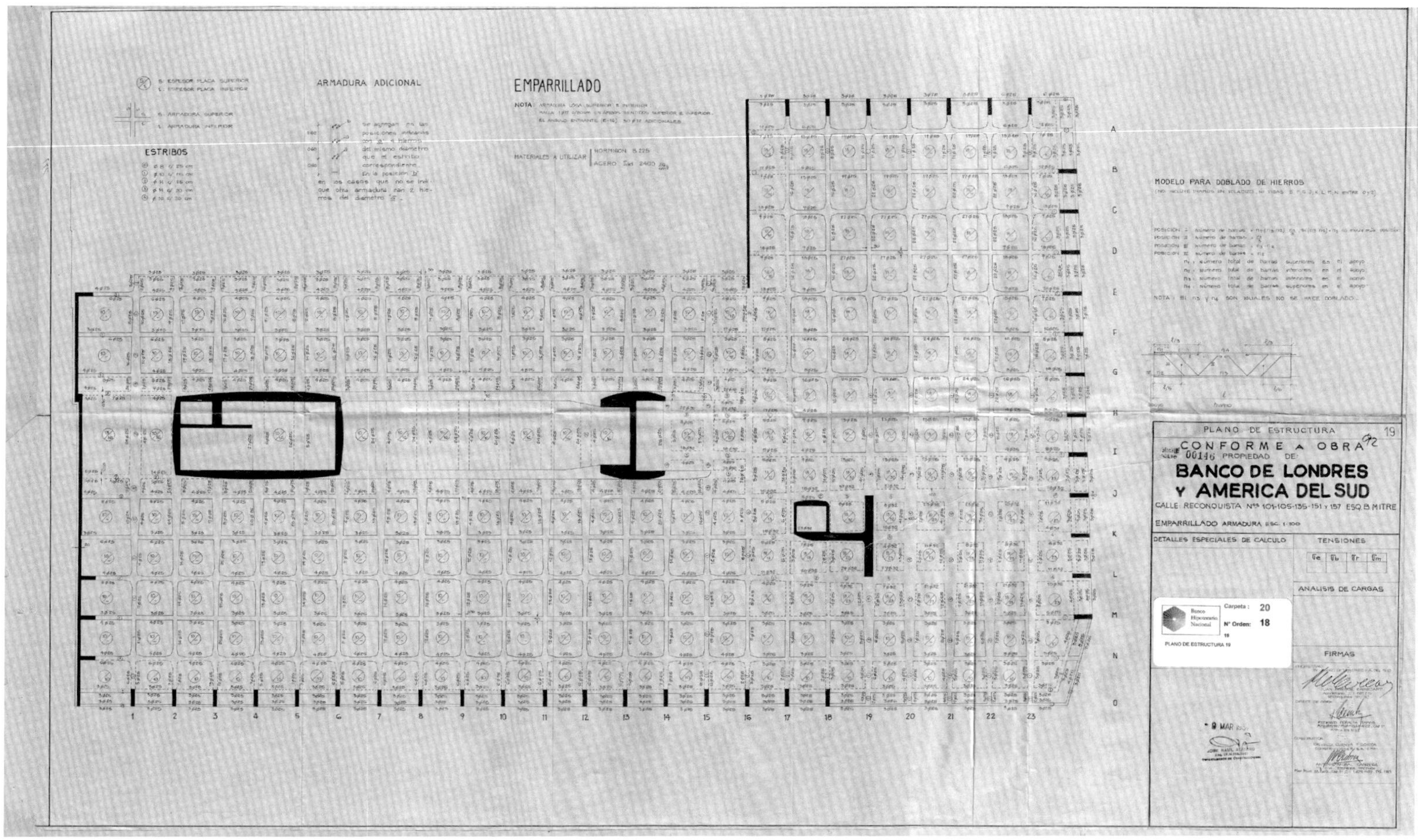

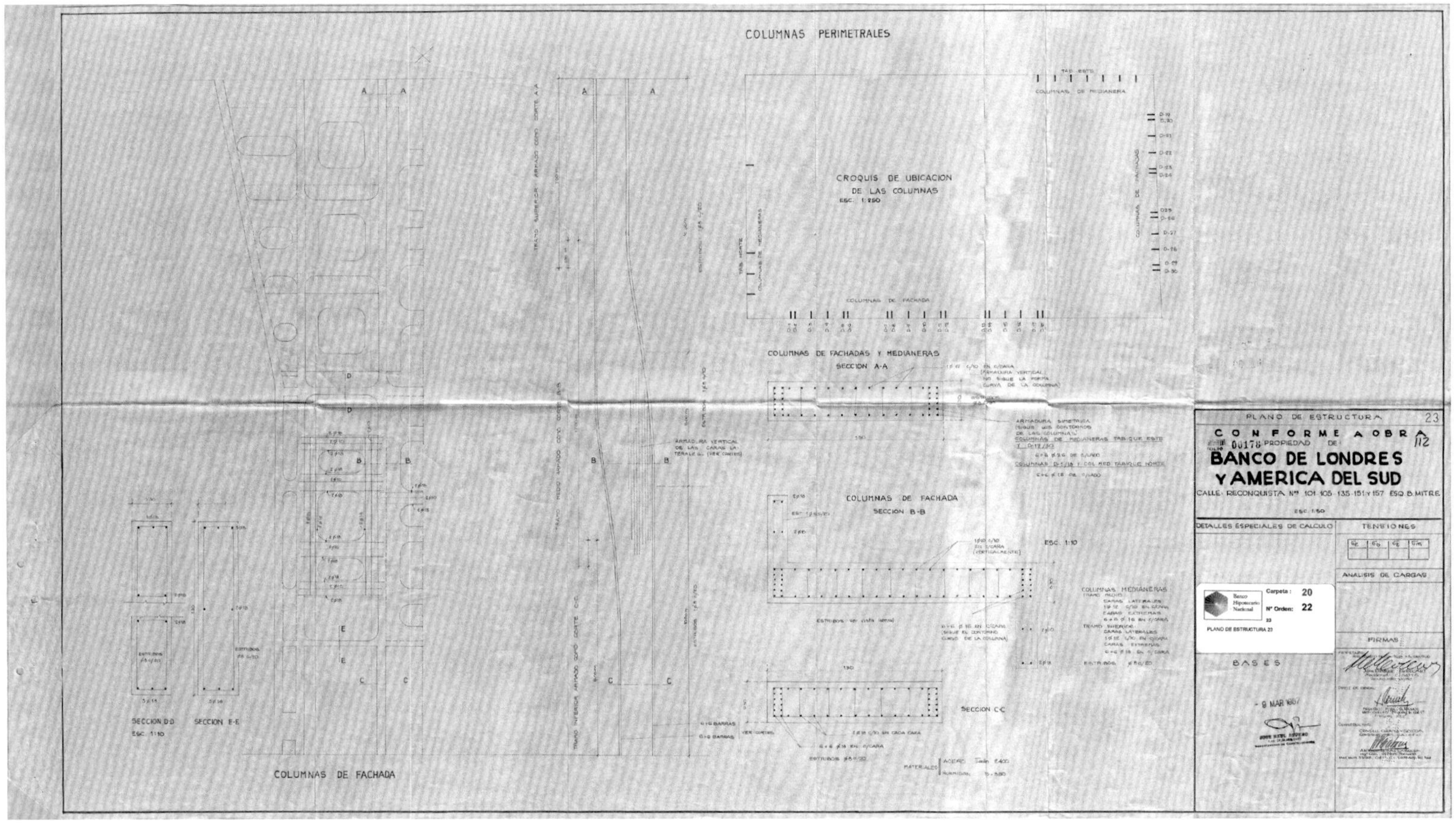
COLUMNAS PERIMETRALES
CROQUIS DE UBICACION
DE LAS COLUMNAS
COLUMNAS DE FACHADAS Y MEDIANERAS
SECCION A-A
COLUMNAS DE FACHADA
SECCION B-B
SECCION C-C
SECCION D-D
SECCION E-E
COLUMNAS DE FACHADA
PLANO DE ESTRUCTURA 23
CONFORME A OBRA
BANCO DE LONDRES
Y AMERICA DEL SUD
CALLE: RECONQUISTA Nº 101·105·135·151 y 157 ESQ. B. MITRE
DETALLES ESPECIALES DE CALCULO
TENSIONES
ANALISIS DE CARGAS
FIRMAS
BASES
Carpeta: 20
Nº Orden: 22

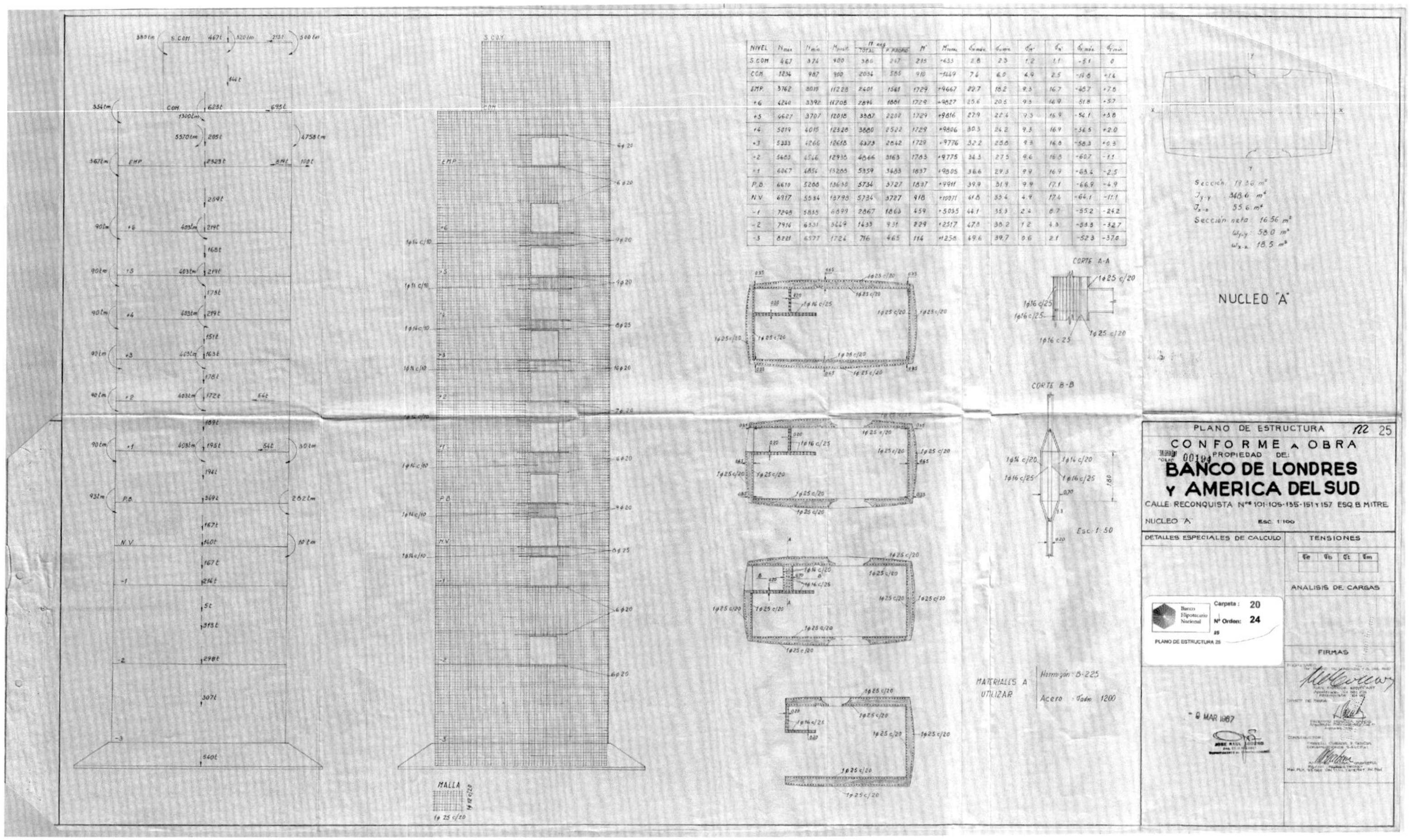

Opposite: Perimeter Columns structure, according to the built structure authorization plan, 1967, Banco Hipotecario's file (box 20, plan 22). Scale 1:125
This page: Structural details of Core A, according to the built structure authorization plan, 1967, Banco Hipotecario's file (box 20, plan 24). Scale 1:250

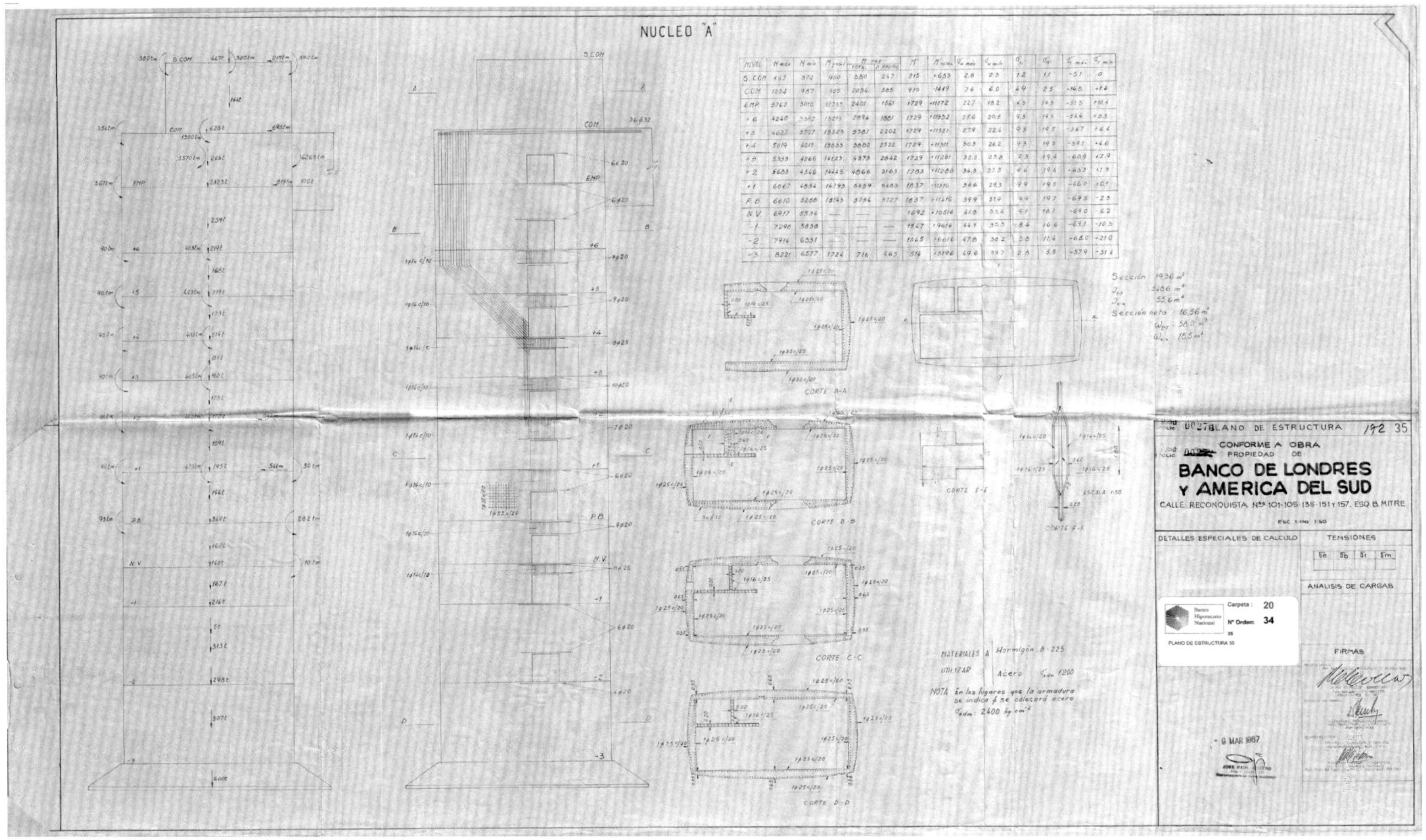
NUCLEO "A"
PLANO DE ESTRUCTURA
35
CONFORME A OBRA
PROPIEDAD DE
BANCO DE LONDRES
Y AMERICA DEL SUD
CALLE: RECONQUISTA Nº 101-105-135-151 Y 157, ESQ. B. MITRE
DETALLES ESPECIALES DE CALCULO
TENSIONES
ANALISIS DE CARGAS
FIRMAS
CORTE A-A
CORTE B-B
CORTE C-C
CORTE D-D
MATERIALES A UTILIZAR
Hormigón B-225
Carpeta: 20
Nº Orden: 34

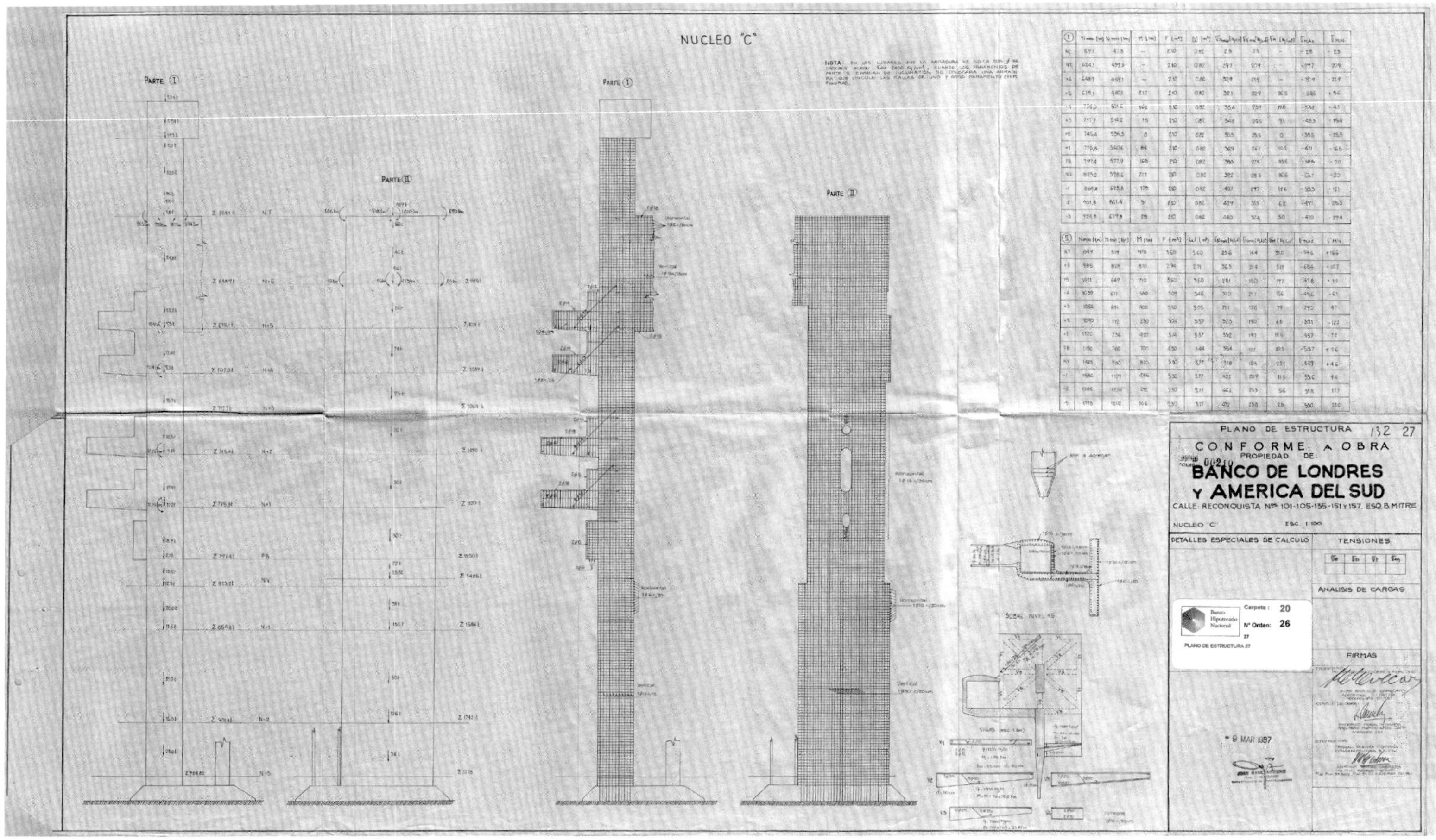

Opposite: Structural details of Core A, according to the built structure authorization plan, 1967, Banco Hipotecario's file (box 20, plan 34). Scale 1:250, 1:125

This page: Structural details of Core C, according to the built structure authorization plan, 1967, Banco Hipotecario's file (box 20, plan 26). Scale 1:250

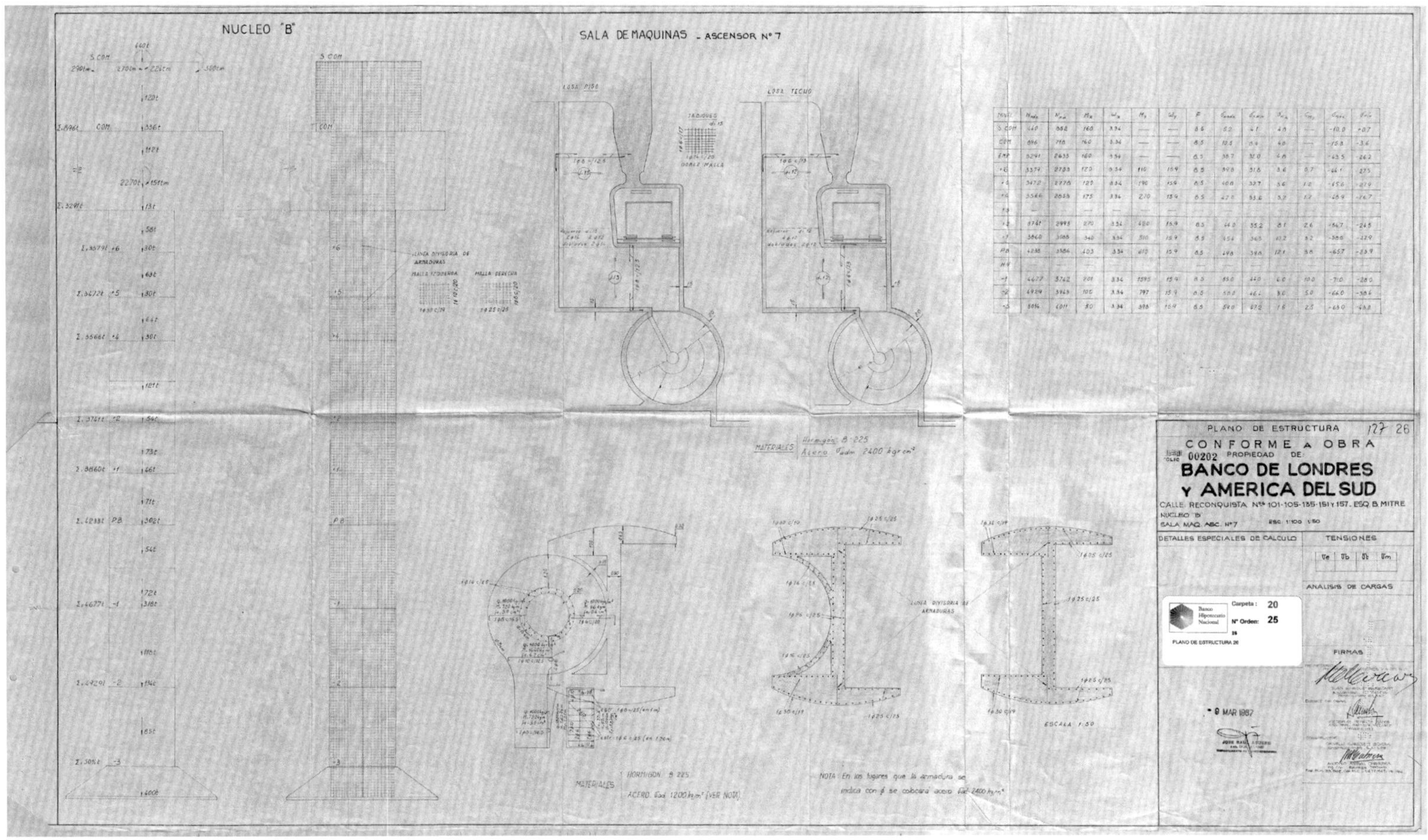
NUCLEO "B"
SALA DE MAQUINAS - ASCENSOR N° 7
PLANO DE ESTRUCTURA
CONFORME A OBRA
PROPIEDAD DE:
BANCO DE LONDRES
Y AMERICA DEL SUD
CALLE RECONQUISTA N° 101-109-135-151 Y 157, ESQ B. MITRE
NUCLEO B
SALA MAQ. ASC. N° 7
DETALLES ESPECIALES DE CALCULO
TENSIONES
ANALISIS DE CARGAS
FIRMAS
Carpeta: 20
N° Orden: 25
PLANO DE ESTRUCTURA 26
ESCALA 1:50

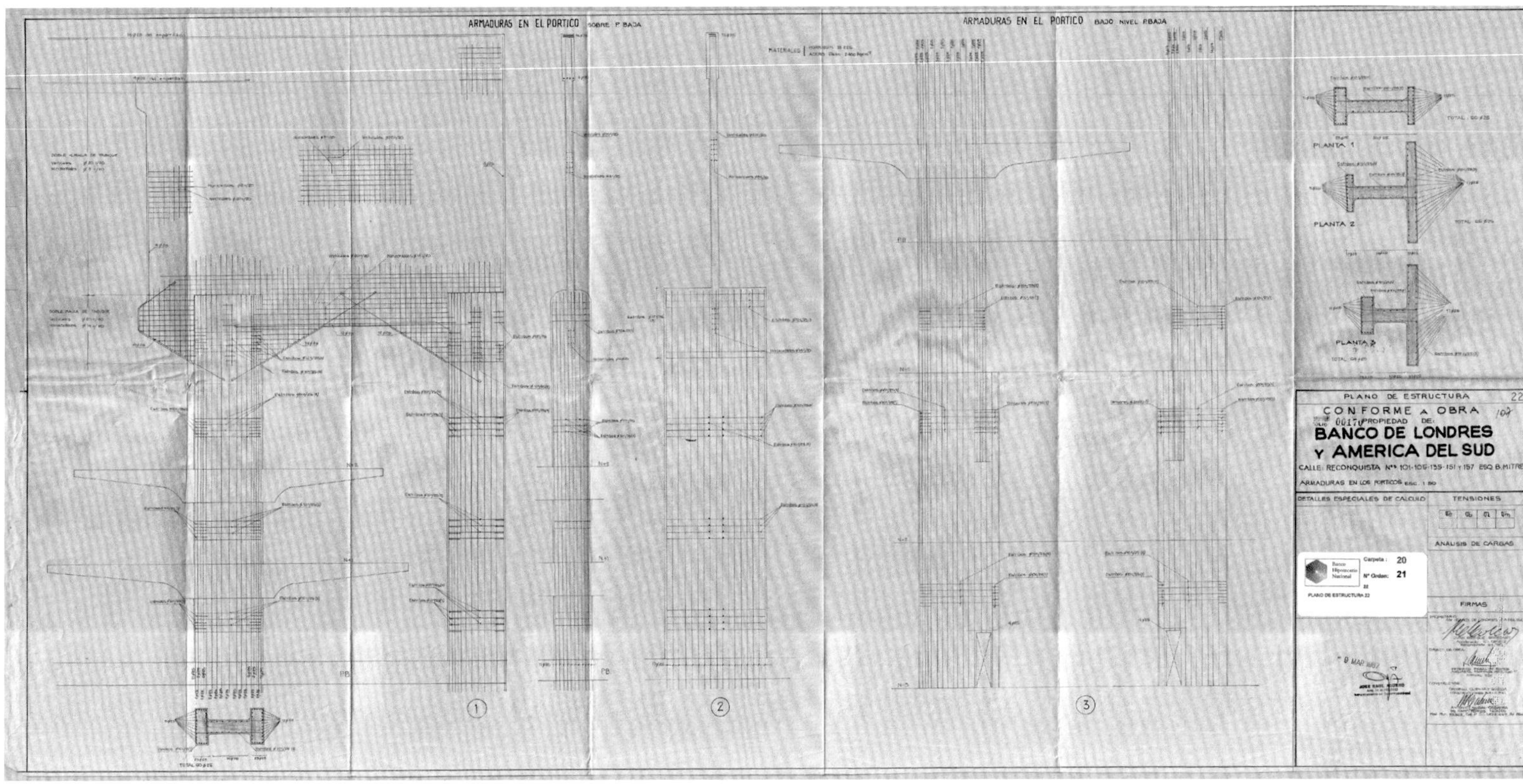

Opposite: Structural details of Core B, according to the built structure authorization plan, 1967, Banco Hipotecario's file (box 20, plan 25). Scale 1:125

This page: Structural reinforcement arcade, according to the built structure authorization plan, 1967, Banco Hipotecario's file (box 20, plan 21). Scale 1:125

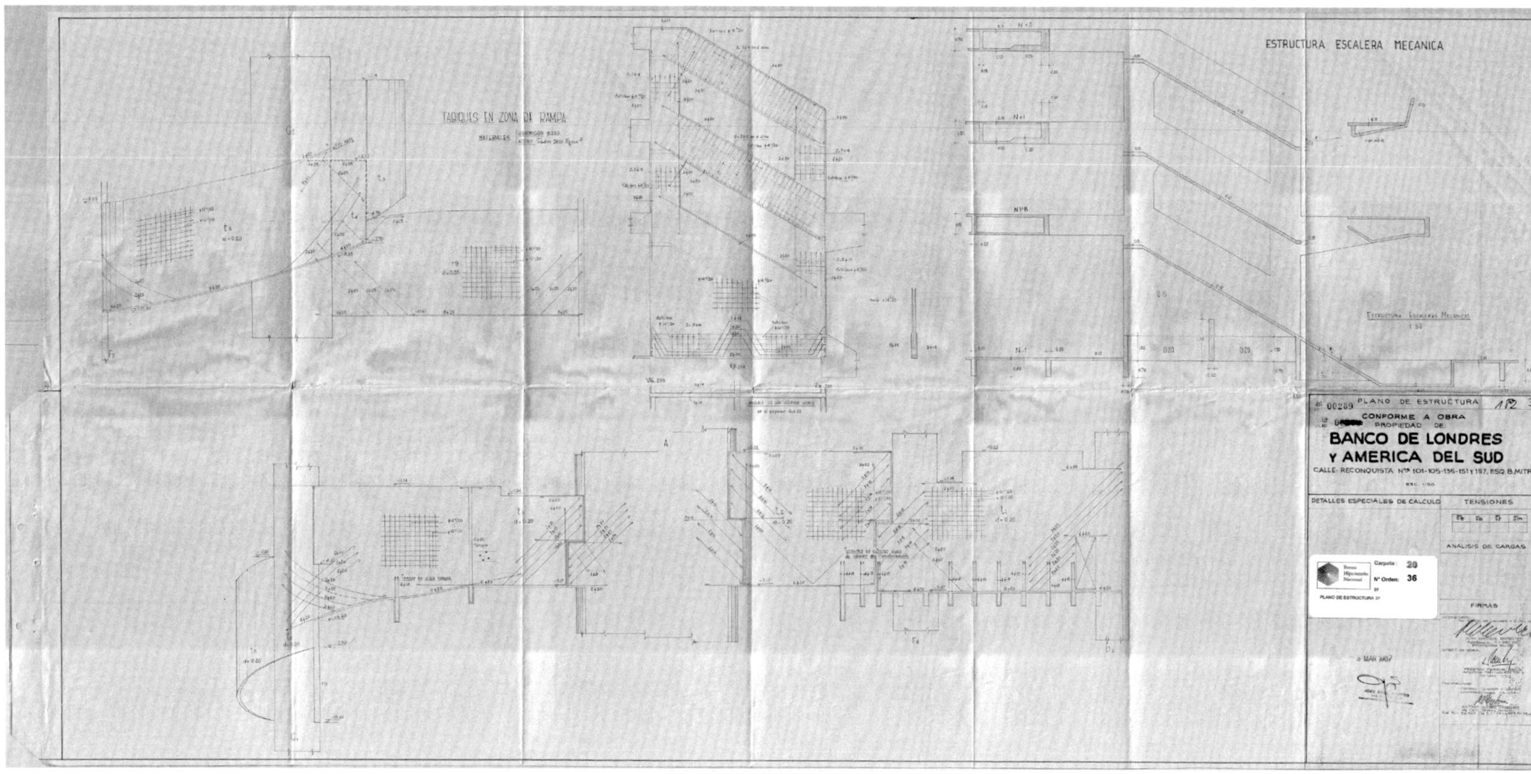
ESTRUCTURA ESCALERA MECANICA
TABIQUES EN ZONA DE RAMPA
PLANO DE ESTRUCTURA
CONFORME A OBRA
PROPIEDAD DE
BANCO DE LONDRES
Y AMERICA DEL SUD
CALLE: RECONQUISTA Nºs 101-105-135-151 y 157, ESQ. B. MITRE
DETALLES ESPECIALES DE CALCULO
TENSIONES
ANALISIS DE CARGAS
FIRMAS
Carpeta: 20
Nº Orden: 36
PLANO DE ESTRUCTURA 37

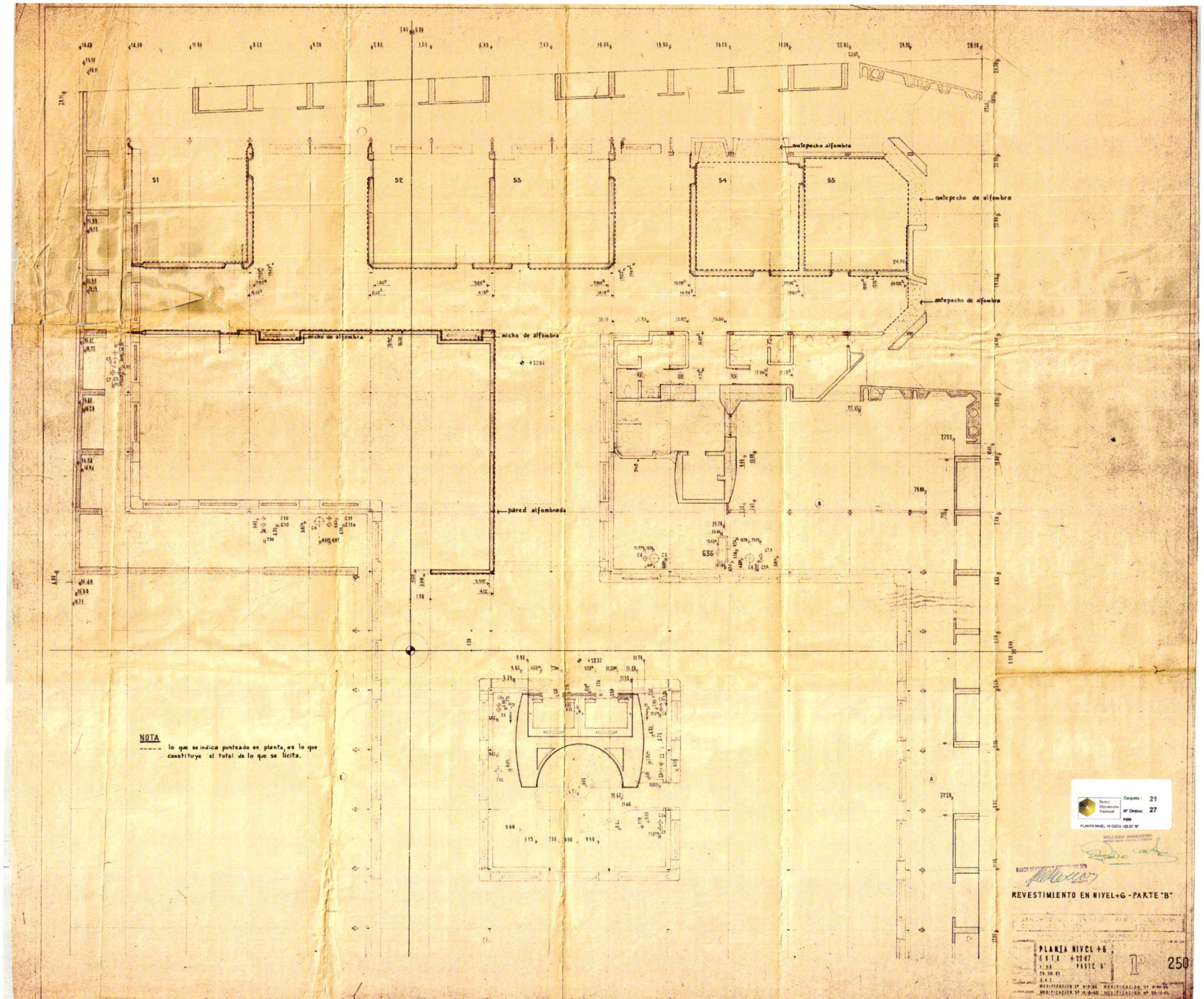

Opposite: Escalator structural details, according to the built structure authorization plan, 1967, Banco Hipotecario's file (box 20, plan 36). Scale 1:125
This page: Level +6, paneling plan, Banco Hipotecario's file (box 21, plan 27)

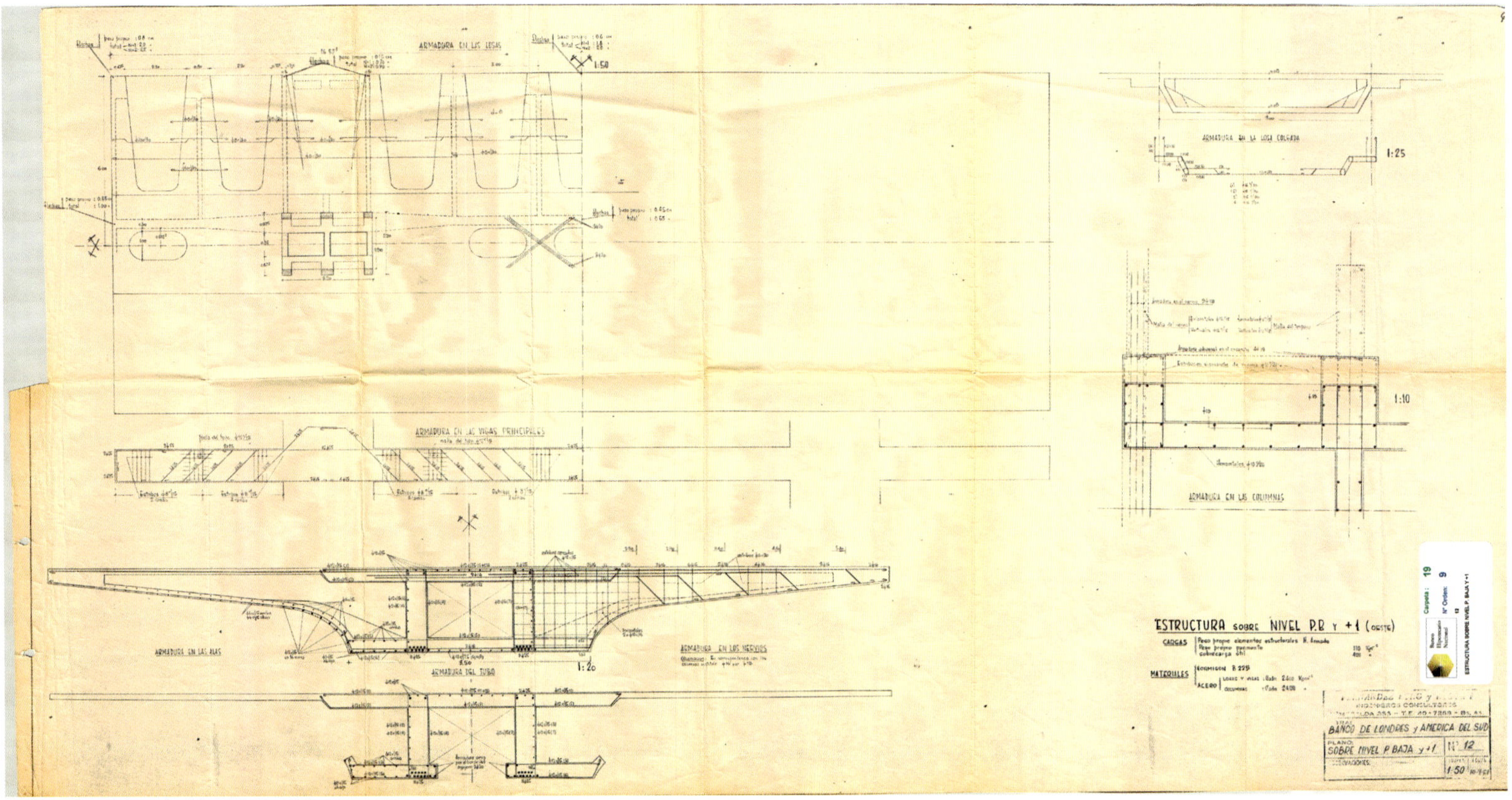

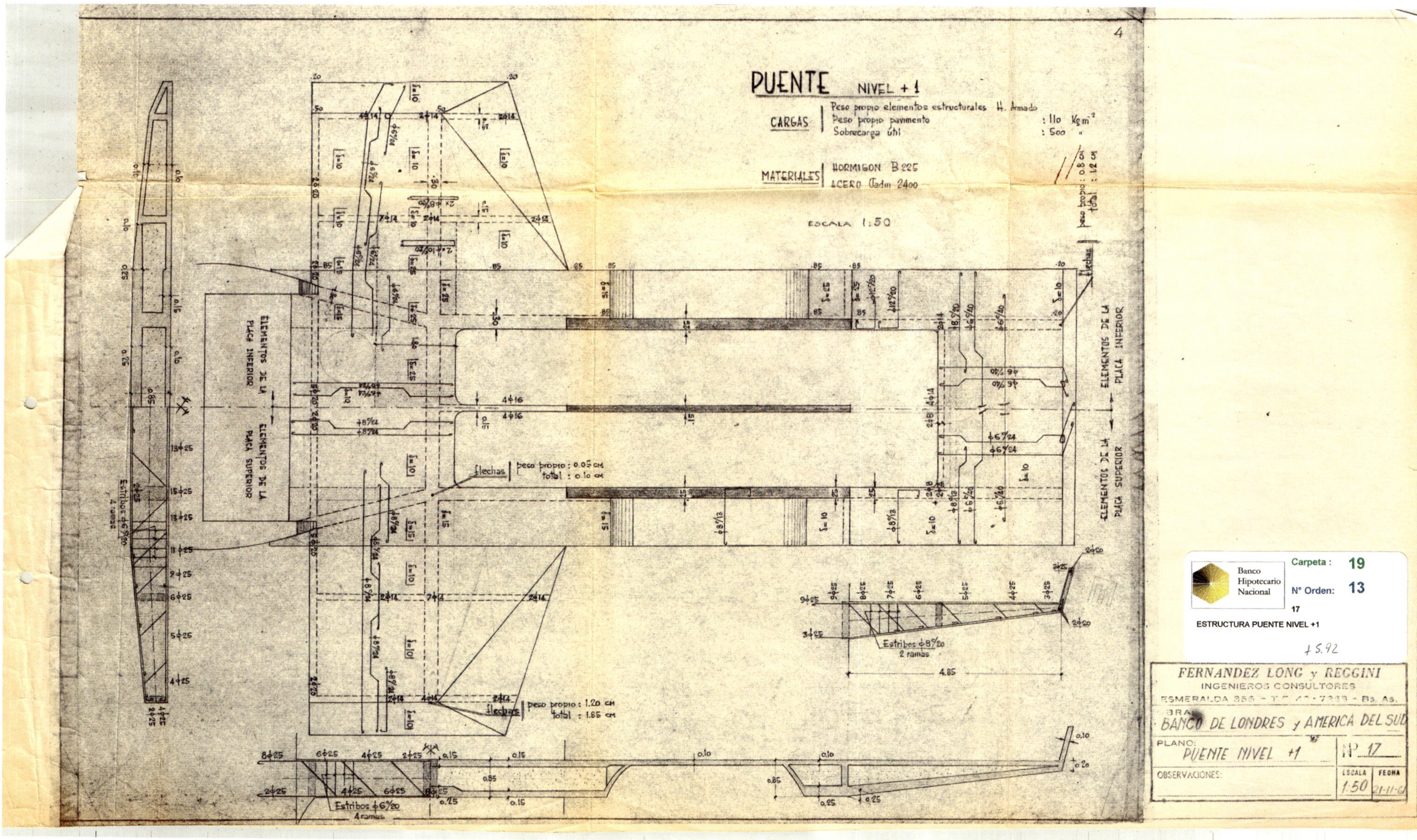

…structure over ground level and over level +1 structure, structure plan, 1961, Banco Hipotecario's file (box 19, plan 9). Scale 1:125

This page: Bridge structure at level +1, structure plan, 1961, Banco Hipotecario's file (box 19, plan 13). Scale 1:125, 1:50

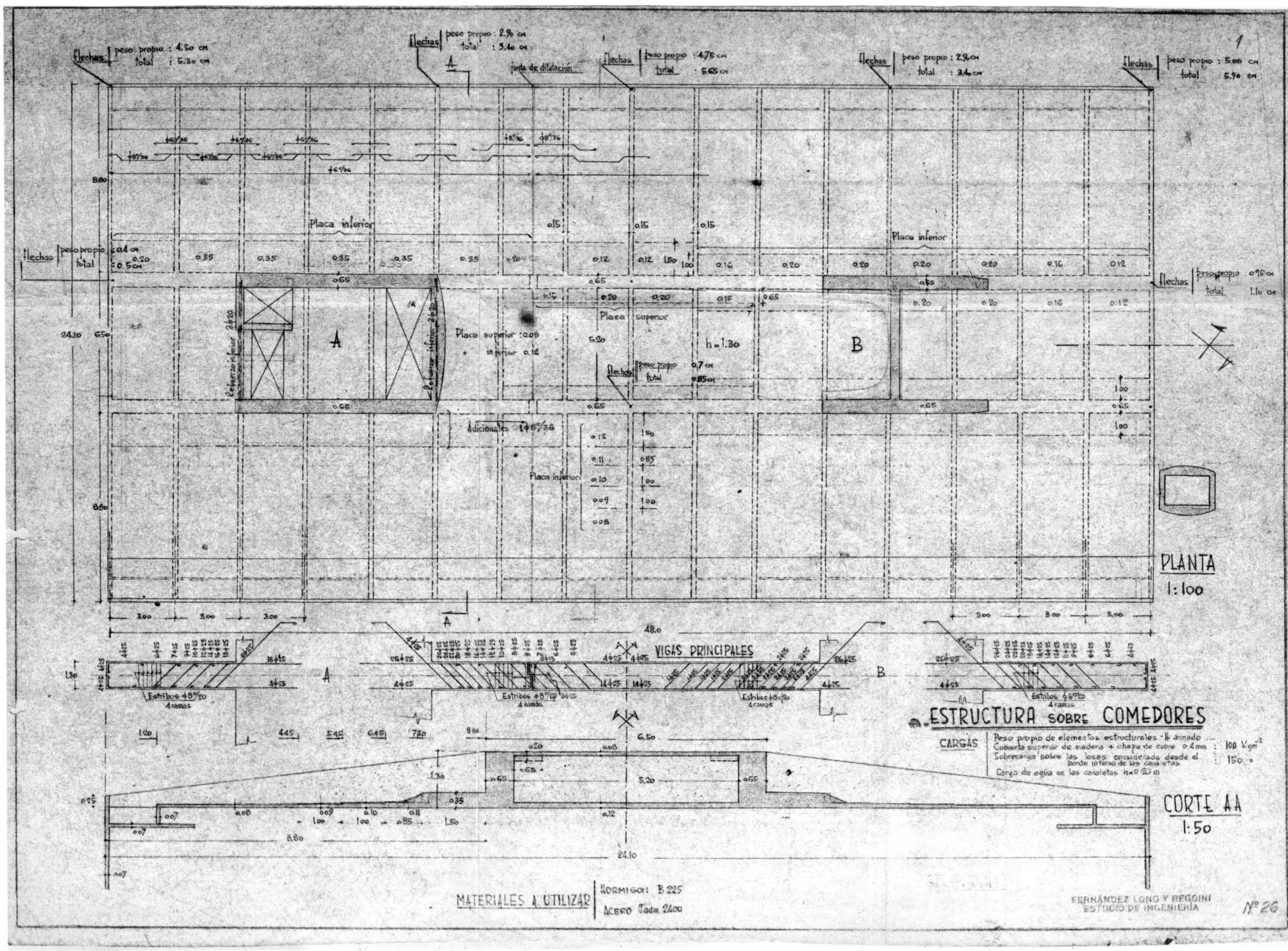

Flechas | peso propio : 4.50 cm | total : 5.30 cm
junta de dilatación
Placa inferior
Placa superior
A
B
h=1.30
PLANTA
1:100
VIGAS PRINCIPALES
ESTRUCTURA SOBRE COMEDORES
CARGAS
Peso propio de elementos estructurales
Sobrecarga sobre las losas
CORTE AA
1:50
MATERIALES A UTILIZAR
HORMIGON B 225
FERNÁNDEZ LONG Y REGGINI
ESTUDIO DE INGENIERÍA
Nº 26

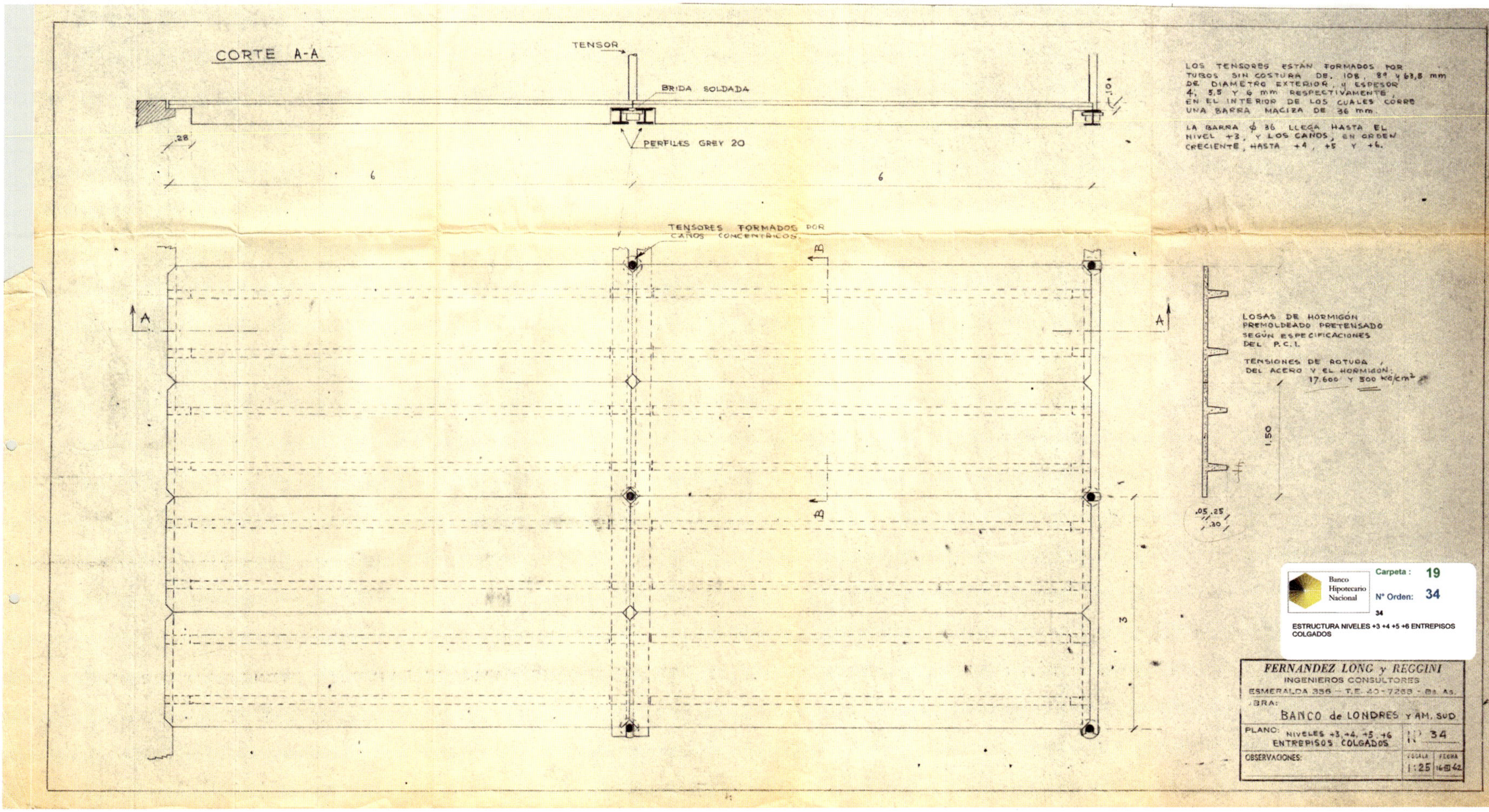

Opposite: Structure over dining hall, structure plan, 1962, Banco Hipotecario's file (box 15, plan 22)
This page: Hanging mezzanine structure, structure plan, 1962, Banco Hipotecario's file (box 19, plan 34). Scale 3:250

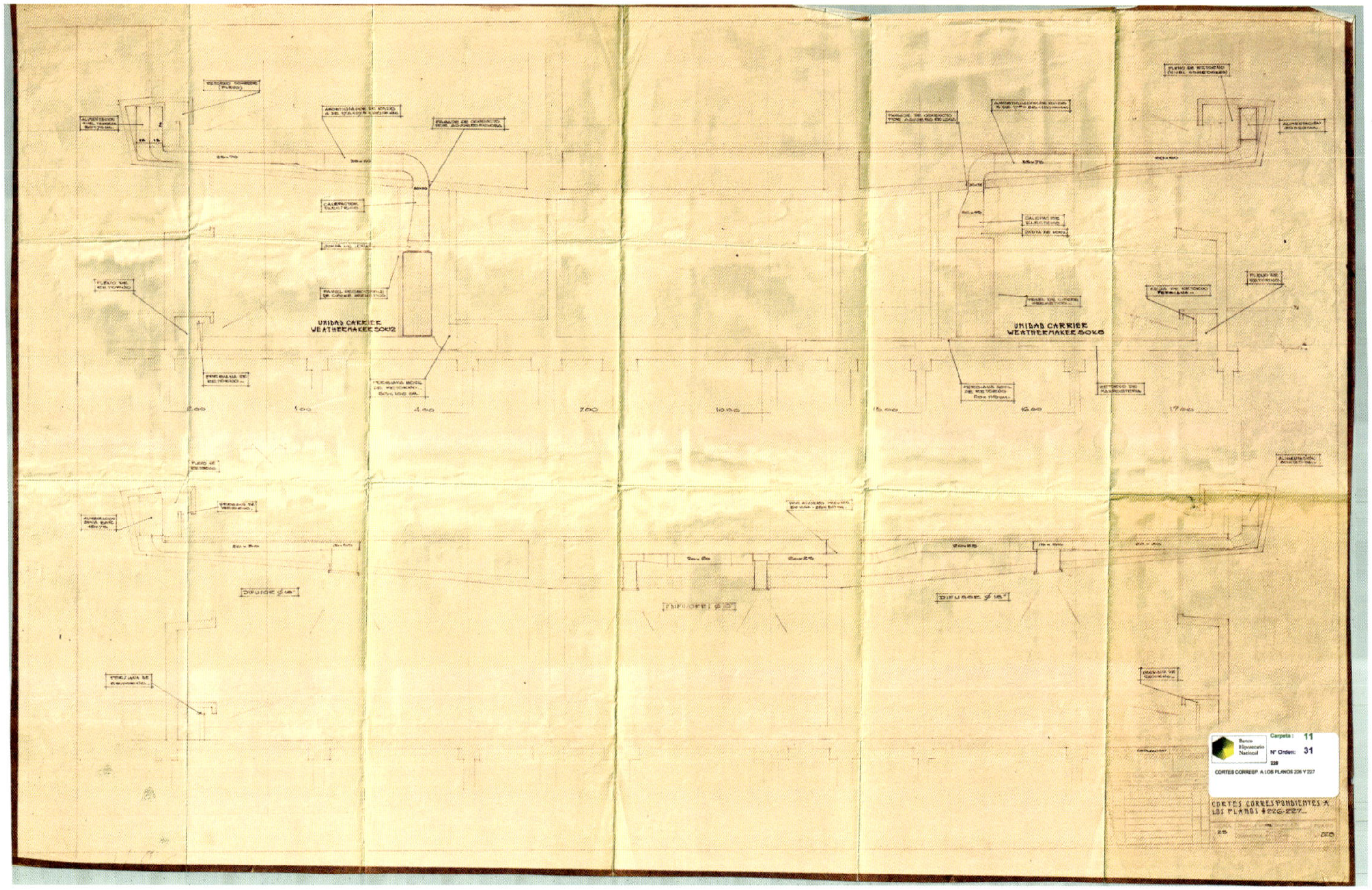
UNIDAS CARRIER
WEATHERMAKER 50K12
UNIDAS CARRIER
WEATHERMAKER 50K6
Banco Hipotecario Nacional
Carpeta : 11
Nº Orden: 31
228
CORTES CORRESP. A LOS PLANOS 226 Y 227
CORTES CORRESPONDIENTES A
LOS PLANOS #226-227
25
228

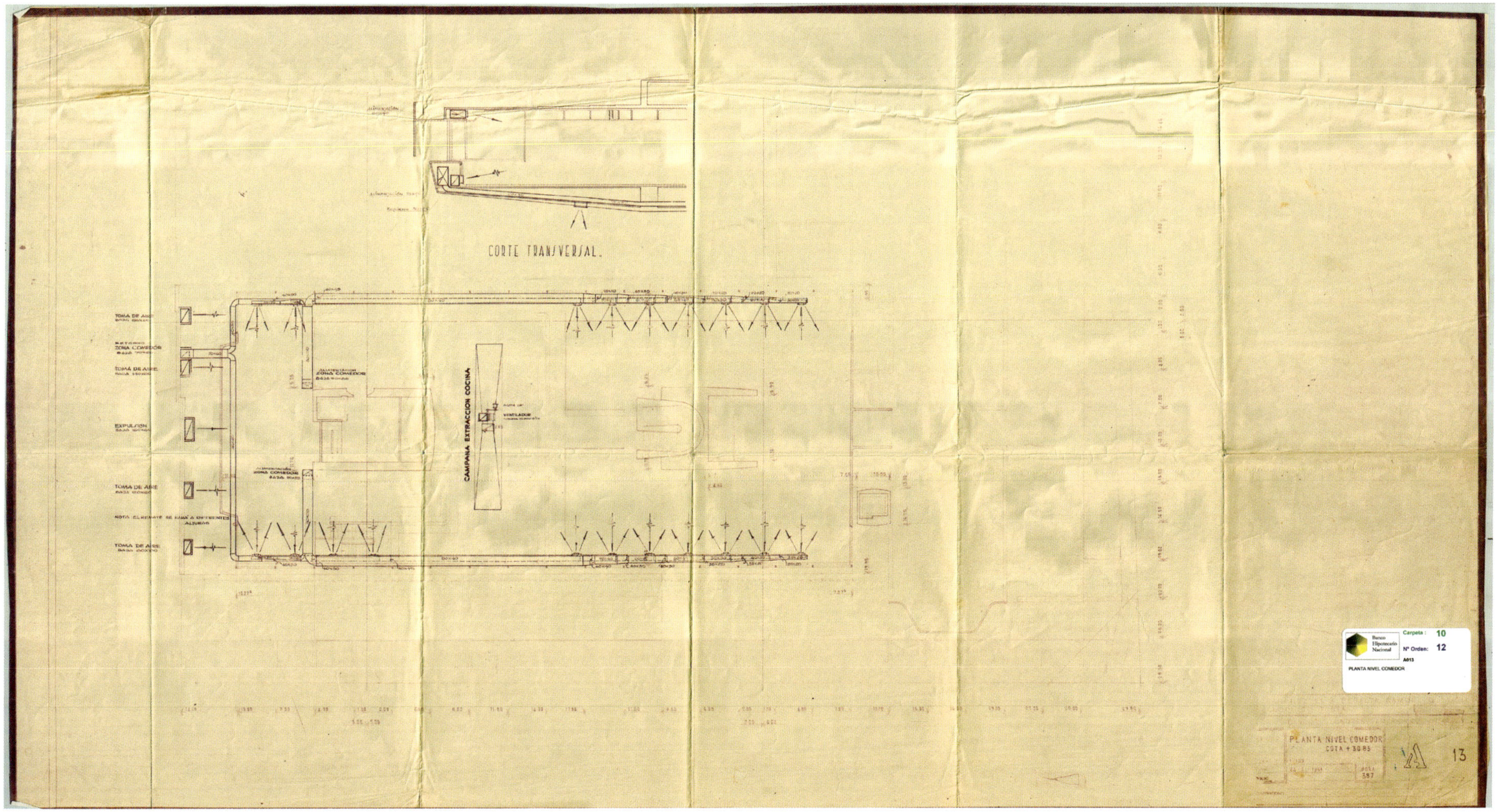

Opposite: Section drawing, air conditioning plan, Banco Hipotecario's file (box 11, plan 31). Scale 3:250
This page: Dining hall level, Fan coils plan, Banco Hipotecario's file (box 10, plan 12). Scale 1:250

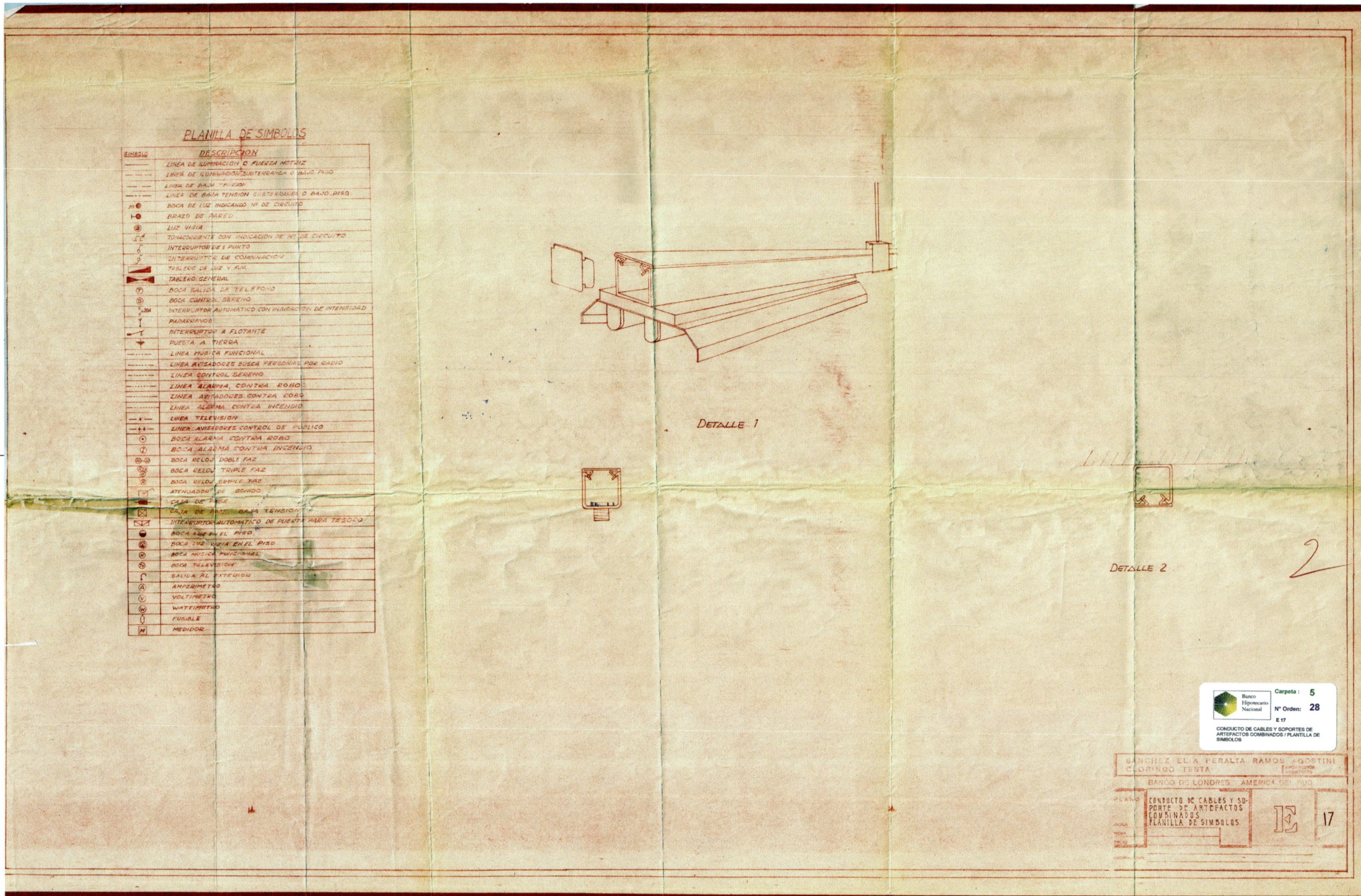
PLANILLA DE SIMBOLOS
SIMBOLO
DESCRIPCION
LINEA DE ILUMINACION O FUERZA MOTRIZ
LINEA DE ILUMINACION SUBTERRANEA O BAJO PISO
LINEA DE BAJA TENSION
LINEA DE BAJA TENSION SUBTERRANEA O BAJO PISO
BOCA DE LUZ INDICANDO Nº DE CIRCUITO
BRAZO DE PARED
LUZ VIGIA
TOMACORRIENTE CON INDICACION DE Nº DE CIRCUITO
INTERRUPTOR DE 1 PUNTO
INTERRUPTOR DE COMBINACION
TABLERO DE LUZ Y F.M.
TABLERO GENERAL
BOCA SALIDA DE TELEFONO
BOCA CONTROL SERENO
INTERRUPTOR AUTOMATICO CON INDICACION DE INTENSIDAD
PARARRAYOS
INTERRUPTOR A FLOTANTE
PUESTA A TIERRA
LINEA MUSICA FUNCIONAL
LINEA AVISADORES BUSCA PERSONAS POR RADIO
LINEA CONTROL SERENO
LINEA ALARMA, CONTRA ROBO
LINEA AVISADORES CONTRA ROBO
LINEA ALARMA CONTRA INCENDIO
LINEA TELEVISION
LINEA AVISADORES CONTROL DE PUBLICO
BOCA ALARMA CONTRA ROBO
BOCA ALARMA CONTRA INCENDIO
BOCA RELOJ DOBLE FAZ
BOCA RELOJ TRIPLE FAZ
BOCA RELOJ SIMPLE FAZ
ATENUADOR DE SONIDO
CAJA DE PASE
CAJA DE PASE BAJA TENSION
INTERRUPTOR AUTOMATICO DE PUERTA PARA TESORO
BOCA LUZ EN EL PISO
BOCA LUZ VIGIA EN EL PISO
BOCA MUSICA FUNCIONAL
BOCA TELEVISION
SALIDA AL EXTERIOR
AMPERIMETRO
VOLTIMETRO
WATTIMETRO
FUSIBLE
MEDIDOR
DETALLE 1
DETALLE 2
2
Banco Hipotecario Nacional
Carpeta : 5
Nº Orden: 28
E 17
CONDUCTO DE CABLES Y SOPORTES DE ARTEFACTOS COMBINADOS / PLANTILLA DE SIMBOLOS
SANCHEZ ELIA PERALTA RAMOS AGOSTINI
CLORINDO TESTA
BANCO DE LONDRES AMERICA DEL SUD
PLANO
CONDUCTO DE CABLES Y SOPORTE DE ARTEFACTOS COMBINADOS
PLANILLA DE SIMBOLOS
E
17

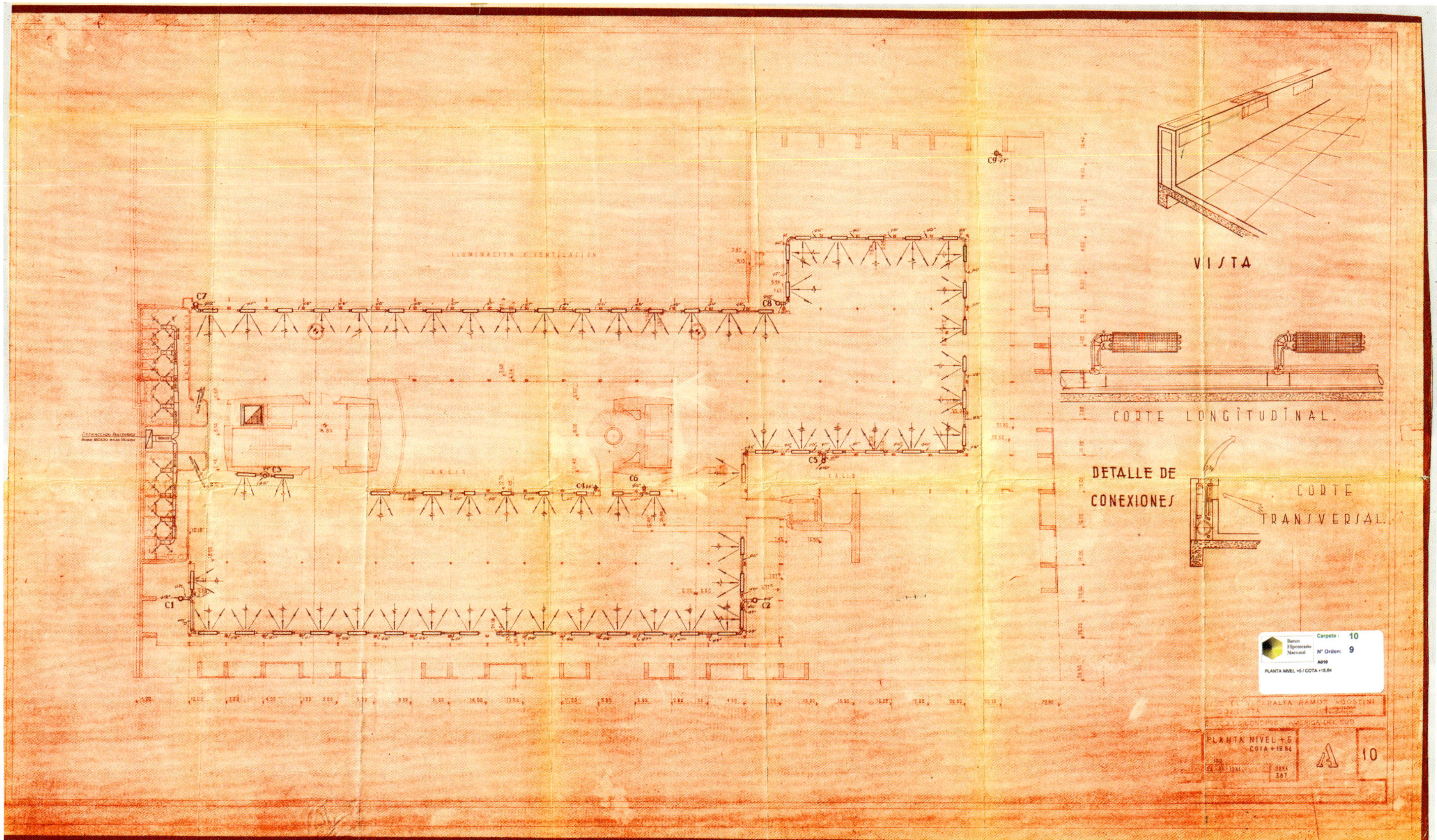

Opposite: Detail drawing of cable ducts and combined media devices, plan symbols, Banco Hipotecario's file (box 5, plan 28)
This page: Level +5, Fan coils plan, Banco Hipotecario's file (box 10, plan 9). Scale 1:250

APROBADO
7/8/64
Nota: El conforme comprende la zona rayada.
Banco Hipotecario Nacional
Carpeta: 3
Nº Orden: 25
141 - 060
FACHADA SOBRE RECONQUISTA / INSTALACION ELECTRICA LUZ
3 JUL 1984
1:50
141 - 60
FACHADA SOBRE RECONQUISTA
INSTALACIÓN ELECTRICA LUZ

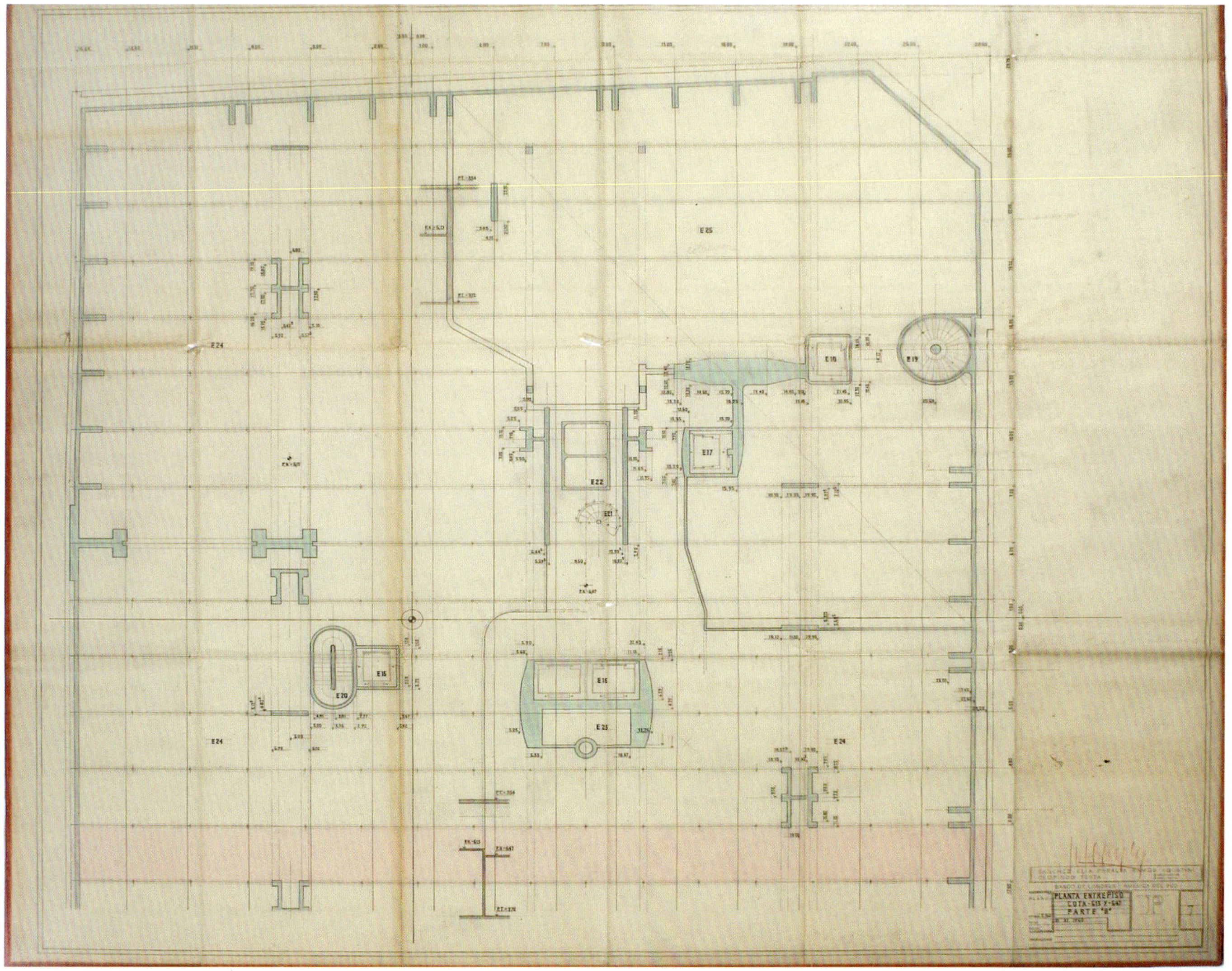

Opposite: Electrical installation of Façade facing Reconquista, 1964. Scale 1:250
This page: Level -6,13m and -5,47m, part B, 1962, SEPRA´s studio file (plan 7). Scale 3:250

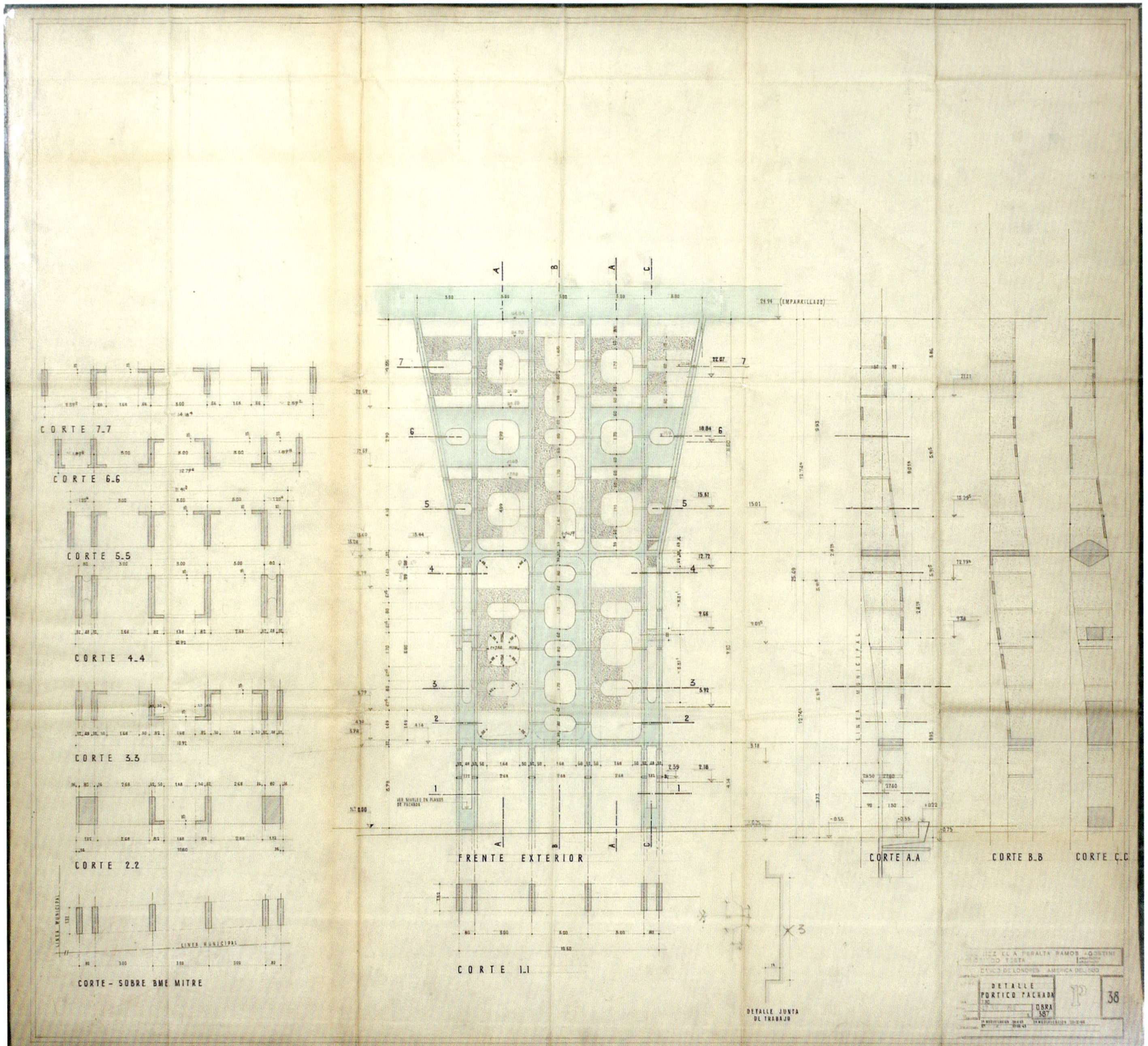
CORTE 7_7
CORTE 6_6
CORTE 5_5
CORTE 4_4
CORTE 3_3
CORTE 2_2
CORTE - SOBRE BME MITRE
FRENTE EXTERIOR
CORTE 1_1
DETALLE JUNTA DE TRABAJO
CORTE A_A
CORTE B_B
CORTE C_C
DETALLE PORTICO FACHADA

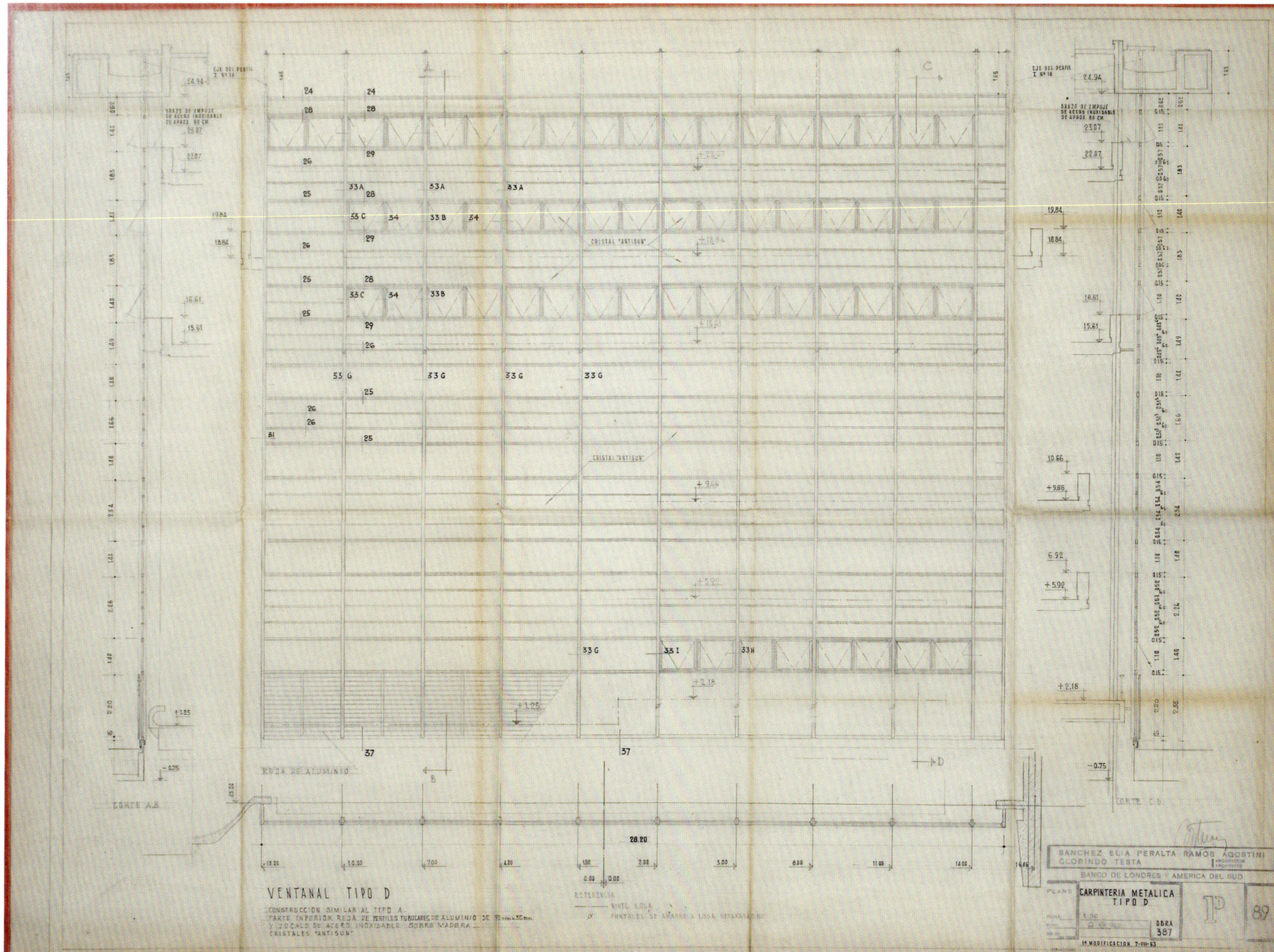

Opposite: Façade detail, 1964, SEPRA's studio file (plan 38). Scale 3:500
This page: Metalwork detail, type D, 1963, SEPRA's studio file (plan 89). Scale 3:250

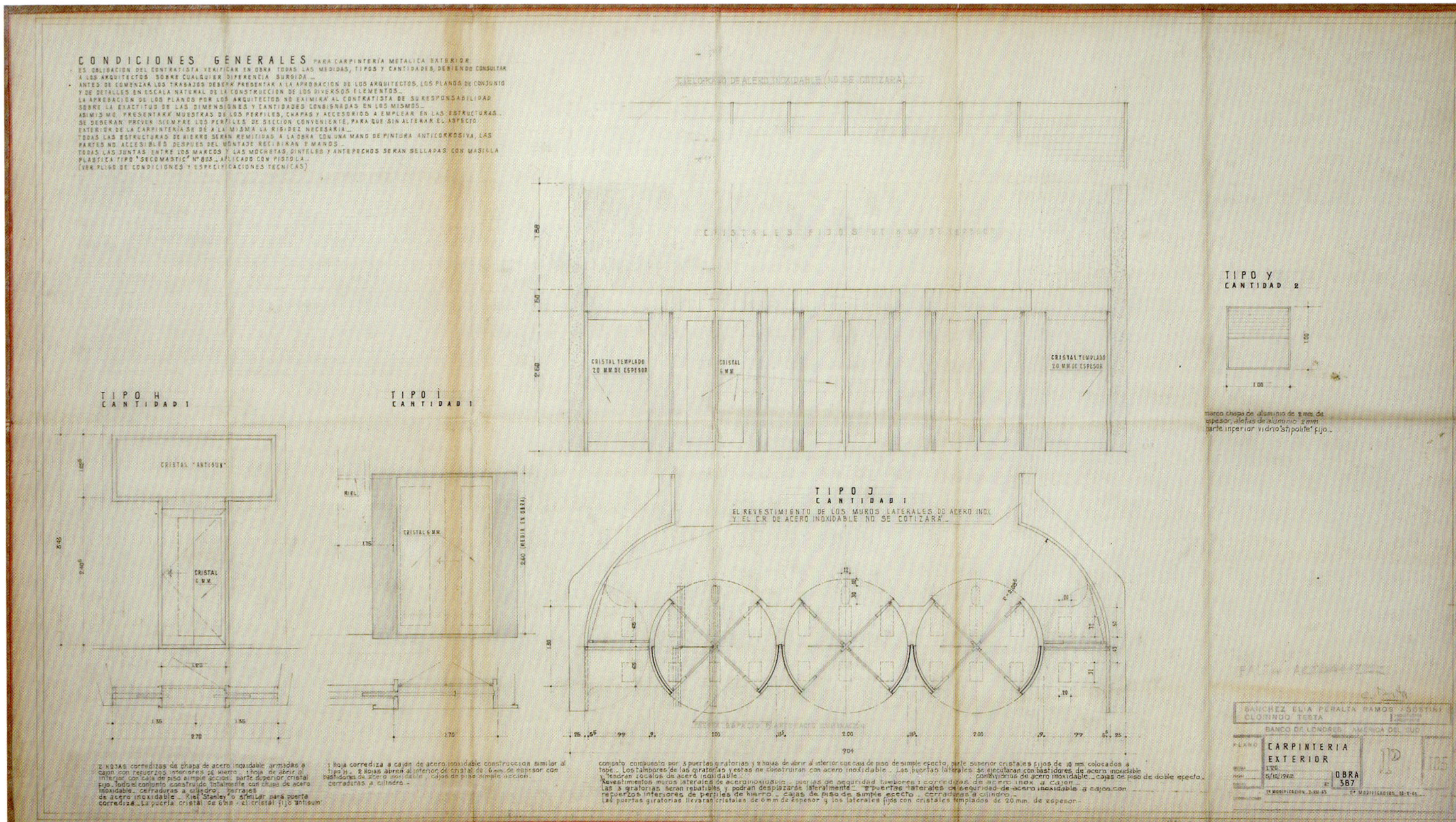

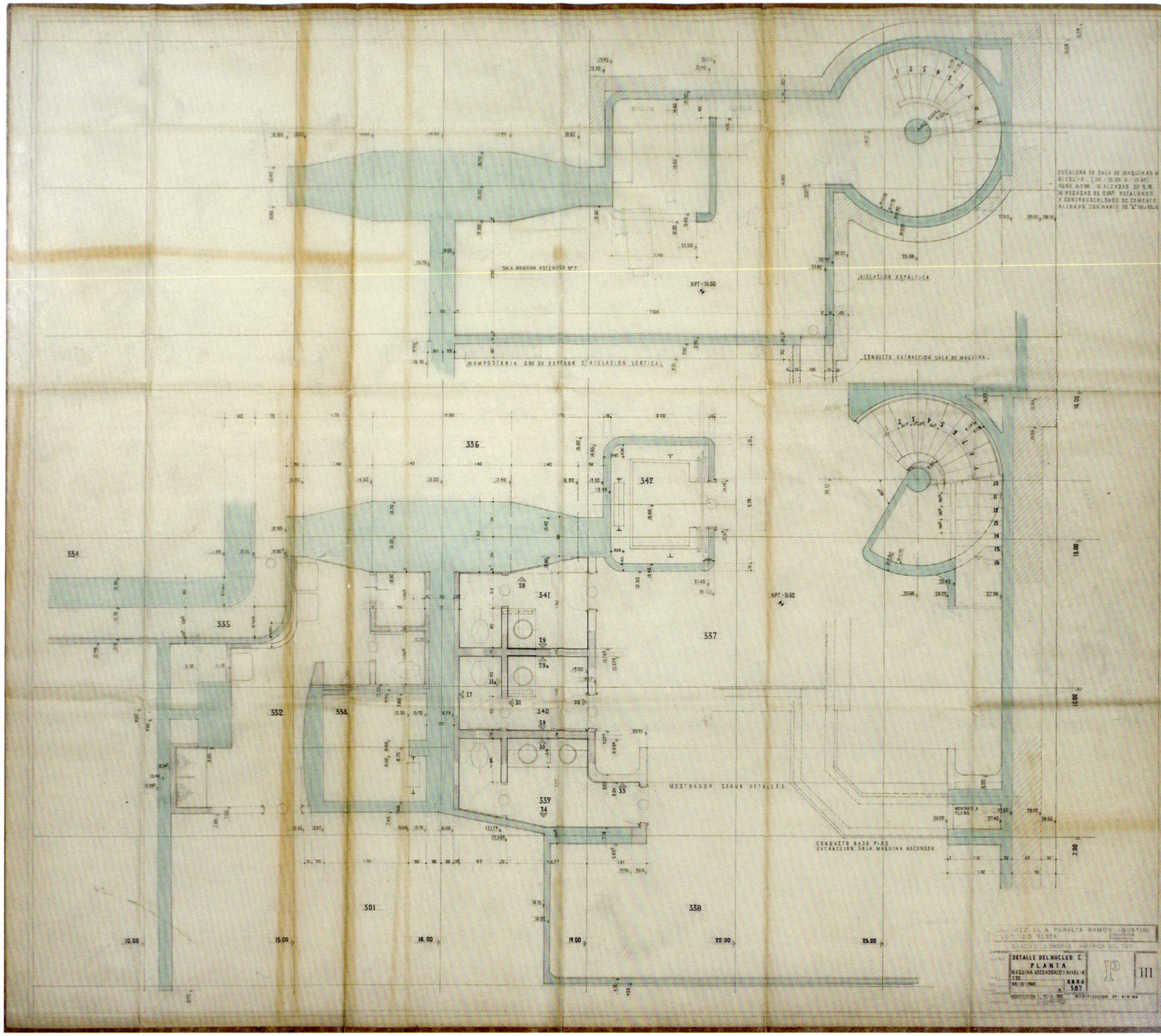

Opposite: Main entrance door, 1965, SEPRA's studio file (plan 105). Scale 3:100
This page: Core C, plan detail, level -3, 1964, SEPRA's studio file (plan 111). Scale 3:100

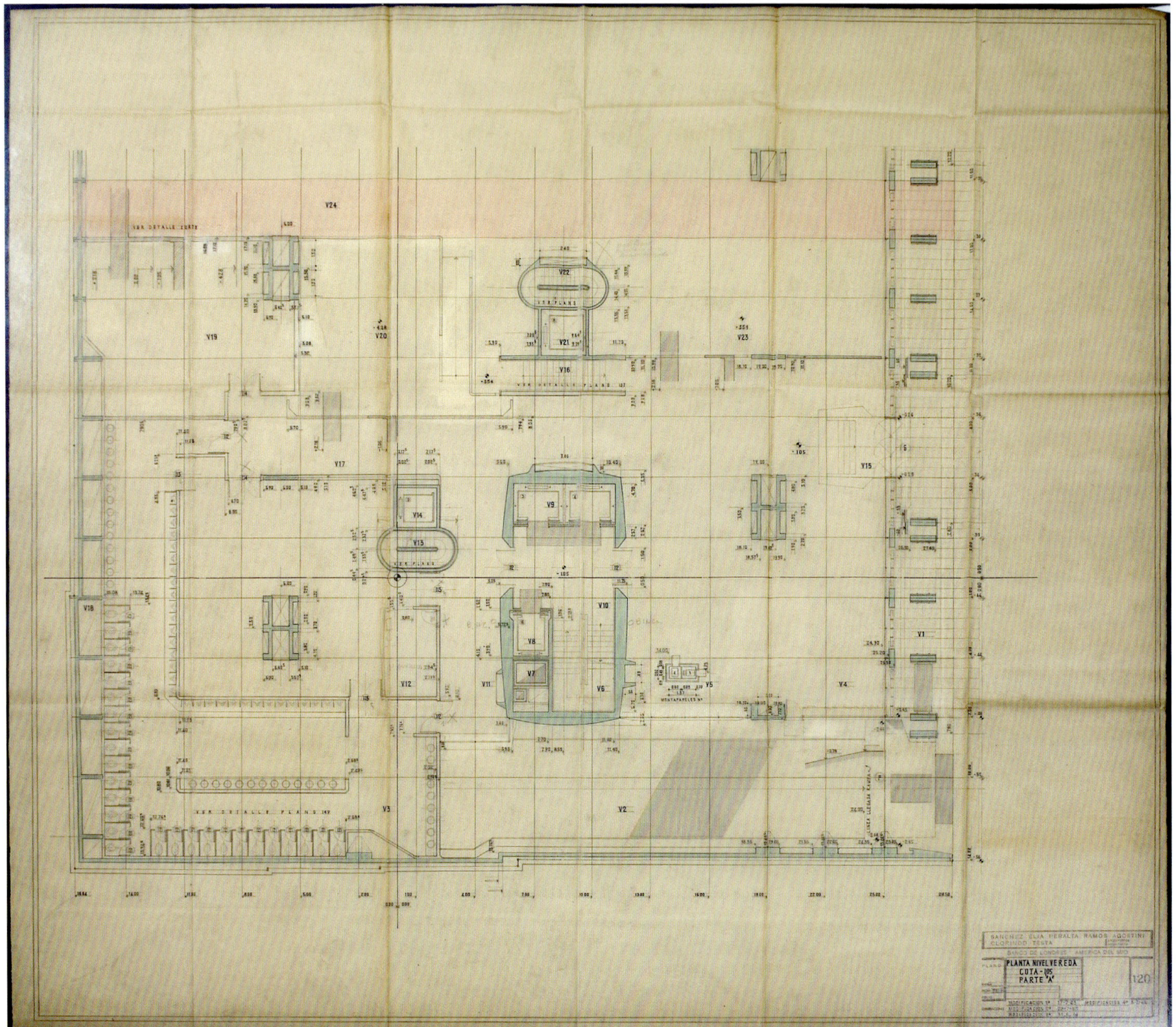
SANCHEZ ELIA PERALTA RAMOS AGOSTINI
CLORINDO TESTA
BANCO DE LONDRES AMERICA DEL SUD
PLANTA NIVEL VEREDA
COTA -1.05
PARTE "A"
120

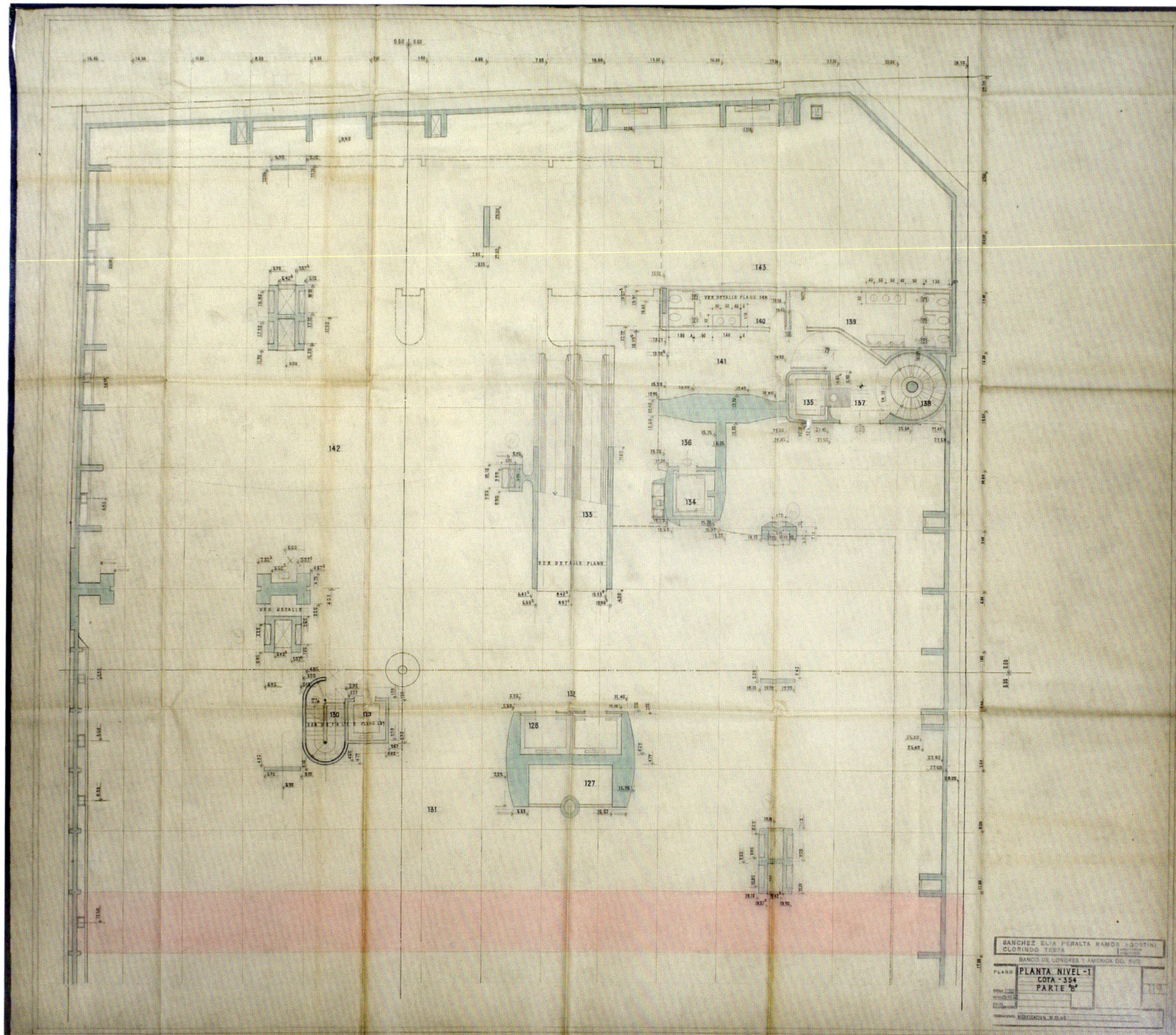

Opposite: Street level, part A, 1965, SEPRA's studio file (plan 120)
This page: Level -1 plan, part B, 1965, SEPRA's studio file (plan 119). Scale 1:5

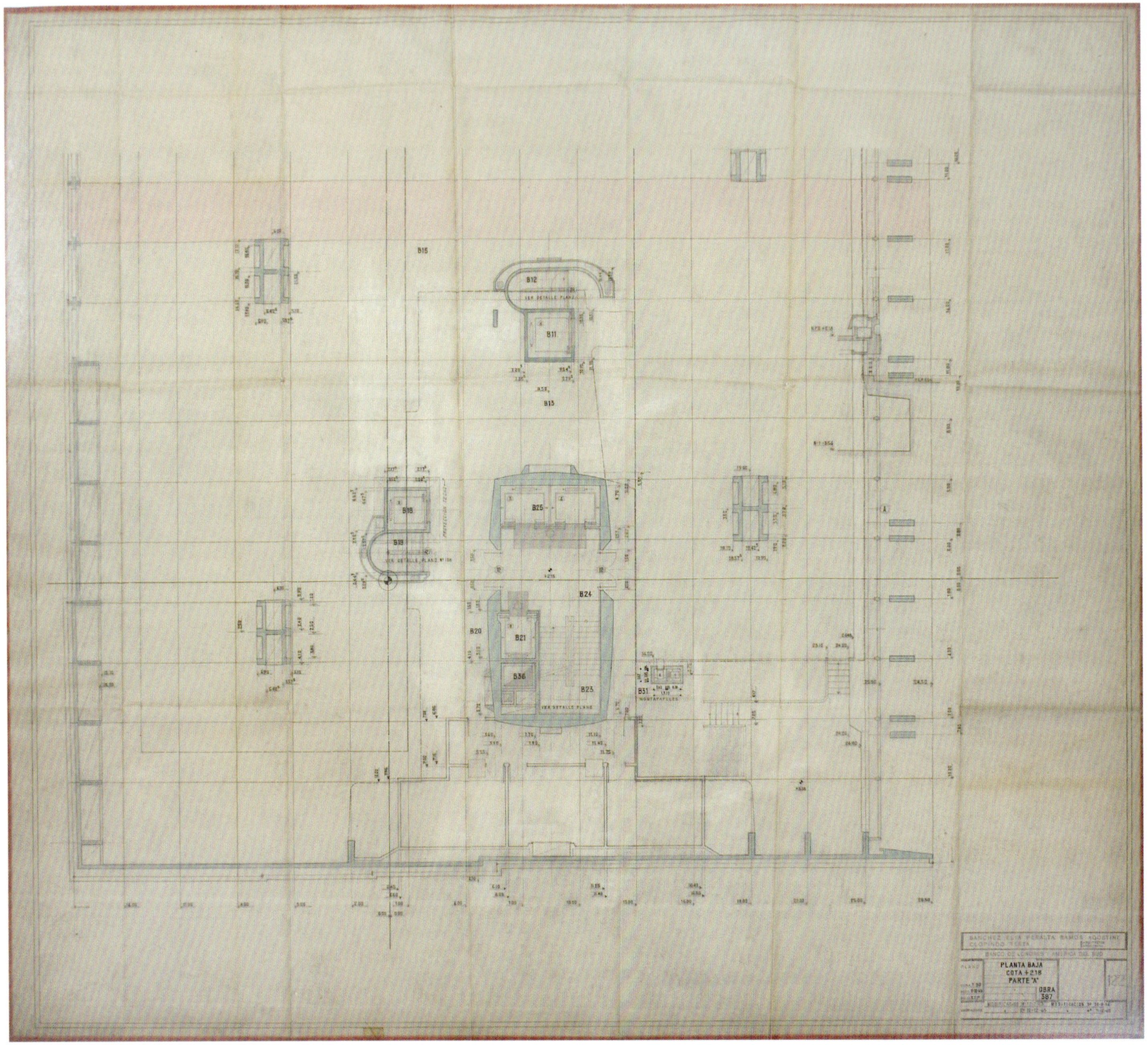
PLANTA BAJA
COTA +216
PARTE "A"
OBRA
387

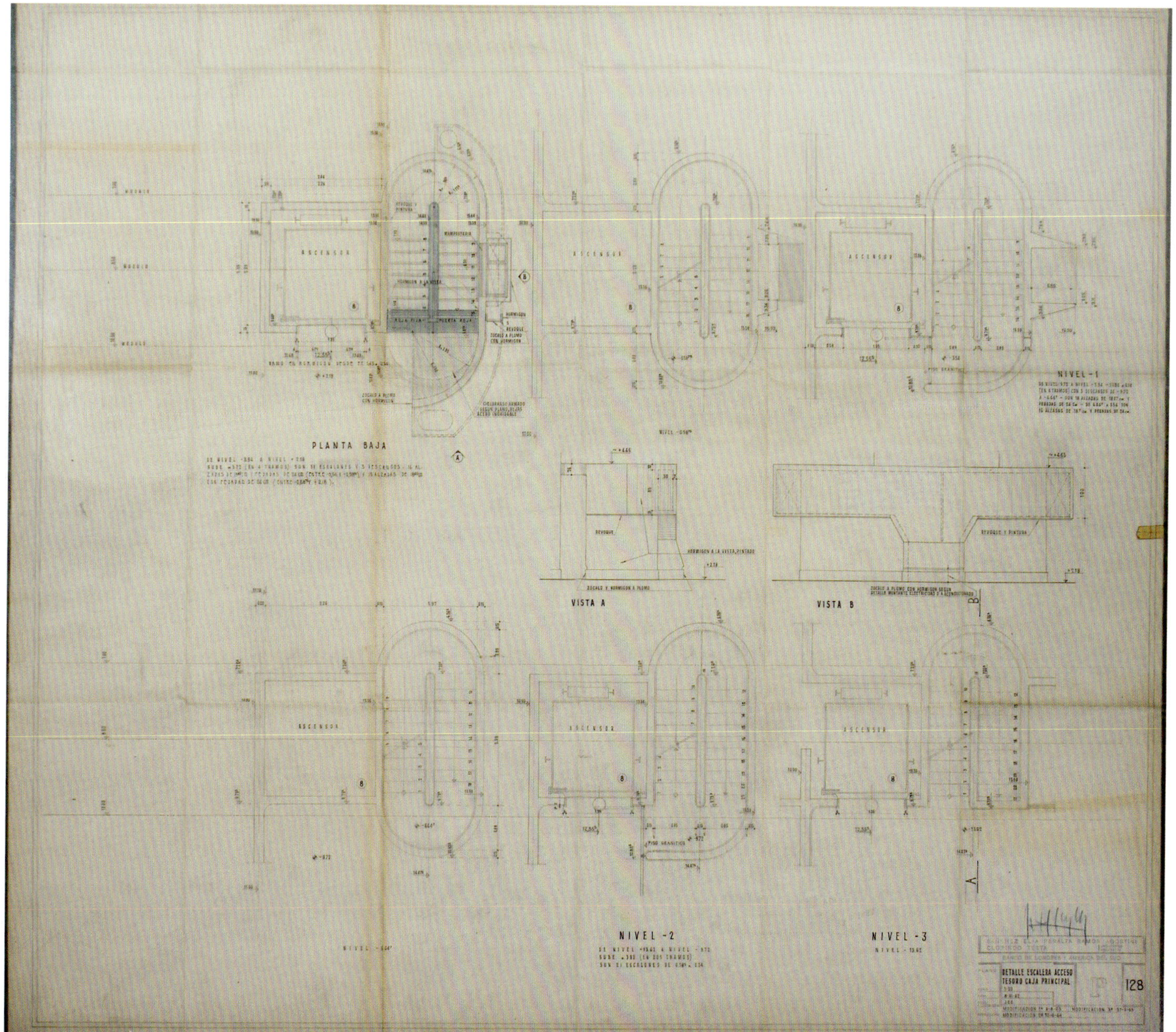

Opposite: Ground floor level, part A, 1965, SEPRA's studio file (plan 122). Scale 3:250
This page: Detail drawings of the stairs to the main safe-deposit boxes, 1965, SEPRA's studio file (plan 128). Scale 3:100

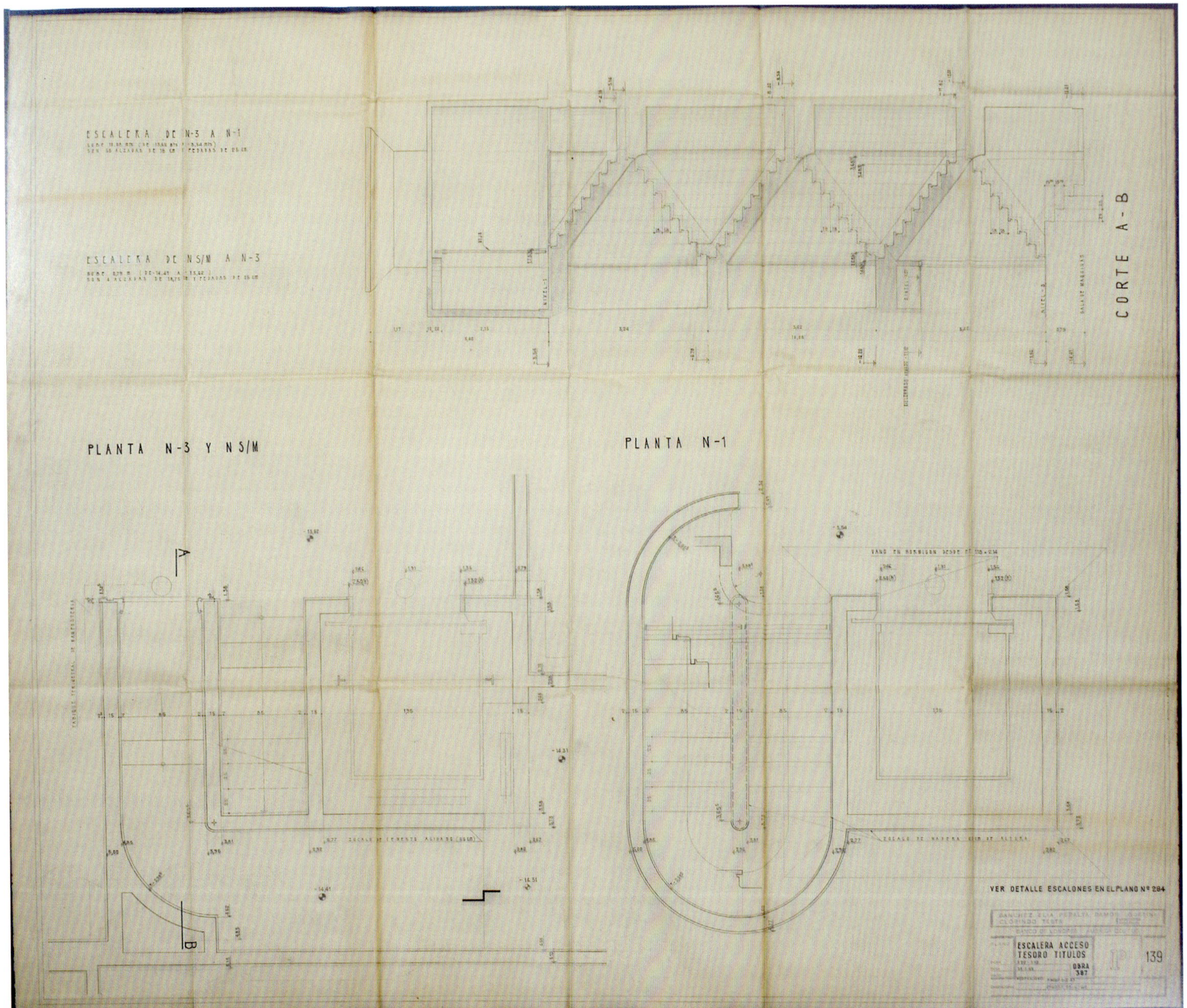
ESCALERA DE N-3 A N-1
ESCALERA DE NS/M A N-3
CORTE A-B
PLANTA N-3 Y NS/M
PLANTA N-1
VER DETALLE ESCALONES EN EL PLANO Nº 284
ESCALERA ACCESO
TESORO TITULOS
OBRA
387
139

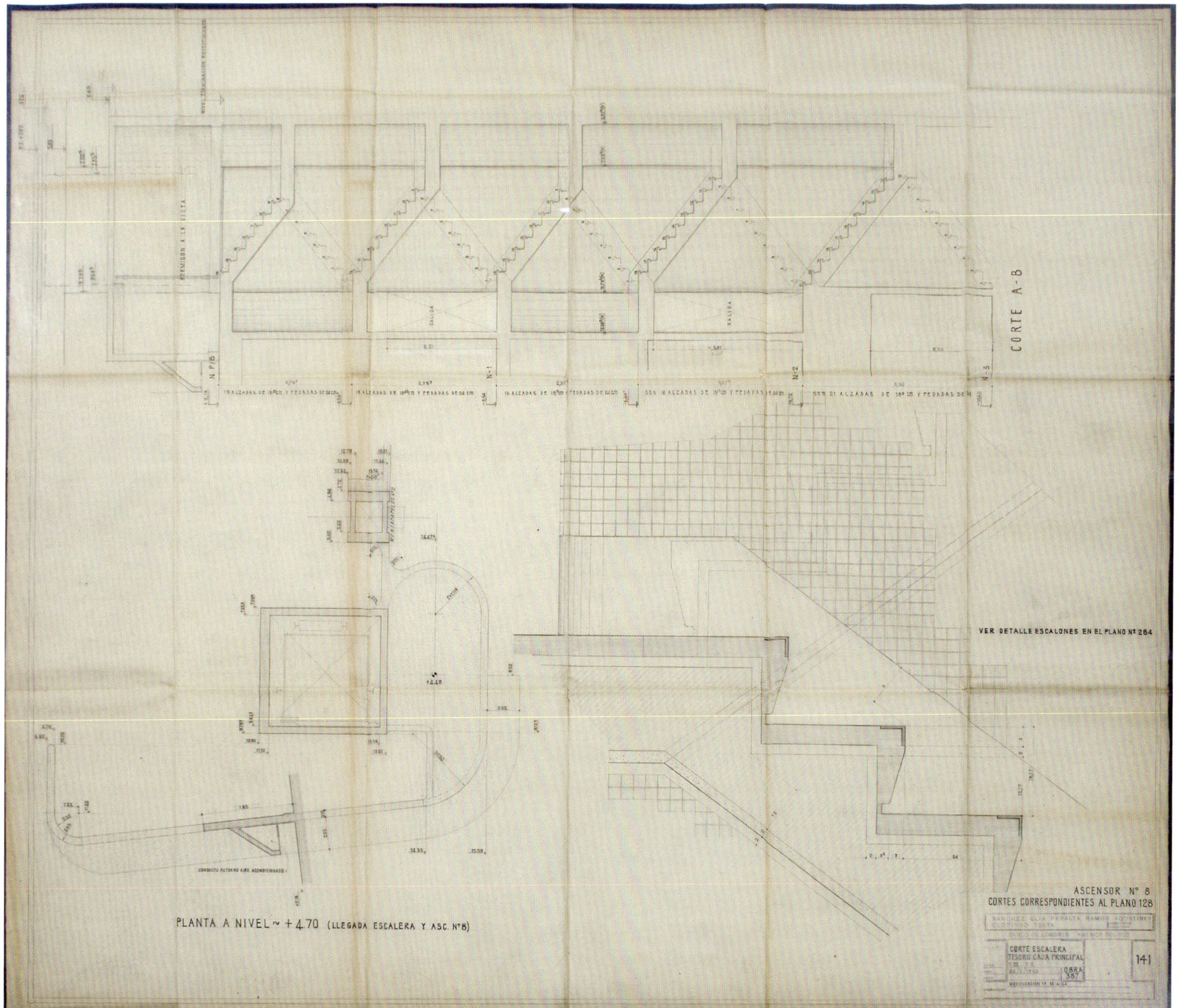

Opposite: Detail drawings of the stairs to the treasure, 1964, SEPRA's studio file (plan 139)
This Page: Detail drawings of the stairs to the safe-deposit boxes, 1964, SEPRA's studio file (plan 141). Scale 3:100, 3:10

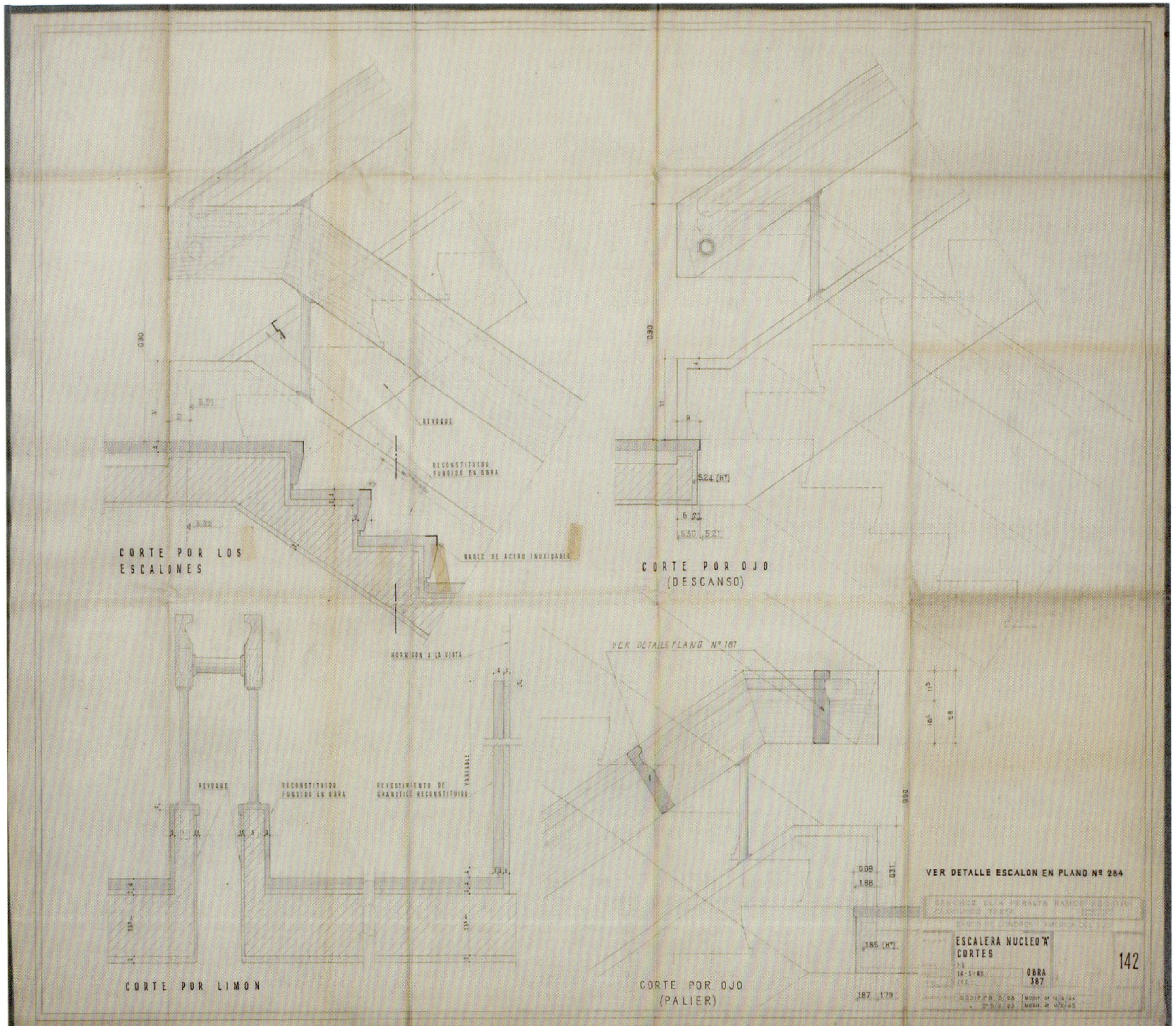
CORTE POR LOS ESCALONES
REVOQUE
RECONSTITUIDO FUNDIDO EN OBRA
NARIZ DE ACERO INOXIDABLE
HORMIGON A LA VISTA
CORTE POR OJO (DESCANSO)
VER DETALLE PLANO Nº 181
CORTE POR LIMON
CORTE POR OJO (PALIER)
VER DETALLE ESCALON EN PLANO Nº 284
ESCALERA NUCLEO "A"
CORTES
OBRA 387
142

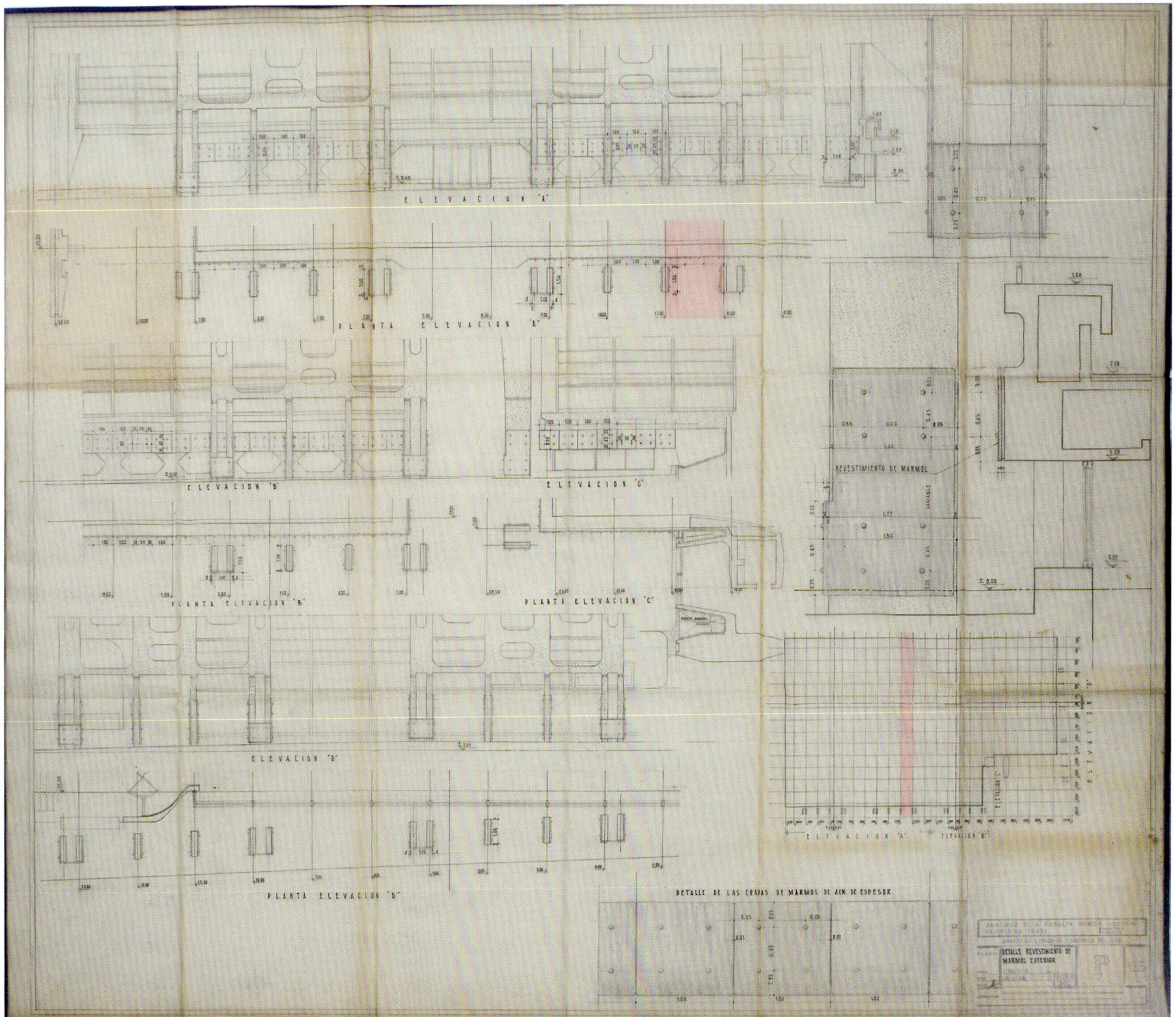

This page: Exterior marble covering detail, 1963, SEPRA´s studio file (plan 155). Scale 3:250, 3:50

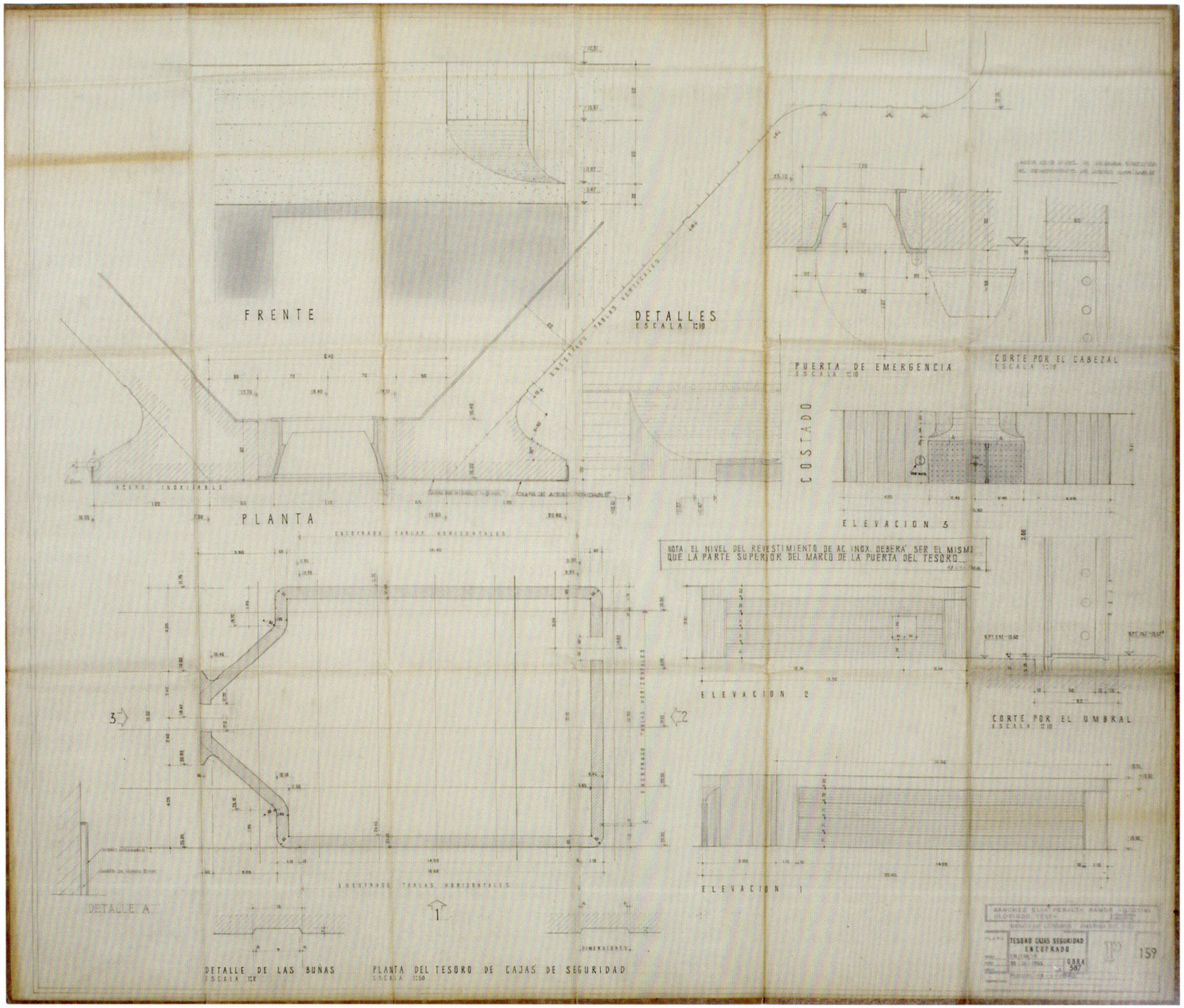
FRENTE
DETALLES
ESCALA 1:10
PLANTA
PUERTA DE EMERGENCIA
CORTE POR EL CABEZAL
COSTADO
ELEVACION 3
NOTA EL NIVEL DEL REVESTIMIENTO DE AC INOX DEBERA SER EL MISMO QUE LA PARTE SUPERIOR DEL MARCO DE LA PUERTA DEL TESORO
ELEVACION 2
CORTE POR EL UMBRAL
ELEVACION 1
DETALLE A
DETALLE DE LAS BUÑAS
PLANTA DEL TESORO DE CAJAS DE SEGURIDAD
TESORO CAJAS SEGURIDAD ENCOFRADO
159

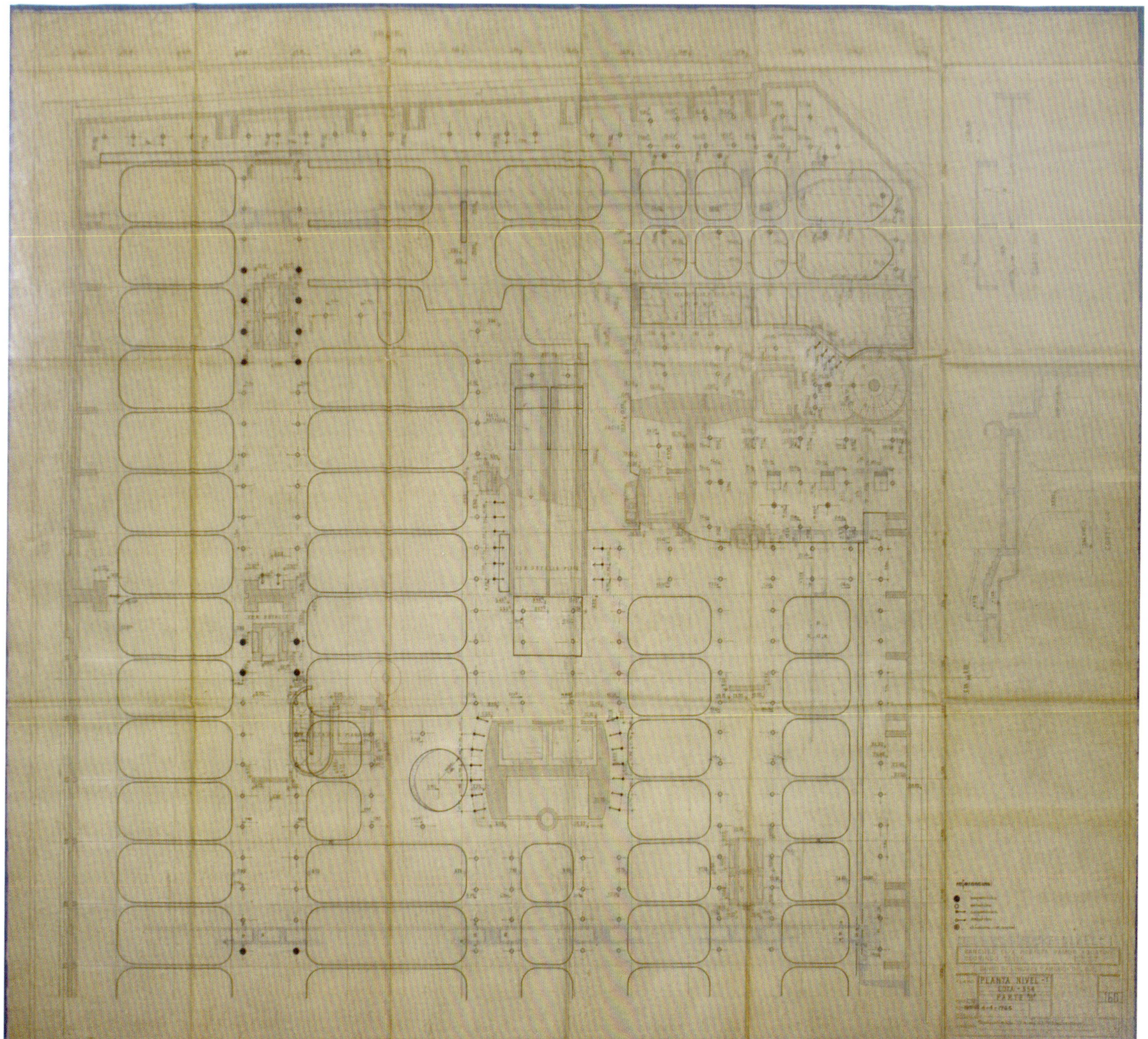

This page: Level -1, part B, 1963, SEPRA's studio file (plan 160). Scale 3:250

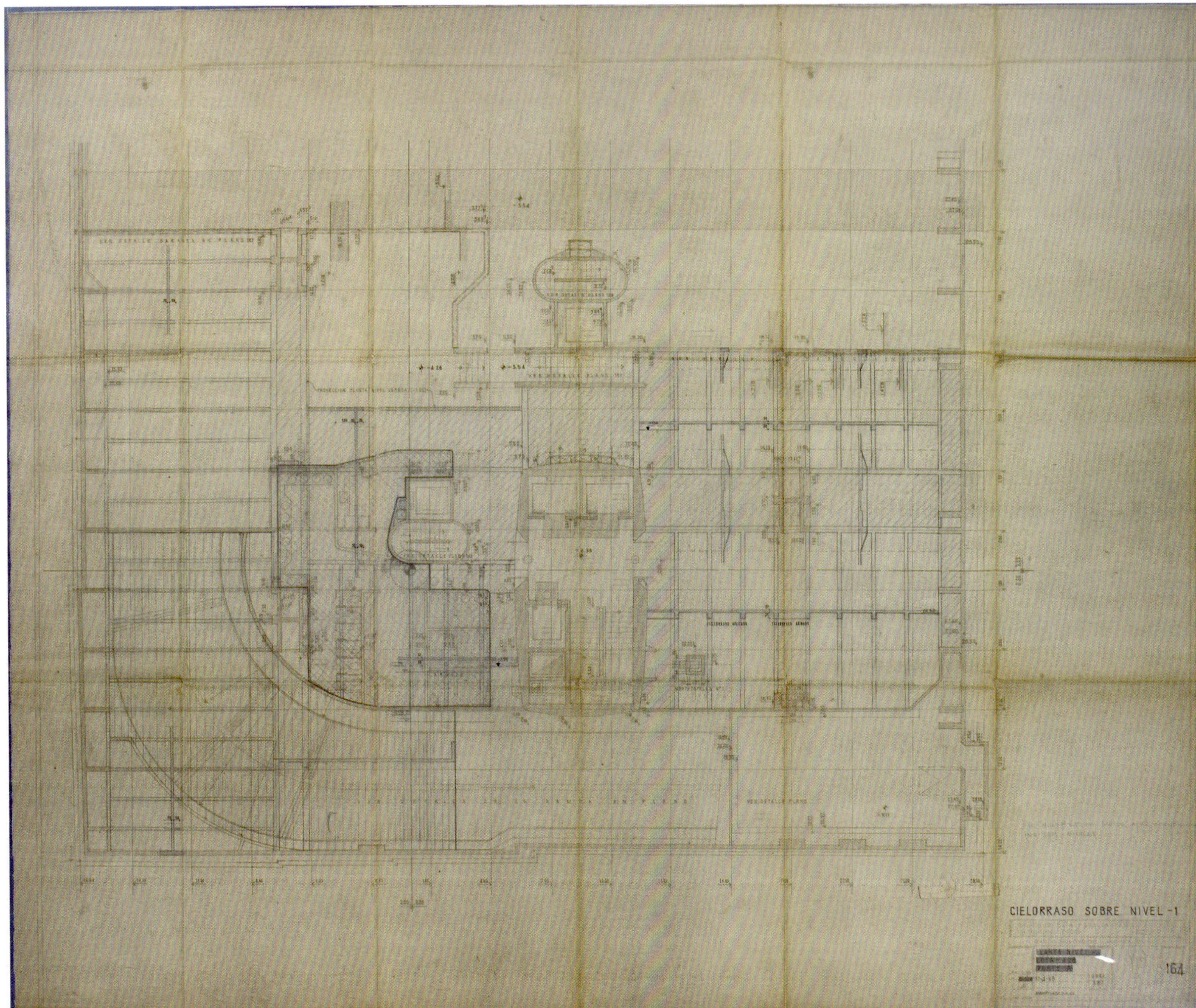
CIELORRASO SOBRE NIVEL -1
164

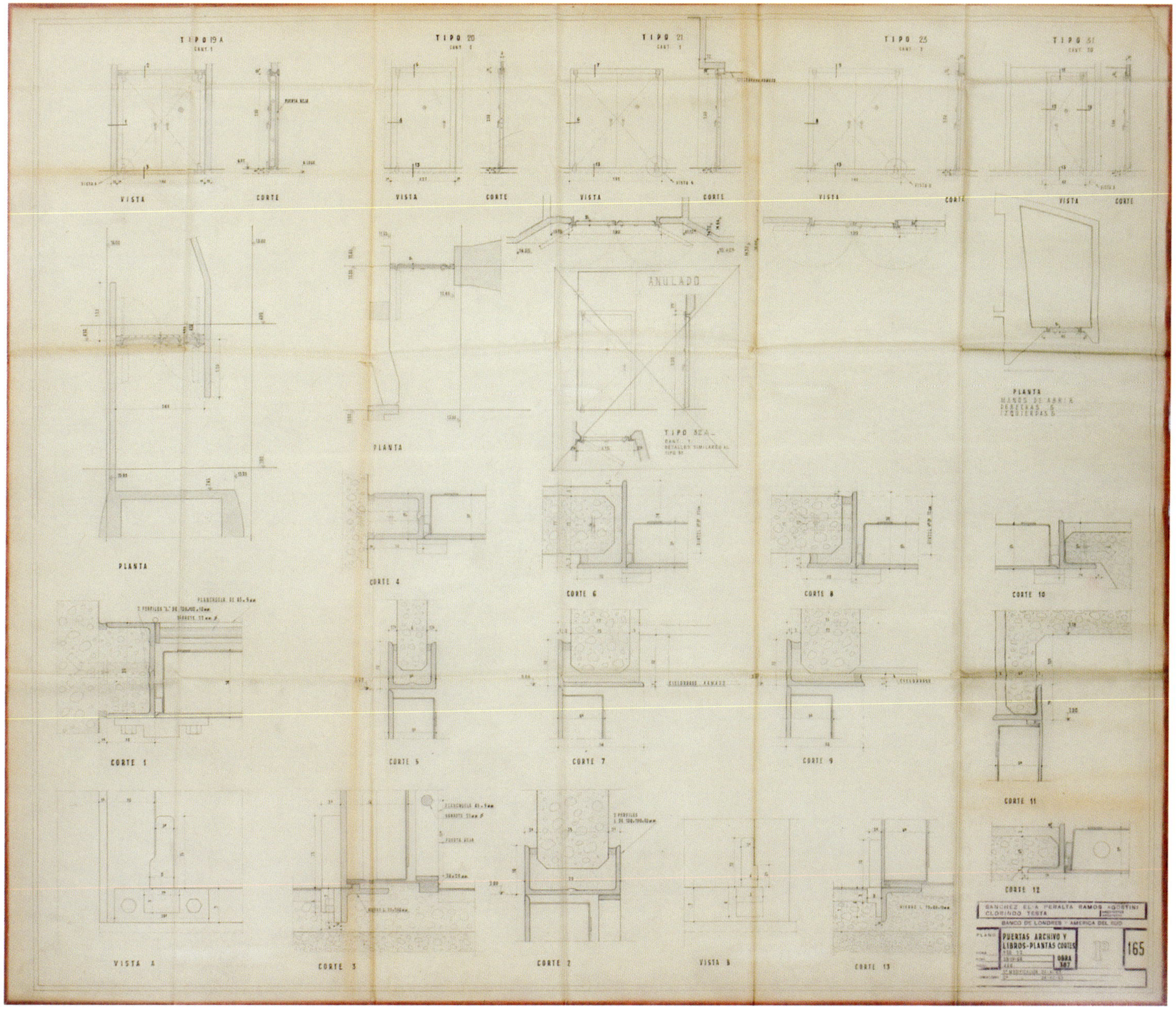

This page: File doors details, 1963, SEPRA´s studio file (plan 165). Scale 3:100

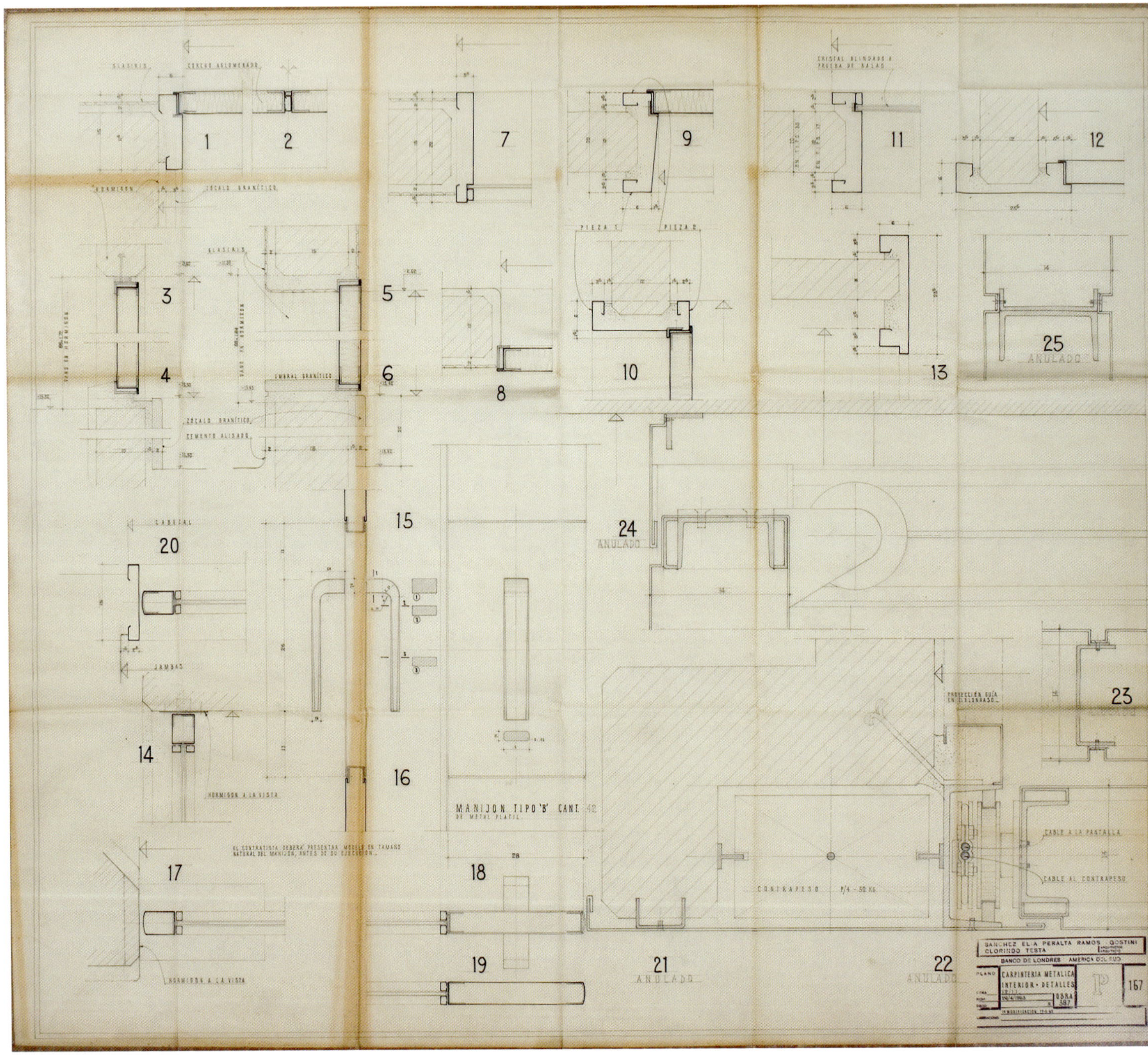

1
2
3
4
5
6
7
8
9
10
11
12
13
14
15
16
17
18
19
20
21
ANULADO
22
ANULADO
23
24
ANULADO
25
ANULADO
CABEZAL
JAMBAS
ZOCALO GRANITICO
CEMENTO ALISADO
UMBRAL GRANITICO
HORMIGON A LA VISTA
MANIJON TIPO 'B' CANT. 42
CONTRAPESO
CABLE A LA PANTALLA
CABLE AL CONTRAPESO
SANCHEZ ELIA PERALTA RAMOS AGOSTINI
CLORINDO TESTA
BANCO DE LONDRES AMERICA DEL SUD
PLANO
CARPINTERIA METALICA
INTERIOR - DETALLES
OBRA 387
167

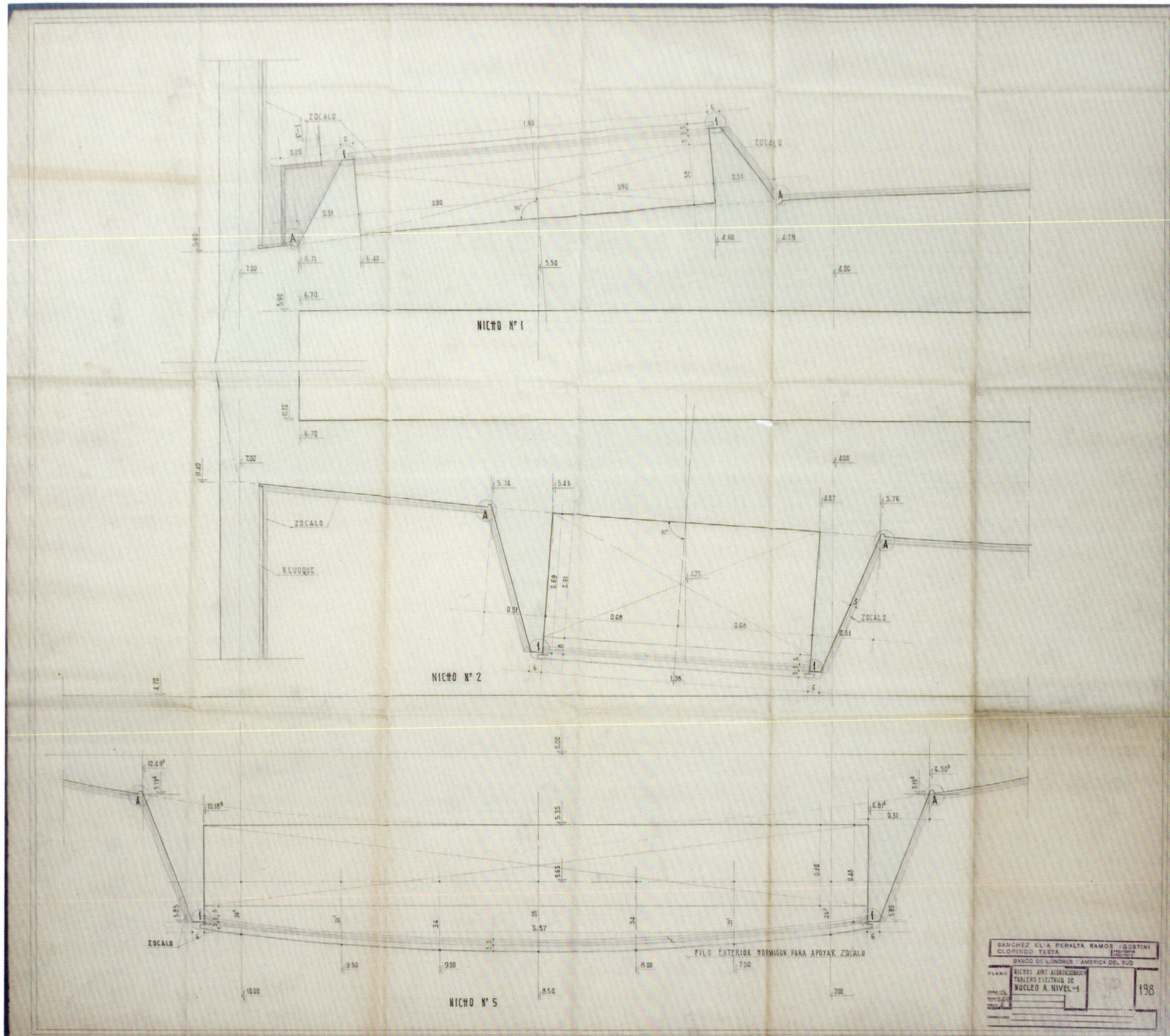

This page: Air Conditioning niches in Core A, level -1, 1963, SEPRA's studio file (plan 198). Scale 3:25

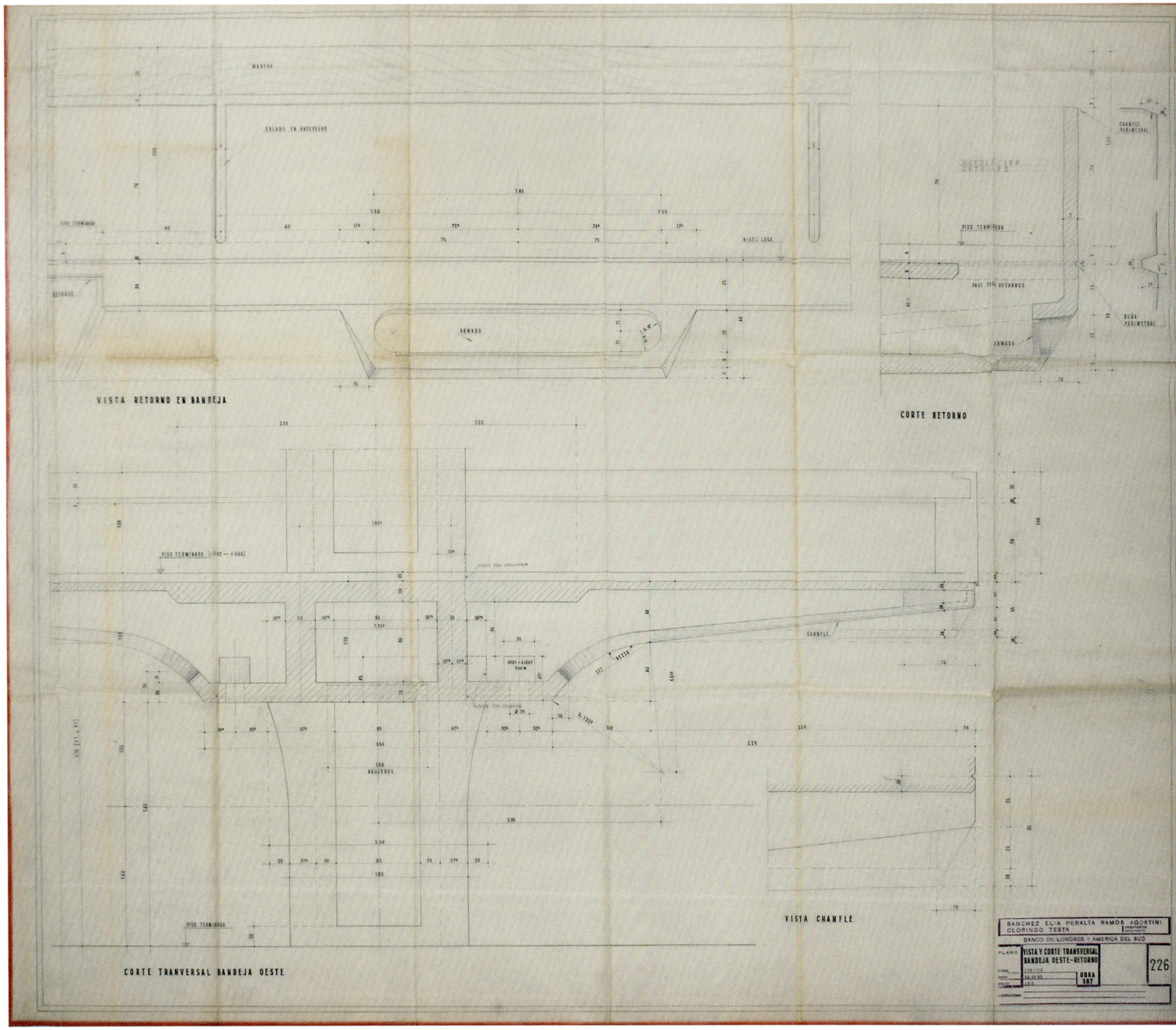

VISTA RETORNO EN BANDEJA
CORTE RETORNO
CORTE TRANVERSAL BANDEJA OESTE
VISTA CHANFLE
CHANFLE
ARMADO
SANCHEZ ELIA PERALTA RAMOS AGOSTINI
CLORINDO TESTA
BANCO DE LONDRES Y AMERICA DEL SUD
PLANO
VISTA Y CORTE TRANSVERSAL
BANDEJA OESTE-RETORNO
OBRA
387
226

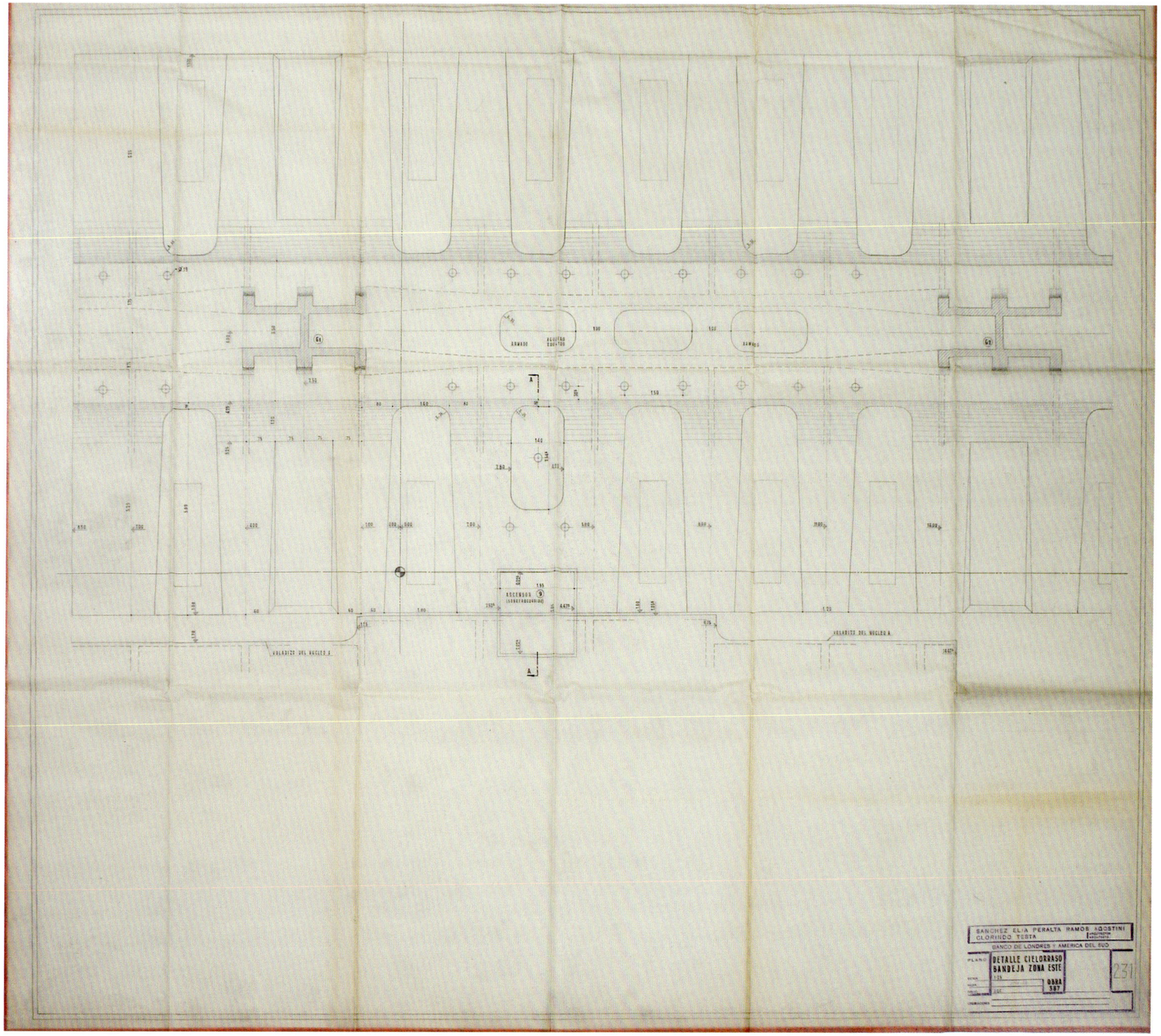

This page: Ceiling detail, East mezzanine, 1963, SEPRA's studio file (plan 231). Scale 3:125

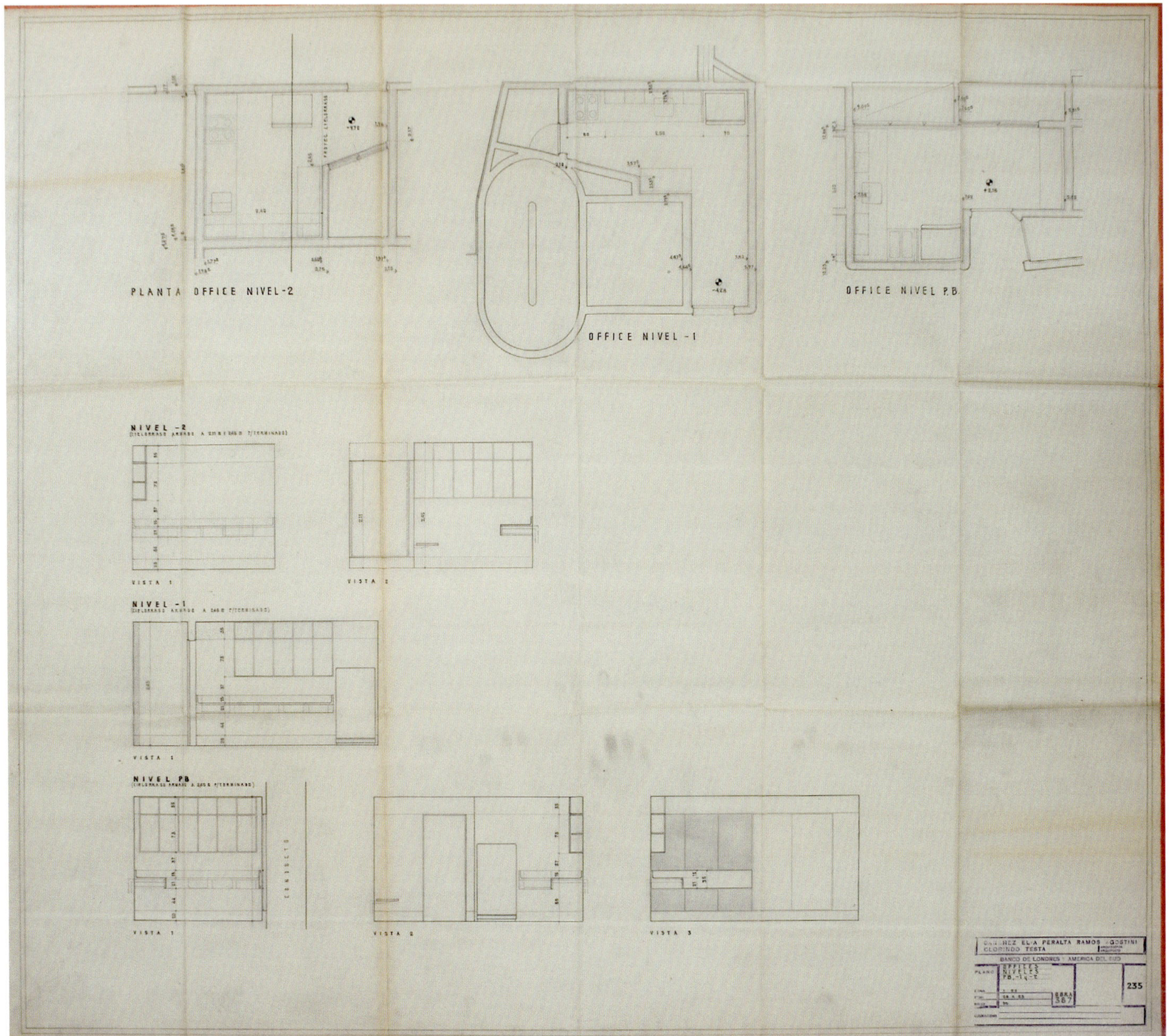
PLANTA OFFICE NIVEL-2
OFFICE NIVEL -1
OFFICE NIVEL P.B
NIVEL -2
NIVEL -1
NIVEL PB
VISTA 1
VISTA 2
VISTA 3
CLORINDO TESTA
BANCO DE LONDRES Y AMERICA DEL SUD
235

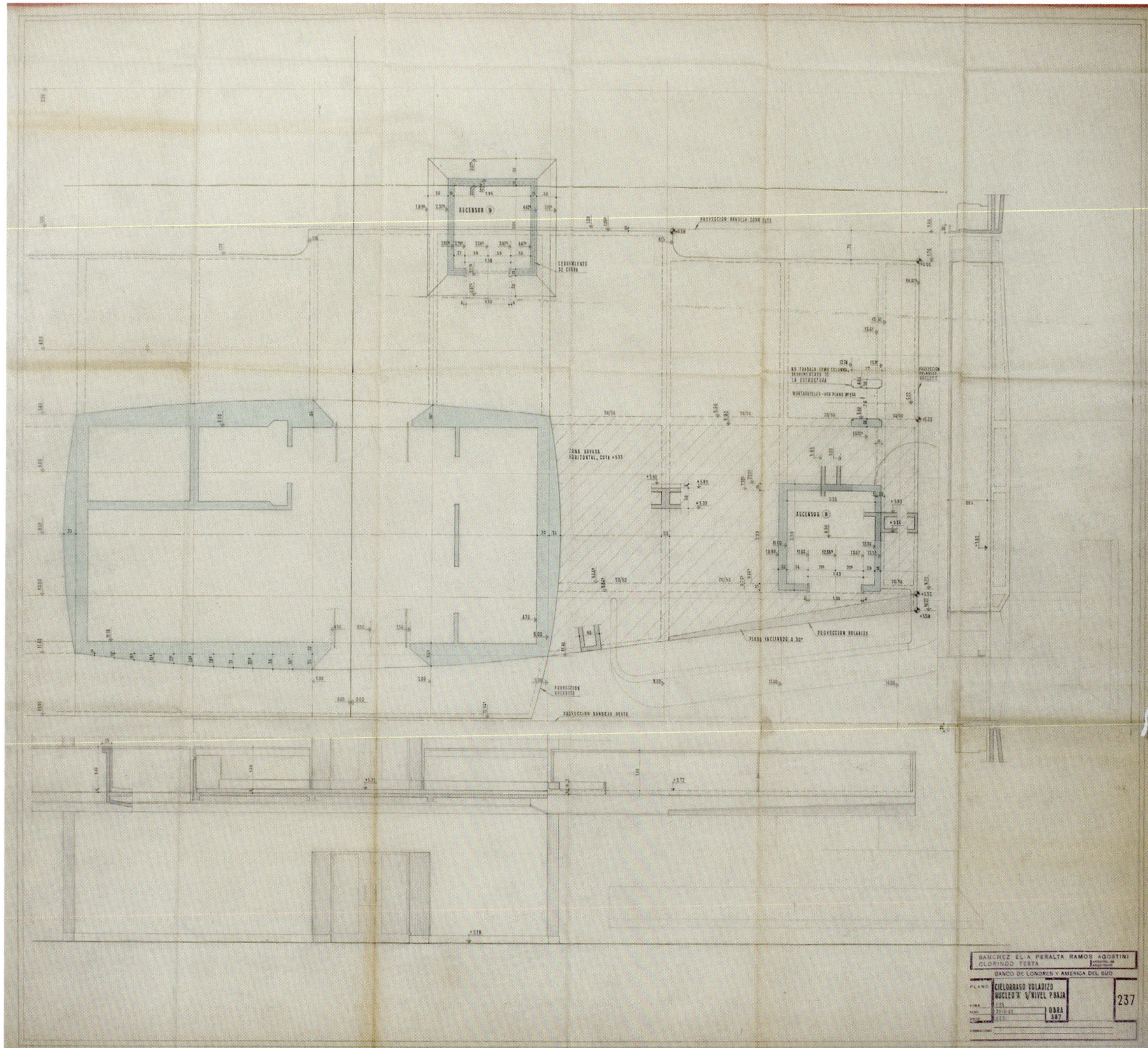

This page: Cantilevered ceiling, Core A, over ground floor, 1963, SEPRA's studio file (plan 237). Scale 3:125

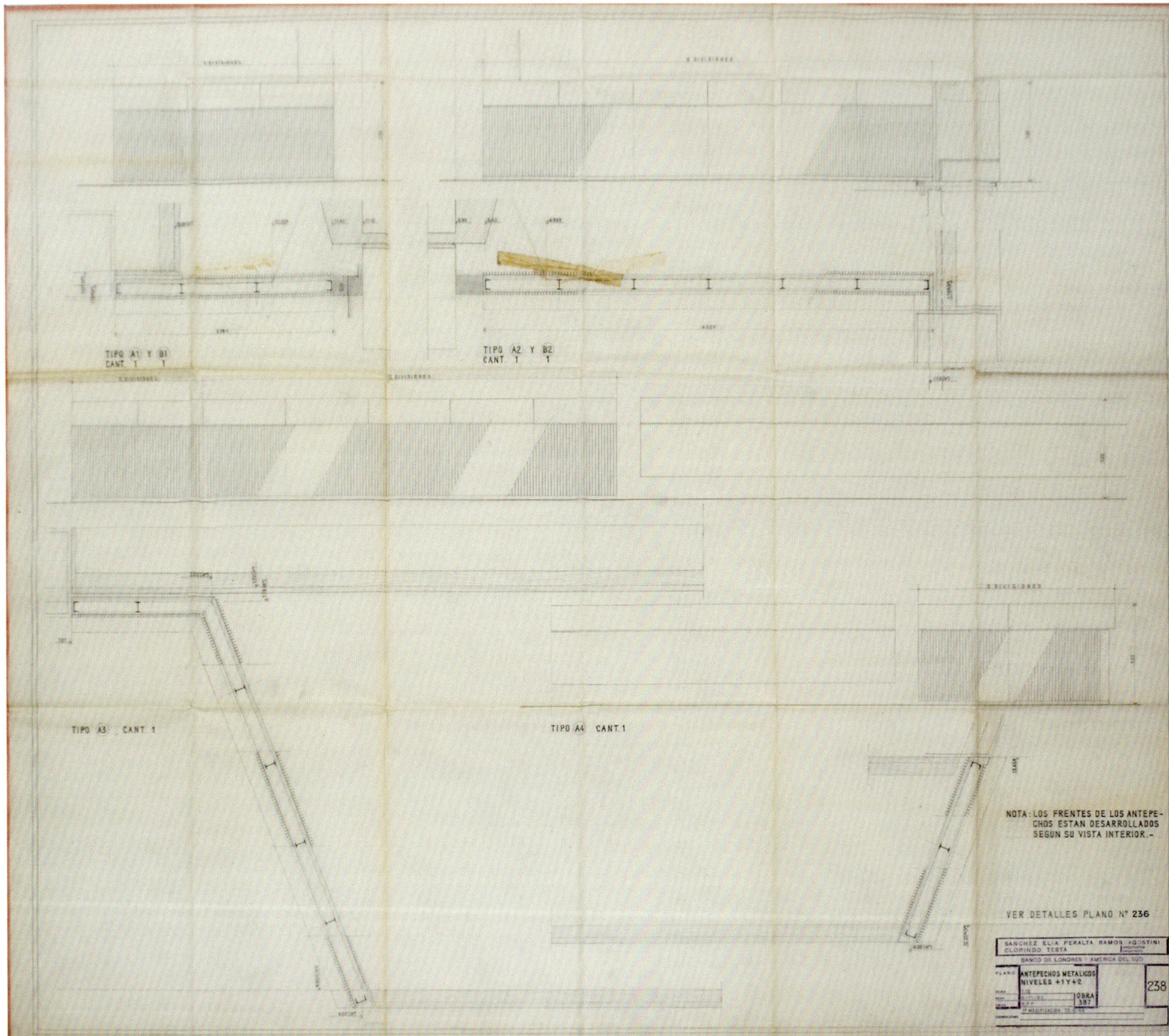

TIPO A1 Y B1
CANT. 1 1
TIPO A2 Y B2
CANT. 1 1
TIPO A3 . CANT. 1
TIPO A4 CANT. 1
NOTA: LOS FRENTES DE LOS ANTEPECHOS ESTAN DESARROLLADOS SEGUN SU VISTA INTERIOR.-
VER DETALLES PLANO N° 236
SANCHEZ ELIA PERALTA RAMOS AGOSTINI
CLORINDO TESTA
BANCO DE LONDRES Y AMERICA DEL SUD
PLANO
ANTEPECHOS METALICOS
NIVELES +1 Y +2
OBRA 387
238

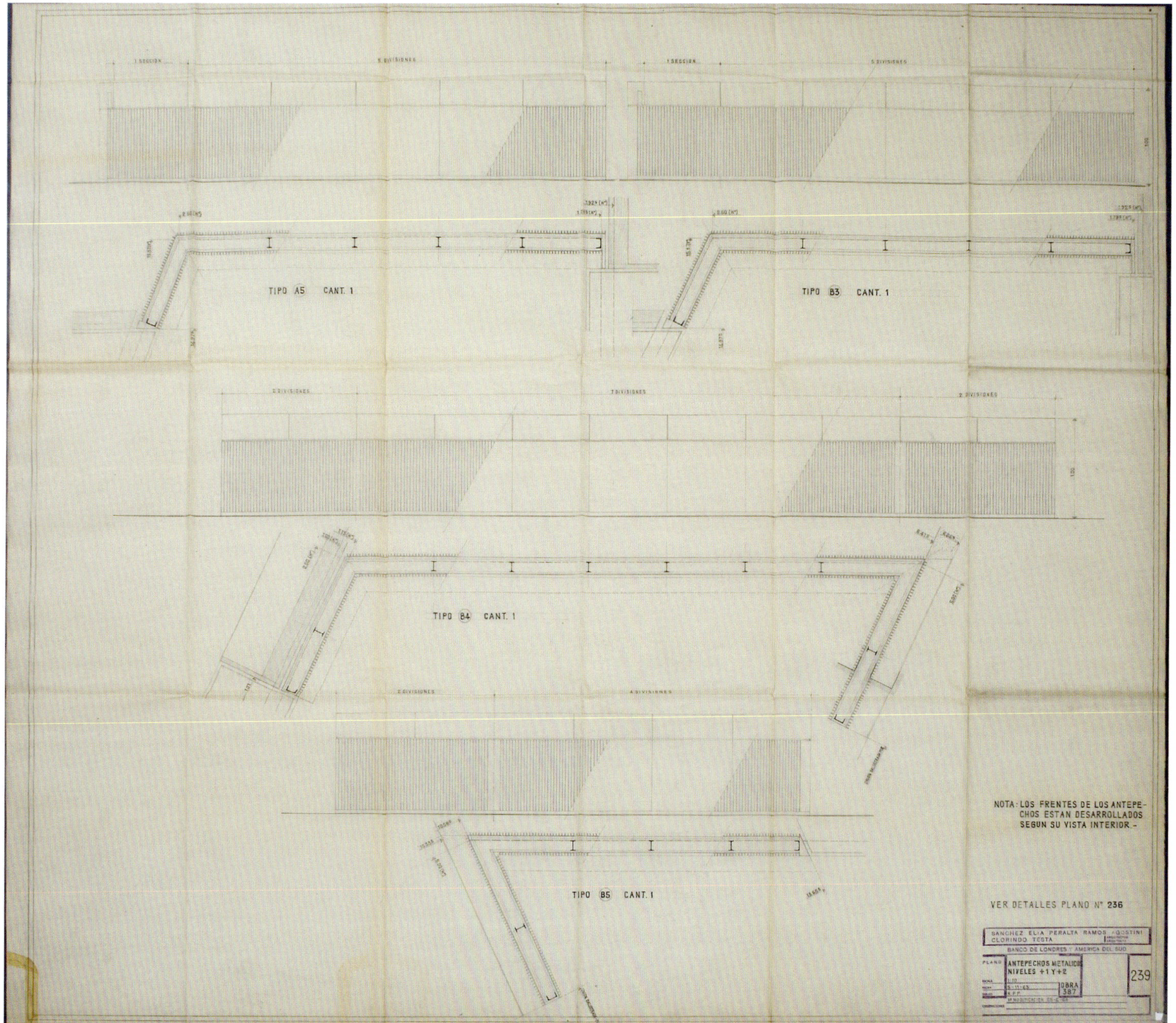

This page: Metal cladding details, level +1 y +2, 1964, SEPRA's studio file (plan 239). Scale 3:50

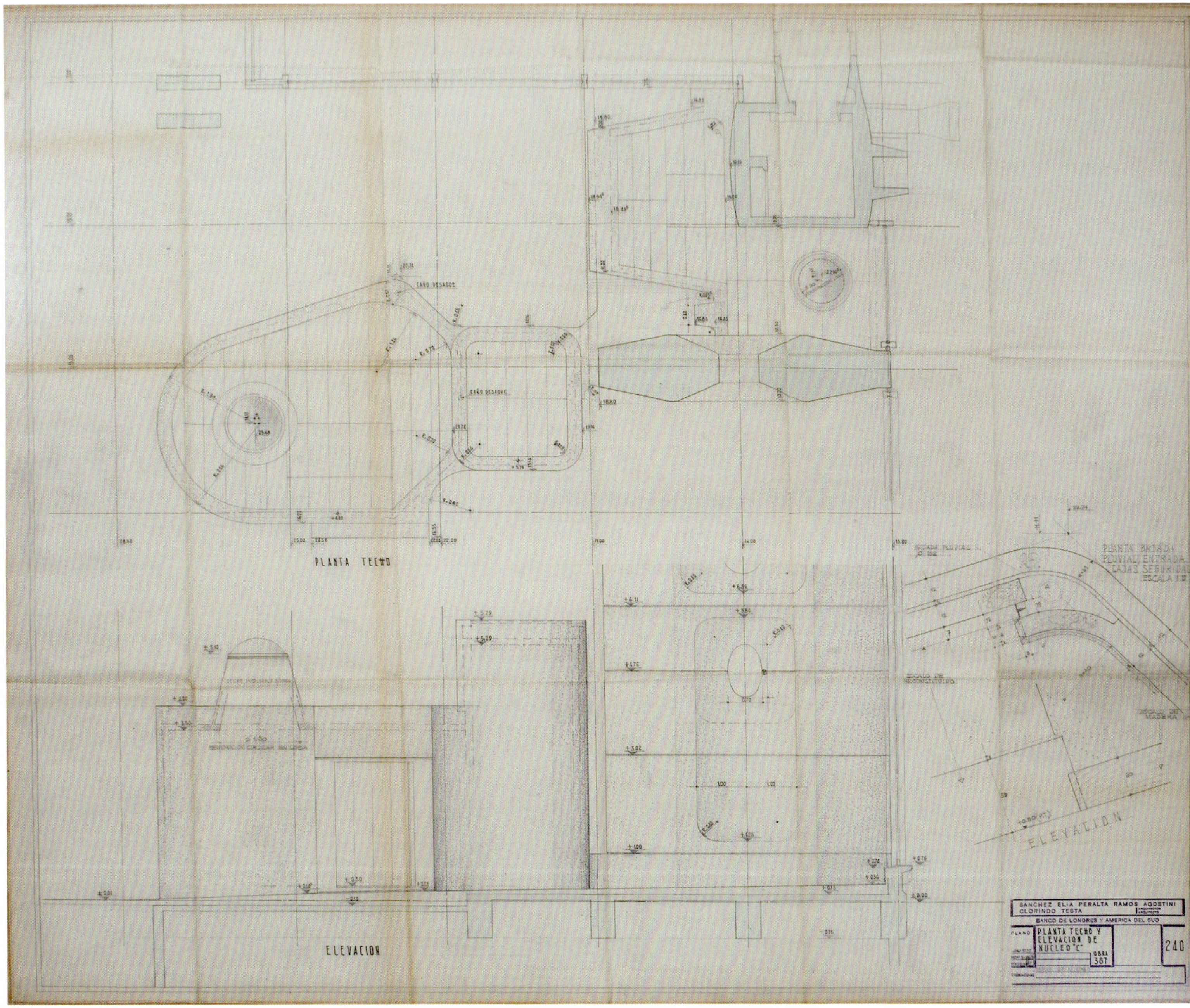
PLANTA TECHO
ELEVACION
ELEVACION
SANCHEZ ELIA PERALTA RAMOS AGOSTINI
CLORINDO TESTA
BANCO DE LONDRES Y AMERICA DEL SUD
PLANO
PLANTA TECHO Y
ELEVACION DE
NUCLEO "C"
OBRA
387
240

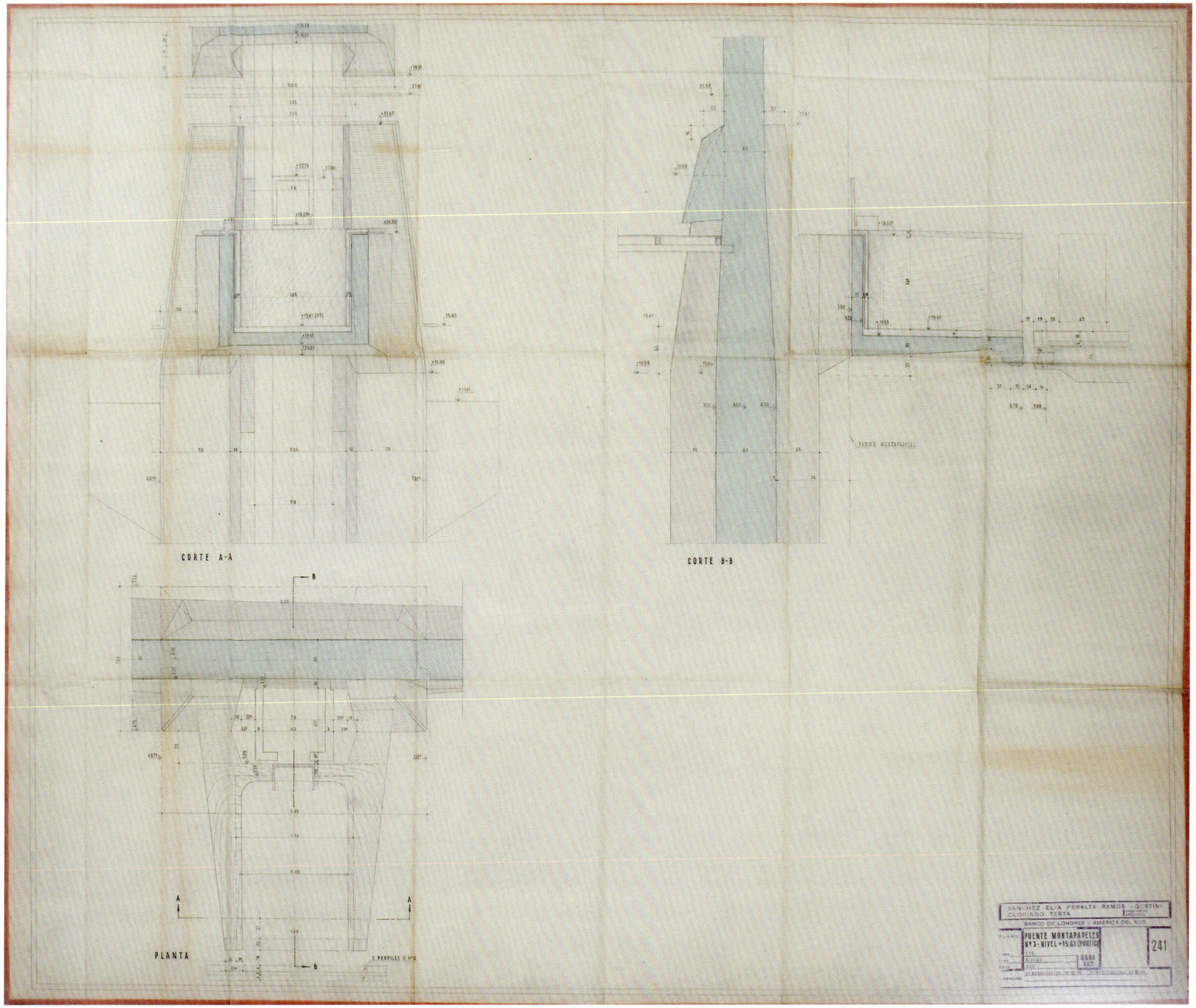

This page: Bridge detail (level +15,61m.), 1964, SEPRA's studio file (plan 241). Scale 3:50

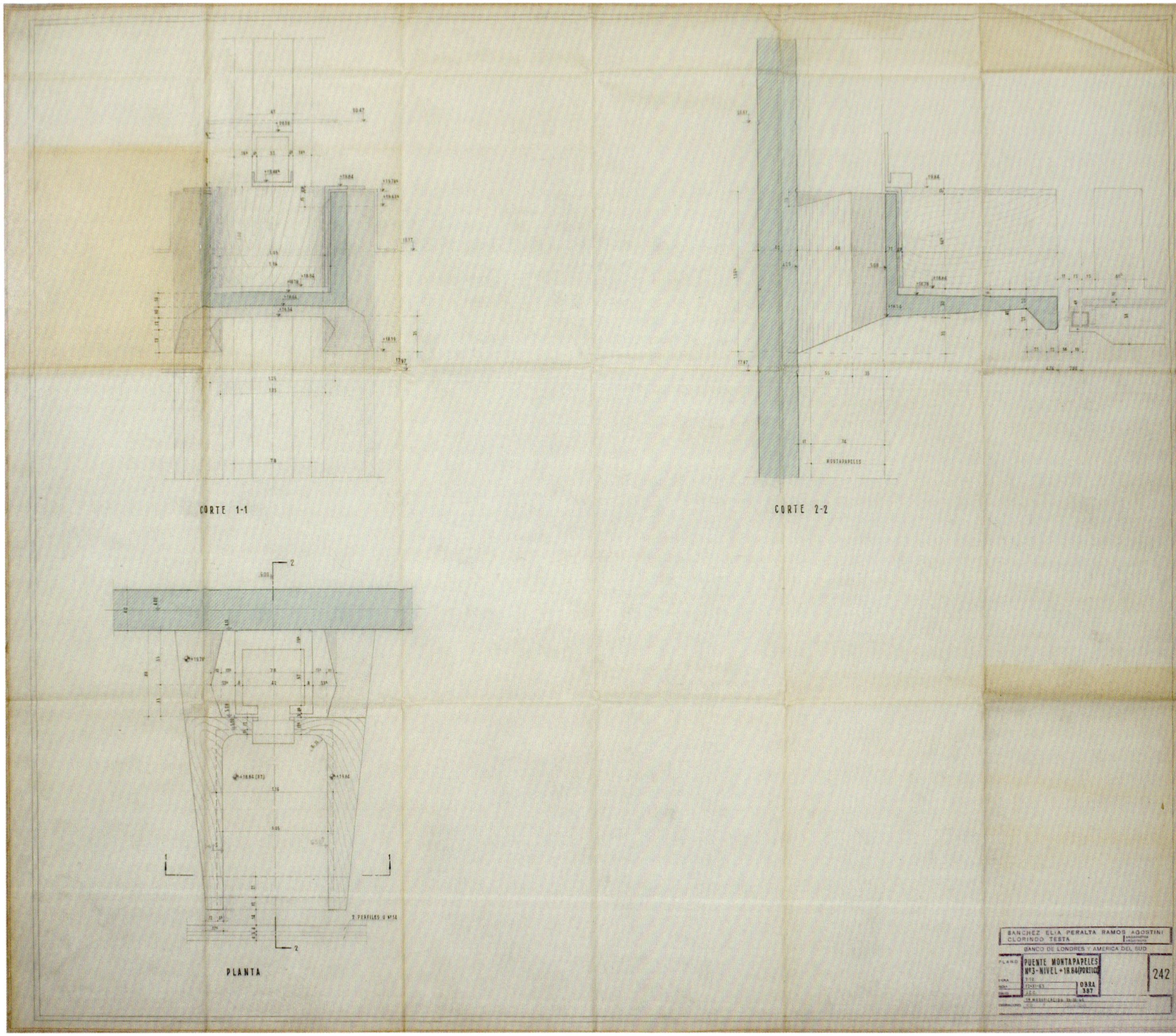
CORTE 1-1
CORTE 2-2
MONTAPAPELES
PLANTA
SANCHEZ ELIA PERALTA RAMOS AGOSTINI
CLORINDO TESTA
BANCO DE LONDRES Y AMERICA DEL SUD
PLANO
PUENTE MONTAPAPELES
Nº3-NIVEL +18.84(PORTICO)
OBRA
387
242

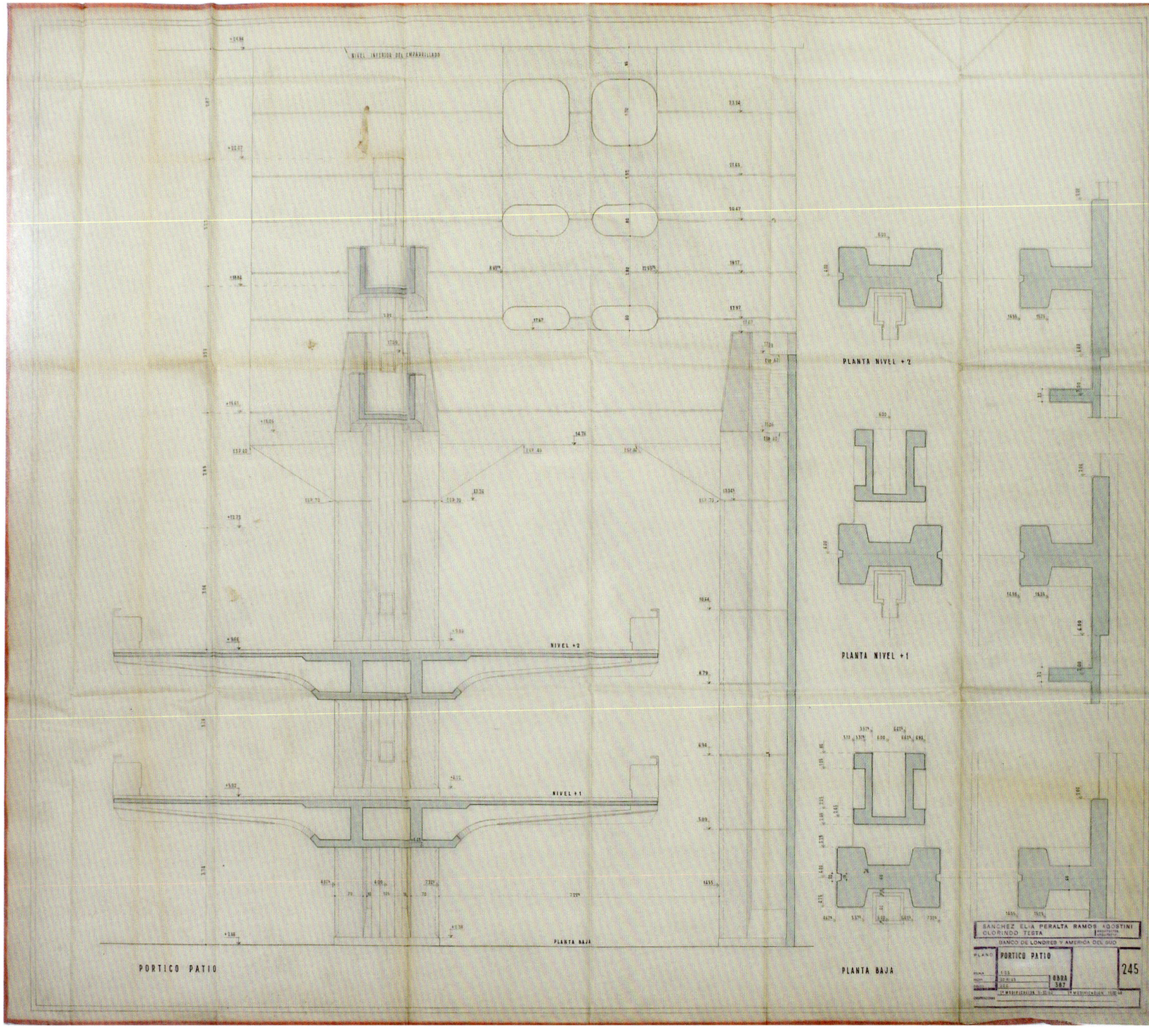

Opposite: Bridge detail (level +15,84m), 1964, SEPRA's studio file (plan 242). Scale 3:50
This page: Patio arcade details, 1963, SEPRA's studio file (plan 245). Scale 3:125

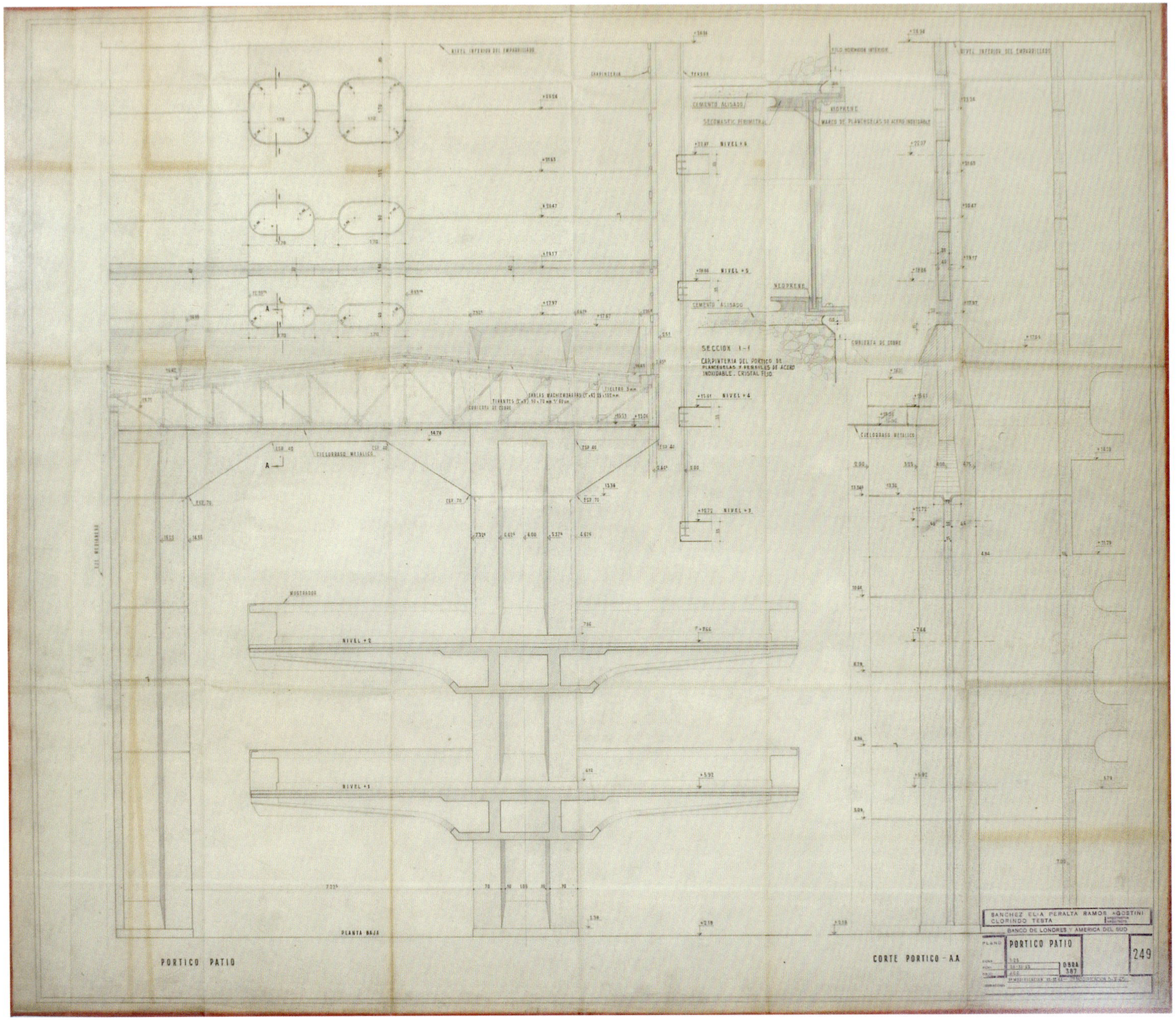

SECCION 1-1
CARPINTERIA DEL PORTICO DE PLANCHUELAS Y PERFILES DE ACERO INOXIDABLE - CRISTAL FIJO
NIVEL +2
NIVEL +1
PLANTA BAJA
PORTICO PATIO
CORTE PORTICO - AA
SANCHEZ ELIA PERALTA RAMOS AGOSTINI
CLORINDO TESTA
BANCO DE LONDRES Y AMERICA DEL SUD
PLANO
PORTICO PATIO
OBRA
387
249

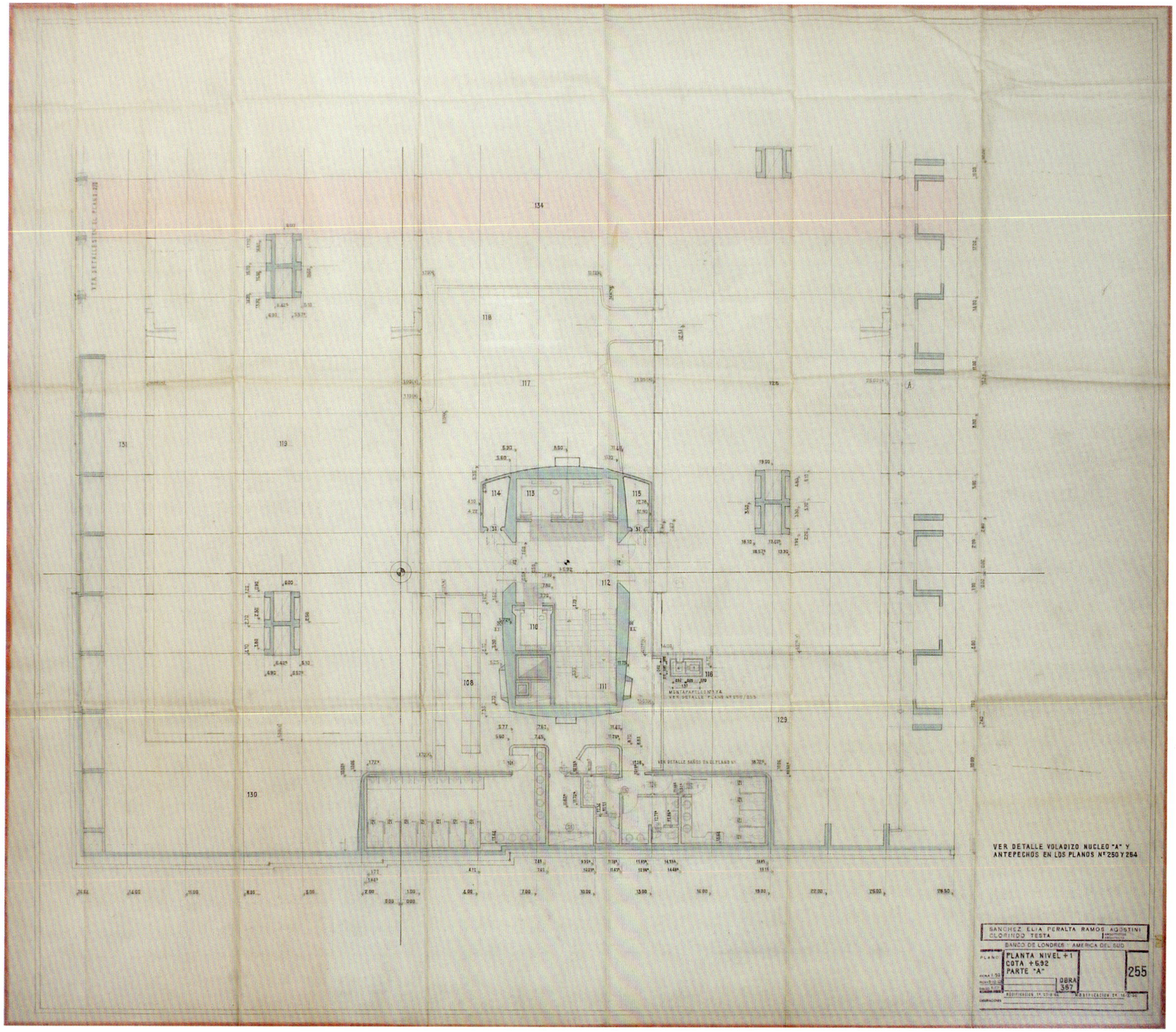

Opposite: Patio arcade details, 1965, SEPRA's studio file (plan 249). Scale 3:125
This page: Level +1 plan, part A, 1964, SEPRA's studio file (plan 255). Scale 1:50

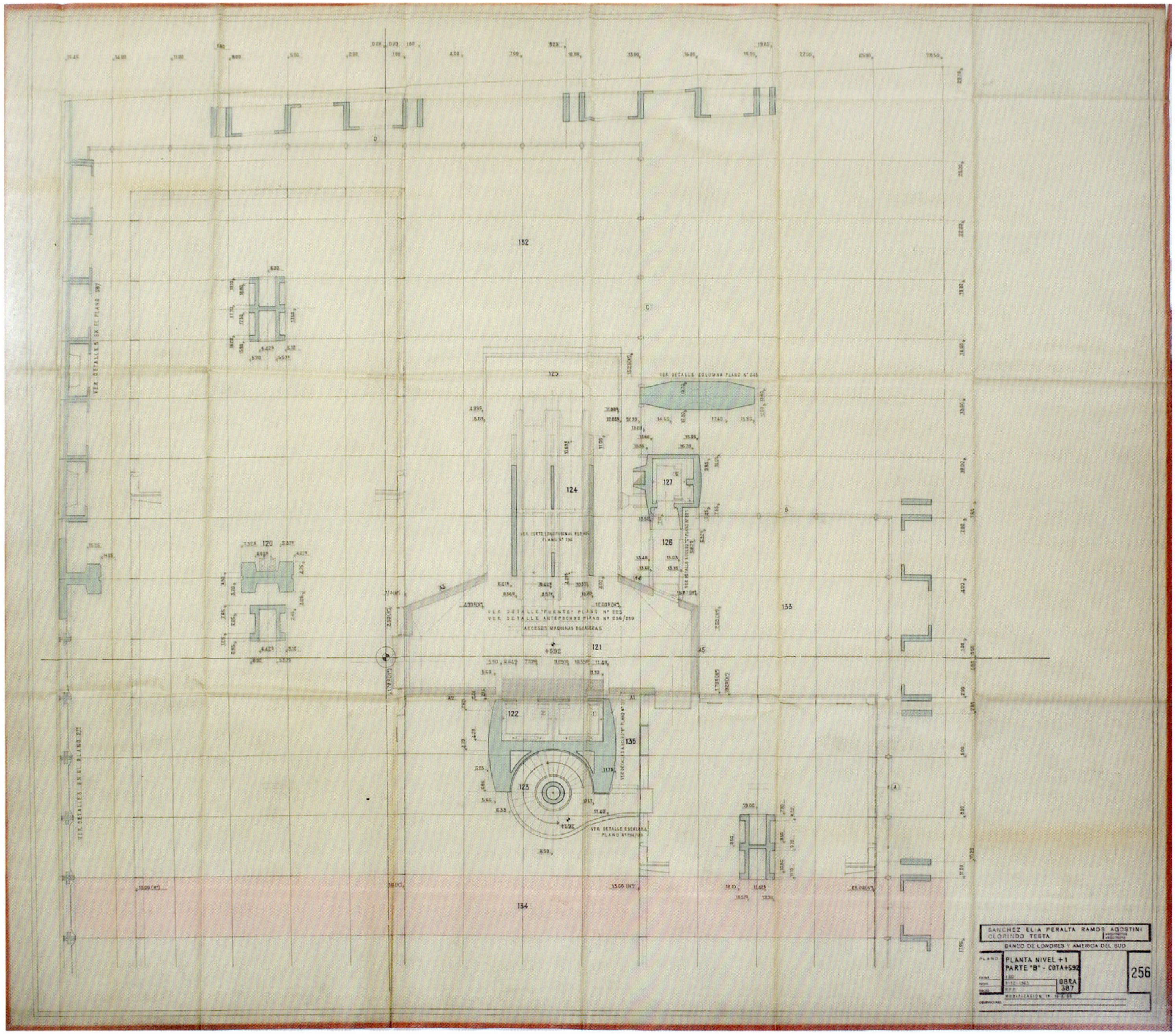
SANCHEZ ELIA PERALTA RAMOS AGOSTINI
CLORINDO TESTA
BANCO DE LONDRES Y AMERICA DEL SUD
PLANO
PLANTA NIVEL +1
PARTE "B" - COTA+592
OBRA 387
256

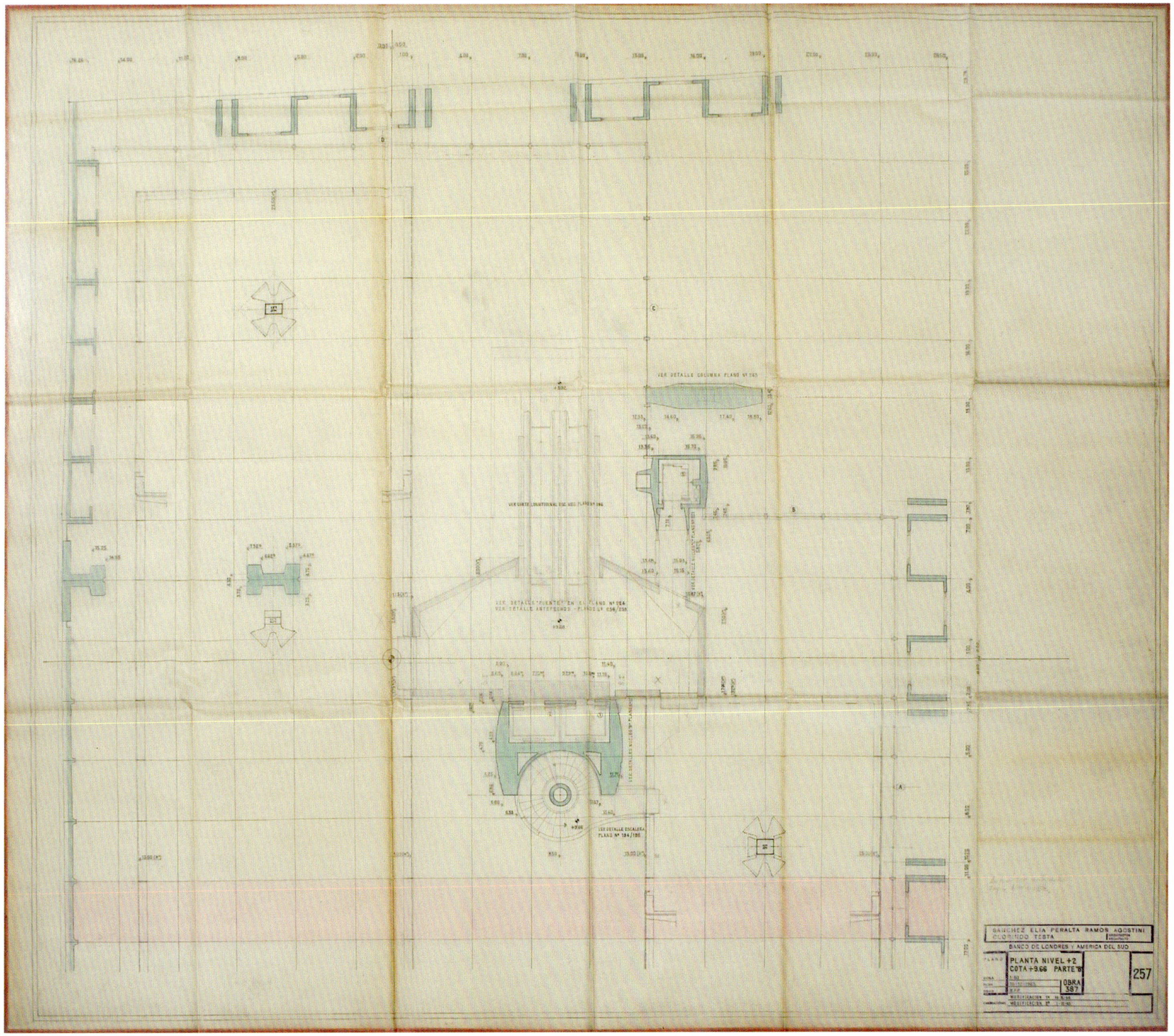

Opposite: Level +1 plan, part B, 1964, SEPRA's studio file (plan 256). Scale 3:250
This page: Level +2 plan, part B, 1965, SEPRA's studio file (plan 257). Scale 3:250

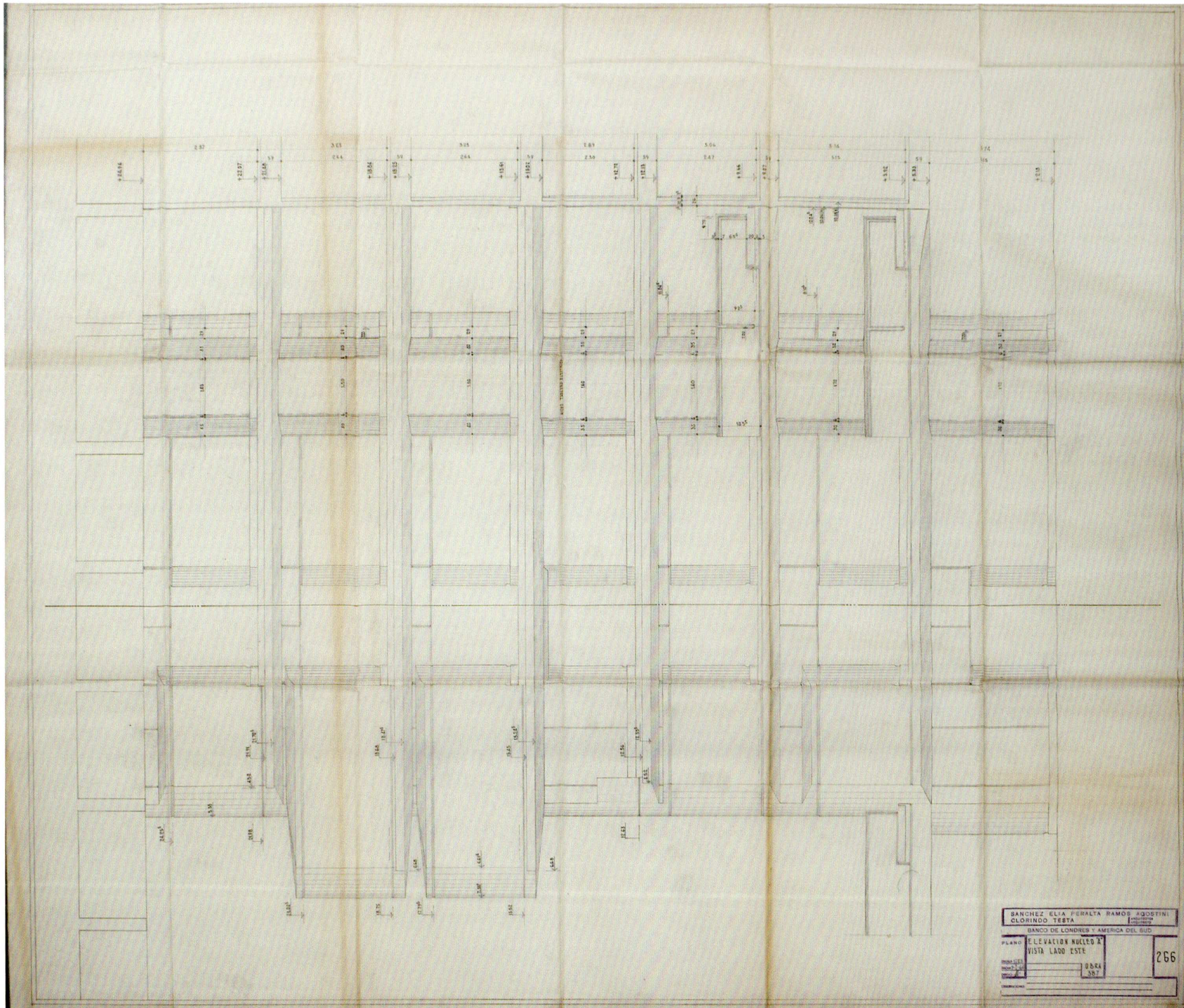
SANCHEZ ELIA PERALTA RAMOS AGOSTINI
CLORINDO TESTA
BANCO DE LONDRES Y AMERICA DEL SUD
PLANO
ELEVACION NUCLEO "A"
VISTA LADO ESTE
OBRA
387
266

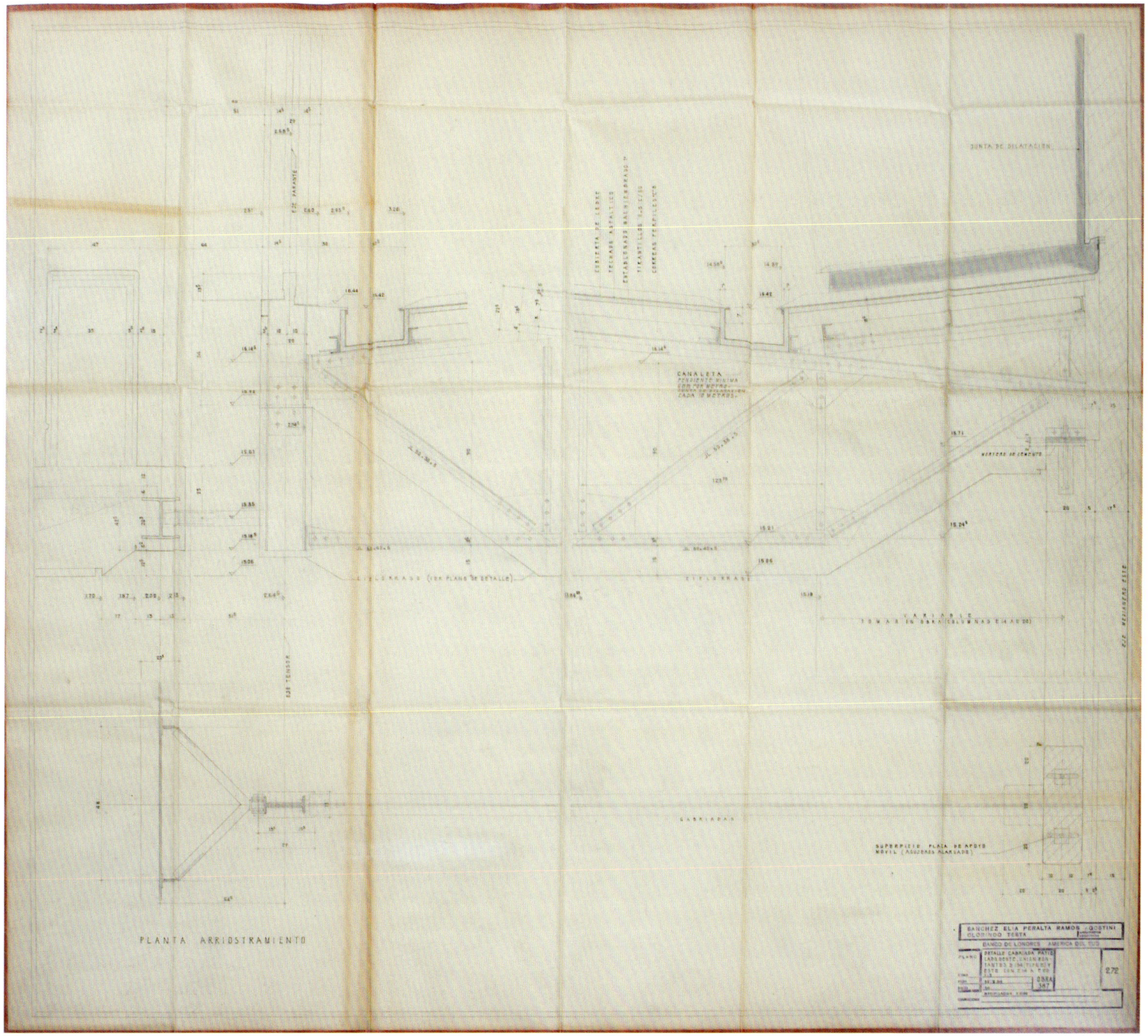

Opposite: Section Core A, East side, 1964, SEPRA's studio file (plan 266). Scale 3:125
This page: Patio's roof detail, 1963, SEPRA's studio file (plan 272)

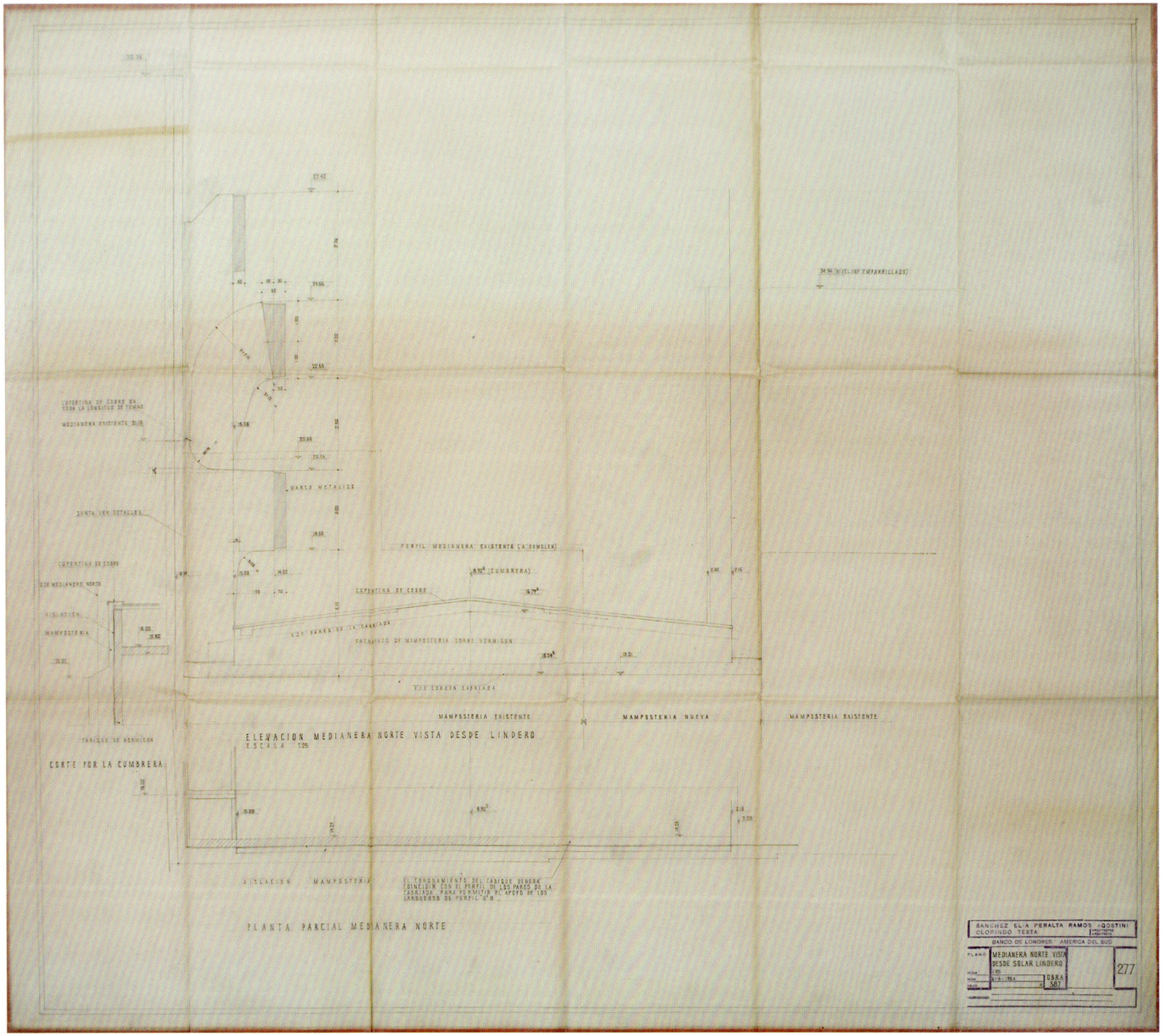
ELEVACION MEDIANERA NORTE VISTA DESDE LINDERO
ESCALA 1:25
CORTE POR LA CUMBRERA
MAMPOSTERIA EXISTENTE
MAMPOSTERIA NUEVA
MAMPOSTERIA EXISTENTE
EJE CORDON CABRIADA
ENCHAPADO DE MAMPOSTERIA SOBRE HORMIGON
TABIQUE DE HORMIGON
AISLACION
MAMPOSTERIA
EL CORONAMIENTO DEL TABIQUE DEBERA COINCIDIR CON EL PERFIL DE LOS PARES DE LA CABRIADA PARA PERMITIR EL APOYO DE LOS LARGUEROS DE PERFIL U 8
PLANTA PARCIAL MEDIANERA NORTE
SANCHEZ ELIA PERALTA RAMOS AGOSTINI
CLORINDO TESTA
BANCO DE LONDRES AMERICA DEL SUD
PLANO
MEDIANERA NORTE VISTA DESDE SOLAR LINDERO
1:25
6-4-1964
OBRA 387
277

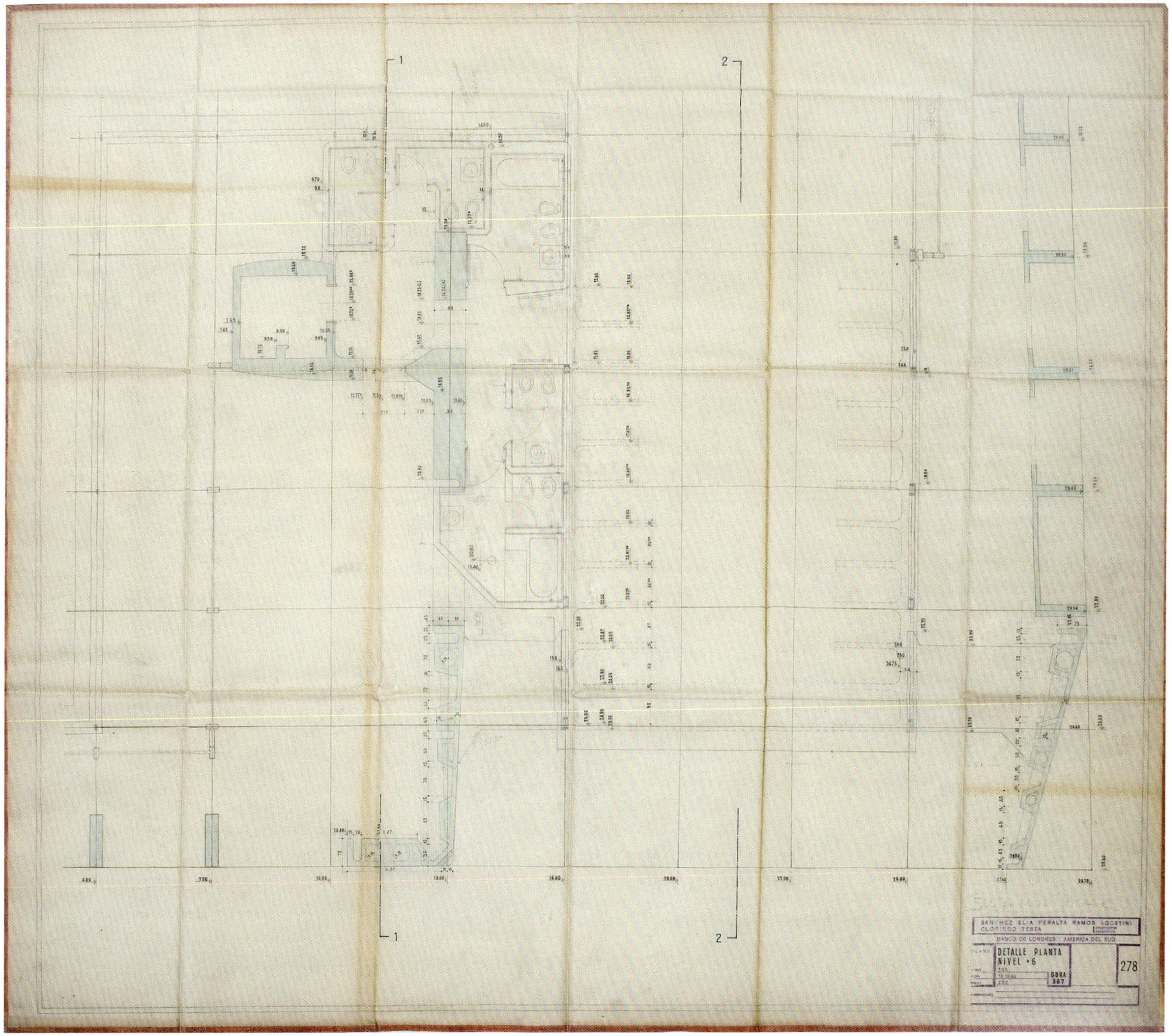

Opposite: North dividing wall (seen from boundary plot, 1964, SEPRA´s studio file (plan 277). Scale 3:125
This page: Level +6 plan detail, 1964, SEPRA´s studio file (plan 278). Scale 3:125

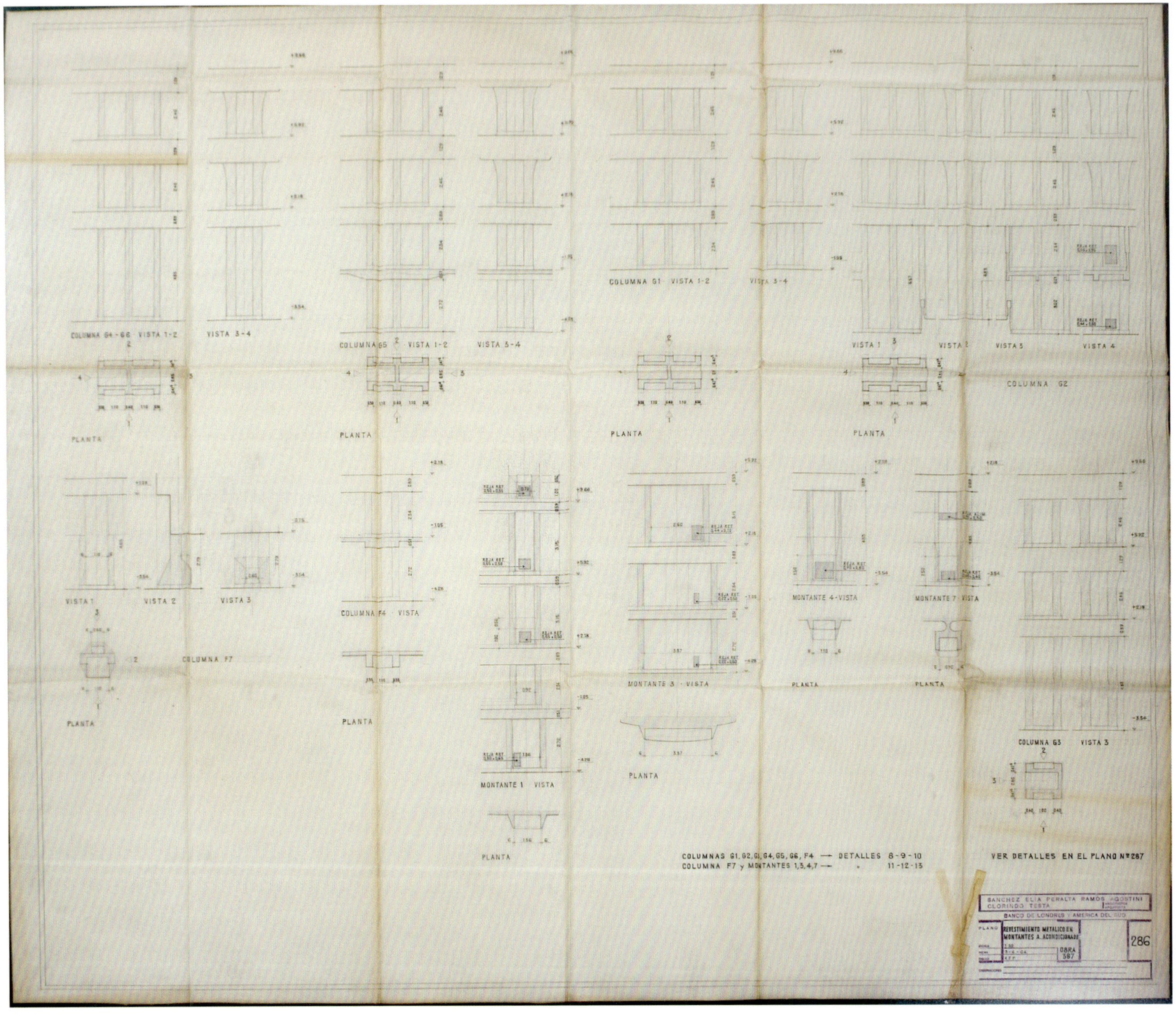
COLUMNA G4-G6 VISTA 1-2
VISTA 3-4
COLUMNA G5 VISTA 1-2
VISTA 3-4
COLUMNA G1 VISTA 1-2
VISTA 3-4
VISTA 1
VISTA 2
VISTA 3
VISTA 4
COLUMNA G2
PLANTA
COLUMNA F7
COLUMNA F4 VISTA
MONTANTE 1 VISTA
MONTANTE 3 VISTA
MONTANTE 4-VISTA
MONTANTE 7 VISTA
COLUMNA G3 VISTA 3
COLUMNAS G1, G2, G3, G4, G5, G6, F4 → DETALLES 8-9-10
COLUMNA F7 y MONTANTES 1,3,4,7 → 11-12-13
VER DETALLES EN EL PLANO Nº 287
SANCHEZ ELIA PERALTA RAMOS AGOSTINI
CLORINDO TESTA
BANCO DE LONDRES Y AMERICA DEL SUD
REVESTIMIENTO METALICO EN MONTANTES A. ACONDICIONADO
OBRA 387
286

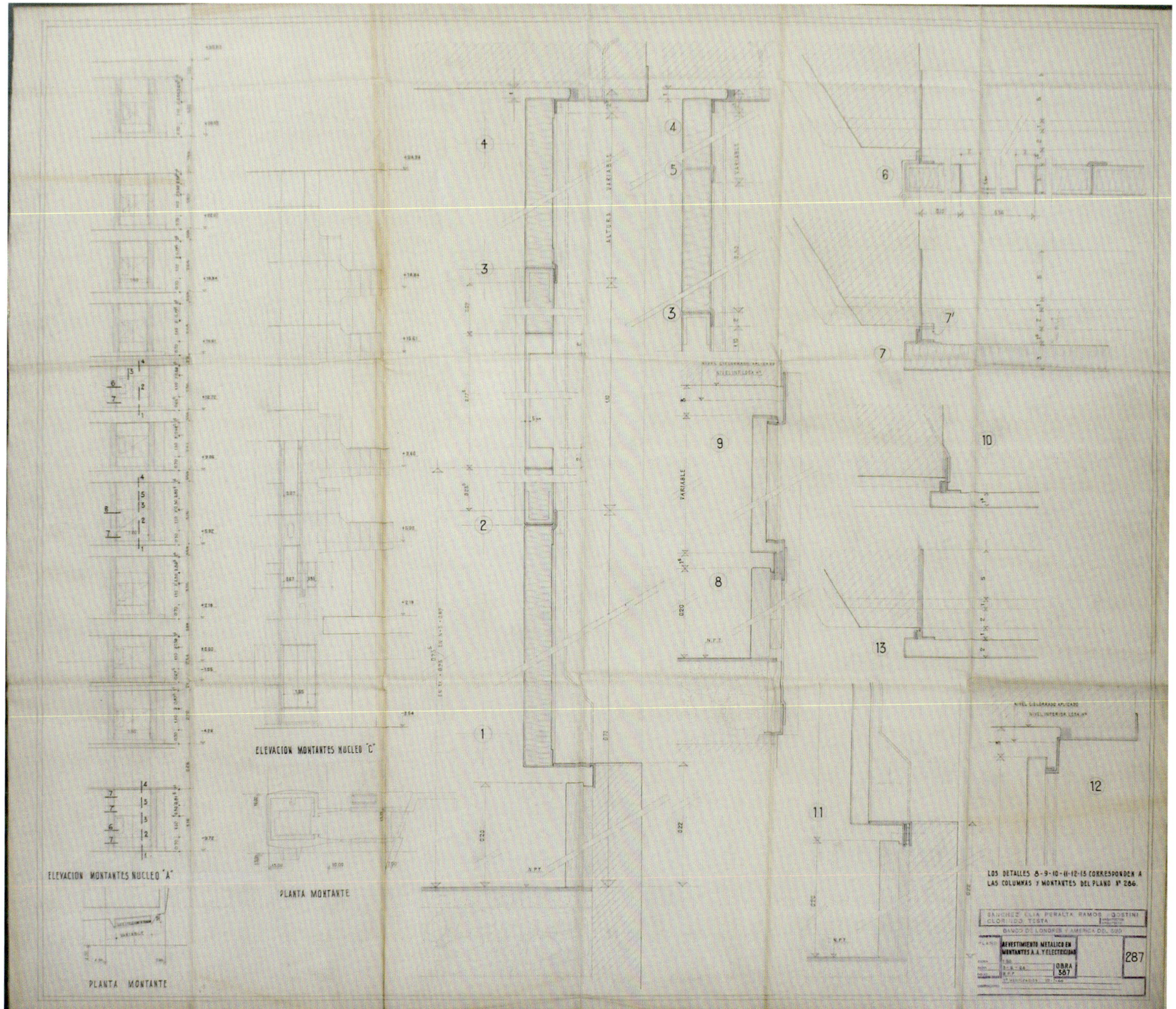

Opposite: Metal cladding of air conditioning ducts, 1964, SEPRA's studio file (plan 286). Scale 3:250

This page: Metal cladding of air conditioning and electricity ducts, 1964, SEPRA's studio file (plan 287). Scale 3:250

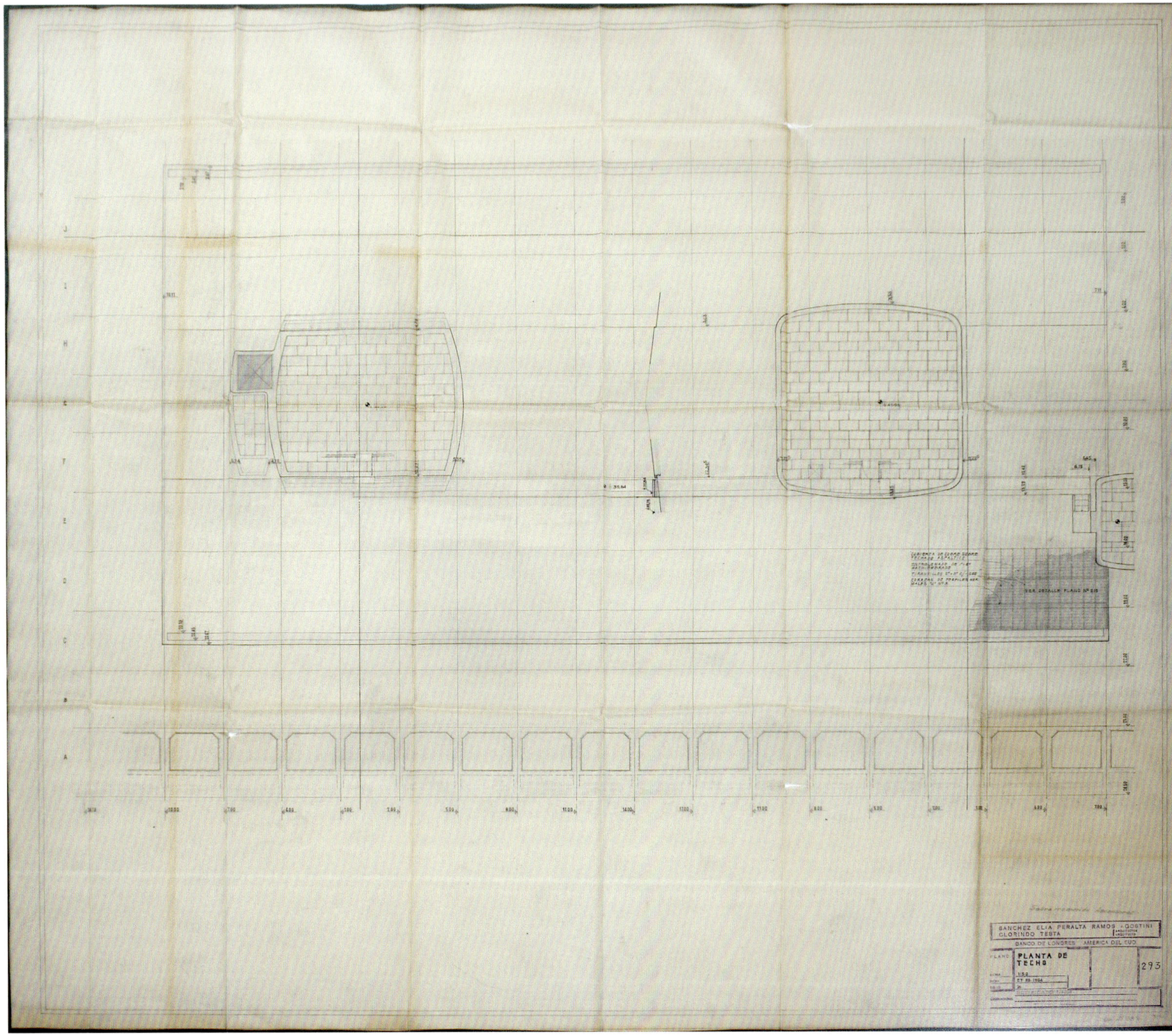
SANCHEZ ELIA PERALTA RAMOS AGOSTINI
CLORINDO TESTA
BANCO DE LONDRES AMERICA DEL SUD
PLANO
PLANTA DE TECHO
293

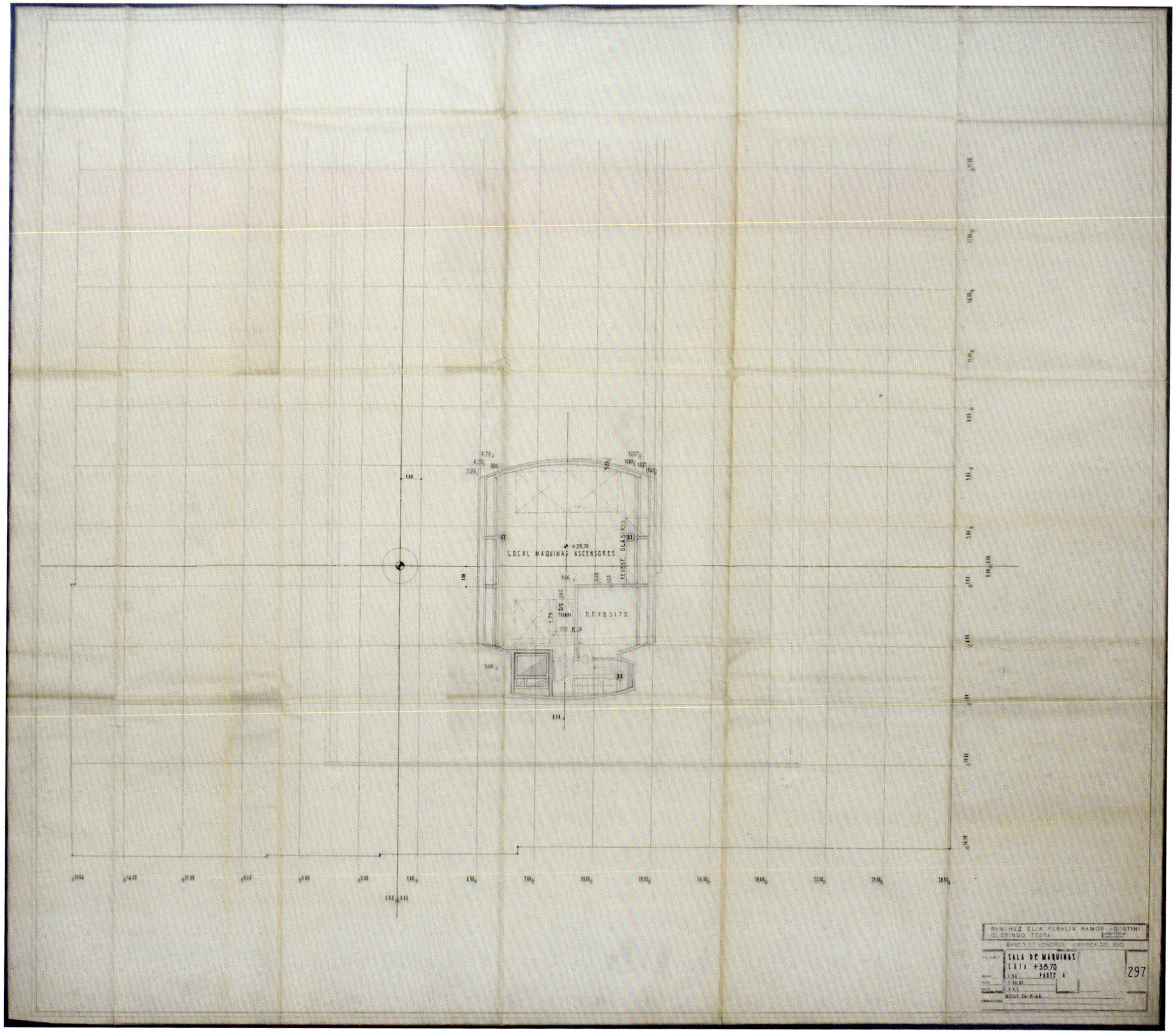

Opposite: Roof plan, 1964, SEPRA's studio file (plan 293). Scale 3:125
This page: Machinery room, part A, 1964, SEPRA's studio file (plan 297). Scale 3:250

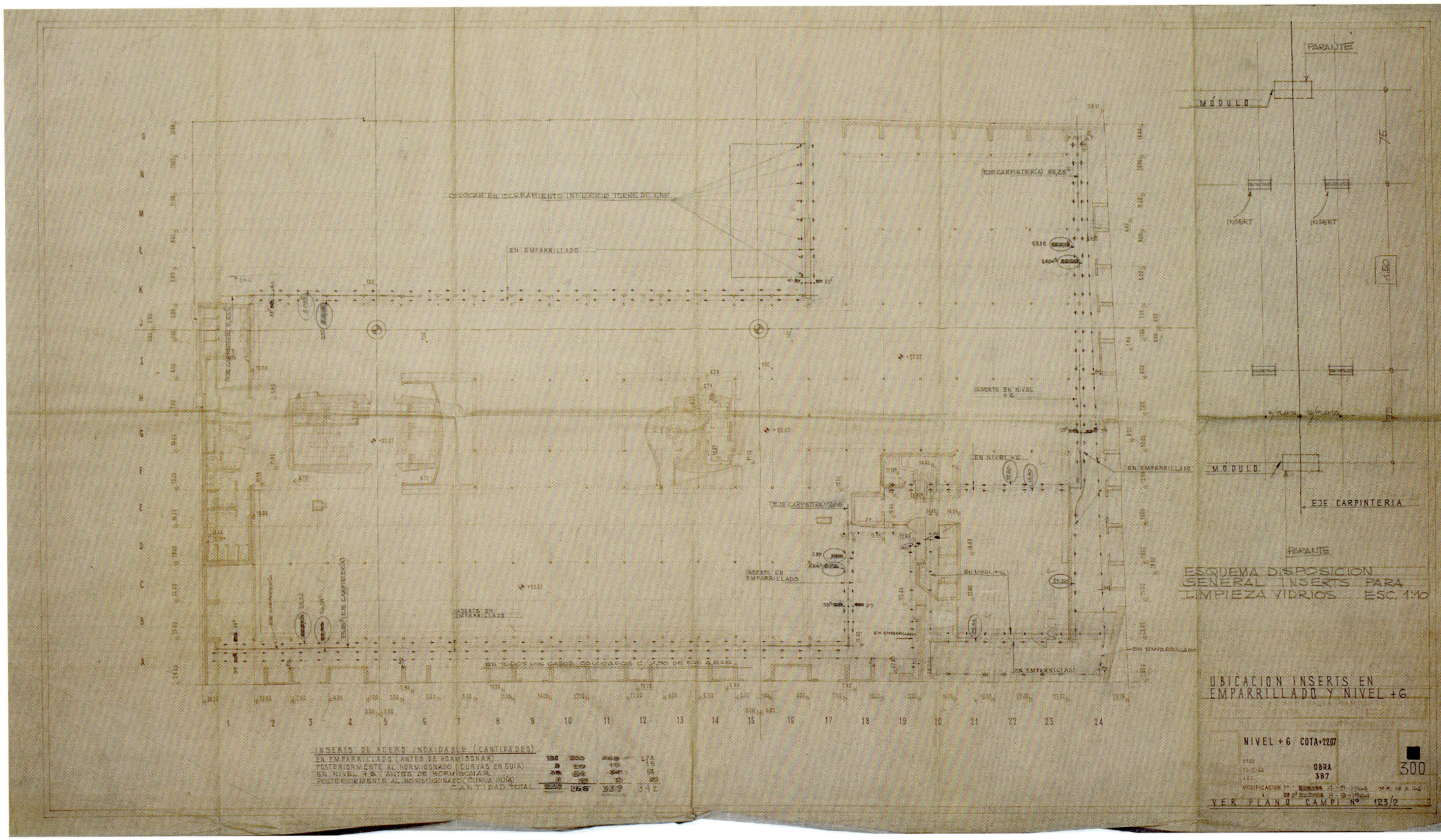
PARANTE
MÓDULO
INSERT
INSERT
1.50
MÓDULO
EJE CARPINTERIA
PARANTE
ESQUEMA DISPOSICION
GENERAL INSERTS PARA
LIMPIEZA VIDRIOS ESC. 1:10
EN EMPARRILLADO
EN NIVEL +6
INSERTS EN EMPARRILLADO
UBICACION INSERTS EN
EMPARRILLADO Y NIVEL +6
NIVEL +6 COTA+22.07
OBRA
387
300
VER PLANO CAMPI Nº 123/2
INSERTS DE ACERO INOXIDABLE (CANTIDADES)
CANTIDAD TOTAL

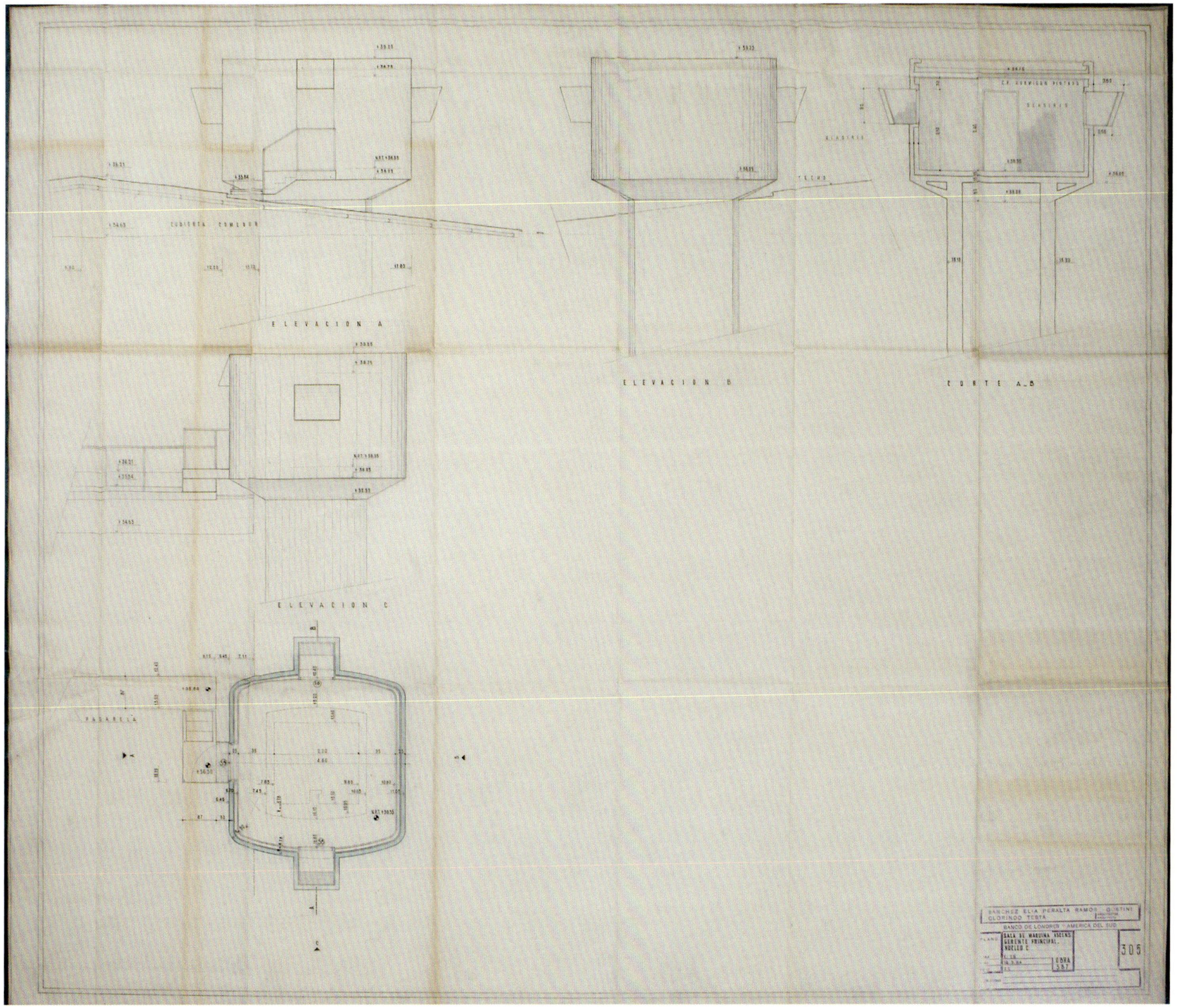

Opposite: Inserts in reinforce and level +6, 1964, SEPRA's studio file (plan 300). Scale 1:100
This page: Elevator Machinery room, Core C, 1964, SEPRA's studio file (plan 305). Scale 3:125

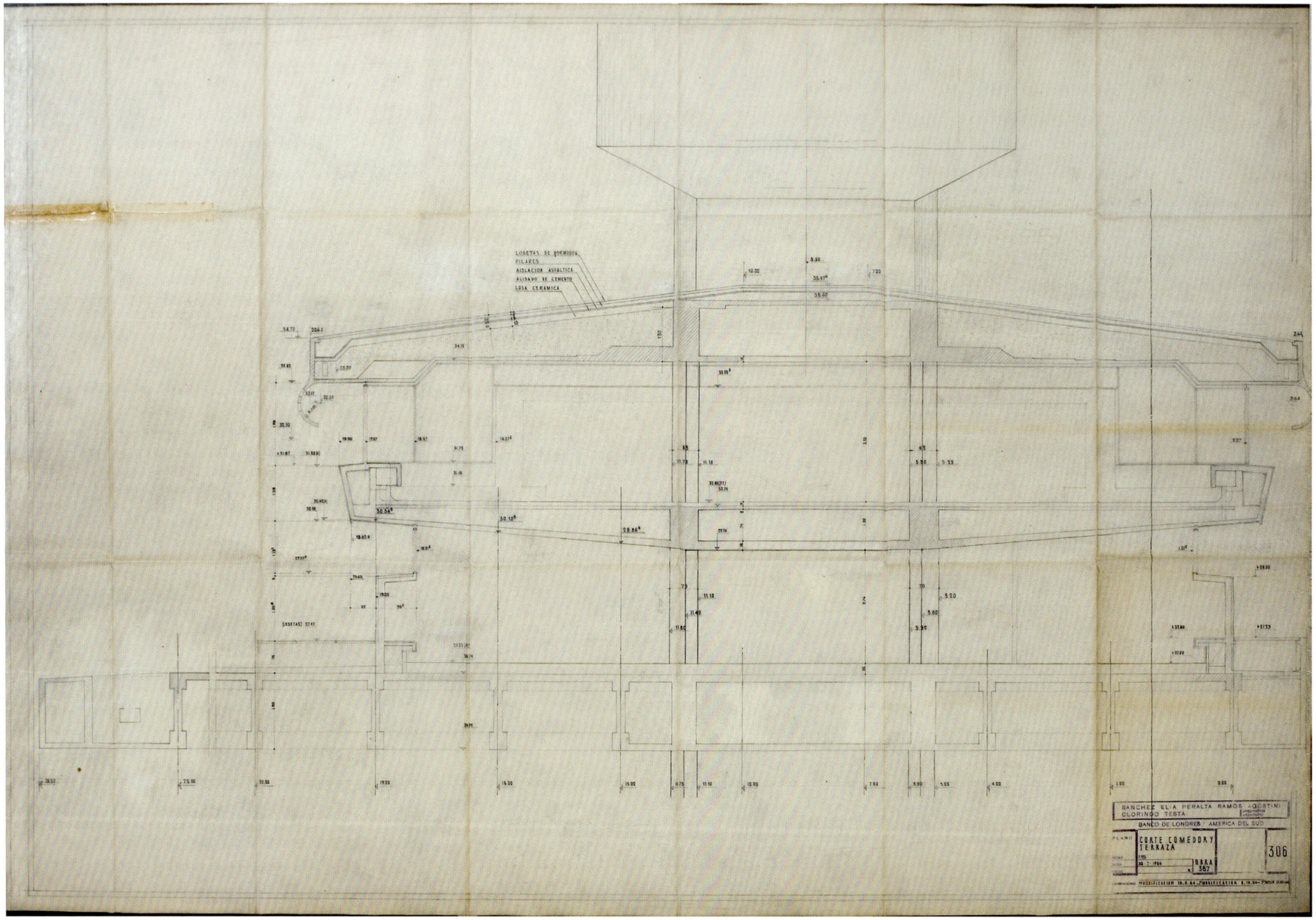
LOSETAS DE HORMIGON
PILARES
AISLACION ASFALTICA
ALISADO DE CEMENTO
LOSA CERAMICA
SANCHEZ ELIA PERALTA RAMOS AGOSTINI
CLORINDO TESTA
BANCO DE LONDRES Y AMERICA DEL SUD
PLANO
CORTE COMEDOR Y TERRAZA
30.7.1964
OBRA 367
306
MODIFICACION 16.9.64 - 2ª MODIFICACION 5.10.64

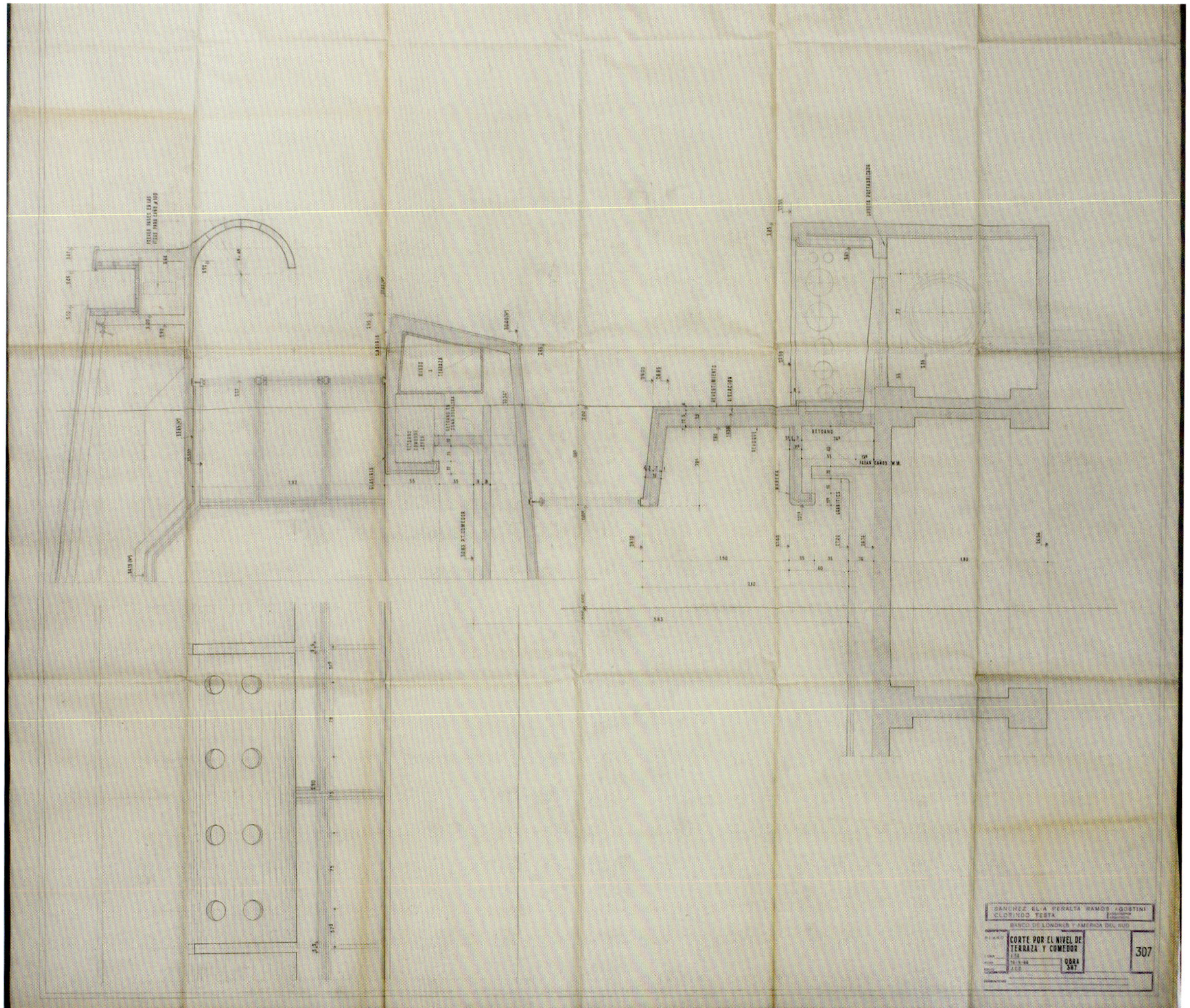

Opposite: Dining hall and terrace section, 1964, SEPRA's studio file (plan 306). Scale 3:125
This page: Dining hall and terrace section, 1964, SEPRA's studio file (plan 307). Scale 3:50

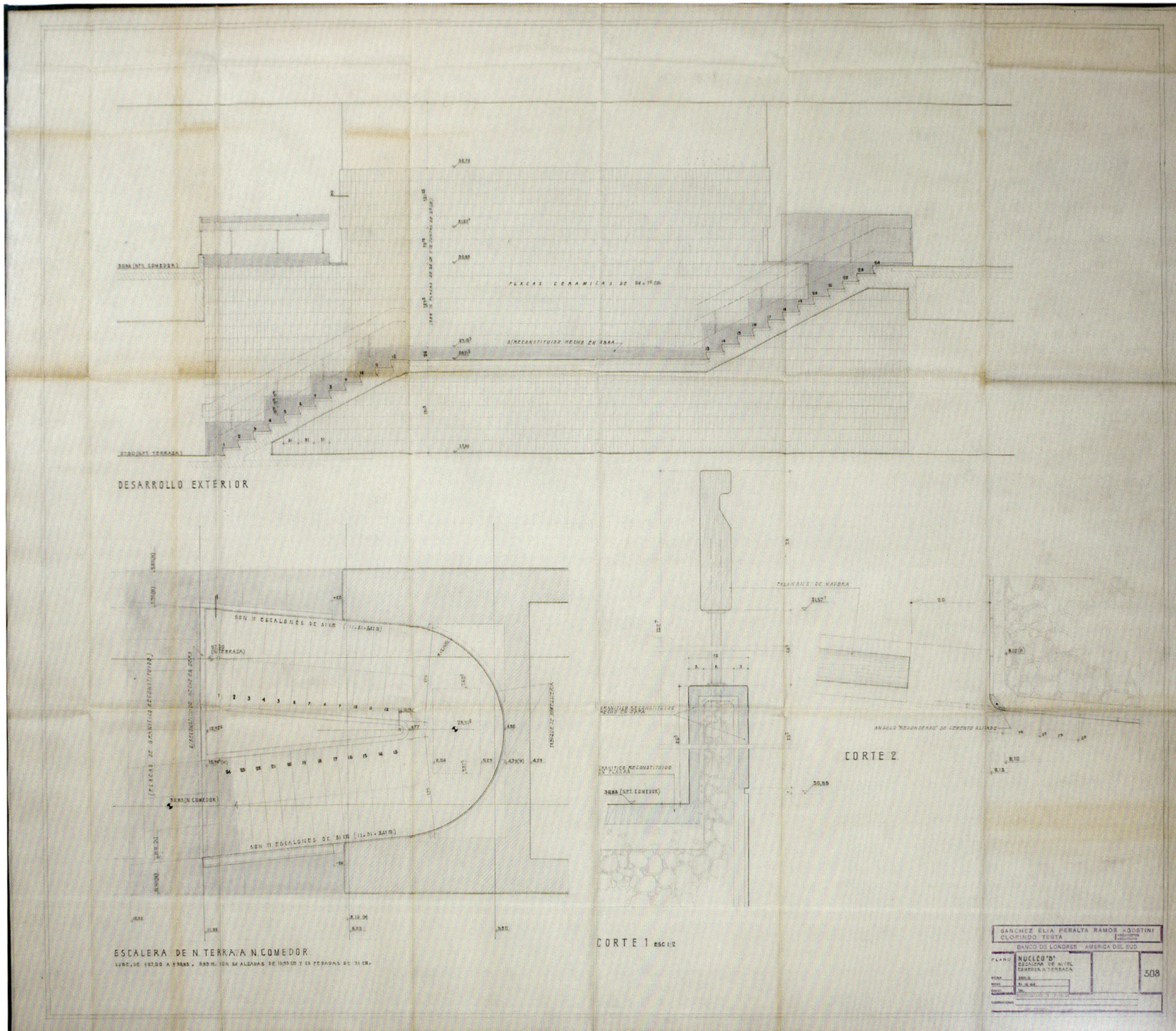
DESARROLLO EXTERIOR
ESCALERA DE N. TERRA A N. COMEDOR
CORTE 1
CORTE 2
SANCHEZ ELIA PERALTA RAMOS AGOSTINI
CLORINDO TESTA
BANCO DE LONDRES AMERICA DEL SUD
PLANO
NUCLEO "B"
308

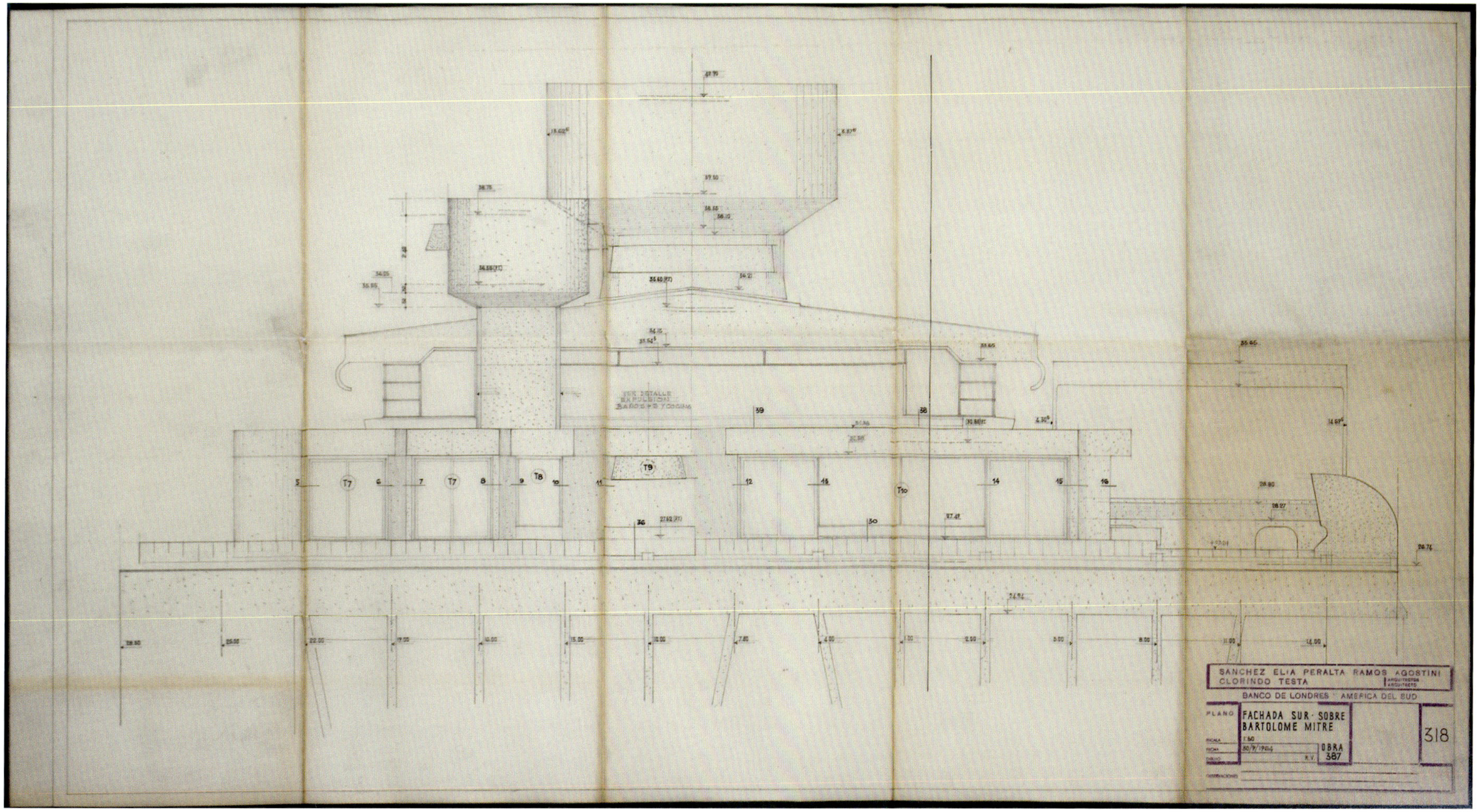

This page: Batolome Mitre st. façade, detail, 1964, SEPRA's studio file (plan 318). Scale 3:250

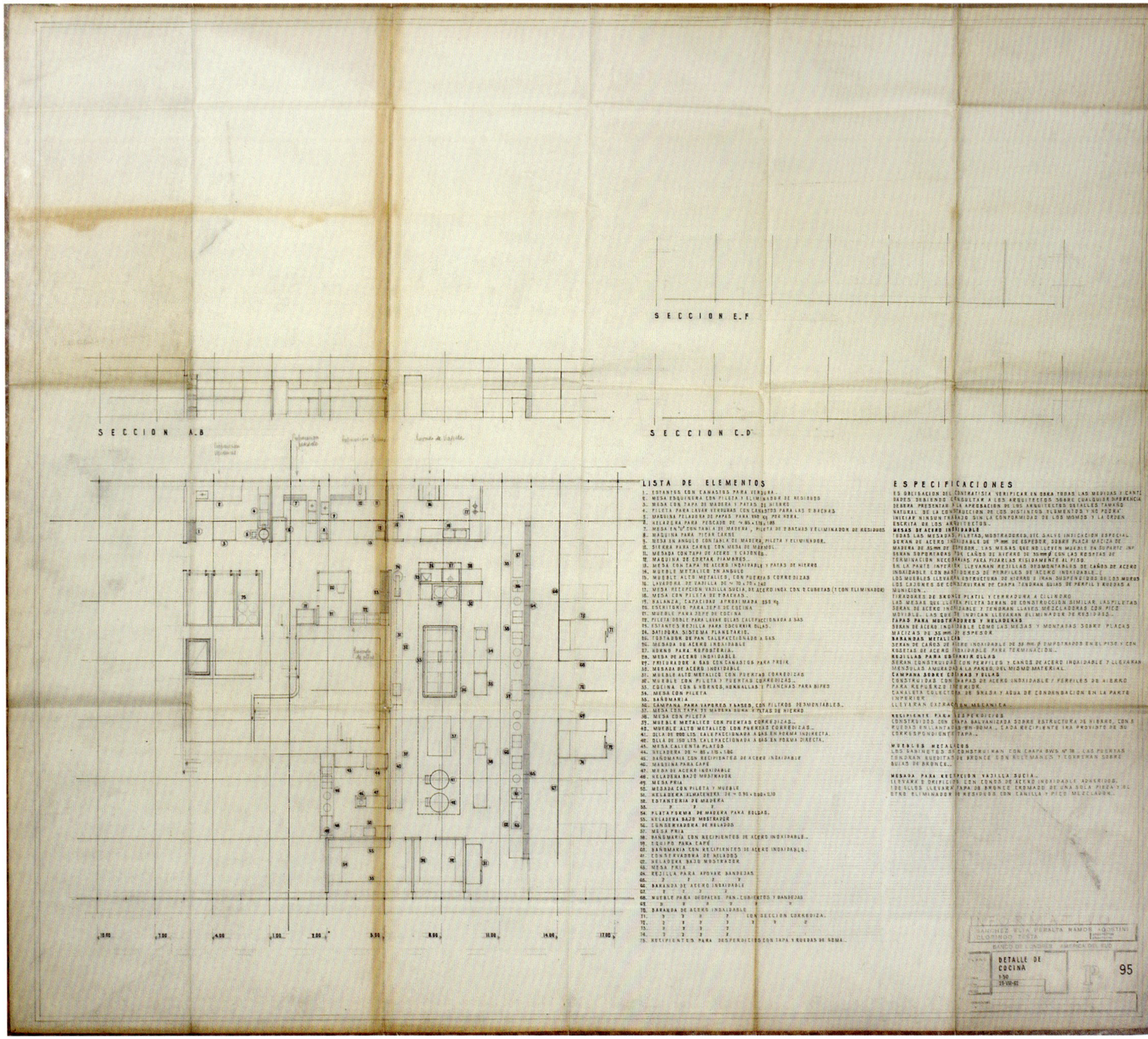
SECCION E.F
SECCION A.B
SECCION C.D
LISTA DE ELEMENTOS
ESPECIFICACIONES
SANCHEZ ELIA PERALTA RAMOS AGOSTINI
CLORINDO TESTA
BANCO DE LONDRES Y AMERICA DEL SUD
DETALLE DE
COCINA
1:50
95

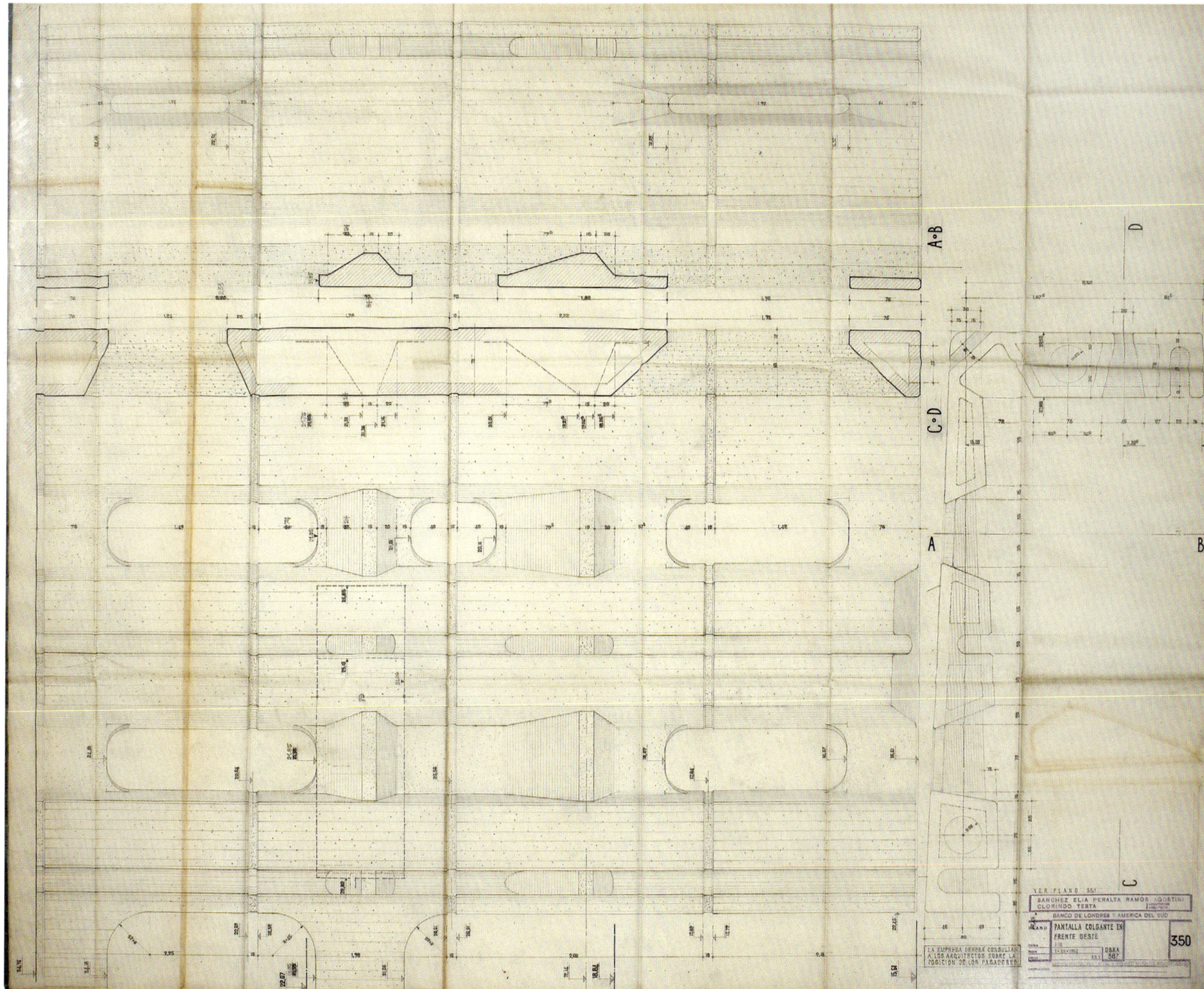

Opposite: Kitchen detail, 1962, SEPRA's studio file (plan 99). Scale 3:250
This page: Hanging screen in west façade, 1964, SEPRA's studio file (plan 350). Scale 3:50

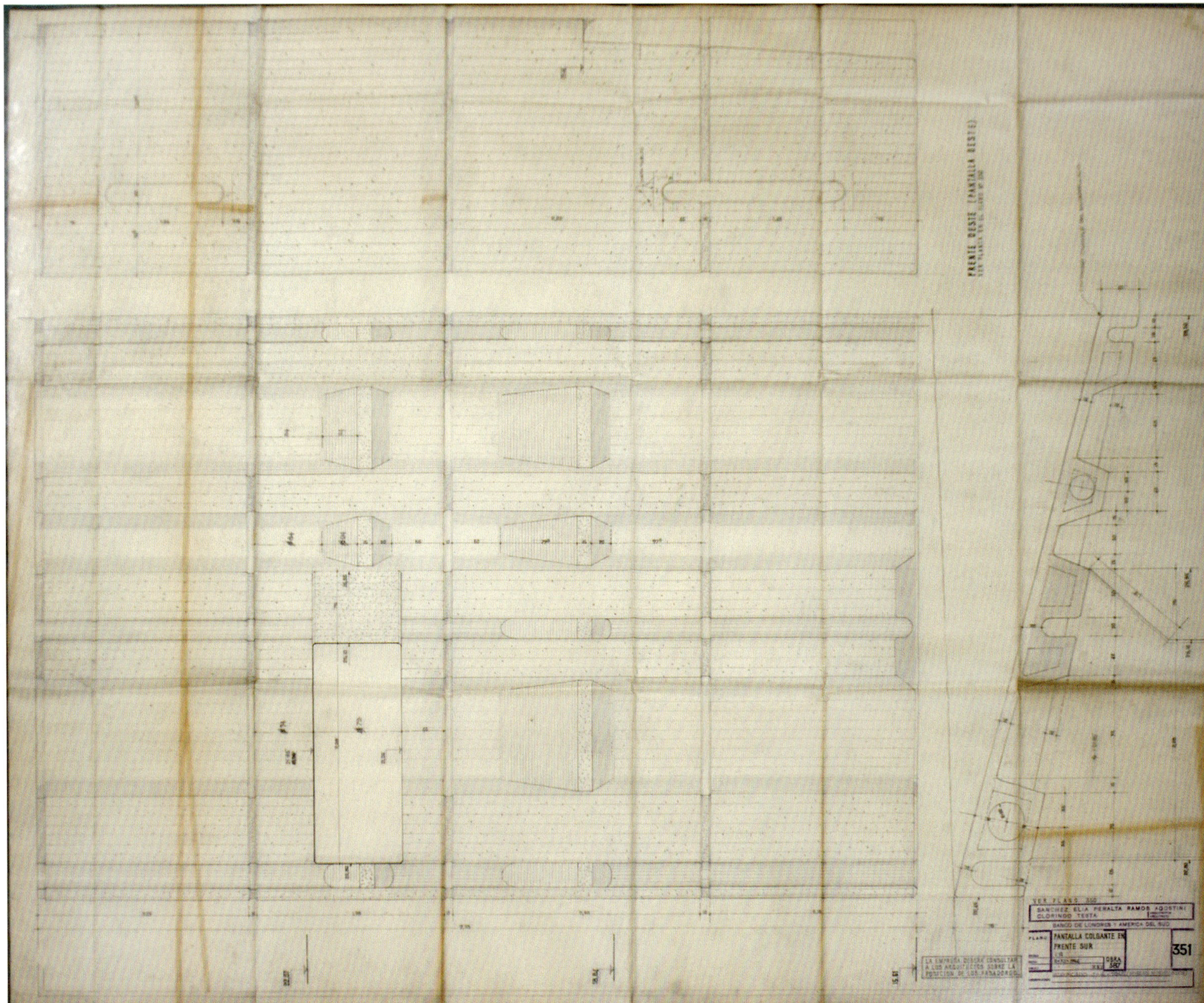
FRENTE OESTE (PANTALLA OESTE)
VER PLANO 350
SANCHEZ ELIA PERALTA RAMOS AGOSTINI
CLORINDO TESTA
BANCO DE LONDRES Y AMERICA DEL SUD
PLANO
PANTALLA COLGANTE EN
FRENTE SUR
OBRA
567
351
LA EMPRESA DEBERÁ CONSULTAR
A LOS ARQUITECTOS SOBRE LA
POSICION DE LOS PASADORES.

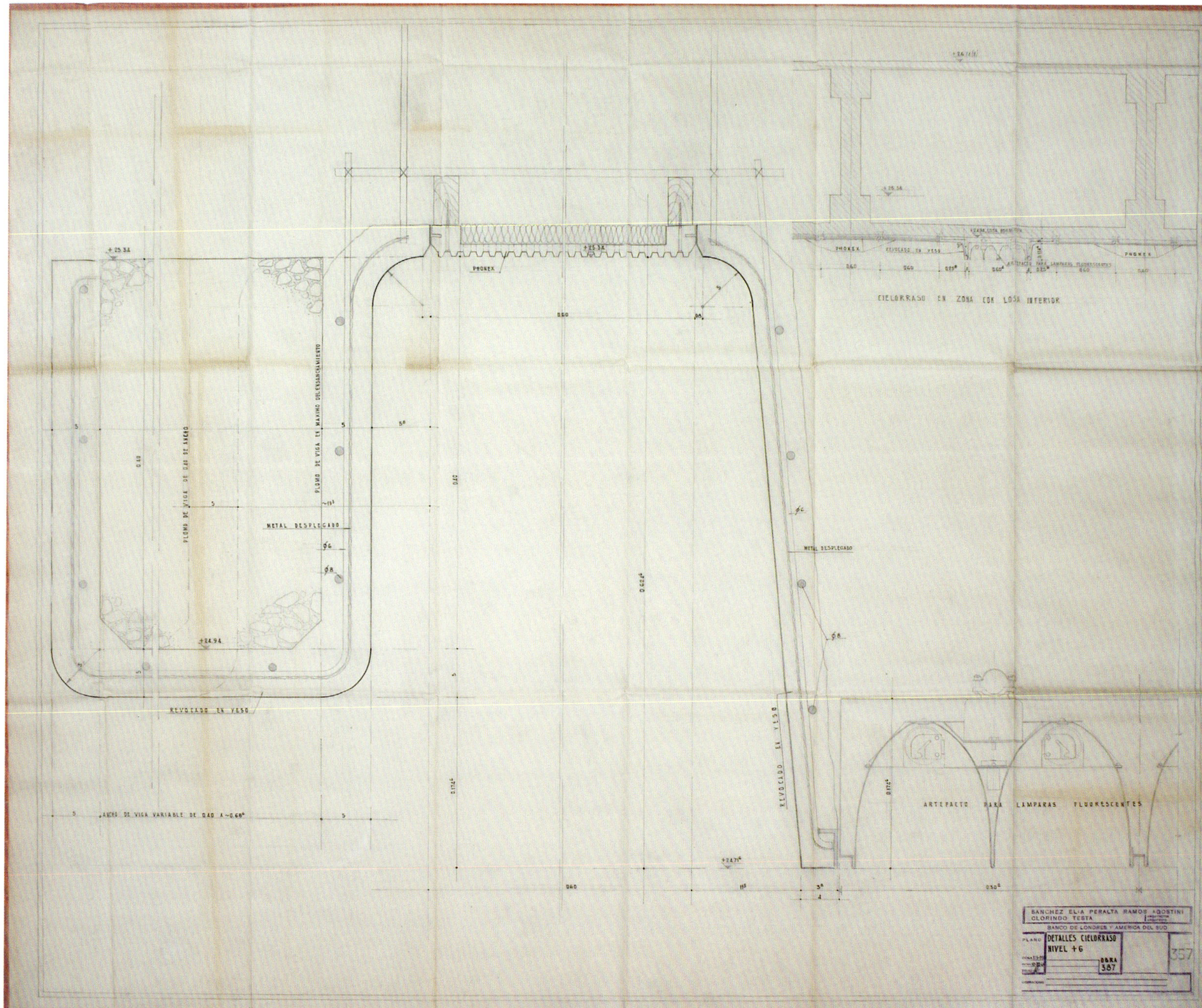

This page: Level +6 ceiling detail, 1964, SEPRA's studio file (plan 357)

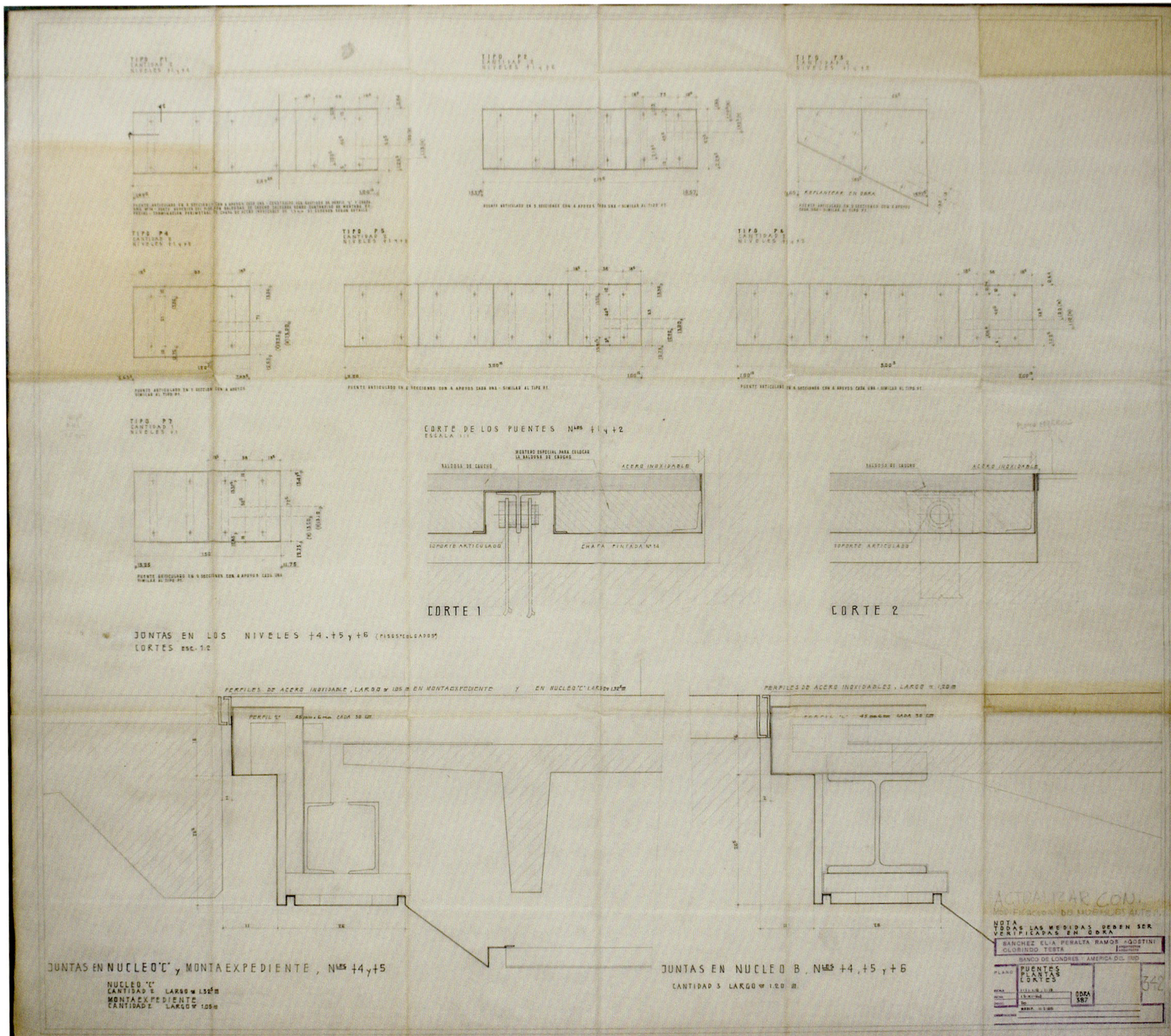
CORTE DE LOS PUENTES
CORTE 1
CORTE 2
JUNTAS EN LOS NIVELES +4, +5 y +6
CORTES ESC. 1:2
JUNTAS EN NUCLEO "C" y MONTAEXPEDIENTE, Nros +4 y +5
JUNTAS EN NUCLEO B, Nros +4, +5 y +6
NOTA
TODAS LAS MEDIDAS DEBEN SER VERIFICADAS EN OBRA
SANCHEZ ELIA PERALTA RAMOS AGOSTINI
CLORINDO TESTA
PUENTES
PLANTAS
CORTES

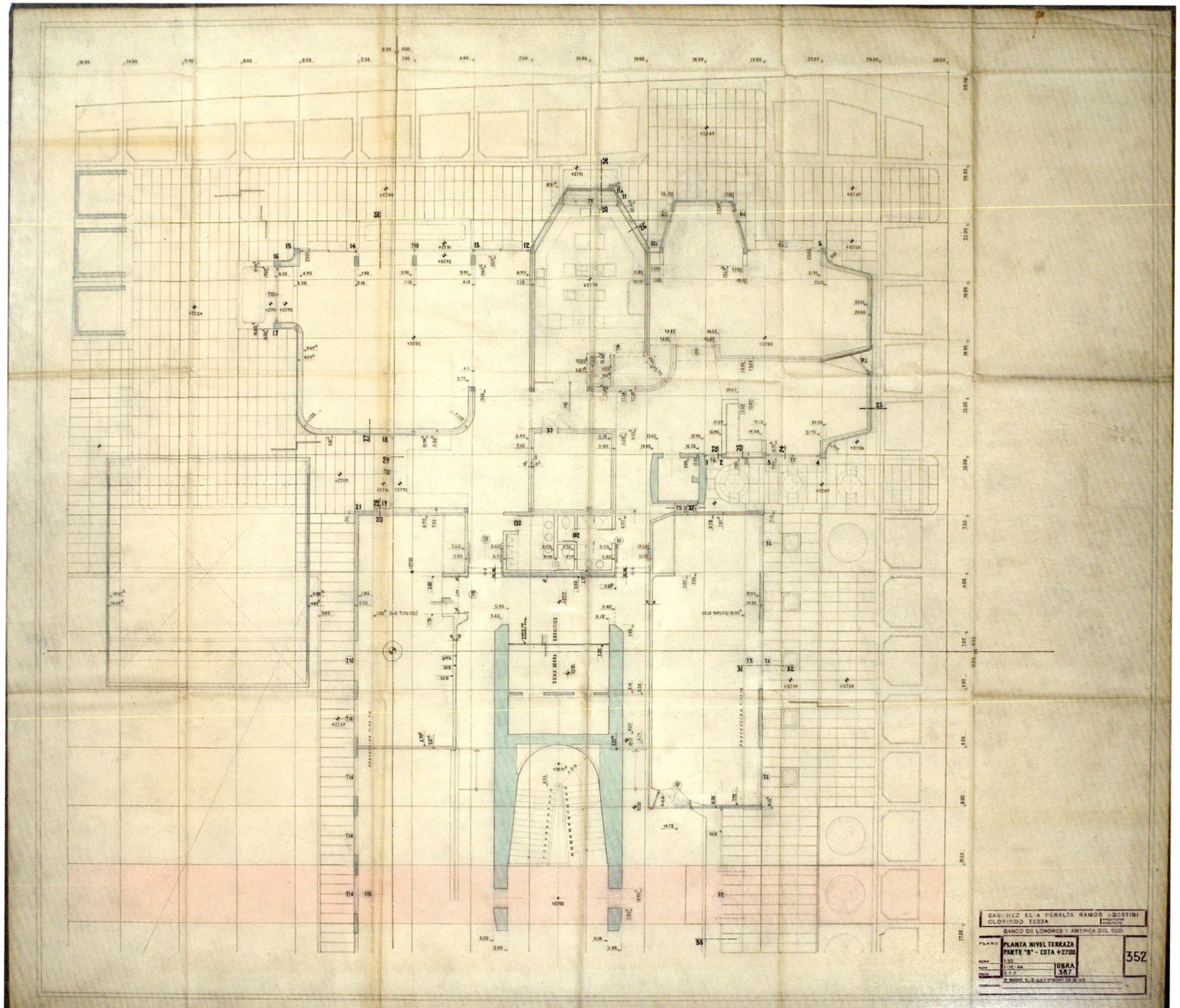

This page: Terrace level plan, part B, 1965, SEPRA's studio file (plan 352). Scale 3:250

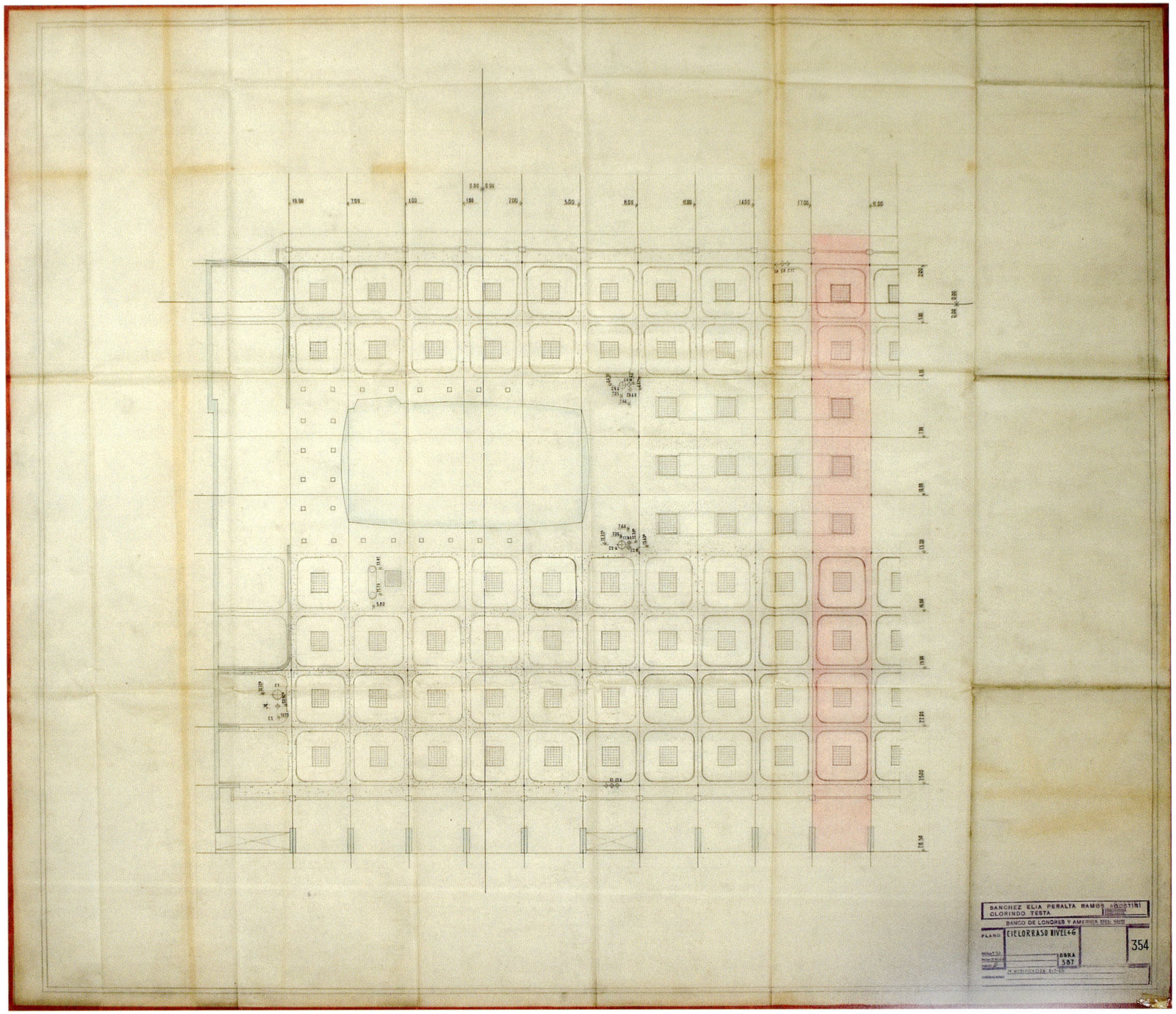
SANCHEZ ELIA PERALTA RAMOS AGOSTINI
CLORINDO TESTA
BANCO DE LONDRES Y AMERICA DEL SUD
PLANO
CIELORRASO NIVEL+6
OBRA
587
354

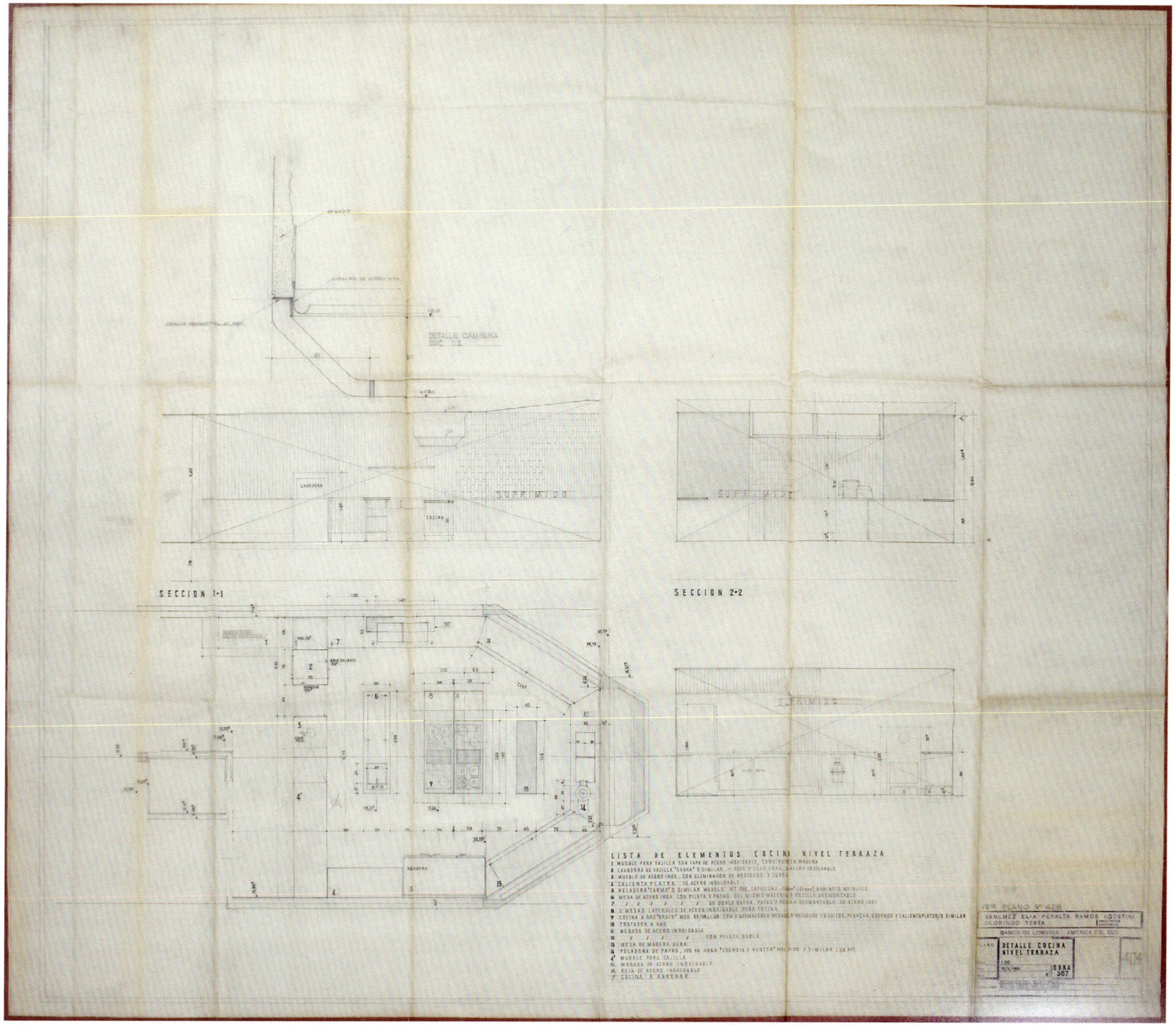

This page: Kitchen detail, 1965, SEPRA's studio file (plan 404). Scale 3:100

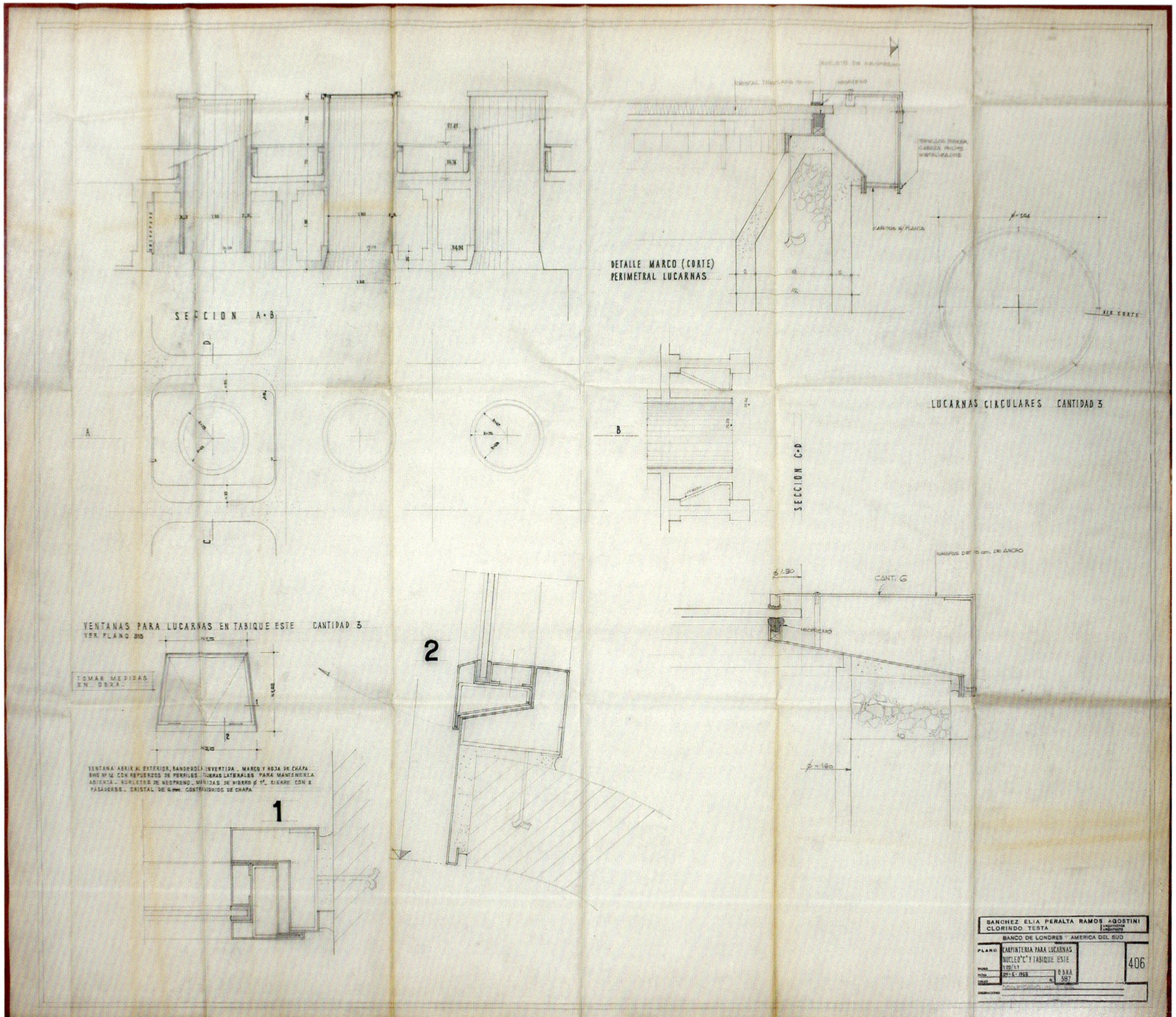
SECCION A-B
DETALLE MARCO (CORTE)
PERIMETRAL LUCARNAS
LUCARNAS CIRCULARES CANTIDAD 3
SECCION C-D
VENTANAS PARA LUCARNAS EN TABIQUE ESTE CANTIDAD 3
TOMAR MEDIDAS EN OBRA
CANT. 6
1
2
SANCHEZ ELIA PERALTA RAMOS AGOSTINI
CLORINDO TESTA
BANCO DE LONDRES Y AMERICA DEL SUD
PLANO
CARPINTERIA PARA LUCARNAS
NUCLEO "C" Y TABIQUE ESTE
1:20/1:1
OBRA
587
406

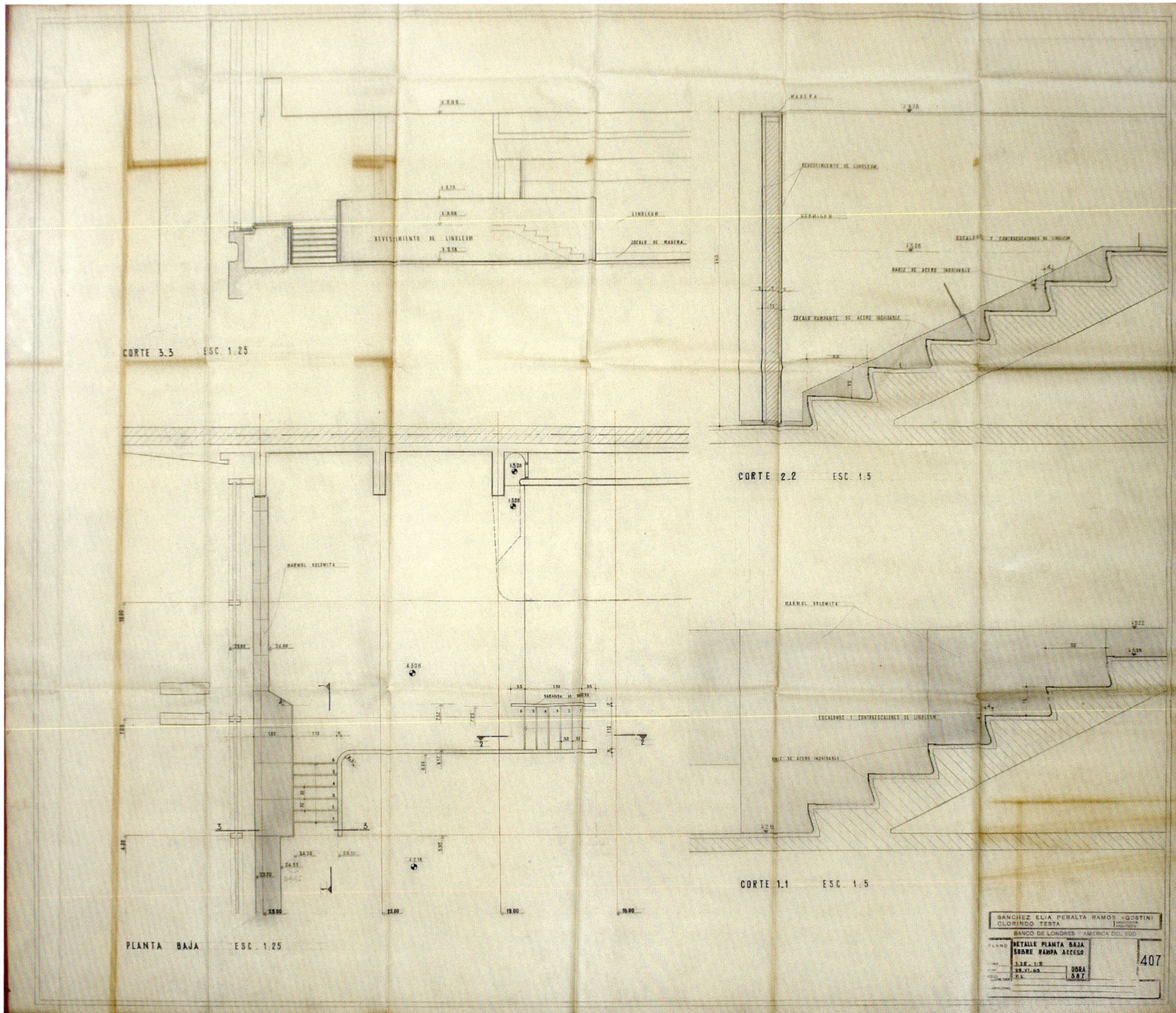

This page: Ground floor detail, over entrance ramp, 1965, SEPRA's studio file (plan 407). Scale 3:125, 3:25

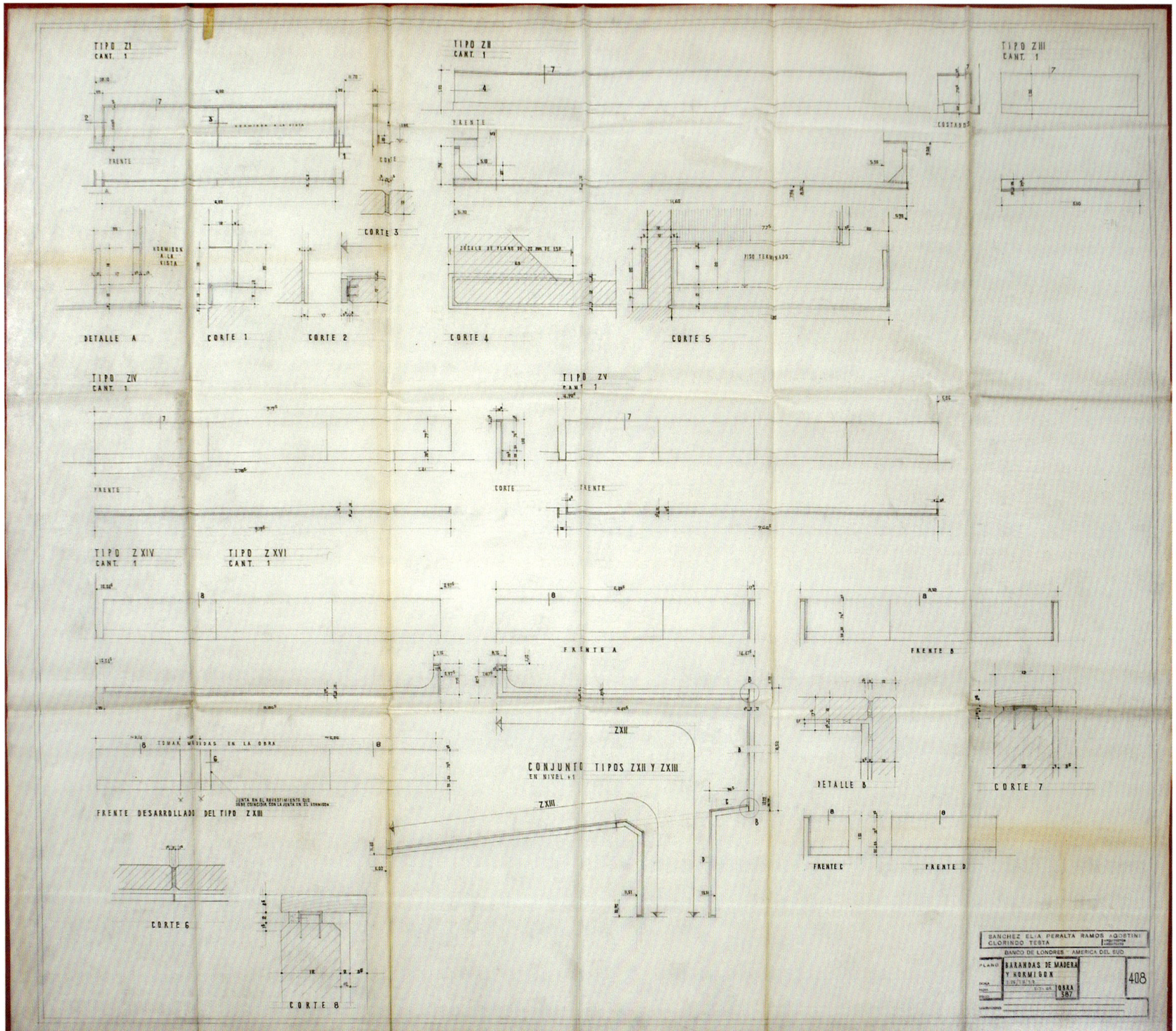
TIPO ZI
CANT. 1
FRENTE
CORTE 3
DETALLE A
CORTE 1
CORTE 2
TIPO ZII
CANT. 1
FRENTE
COSTADO
CORTE 4
CORTE 5
TIPO ZIII
CANT. 1
TIPO ZIV
CANT. 1
FRENTE
CORTE
TIPO ZV
CANT. 1
FRENTE
TIPO Z XIV
CANT. 1
TIPO Z XVI
CANT. 1
FRENTE A
FRENTE B
TOMAR MEDIDAS EN LA OBRA
FRENTE DESARROLLADO DEL TIPO Z XIII
CONJUNTO TIPOS ZXII Y ZXIII
EN NIVEL +1
ZXII
ZXIII
DETALLE B
CORTE 7
FRENTE C
FRENTE D
CORTE 6
CORTE 8
SANCHEZ ELIA PERALTA RAMOS AGOSTINI
CLORINDO TESTA
BANCO DE LONDRES Y AMERICA DEL SUD
PLANO
BARANDAS DE MADERA
Y HORMIGON
OBRA
387
408

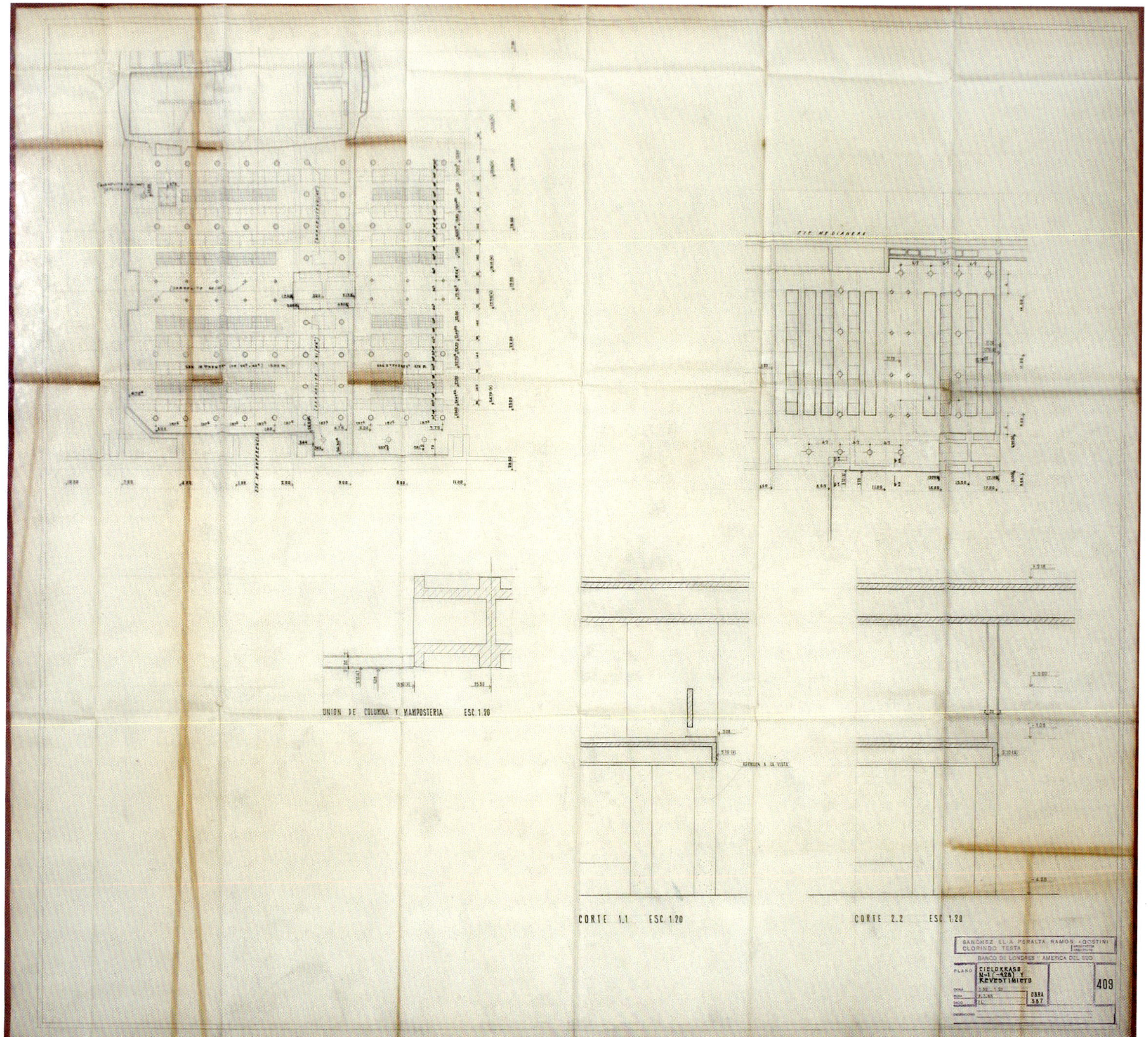

This page: Ceiling level -1, 1965, SEPRA's studio file (plan 409)

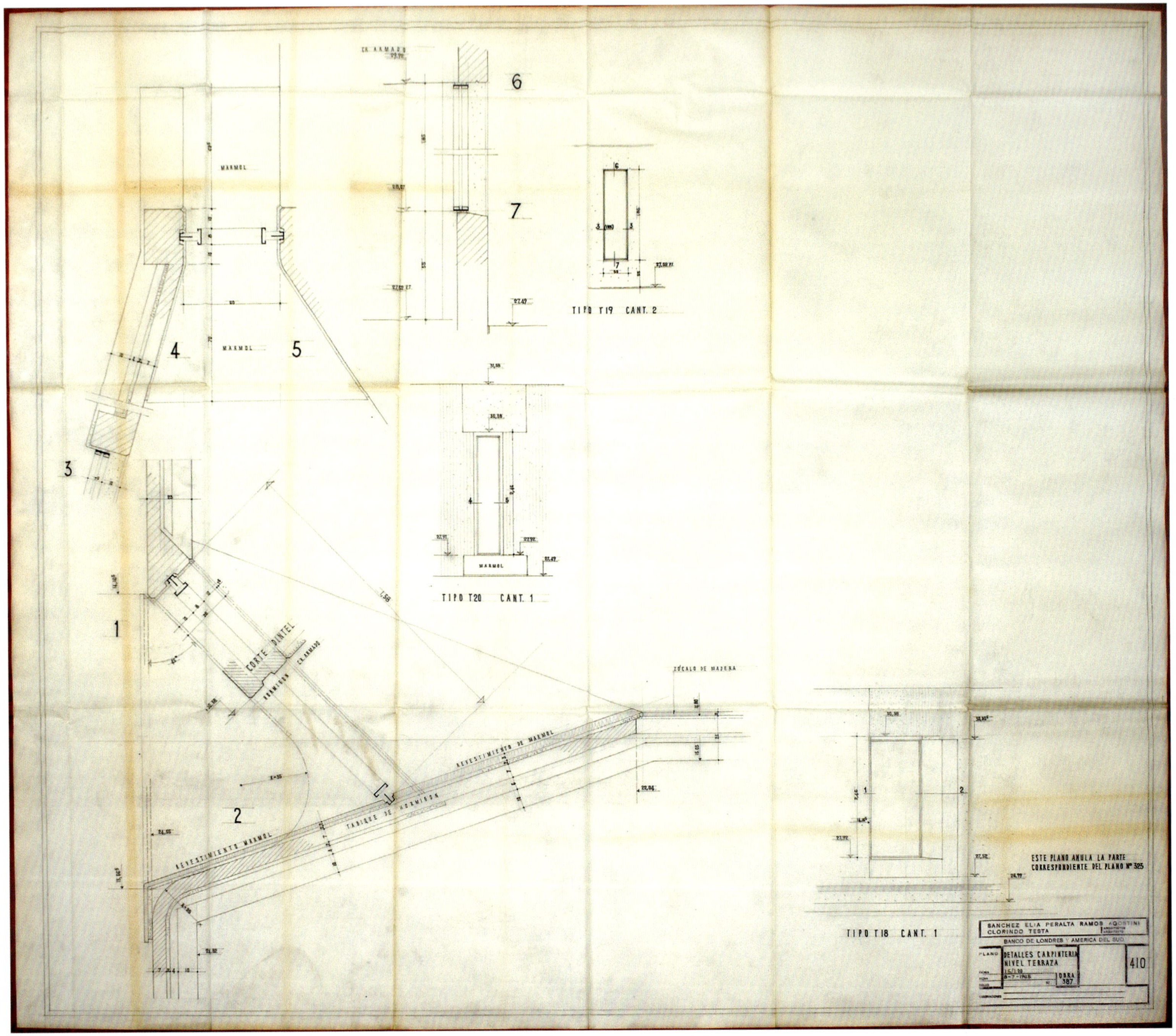
6
7
MARMOL
4
MARMOL
5
3
TIPO T19 CANT. 2
TIPO T20 CANT. 1
1
CORTE DINTEL
ZOCALO DE MADERA
REVESTIMIENTO DE MARMOL
TABIQUE DE HORMIGON
REVESTIMIENTO MARMOL
2
TIPO T18 CANT. 1
ESTE PLANO ANULA LA PARTE
CORRESPONDIENTE DEL PLANO Nº 325
SANCHEZ ELIA PERALTA RAMOS AGOSTINI
CLORINDO TESTA
BANCO DE LONDRES Y AMERICA DEL SUD
PLANO
DETALLES CARPINTERIA
NIVEL TERRAZA
8-7-1965
OBRA
387
410

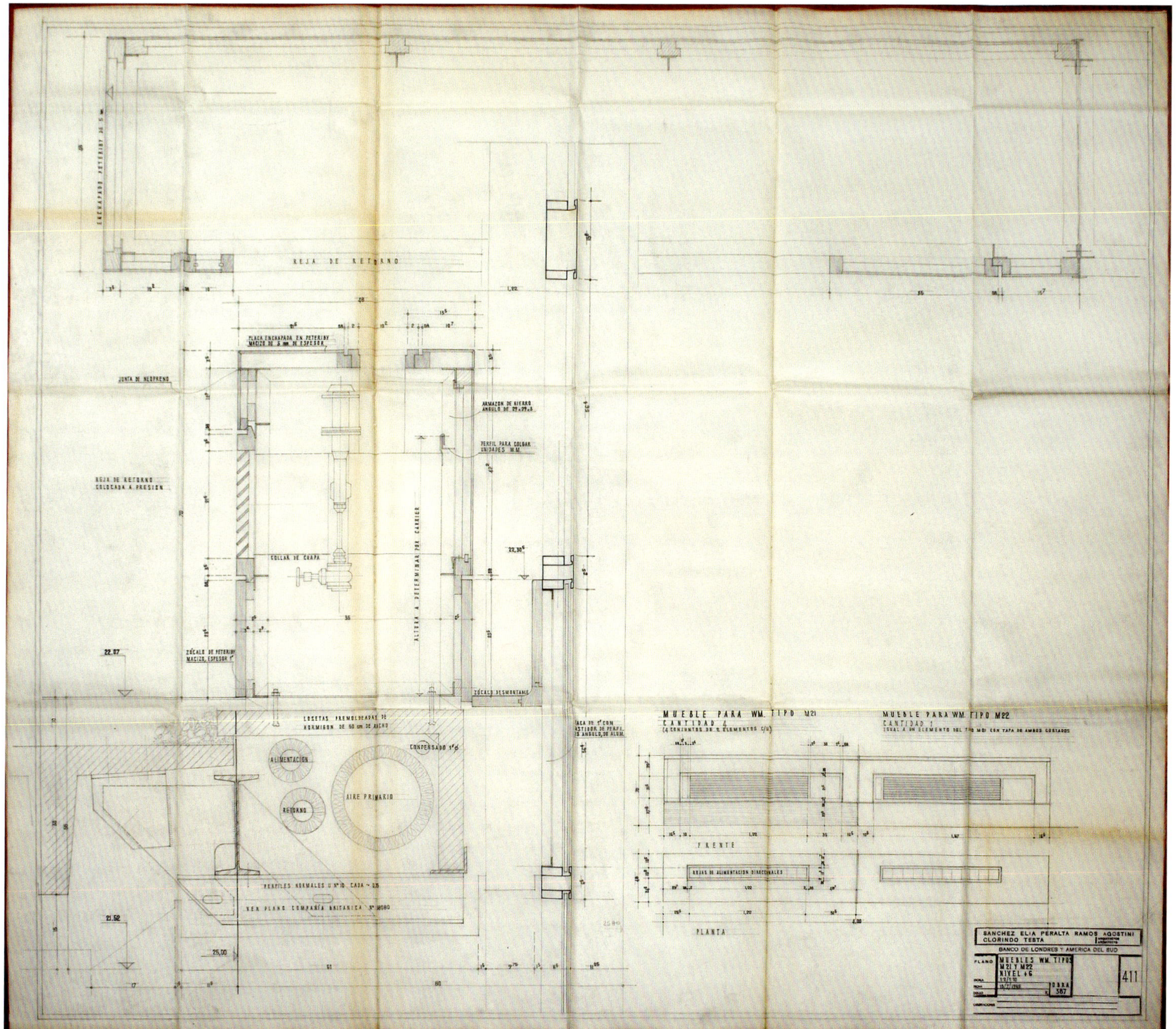

Opposite: Detail drawings of the windows at terrace level, 1965, SEPRA's studio file (plan 410)
This page: Fitted furniture details, 1965, SEPRA's studio file (plan 411). Scale 3:10, 3:50

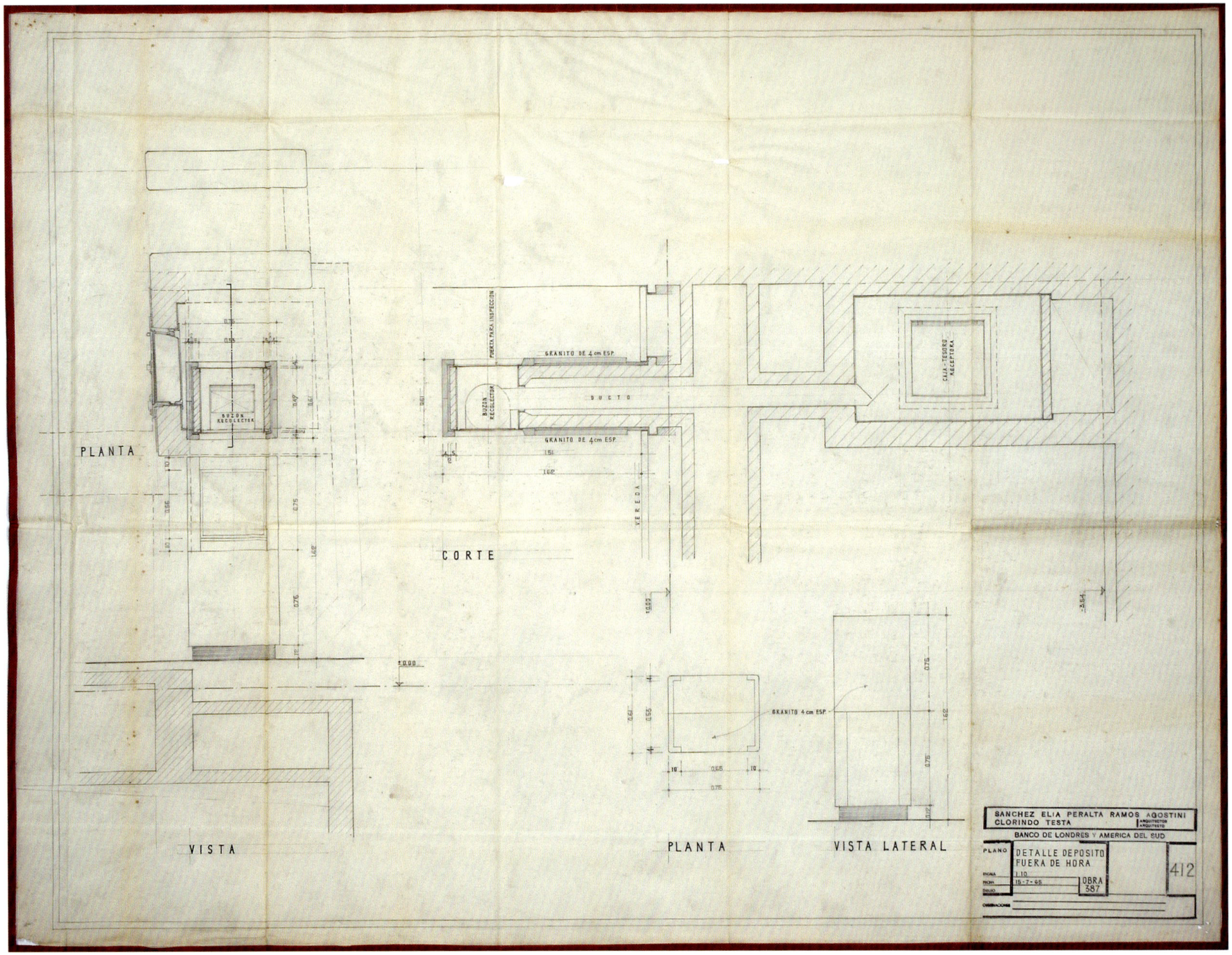
PLANTA
CORTE
VISTA
PLANTA
VISTA LATERAL
GRANITO DE 4 cm ESP.
DUCTO
VEREDA
SANCHEZ ELIA PERALTA RAMOS AGOSTINI
CLORINDO TESTA
BANCO DE LONDRES Y AMERICA DEL SUD
DETALLE DEPOSITO
FUERA DE HORA
OBRA 387
412

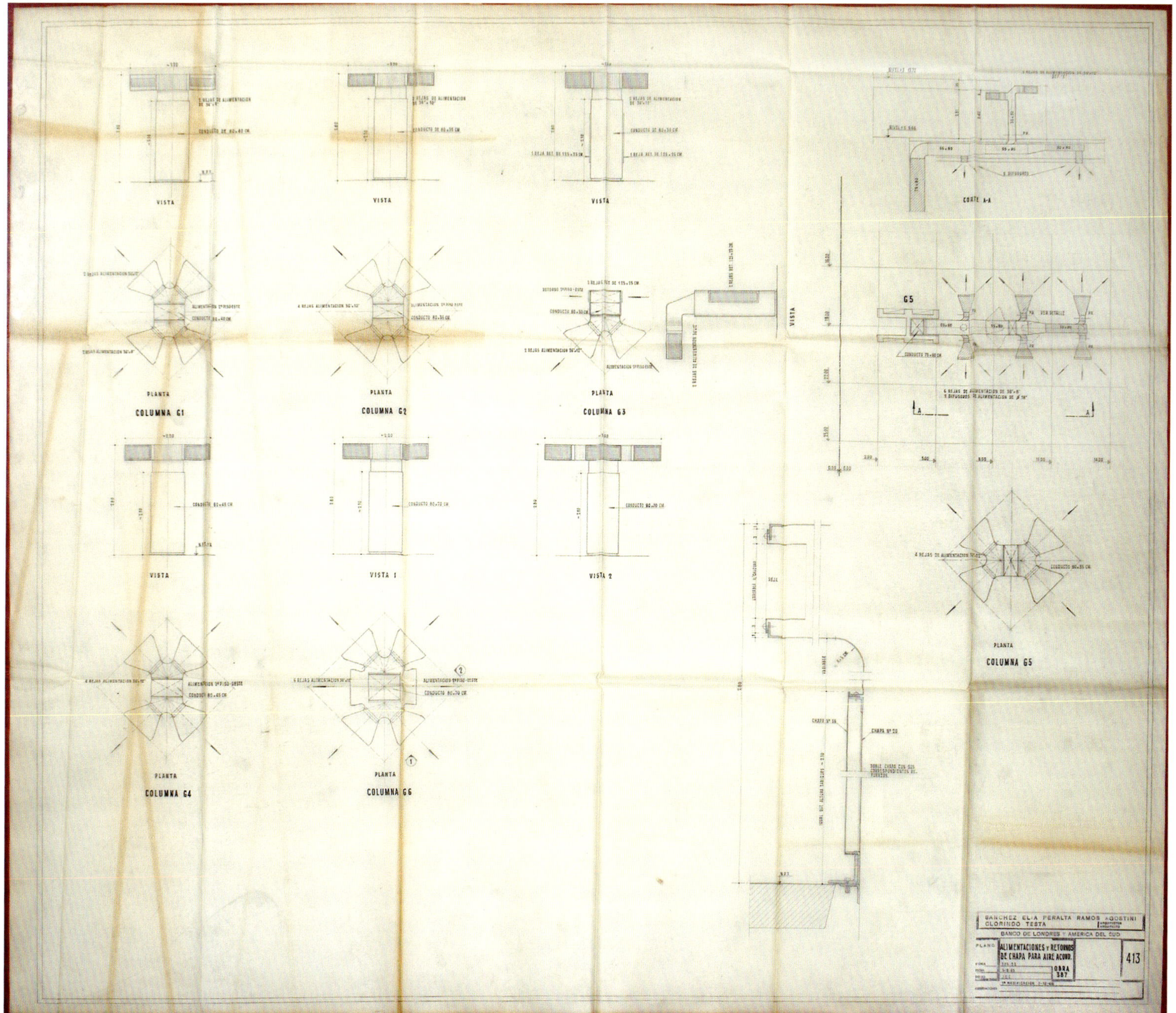

Opposite: Night time deposit box detail, 1965, SEPRA's studio file (plan 412). Scale 3:50
This page: Air conditioning duct detail, 1965, SEPRA's studio file (plan 413). Scale 3:125, 3:10

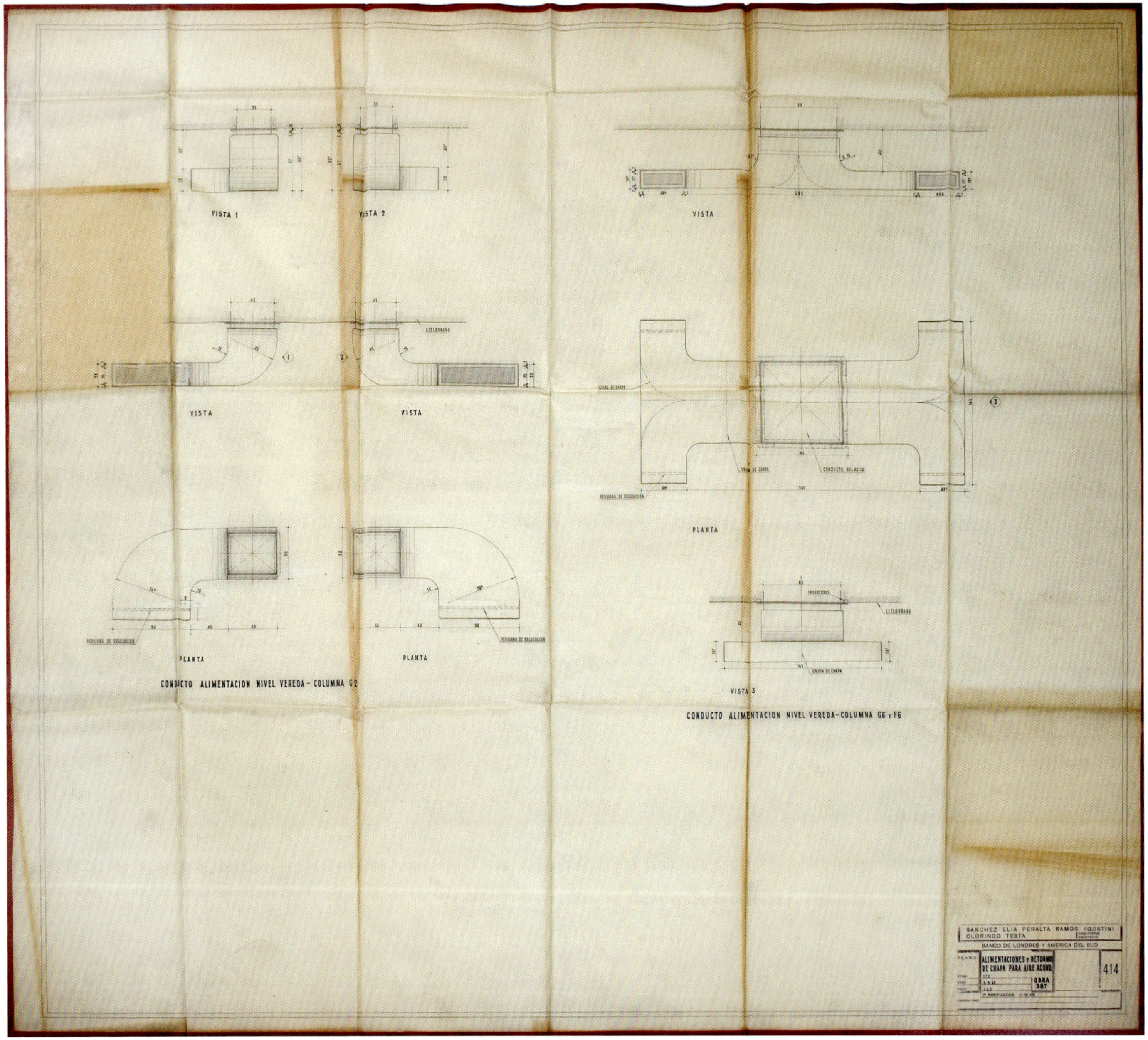
VISTA 1
VISTA 2
VISTA
CIELORRASO
VISTA
VISTA
PLANTA
PLANTA
PERSIANA DE REGULACION
CONDUCTO ALIMENTACION NIVEL VEREDA - COLUMNA G2
PLANTA
VISTA 3
INYECTORES
CIELORRASO
UNION DE CHAPA
CONDUCTO ALIMENTACION NIVEL VEREDA - COLUMNA G6 y F6
SANCHEZ ELIA PERALTA RAMOS AGOSTINI
CLORINDO TESTA
BANCO DE LONDRES Y AMERICA DEL SUD
ALIMENTACIONES y RETORNOS DE CHAPA PARA AIRE ACOND.
OBRA 387
414

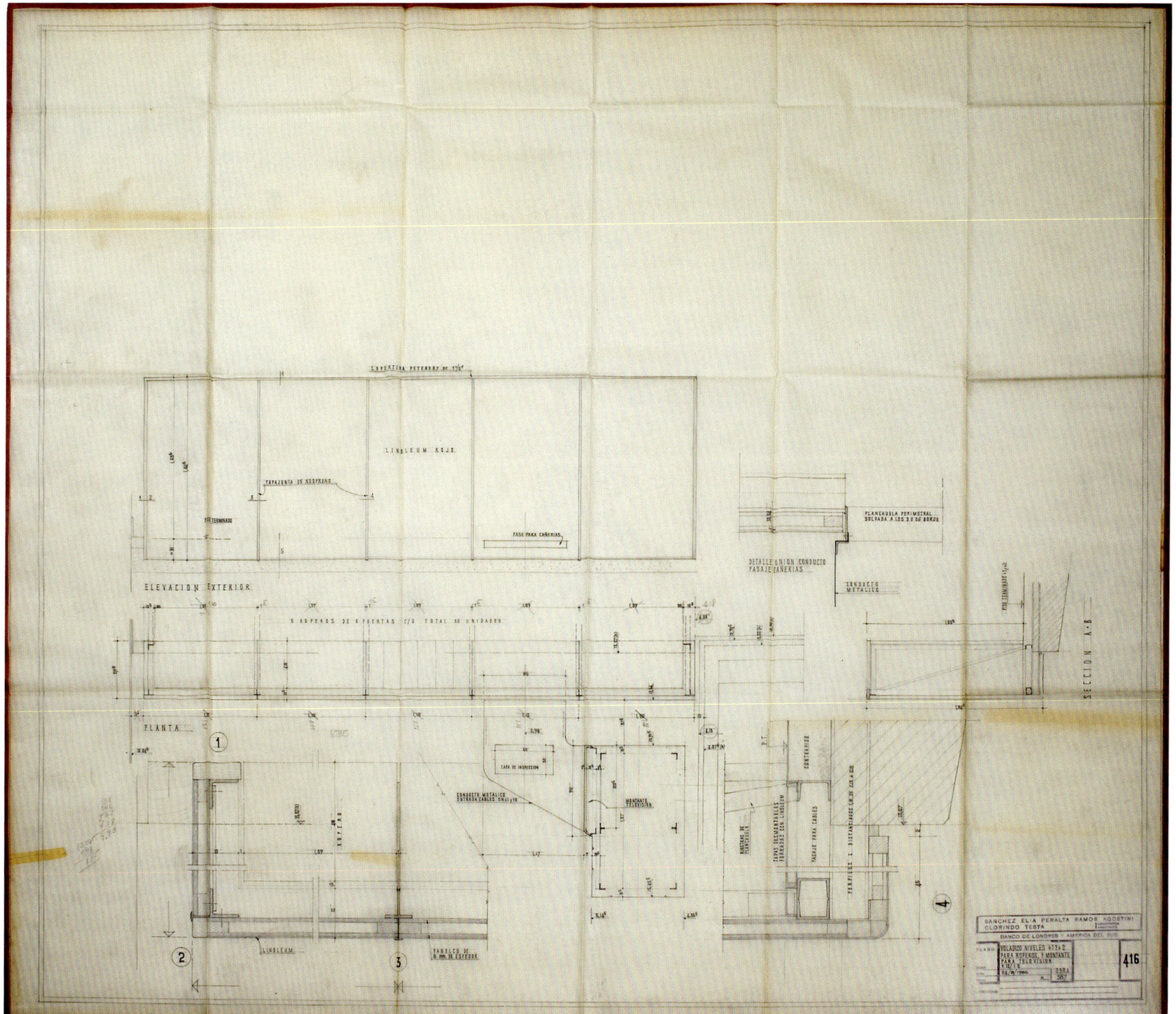

Opposite: Air conditioning duct detail, 1965, SEPRA's studio file (plan 414). Scale 3:50
This page: Cantilever details for wardrobes and TV, 1965, SEPRA's studio file (plan 416). Scale 3:50, 3:10

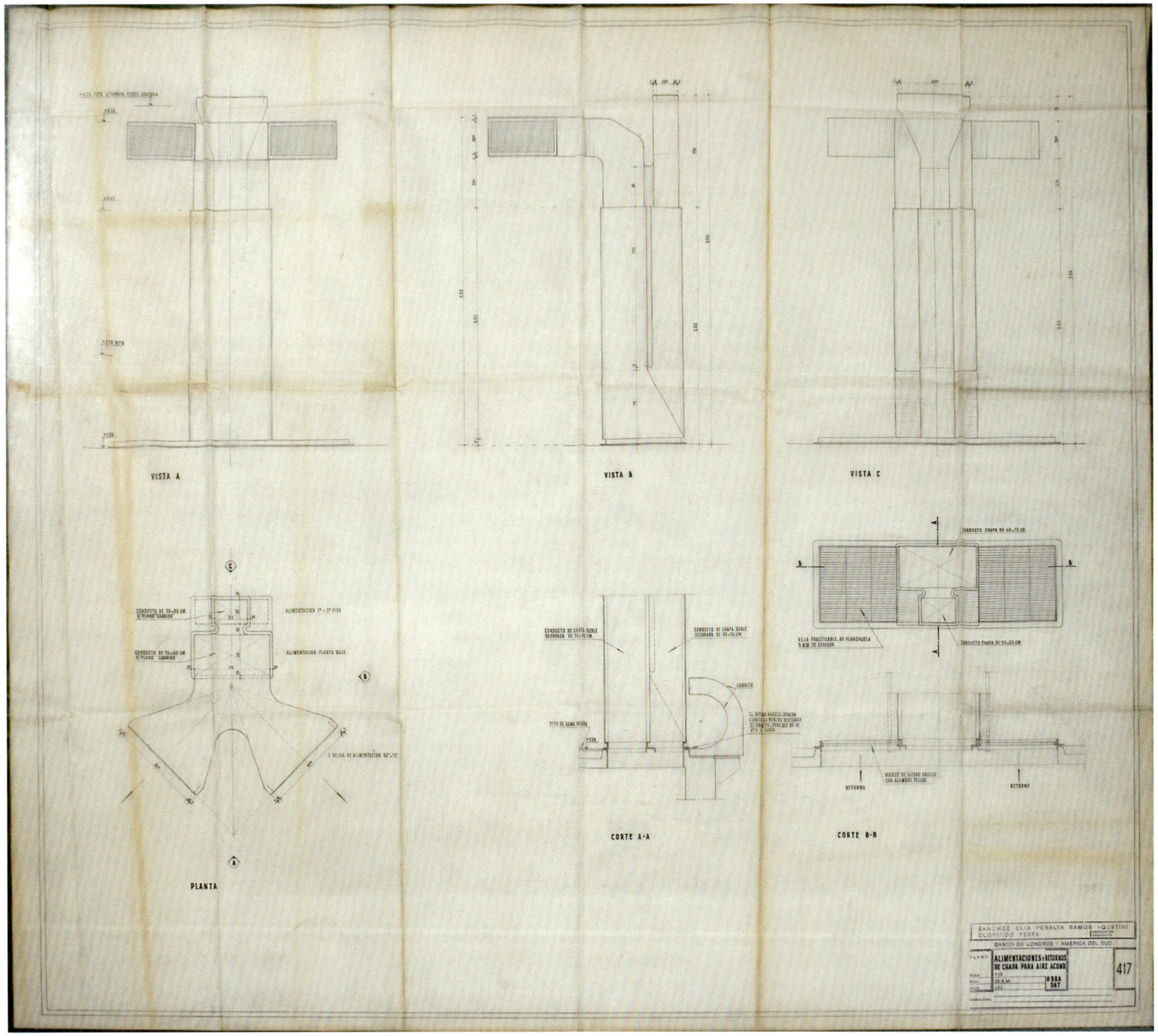

VISTA A
VISTA B
VISTA C
PLANTA
CORTE A-A
CORTE B-B
SANCHEZ ELIA PERALTA RAMOS AGOSTINI
CLORINDO TESTA
BANCO DE LONDRES Y AMERICA DEL SUD
PLANO
ALIMENTACIONES y RETORNOS DE CHAPA PARA AIRE ACOND.
OBRA 387
417

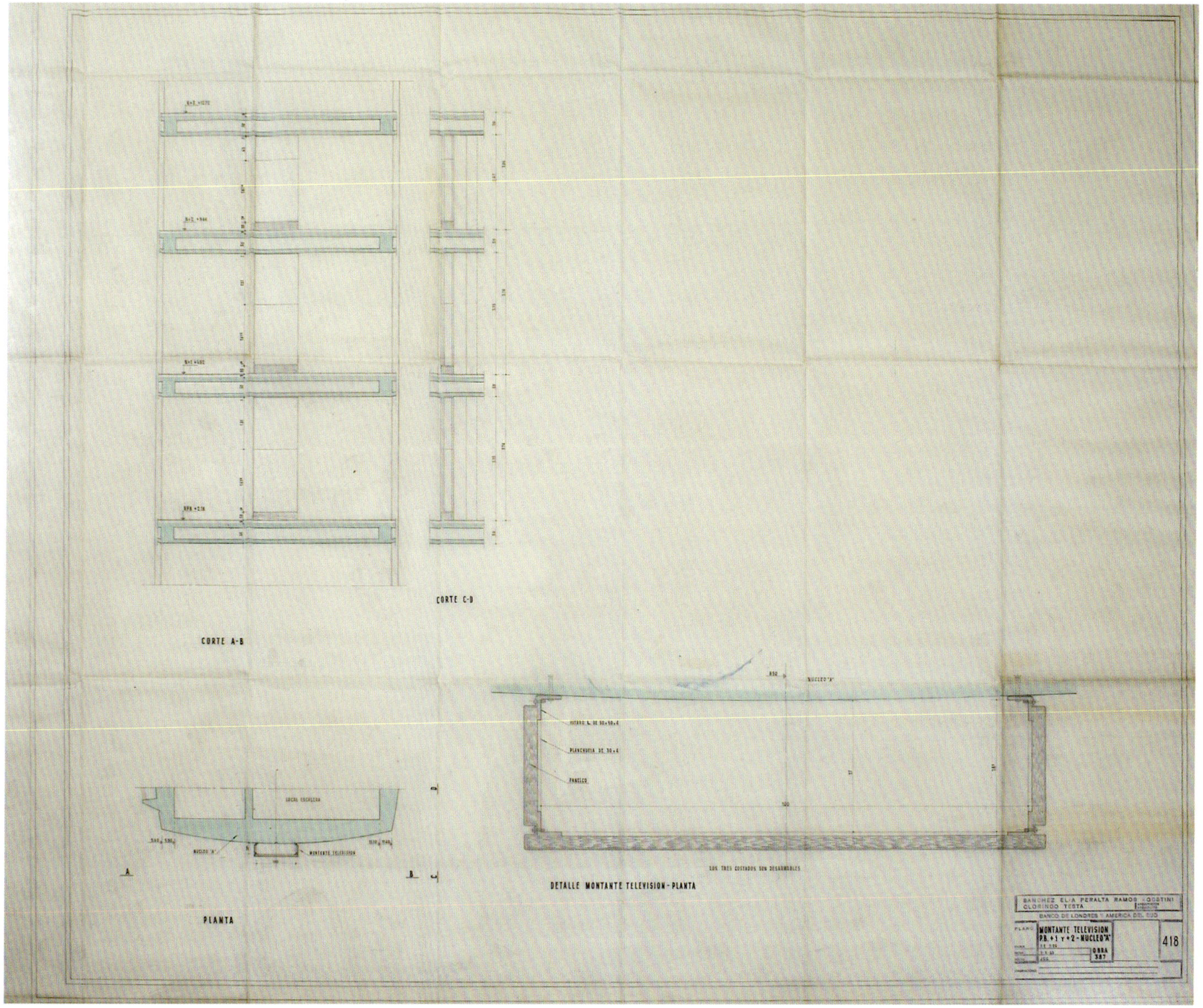

Opposite: Air conditioning duct detail, 1965, SEPRA's studio file (plan 417). Scale 3:50
This page: TV duct at Core A, levels: ground floor, +1, +2, 1963, SEPRA's studio file (plan 418). Scale 3:10, 3:125

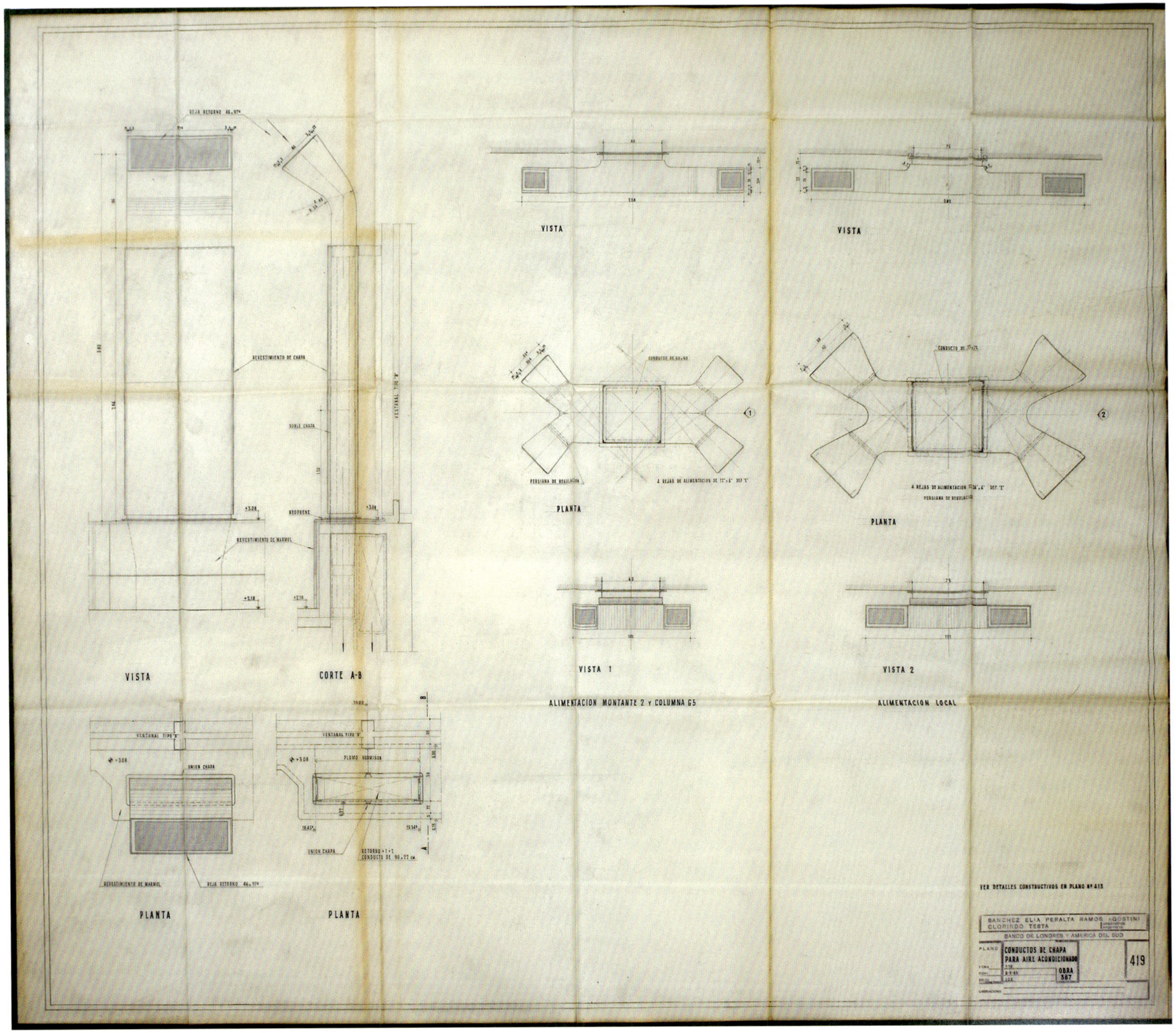
VISTA
CORTE A-B
PLANTA
PLANTA
VISTA
VISTA
PLANTA
PLANTA
VISTA 1
VISTA 2
ALIMENTACION MONTANTE 2 y COLUMNA G5
ALIMENTACION LOCAL
VER DETALLES CONSTRUCTIVOS EN PLANO Nº 413
SANCHEZ ELIA PERALTA RAMOS AGOSTINI
CLORINDO TESTA
BANCO DE LONDRES Y AMERICA DEL SUD
CONDUCTOS DE CHAPA PARA AIRE ACONDICIONADO
OBRA 587
419

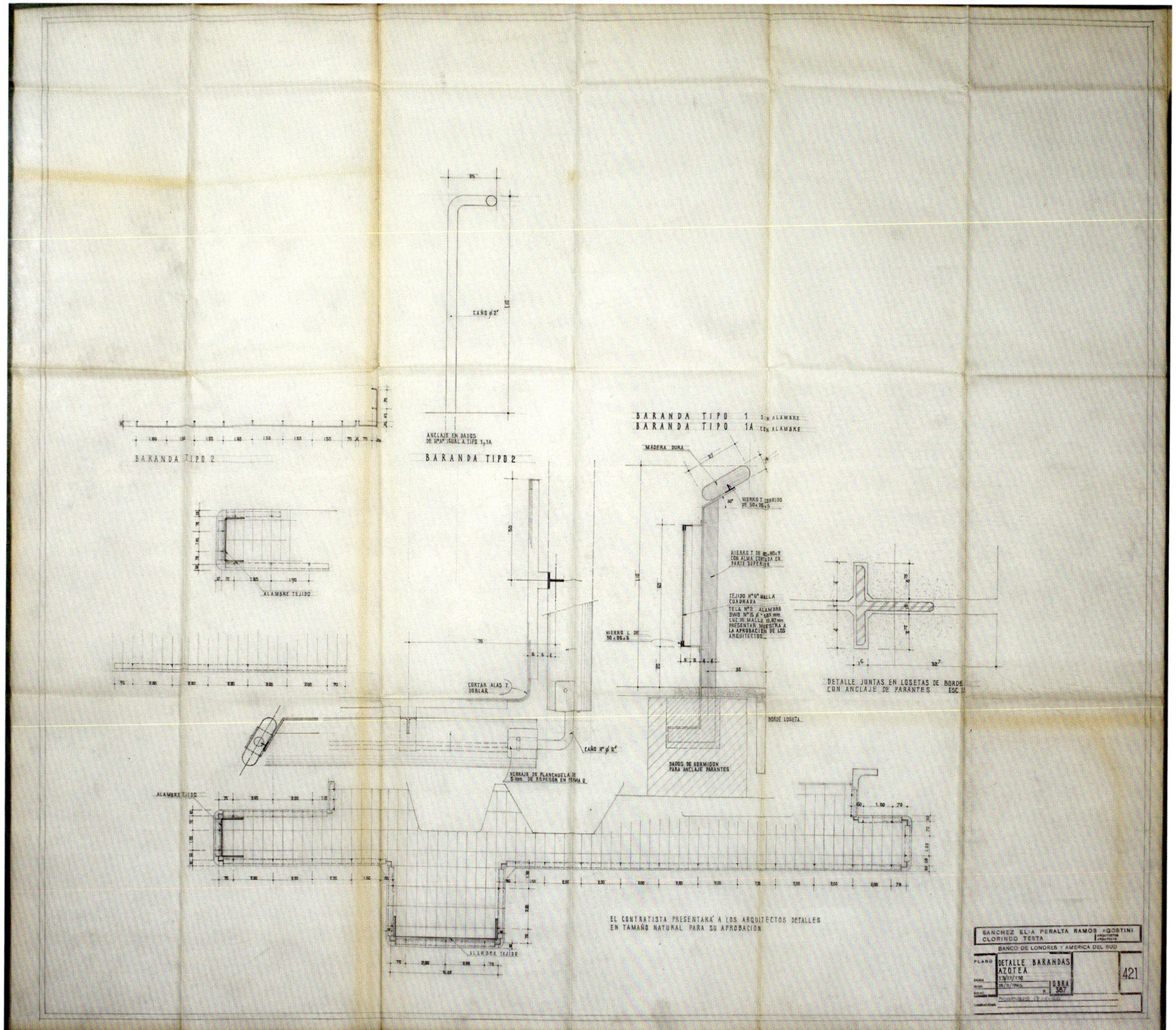

Opposite: Air conditioning duct detail, 1965, SEPRA's studio file (plan 419). Scale 3:50
This page: Detail drawings of the terrace handrail, 1965, SEPRA's studio file (plan 421). Scale 3:25

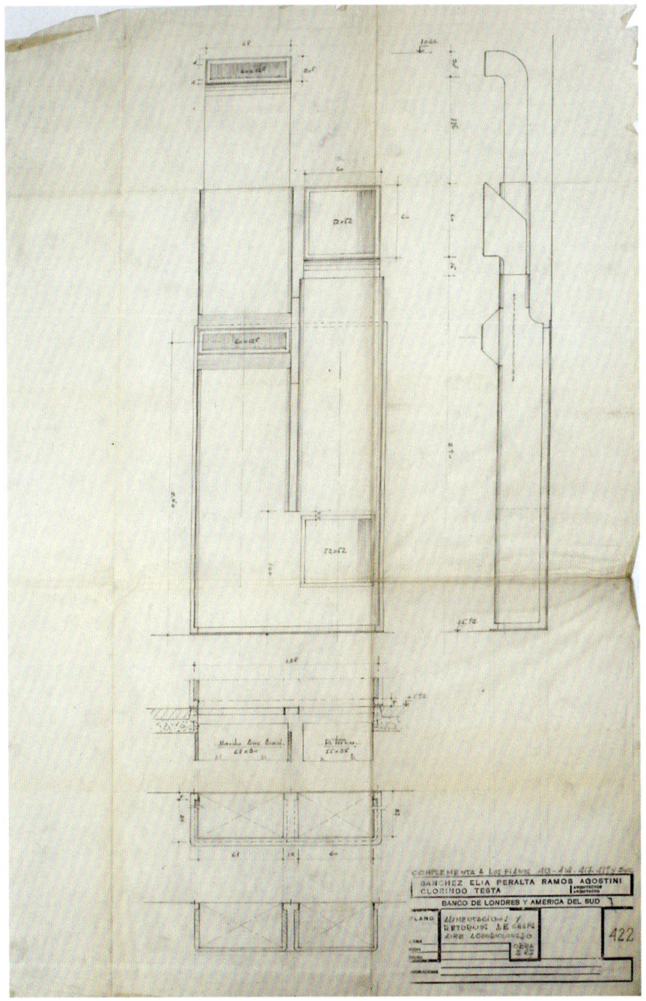
SANCHEZ ELIA PERALTA RAMOS AGOSTINI
CLORINDO TESTA
BANCO DE LONDRES Y AMERICA DEL SUD
PLANO
422

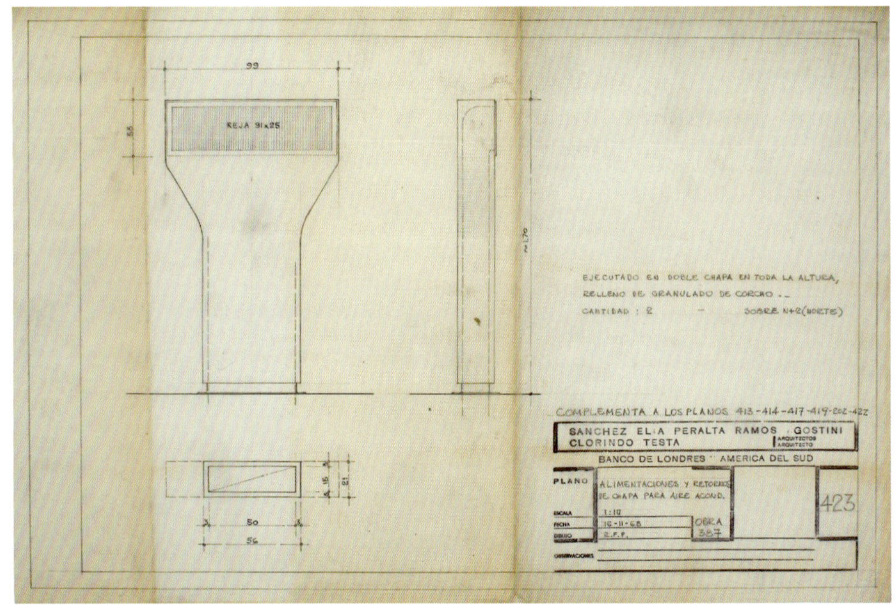
99
REJA 91x25
EJECUTADO EN DOBLE CHAPA EN TODA LA ALTURA,
RELLENO DE GRANULADO DE CORCHO .-
CANTIDAD : 2 - SOBRE N+2(NORTE)
COMPLEMENTA A LOS PLANOS 413-414-417-419-202-422
SANCHEZ ELIA PERALTA RAMOS GOSTINI
CLORINDO TESTA
ARQUITECTOS
ARQUITECTO
BANCO DE LONDRES AMERICA DEL SUD
PLANO
ALIMENTACIONES Y RETORNOS
DE CHAPA PARA AIRE ACOND.
ESCALA
1:10
FECHA
16-11-68
DIBUJO
OBRA
387
OBSERVACIONES
423
50

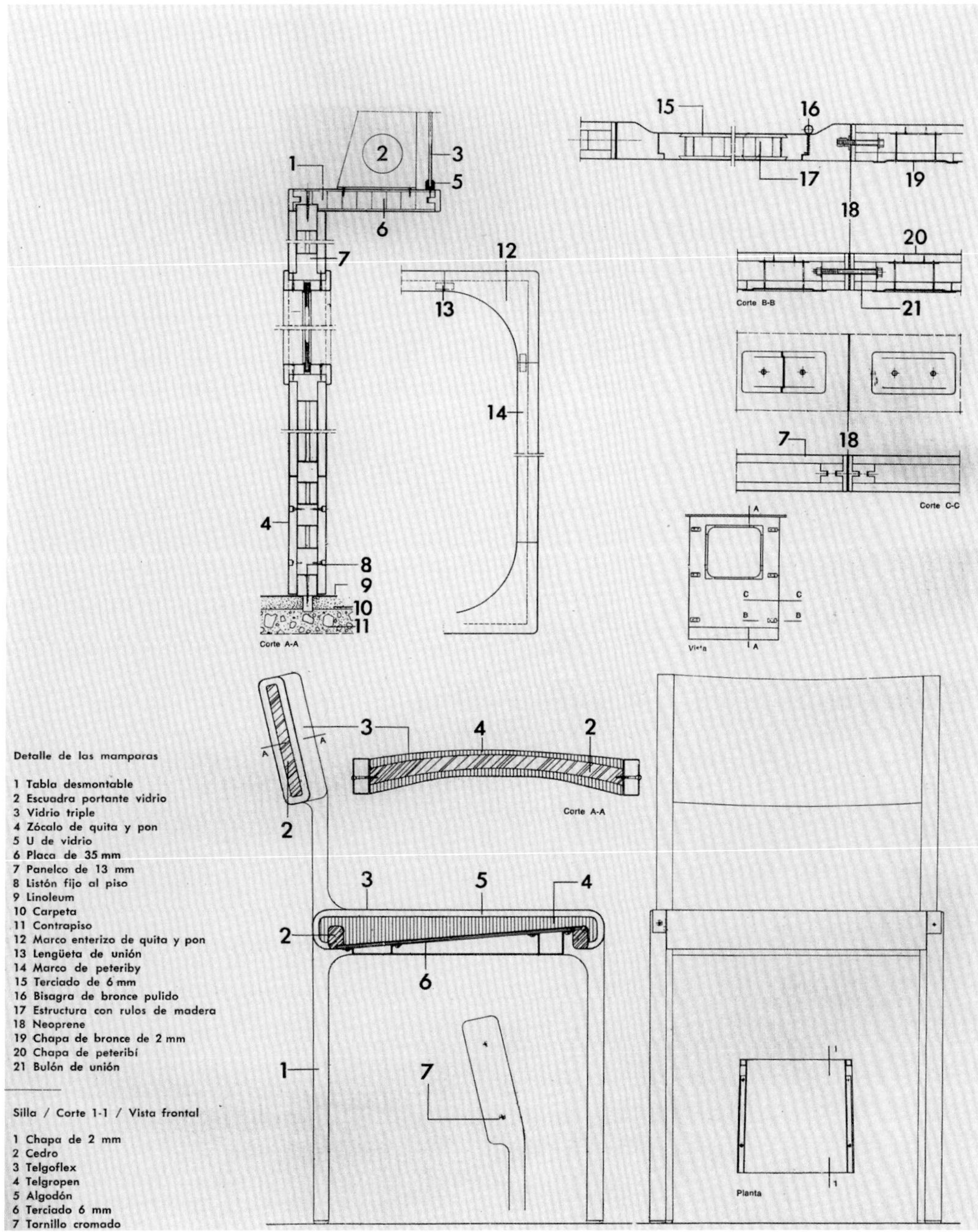

Opposite: Air conditioning duct detail, 1965, SEPRA's studio file (plan 422)
Air conditioning duct detail, 1965, SEPRA's studio file (plan 423). Scale 1:10
This page: Chair and screen details, published in Summa 6-7, 1966, Pag. 37.

Photographs

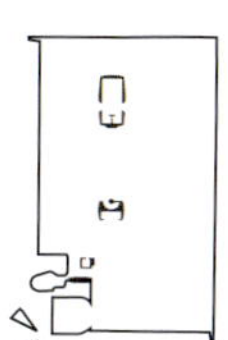

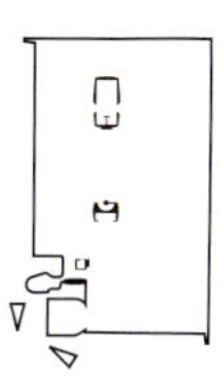

dor de dueños

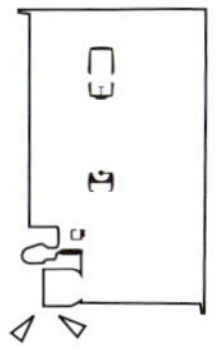

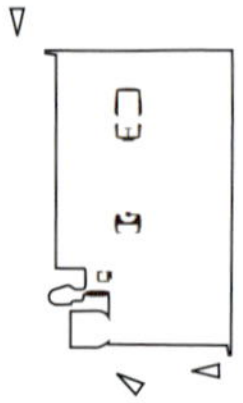

BBVA
Banco
Francés

EL PODER

BBVA
Banco
Francés
Solo
Acceso a
Cocheras

rio
creador de dueños

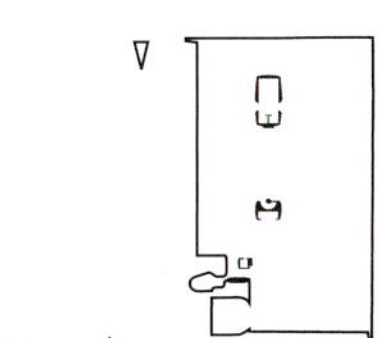

O'NFM 4

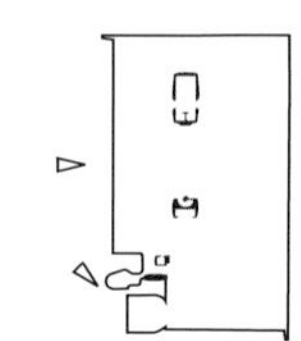

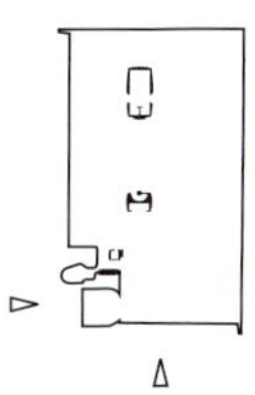

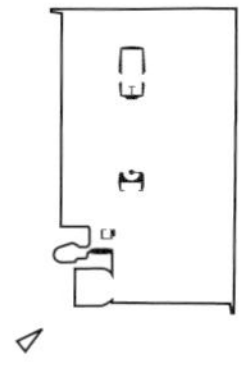

197

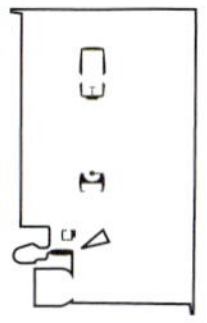

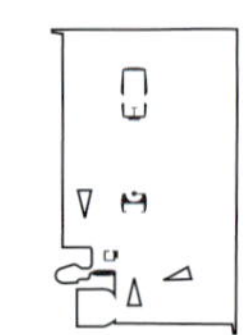

Acérquese
asesoramiento
Tarjetas de crédito
cajas de ahorro,
préstamos
seguros.
Atención al cliente
SALIDA

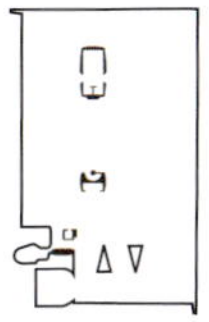

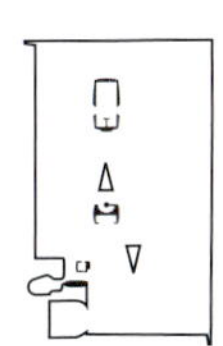

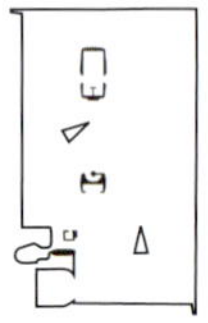

O'NFM 4

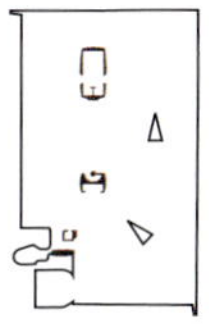

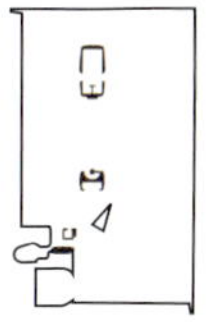

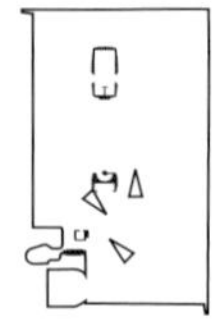

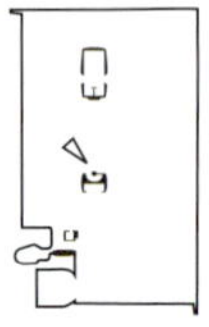

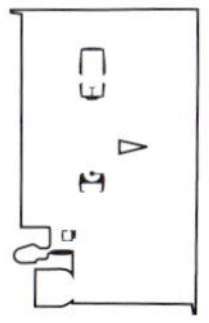

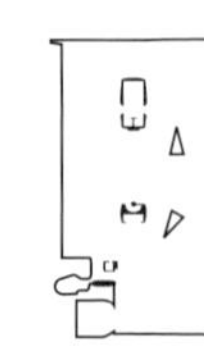

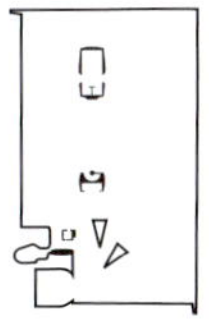

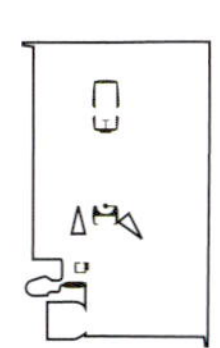

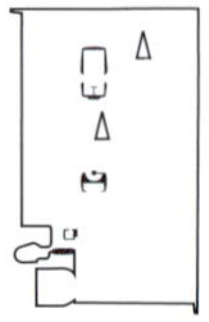

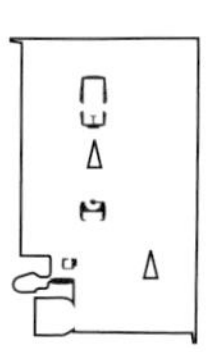

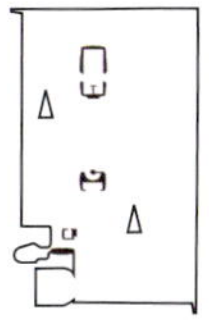

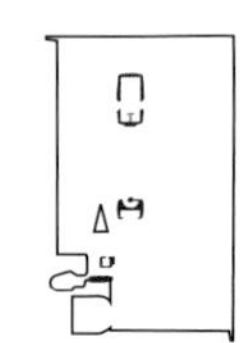

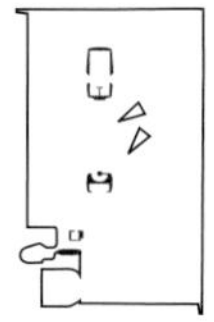

Interview, Biographies & Credits

Interview

50 years later: a conversation with Clorindo Testa
Buenos Aires 2010
Interviewers: Manuel Cuadra and Wilfried Wang
Translation: Ilan Vit

FIRST SESSION:

MC: *Clorindo, we would like to understand the architecture of the Banco de Londres y América del Sud and, especially, its effect: it is a mysterious work, which signifies a lot to those who are exposed to it, either local people or those who come from far away to contemplate it. We would like to see what lies behind it. We could begin to talk about the concrete circumstances and the moment in which you came up with the conceptualization of this project by the end of the 1950s.*

CT: By the end of 1959, Sánchez Elía, Peralta Ramos and Agostini called me to participate in an international competition for the monument to Batle y Ordóñez in Montevideo. So we entered the competition, and three proposals were selected for a second round: one was French, another one was Spanish, and the third one was ours. By the end of the second round, the first prize was declared void and the second one was given to the French proposal, and for us a mention. That was the beginning of my relationship with Sánchez Elía, Peralta Ramos and Agostini. The following year, the Banco's London headquarter had sent an architect, Gerald Wakeham, to Buenos Aires to set up a competition and select the architects that would be invited to participate, among them the studio of Sánchez Elía, Peralta Ramos and Agostini. Just as in the case of the competition for the Batle y Ordóñez Monument, they asked me if I wanted to participate.

Gerald Wakeham then reviewed the proposals. The others were more conventional. For example, the direction of the Banco asked to widen the street. We thought that it was not convenient to break the block's alignment, so we pushed the façade on the lower level to the back, but, in the upper levels it remained in place, so the block's envelope would not be broken. The Banco's Board of Directors decided to follow Wakeham's criteria. After the competition, everything flowed smoothly. The tender documents were sent out and construction began. The Banco intervened: one of its rules was that none of the Banco's functionaries could call the architects asking for specific changes. Everything had to go through Gerald Wakeham, who analyzed the request and determined if it was appropriate or not.

MC: *A stupendous regulation!*

CT: Yes, fantastic:our only relation was with Wakeham.

MC: *...with a fellow architect...*

CT: Gerald Wakeham was very smart. I remember that every single month a note on the construction's advancement would come out in the magazine "Sucesos Argentinos", which made it a well known enterprise. On inauguration day, 25,000 persons entered the Banco as soon as it opened its doors. And I remember that the first person who entered received a bouquet of roses, and, afterwards, the poor guy did not know what to do with it...

MC: *How do you explain to yourself the Banco's impact?*

CT: The building was different from what people used to see in Buenos Aires. Its covered space, its transparency, because when one looks from the inside out, the façade is not the Banco's façade, but the façade of the Banco de la Nación on the other side of the street.

MC: *And where did the idea for such a space come from?*

CT: Because it functioned properly. Sánchez Elía was a very energetic, fantastic construction leader. Agostini was a smart and alert architect, so, with him and Sánchez Elía – because Peralta Ramos was in charge of other works – we made the project. How did we come up with it? I do not remember. We wanted to make

Figurine collection of Clorindo Testa
Manuel Cuadra, 2010

a central space; you know what I mean? We wanted a clear distinction between the Banco's public area and its inner functions: the latter is suspended from the upper slab, and the former is beneath.

MC: *Everything with "legs" is public and that which is suspended...*

CT: Yes: what is suspended is internal. The Banco practically did not have any enclosed spaces, only those for the directors were closed.

MC: *What you were able to develop sounds very natural, but, on the other side it was completely different.*

CT: Yes. But I do not recall having thought with either Peralta or Agostini that what we were doing something completely different. It all started as a natural way to respond to the Banco's requests.

MC: *Knowing SEPRA's work, I understand how Sánchez Elía contributed to provide the building with its outstanding material quality.*

CT: Yes, and the contractors worked extremely well.

MC: *Agostini's contribution is understood as that of a colleague with whom you could speak. But the conceptualization of the project itself is more your thing, isn't it?*

CT: In regards to the project, those who solved its problems were Agostini and me...And Sánchez Elía, who supported us...

MC: *Agostini died young...*

Clorindo Testa's Office, Buenos Aires

CT: Yes, in fact, all three have died. All of them were more or less ten years older than me.

MC: *Why do they not have equivalent works?*

CT: Works of quality they have...

MC: *...but this is not their kind of architecture...*

CT: ...no, it is not.

MC: *....maybe it is more yours...*

CT: ...yes...It is a thing of the moment... There was a good dynamic in the team with Sánchez Elía, Peralta and Agostini.

MC: *It was an exceptional moment.*

CT: Yes, it was. Everything started with the Batle y Ordóñez Monument. The place selected for the commemoration had a unique landscaping quality, because it was a mound on an island near the coastline.

MC: *Was your proposal for the Batle y Ordóñez Monument a prelude to what was to come later with the Banco?*

CT: Facing Montevideo there was a circle, partially open, with a ramp going upwards. That was the idea: to see the city from afar, through the monument. MC: *I love what you are saying, because you are describing a landscape above all: what you proposed was a point of view and a promenade.*

MC: *This type of work with the landscape, could also be related to the Banco?*

CT: It could, because we worked, let us say, with the surroundings of the Banco.

MC: *Perhaps, the Bank also proposes an inner landscape?*

CT: It is like a covered plaza. That was our idea.

MC: *It is a covered plaza that offers a promenade and different points of view…*

CT: There are the mechanical stairs, and after that, the spiral staircase, the elevators. And on the back, the Banco's inner circulation.

MC: *It all sounds very natural, quite simple, very logical. But is this enough to explain the fascination posed by this type of architecture?*

CT: I do not know.

MC: *The building functions extremely well and its structure is very clear. But, that does not explain the charm it has on people…*

CT: Yes, I do not know.

MC: *You said, if we look at the building from the outside, of getting rid of the façade to widen the street.*

CT: The competition asked to widen the street because it was very narrow, and we thought the neighborhood's alignment, up above, should remain continuous, like everywhere else.

MC: *That is an aspect of the façades designs…*

CT: After that are the "legs." The upper module is a reticulated slab of three by six meters. That is, the legs are separated by three meters each. But, to avoid closing the space beneath, some columns would open and join some of their neighbors: there are three legs that remain straight, and two others that join together. After that, the legs received the perforated screens, what made them rigid. In the original proposal there were circles, and the only thing that the Banco's Director asked us, through Gerald Wakeham, was if we could change a little those circles, because they reminded him of a Gruyère cheese. Then from the circles we shifted to squares with rounded corners.

MC: *That is fine, I understand such logic and its results.*

CT: What I was telling you before, that the façade is transparent and that you do not see the "legs" from the inside, but from

Clorindo Testa's Office, Buenos Aires

the Banco de la Nación, well that came about later. It is not like we thought about it, at that moment.

MC: *Yes, but even so, it is wonderful: that the pillars below start thin and as they rise become wider. When you are inside looking out, those pillars enable you to orient yourself, they tell you if you are at a lower or upper level, according to the truss you have in front of you. And that is a great quality: it individualizes each point in which one finds oneself…*

CT: Yes, that also happens.

MC: *What I wonder is what do people, who know nothing about architecture, see in the building, because the interest of someone who knows nothing is...*

CT: I think the building still has attraction, because it is still very different from any other bank, or any other place in Buenos Aires.

MC: *At its moment, it must have had something futuristic.*

CT: And distinct. That is why twenty five thousand people came the day it opened.

MC: *A second subject, we would like to talk about, has to do with the fact that you, besides being an architect, you are also a painter. What were you painting in that period?*

CT: The same as today.

MC: *Your paintings, your drawings, have different motifs over time...*

CT: Around the 1960s it was a more abstract type of painting.

MC: *What attracted you? Do you remember?*

CT: No, because I think I have always done the same thing.

MC: *How did you start painting?*

CT: I started to paint because I was always drawing.

MC: *Since childhood...*

CT: Yes. Three years after graduation, almost four, when I was in Europe, Franz van Riel, whose father had an art gallery in calle Florida, told me, when you come back to Buenos Aires, come by, so we can make an exhibition. The drawings I did back then, were those of an architect...When I had to prepare the exhibition, I started to change my manner of drawing doing both things simultaneously: architecture and painting.

MC: *Once a painter: what kind of interests have you had, what kind of themes?*

CT: They keep on changing, because that was the year 1950, and now we are in 2010, things change, and you keep on moving according to the times.

Sketching, Clorindo Testa

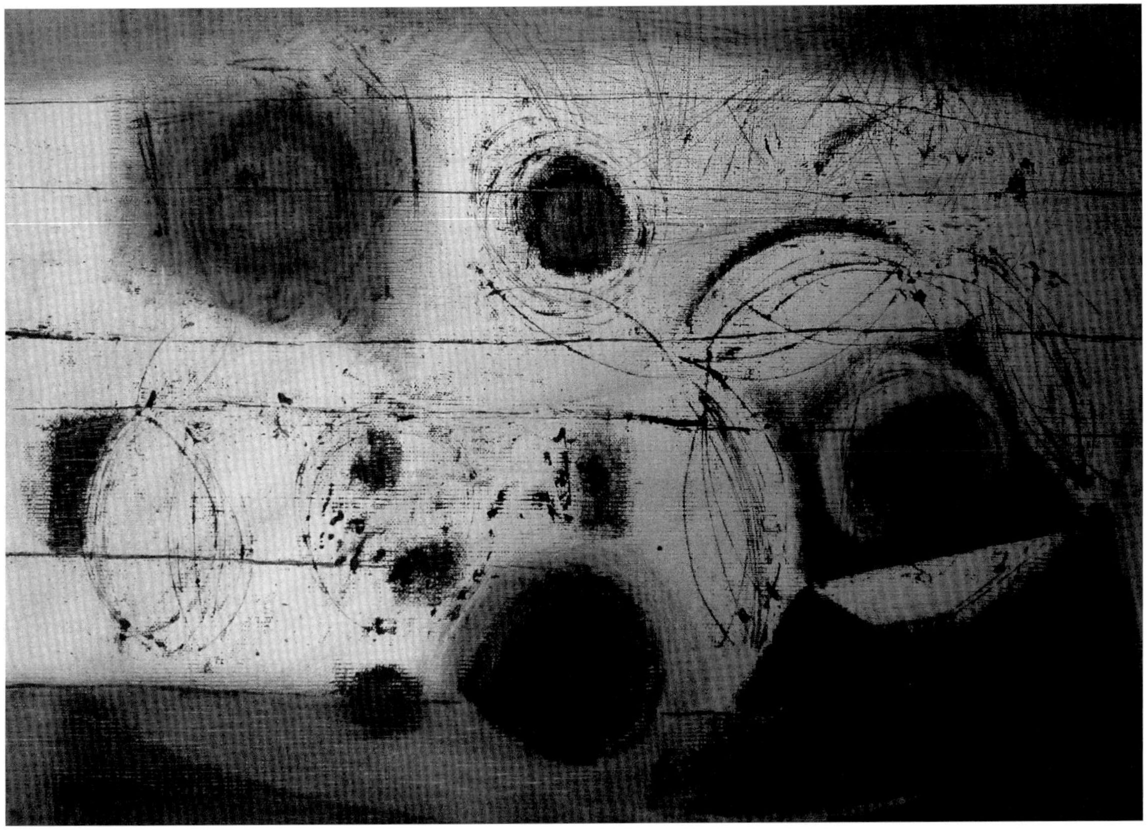

Painting, Clorindo Testa

MC: *When you speak about the Banco, you make all references to more or less objective requirements. Regarding your painting, are you also that objective, or there are no words for that?*

CT: All things are always thought. The Banco responded very well and keeps on responding to its inner function.

MC: *And in painting?*

CT: I think in painting a similar thing happens. That is, things are never improvised. There are painters who do it just like that and they are excellent, those who throw paint against the canvas. That is one way of painting. Another way is the one in which you know what you are about to do. After that things evolve, certainly. But, you more or less know. You do not stand against the empty canvas, and say: what should I do now?

MC: *You say you have a painting from 1960 or so, hanging somewhere...*

CT: Yes, I think it is from 1961.

MC: *If you like, could you tell what it is about?*

CT: There are circles and lines. They seem to resemble bicycles, but they are not so. And that one is also from the 1960s, I think...let me see...I have to take a look...57. Yes, it is from 1957.

MC: *And how it may have come about, let us say, what was the subject or the question you posed yourself at the time?*

CT: I do not remember.

MC: *Is the theme an attempt to organize figures?*

CT: Yes. It was an abstract painting, that was the trend of the time...

MC: *When you say you make architecture and make paintings, does one have something to do with the other, or is there no connection between them?*

CT: No, in fact, they have nothing in common. The way in which I face both is the same.

Clorindo Testa living room

You think things through.

MC: When I stand in front of a painting, one of yours, for example, either something happens between the painting and me or nothing happens: that is what enables one to talk about a work of art or not. I wonder if something similar happens with a work of architecture, like the Banco. People who visit the building, though they know little about architecture, are moved...

CT: Yes, I think it is so. But why?

SECOND SESSION:

WW: How do you divide your time in terms of working on projects and working on paintings?

CT: My activities in one and the other have always been together for a long time ago. As I sit here, I can do something about architecture, then, stand up and paint. Generally on Saturday mornings is when I finish my paintings.

WW: And you don't just make paintings, you also make objects and installations.

CT: Certainly, but they always have a specific aim. This, for instance, is a glyptodont... an animal that used to live in Patagonia, thousands of years ago. It was fun, because...Did you see the Biblioteca Nacional – the National Library?...which has four "legs," and the auditorium as a kind of belly.When excavation began for its construction, the carapace of a glyptodont was uncovered. Afterwards I realized that if you draw the glyptodont, like this, there is a certain likeness...Then I had the occurrence to say that the glyptodont had been there for years, but, when the animal that soon enough would replace it, appeared, the other one could leave, because its task had been fulfilled.

MC: As we can see, art and architecture are intimately tied in your character...

CT: Of course, but, over here there are many architects that paint. I am not the only one.

WW: No, not so many...

CT: Well, I am more devoted to art. But there are many who paint, and there are also physicians who paint. That is why, I think anyone may perform these activities...

MC: The question would be, what is the relationship between both of them?

CT: I believe all activities are bound together. In Venice, physicians used to use masks with large noses? It was to avoid touching the sick, so that physicians could look and make the diagnostic from a distance, imagining in their minds what the patient might have. In fact, architects have a similar ability. They think beforehand, they know what they are going to do beforehand. They know how to offer solutions...Someone tells you: a hospital. Then, you imagine the hospital in your mind; you do not need to draw it all the time. That is, I think there are some parallelisms and anyone can do a little bit of everything.

WW: Yesterday we spoke about a drawing and I asked you, how do you develop your forms. You said you had all developed in your head, and then you start drawing.

CT: Yes, that is what I was telling you. That is, first one thinks, then one draws.

WW: But what about painting, do you know what you are painting before you start painting?

CT: Yes, more or less.

WW: But only more or less...

CT: More or less, because as you develop your ideas, things change. Because, in the Biblioteca Nacional's case, a competition I made with Francisco Bullrich and Alicia Cazzaniga, his wife, when we started to talk about the project, we thought it was a quadruped, but, afterwards, I think it was Francisco, who said that if the engineer later on would request instead of four, six "legs," changing it from a quadruped to a hexapod, then, the project would have to be changed completely, because six legs would be too much for the Library. Four would be fine.

WW: So, when you spoke about this just now, you are clear about how you want people to read something. This is like an animal for example.

CT: Yes. But, we realized this ten or twenty years afterwards, that in fact this thing here, the glyptodont had something in common with the building. And then you could say that the former had been there waiting many centuries for another animal to arrive and replace it. But, you do not think about this when you are designing the Library, you do not think it should look like an animal...

MC: Is there a similar metaphor for the Banco?

CT: No. With the Banco's project we aimed for a covered space that resembled a public square.

MC: Did you think it so, since the beginning?

CT: Not exactly the way I just described it, but, we did aim for an open space for the public.

MC: And where did this idea come from?

CT: I do not know.

WW: Looking back now, you see different glass technology. The facade used in the Banco has aluminum profiles. Now, but nowadays one can make it of very small pieces and a lighter structure. If you could make it again, would you consider making with a lighter glazing system?

CT: I never think how I would do something today that I did forty years ago, or what did we accomplish. I would do it differently, of course. All that carpentry hangs from above. There are iron tensile rods covered with aluminum. But anyway, when you are at the Banco's interior, it is like the façade has completely vanished, even the heavy, concrete "legs" disappear.

WW: In many ways, what I find very powerful about the Banco is the relationship between its facade and the historicist facades around, and if one thinks about the historicist facades, the origins of classical architecture is also very rational... In the case of the Banco there is are logical supports of piers, you have beams, and then the ornament became very specific, as in the iconography of classical architecture. Your description also begina with a rational idea, gathering the supports below so that you have wider a transparency between inside and outside at street level.

CT: I do not know that we thought about it right at the beginning, but, I think it was there as a seed since the beginning. I

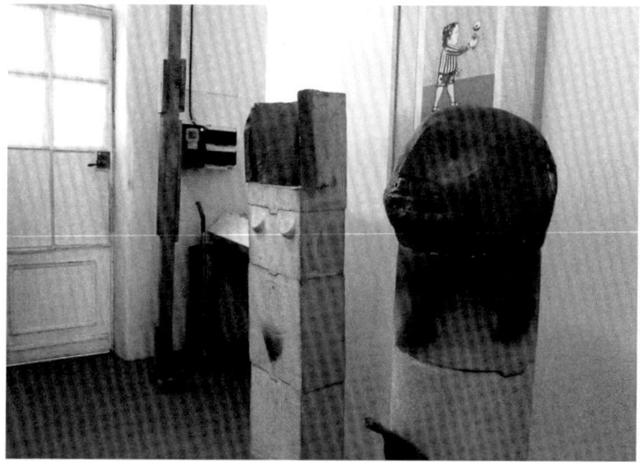

Sculpture collection of Clorindo Tsta

am sure we did not want the space to be enclosed with columns every three meters; hence, we opened it up. Then when you look up, you say: How well does the Banco de la Nación look from over here! You realize that the element defining that space is the building on the other side of the street; don't you think so?

WW: But there is then a very powerful engagement between the two.

CT: Yes.

WW: Based on a rational origin, they then enter into something more figurative, they do not just stay in the rationalistic line of vertical supports and horizontal beams... this would be very typical of the hard functionalist... but they are more sculptural, and they are also more sculptural in the way that classical architecture is more sculptural. It's also more figurative, so there is a difference between the purely rationalist architecture of the time, and something that has more expression.

CT: Yes, of course..

MC: On one hand, there is the rational origin of the façade's elements, and, on the other one, the associations awakened by such elements. Anyone, simply looking at the facades, could say: on one side there is a Neoclassical building and, on the other one, referring to the Banco, there is another one with elements that seem more Neogothic…

CT: Yes, of course… I can tell you that we are not bothered by the presence of the Banco de la Nación in front of our site. We thought it was OK, it was designed by Bustillo. It is a prolific and strong façade. We liked the idea of keeping its presence and letting it be seen, thus becoming the element that encloses the Banco on its opposite end.

MC: What type of architecture or buildings are the Banco's cousins or brothers? Is it a close relative to the Banco de la Nación or to those buildings with glass facades, those with curtain walls, which may be found in the neighborhood, as well?

CT: I think it is closer to the Banco de la Nación than to a glass façade.

WW: When you have a curtain in a window and it is closed it looks like a normal piece of textile. And when you open it and its bundle together it has something of the quality of a Doric column, it is fluted.

CT: Yes, in fact, this drawing I made could be like me pulling and putting the curtains together.

WW: Did you ever come across an architect from the USA called Paul Nelson?

CT: Nelson? No. When did Nelson practice?

WW: He was working in the 30s to 50s... and he made some hospitals and an interesting house. Not built, just a project. And it was called the maison suspendue. It had a steel roof from which galleries were suspended.

CT: No, I did not know him.

WW: You speak about making a public space, on the other hand, because of the monumental character of the exterior one also gets an sense that is this like a protection for the Banco. It's like a cage. like a box. Was this not what you were interested in?

CT: No, we thought it should be like a box on the outside and inside it should be different. That is, it should be independent.

MC: Were all those pieces built on site?

CT: Yes, with exception of the slabs that are suspended from the roof; they measured three by six meters. Those slabs were placed afterwards, on the steel structure.

MC: That means all the suspended slabs were assembled as prefabricated slabs.

CT: And everything underneath was built on site.

MC: The entrance of the building suggests that it used to be closed until someone opened the curtains, letting the blue cabin above be seen.

CT: Of course, that was the director's offices.

WW: So there is this panel there…

CT: Do you mean the one that descends from the upper roof?

WW: Why is it like an angle? Is it to refer to these diagonals of the other buildings across the street?

CT: I do not remember if it is inclined or not. We did it to close the space. When you are above, it is like a screen that takes you toward the corner.

MC: Does it not have something to do with solar protection?

CT: No, not at all...

MC: And does it support the upper area, the director's cabin?

CT: No. It is like a curtain hanging from above. It was designed to close the space. And, at the same time, it helped the structure, as a counter balance.

WW: This building is beyond what you call a rational structure. When one looks at all the elements, even down to details as the seats or the air conditioning pieces, they all have a figure, they all are sculpture, they all are expressive, and this is something which makes the difference between this building and...

CT: ...and other buildings, yes...

WW: ...but you have to think of all those forms, you have to think about what this movements do when the air comes out of there.

CT: Well, that was necessary because we had to separate the openings for the air conditioning.

WW: But it is almost like the shape of a human.

CT: Ah...I had not thought about it like that.

MC: There is a particularly figurative element. The main entrance is like a perforation made to the suspended façade and in many modern buildings it would simply be that: a perforation that is usually closed with a sliding door or something like that. In contrast with such custom, the Banco offers almost a veritable Triumphal Arch.

CT: The idea was something like that: because if you do not do so, any place could be the entrance.

MC: Everything related to visual communication was very well thought, indeed.

CT: Yes! Of course.

Selected Bibliography

Bibliography of SEPRA

Ortiz, Federico, "SEPRA", *Instituto de Arte Americano*, Buenos Aires, 1964.

"La unión hace la fuerza: SEPRA", in *Nuestra Arquitectura*, no. 425, Jun 1965, pp. 22-23.

"General Motors S.A.", in *Summa*, no. 5, Jul 1966, pp. 25-29.

"Kaiser Aluminio S.A.", in *Summa*, no. 5, Jul 1966, pp. 30-33.

"Edificio de departamentos, Austria 2624, Buenos Aires", in *Summa*, no. 16, Apr 1969, pp. 28-31.

"CIAE, Subestación transformadora Melo, Buenos Aires, 1969", in *Summa*, no. 25, May 1970, pp. 42-45.

"Hotel Buenos Aires Sheraton, Avdas. Leandro N. Alem, Eduardo", in *Summa*, no. 35, Mar 1971, pp. 41-45.

"Editorial Atlántida S.A.", in *Summa*, nos. 45-46, Jan-Feb 1972, pp. 21-24.

"SEPRA. últimas realizaciones", in *Summa*, no. 47, Mar 1972, pp. 18-52.

Ortiz, Federico, "SEPRA, retrospectiva 1936-1966" in *Summa +*, no. 47, Mar 1972, pp. 9-24.

"10 años 10 obras", in *Summa*, no. 50, Jun 1972, pp. 51-56.

"Hotel Sheraton", in *Nuestra Arquitectura*, no. 479, 1972, pp. 26-46.

"Edificio Torre Catalinas Norte" in *Construcciones*, no. 251 Jan-Feb 1975, pp. 319-328.

"Planta impresora para Editorial Atlántida" in *Construcciones*, no. 253, May-Jun 1975, pp. 396-408.

"Compania sudamericana BTB SA", in *Summa*, no. 89, May 1975, pp. 51-53.

"Torre Catalinas Norte", in *Summa*, no. 97, Jan 1976, pp. 40-41.

"Edificio para el Hotel Libertador" in *Construcciones*, no. 263, Jan-Feb 1977, pp. 1-10.

"Edificio Diario La Razón" in *Construcciones*, no. 267, Sep-Oct 1977, pp. 1-8.

"Estadio Córdoba", in *Construcciones*, no. 268, Nov-Dec 1977, pp. 1-18.

"Nave de Pescado, Mercado Central", in *Nuestra Arquitectura*, no. 500, 1977, pp. 76-79.

"Hotel de Turismo Internacional", in *Nuestra Arquitectura*, no. 500, 1977, pp. 83-86.

"Hotel Ayuí, Concordia, provincia de Entre Ríos", in *Summa*, no. 123, Apr 1978, pp. 87-88.

"Hotel Libertador Maipú 783, Capital Federal", in *Summa*, no. 123, Apr 1978, pp. 45-52.

"Estadio de Córdoba", in *Summa*, no. 125, Jun 1978, pp. 65-76.

"Edificio para oficinas, Corrientes 409, Capital Federal", in *Summa*, no. 144, Dec 1979, pp. 45-47.

"Mercado Central de Buenos Aires" in *Construcciones*, no. 280, Nov-Dec 1979, pp. 1-8.

"Plan municipal de escuelas", in *Summa*, special no., Feb 1981, pp. 15-32.

"Escuela de Ingeniería Delta, Campana, provincia de Buenos Aires", in *Summa*, special no., Feb 1981, pp. 33-35.

"Edificio Diario La Nación, Bouchard 557, Buenos Aires", in *Summa*, no. 160, Mar 1981, pp. 31-38.

"Plan municipal de 60 escuelas para la ciudad de Buenos Aires" in *Construcciones*, no. 289-290 May-Aug 1981, pp. 2-33.

"Mercado Central de Buenos Aires", in *Summa*, no. 164, Jul 1981, pp. 33-46.

"Banco de la Nación Argentina. Sucursal San Pablo, Brasil. Sucursal San Miguel de Tucumán", in *Summa*, no. 173, Apr 1982, pp. 39-45.

"Hotel Libertador Maipú 783, Capital Federal", in *Summa*, special no., Jul 1982, pp. 47-51.

"Hipermercado Carrefour, Vicente López" in *Construcciones*, no. 305-306, Jan-Apr 1984, pp. 2-20.

"Chase Manhattan Bank" in *Construcciones* No. 305-306 Jan-Apr1984, pp. 47-54.

"Facultad de Ingeniería de la Universidad Católica Argentina", in *Summa*, no. 202, Jul 1984, pp. 61-68.

"Chase Manhattan Bank, Buenos Aires", in *Summa Temática*, no. 3, 1984, pp. 68-69.

"Dos casos de equipamiento de locales bancarios", in *Summa Temática*, no. 1, 1986, pp. 58-61.

"Edificio torre in Avenida de Mayo, Chacabuco y Rivadavia" in *Construcciones*, no. 315, Oct 1987, pp. 23-28.

"Embajada de Brasil. nueva sede de la cancillería", in *Summa*, no. 266-267, Oct-Nov 1989, pp. 76-81.

"Mc Donald's", in *Summa*, no. 268, Dec 1989, pp. 42-45.

"Torre Libertador y Suipacha", in *Summa*, no. 277-278, Sep-Oct 1990, pp. 128-131.

"Hotel Park Hyatt", in *Summa*, no. 282-283, Feb-Mar 1991, pp. 60-70.

Brandariz, Gustavo Andres, "SEPRA. medio siglo de arquitectura", in *Revista de Arquitectura*, no. 155, Nov-Dec 1991, pp. 42-70.

"Lopez, Juan C., Peralta Ramos SEPRA, Robirosa-Beccar Varela-Pasinato, Dique 4 - Docks 1 y 2" in *Arquis*, no. 1, Jan 1994, pp. 36-41.

"Entre la city y el puerto", in *Summa +*, no. 4, Dec 1993-Jan 1994, pp. 84-87.

"Hotel Cesar Park. Posadas 1232" in *Summa +*, no. 5, Feb-Mar 1994, pp. 62-67.

"Invasión inteligente", in *Summa +*, no. 6, Apr-May 1994, pp. 38-39.

"Dos in una", in *Summa +*, no. 6, Apr-May 1994, pp. 40-41.

"Torre Fortabat: Viamonte y Bouchard" in *Summa +*, no. 6, Apr-May 1994, pp. 40-41.

"Torre Bouchard Plaza: Bouchard, Lavalle y Madero" in *Summa +*, no. 6, Apr-May 1994, pp. 38-39.

"Alvarez, Mario; Sanchez Elia SEPRA. Torre Le Parc, Oro y Cerviño" in *Summa +*, no. 6, Apr-May 1994, pp. 26-29.

"Robirosa-Beccar Varela-Pasinato ; Sanchez Elia Sepra ; Lopez, Juan C.Puerto. Viamonte 1 y 2" in *Summa +*, no. 11, Feb-Mar 1995, pp. 24-25.

"Alvarez, Mario ; Sanchez Elia SEPRA. Torre Le Parc. La estructura de hormigón armado más alta del país" in *Casa Nueva*, no. 87, Oct 1995, pp. 32-36.

Corona Martinez, Alfonso, "Torres pensantes: Torres Bouchard y Fortabat" in *Summa +*, no. 16, Dec 1995-Jan 1996, pp. 34-40.

"Peralta Ramos - Sepra; Robirosa-Beccar Varela. Edificio Torre Fortabat" in *Architector*, no. 9, Dec 1996, pp. 12-26.

"El Rosedal reencontrado", in *Summa +*, no. 25, Jun-Jul 1997, pp. 94-97.

"Sanchez Elía - Sepra; Robirosa-Beccar Varela-Pasinato. Barrios: Laguna del Sol y Santa Bárbara, Ruta Panamericana, Camino a Nordelta, Pueblo privado estancias del Pilar, Ramal a Pilar" in *Summa +*, no. 69, Nov 2004, pp. 120-131.

"Centro de Convenciones de la Provincia de Salta" in *Architector*, no. 61, 2009, pp. 10-18.

Banco de Londres y América del Sud

"Sanchez Elia-Peralta Ramos-Agostini. Banco de Londres y América del Sud" in *A & P*, no. 2, 1963, pp. 32-34.

"Sánchez Elía-Peralta Ramos-Agostini ; Testa, Clorindo. La nueva sede del Banco de Londres y América del Sud. Bme. Mitre y Reconquista" in *Construcciones*, no. 191, Jul-Aug 1964, pp. 563-572.

Fox, Arthur; J. "Argentine Architects Produce a Real Winner", in *Engineering News Record*, 11 Aug 1966.

Dufan, Pierre; *Techniques et Architecture*, Paris 1966.

"Testa, Clorindo ; Sanchez Elía-Peralta Ramos-Agostini. Nuevo edificio para la sede central del Banco de Londres y América del Sur" in *Construcciones*, no. 200, Jan-Feb 1966, pp. 52-72.

"Sanchez Elia-Peralta Ramos-Agostini. Edificio para el Banco de Londres y América del Sur, Reconquista y Bartolome Mitre" in *Nuestra Arquitectura*, no. 436, Dec 1966, pp. 31-48.

Bullrich, Francisco; Pando, Horacio; Payssé Reyes, Mario; García Vazquez, Francisco; Mendez Mosquera, Carlos. "Opiniones: Banco de Londres" in *Summa*, no. 6-7, Dec 1966, pp. 49-51.

"Sanchez Elia-Peralta Ramos-Agostini Testa, Clorindo. Banco de Londres y América del Sur" in *Summa*, no. 6-7, Dec 1966, pp. 27-46.

Manser, Michael, "Bank in Buenos Aires: Building an image abroad", in *Design*, no. 254, London 1968, pp. 68-69

"Sanchez Elía-Peralta Ramos-Agostini ; Testa, Clorindo. Banco de Londres y América del Sud, casa central". *GA*, no. 65, Tokyo, 1984.

Pronsato, Graciela; Capelli, Roberto; *Las 7+1 Lámparas de la Arquitectura Argentina*, Ediciones Copro, Buenos Aires, 1993.

Cook, Peter; "Clorindo Testa. bank of London and South America Buenos Aires", in *Architectural Design*, no. 5 Sep 2001, pp. 44-49.

"Testa, Clorindo; Sanchez Elia - Peralta Ramos - Agostini. Banco de Londres" in Clarín - Vanguardias Argentinas. Obras y movimientos in el siglo XX. No. 3: *Arquitectura Contemporánea* I, 2005, pp. 78-89.

"Testa, Clorindo; Sánchez Elia - Peralta Ramos - Agostini. Banco de Londres, Bartolomé Mitre y San Martín" in Gonzalez Montaner, Berto (editor); *Guías de Arquitectura Latinoamericana: Buenos Aires*, 2008, pp. 94-99.

Banco de Londres y América del Sud, other branches

"Spandri, Alfonso. Banco de Londres y América del Sud. Avda. Pueyrredon 127. Agencia Once" in *CACYA*, no. 88, Sep 1934, pp. 119-120.

"Sanchez Elia-Peralta Ramos-Agostini ; Testa, Clorindo. Banco de Londres y América del Sur, Santa Fe y Junín" in *Nuestra Arquitectura*, no. 418,, Sep 1964, pp. 32 y 53-55.

"Caffarini, Luis. Banco de Londres y América del Sur, Sucursales: Hipólito Yrigoyen 1000 y Cabildo 1939" in *Nuestra Arquitectura*, no. 418, Sep 1964, pp. 48-52.

"Sanchez Elia-Peralta Ramos-Agostini. Banco de Londres y América del Sur, Santa Fe y Junín", in *Nuestra Arquitectura*, no. 426, Jul 1965, p. 26-29.

"Sanchez Elia-Peralta Ramos-Agostini. Banco de Londres y América del Sur", sucursal Constitución. *Summa*, no. 12, Jul 1968, pp. 62-63.

"Sanchez Elia-Peralta Ramos-Agosti. Banco de Londres in Constitución, Bernardo de Irigoyen 1240" in *Nuestra Arquitectura*, no. 453, Sep 1968, p. 36.

"Larumbe-Rault. Banco de Londres, Avda. Independencia esq. Avda. Luro, Mar del Plata" in *Summa*, no. 33-34, Jan-Feb 1971, p. 51.

"Sanchez Elia-Peralta Ramos-Agostini. Banco de Londres y América del Sud. Sucursal Rosario" in *Construcciones*, no. 242, Jul-Aug 1973, pp. 129-138.

Clorindo Testa

Testa, Clorindo; Arquitectura, pintura y otras cosas. *Catálogo de la Exposición*. Fundación Banco Patricios, 6-30 Nov 1966.

Katzenstein, Ernesto ; Testa, Clorindo ; Lacarra, Hector ; Lanari, Luis ; Sivori, Jose ; Sprovieri, Eduardo ; Valera, Jose ; Aroma, Eduardo ; Viñoly, Rafael. "Mesa redonda. Catalinas Norte pro y contra" in *Summa*, no. 97, Jan 1976, pp. 48-57.

Testa, Clorindo; Quaglia, Carlos; Guth, Erik. "Diagnóstico y pronóstico sobre arquitectura hospitalaria. Mesa Redonda" in *Summa*, no. 107, Dec 1976, pp. 22-26.

CAYC Group; Bedel, Jacques ; Benedit, Luis ; González Mir, Jorge ; Grippo, Victor ; Maler, Leopoldo ; Marotta, Vicente ; Pazos, Luis ; Portillos, Alfredo ; Testa, Clorindo ; Glusberg, Jorge. The Group of the Thirteen at the XIV Bienal de São Paulo, Oct 1977. Buenos Aires : *Cayc*, 1977.

"Ampliación y remodelación del Plaza Hotel de Buenos Aires" in *Construcciones*, no. 268, Nov-Dec 1977, pp. 18-20.

"Edificio Rodríguez Peña 2043, Capital Federal" in *Summa*, no. 131, Dec 1978, pp. 43-49.

Borghini, Sandro ; Minond, Edgardo ; Carriquiry, Jorge ; Hilger, Carlos ; Durmüller, Teresa ; Soler,Oscar ; Frangella, Roberto ; Testa, Clorindo ; Ramos, Carlos ; Petrina, Alberto ; Rosso, Ricardo ; Camdessus, Hugo ; Schere, Rolando ; Fervenza, Juan ; Antonini, Antonio ; Sorondo, Rodolfo ; Sbarra, Alberto ; Delgado Oro, Gustavo. "Perspectivas de arquitectos: algunos ejemplos argentinos" in *Summa*, no. 132, Jan 1979, pp. 41-56.

"Country club" in *Nuestra Arquitectura*, no. 516, 1981, pp. 16-17.

CAYC Group; Bedel, Jacques ; Benedit, Luis ; Glusberg, Jorge ; Gonzalez Mir, Jorge ; Grippo, Victor ; Maler, Leopoldo ; Marotta, Vicente ; Portillos, Alfredo ; Testa, Clorindo. CAYC Group at the Musée Cantonal des Beaux Arts. Buenos Aires : *Cayc*, 1981.

"Testa, Clorindo. Formación del arquitecto" in *Dos Puntos*, no. 4, Mar-Apr 1982, pp. 86-87.

"Restauración in Montserrat. Vivienda de y para Jacques Bedel", in *Dos Puntos*, no. 6, Sep 1982, pp. 47-48.

"Casa in Belgrano, Buenos Aires" in *Summa Tematica*, no. 4, 1983, pp. 28-33.

"Como proyecta y construye Clorindo Testa" in *Trama*, no. 9, 1984, pp. 6-13.

"Conjunto de edificios in Barrio Parque, Buenos Aires" in *Summa Tematica*, no. 4, 1985, pp. 32-34.

"Casa Capotesta, Pinamar" in *Summa Tematica*, no. 28, Nov-Dec 1988, pp. 34-41.

Cook, Peter; "Clorindo Testa", in *World Architecture*, no. 5, 1990, pp. 36-39.

Dagnino, Tomas; "Once upon a time in America..." in *World Architecture*, no. 5, 1990, pp. 51-53.

Glusberg, Jorge; "Where ideas become concrete", in *World Architecture*, no. 5, 1990, pp. 40-50.

Antonini, Antonio ; Lebrero, Carlos ; Schere, Rolando ; Solsona, Justo ; Testa, Clorindo ; Varas, Alberto. "La arquitectura de la Década del '80" in *Revista de Arquitectura*, no. 151, Mar-Apr 1991, pp. 42-63.

Alvarez, Mario ; Díaz, José I. ; Manteola-Sánchez Gómez-Santos-Solsona ; Pelli, César ; Testa, Clorindo ; Antonini-Schon-Zemborain ; Aslan-Ezcurra ; Gramatica-Guerrero-Morini-Pisani ; Viñoly, Rafael ; Roca, Miguel. "Premio Konex de Platino quinquenio 1987-1991 y Premio Konex 1992" in *Revista de Arquitectura*, no. 162, Jan-Feb 1993, pp. 70-76.

Moscato, Jorge. "Clorindo Testa y los mecanismos de la creación" in *Elarqa*, no. 9, Dec 1993, pp. 16-19.

"Concurso Sociedad Hebraica Argentina" in *Revista de Arquitectura SCA*, no. 170, May-Jun 1994, pp. 15-64.

Irace, Fulvio. "Clorindo Testa" in *Abitare*, no. 342, Jul-Aug 1995, pp. 112-119.

Acosta, Wladimiro ; Alvarez, Mario ; Testa, Clorindo ; Diaz, Jose I. ; Manteola-Sanchez Gomez-Santos-Solsona ; Gramatica-Guerrero-Morini-Pisani-Urtubey ; Antonini-Fervenza-Hall-Schon-Zemborain ; Aslan-Ezcurra ; Urgell-Fazio ; Baudizzone-Lestard-Varas ; Lier-Tonconogy ; Roca, Miguel ; Benadon-Berdichevsky-Cherny ; Robirosa-Beccar Varela-Pasinato ; Lopez, Juan C. "Colección y Hallazgos. Dibujos de arquitectos" in *Arquis*, no. 7, Oct 1995, pp. 10-23.

"Conversaciones in el 2: Clorindo Testa" in *Rd2*, no. 27, 1995, pp. 35-38.

"Clorindo Testa. Arquitectura, pintura y otras cosas" Catálogo de la Exposición Nov de 1996. Buenos Aires : Fundación Banco Patricios, 1996.

Testa, Clorindo. "Un colectivo para todos" in *Arquis*, no. 8, Mar 1996, pp. 94-95.

Doval, Pablo; "Un Pato decorado o la apasionada búsqueda de la libertad", in *Summa +*, no. 21, Oct-Nov 1996, pp. 42-51.

Chandler, Miriam ; Iribarne, Jorge. "Reportaje a Clorindo Testa" in *Revista de Arquitectura*, no. 183, Nov-Dec 1996, pp. 44-59.

Fernandez, Roberto; "Teatro de la arquitectura" in *Summa +*, no. 28, Dec 1997-Jan 1998, p. 152.

Alvarez, Mario; Dujovne, Berardo; Lier, Raúl; Miani, Rodolfo; Solsona, Justo; Testa, Clorindo; Keselman, Jul; "7 opiniones expertas. Patrimonio: ¿propiedad de los preservacionistas?" in *Revista de Arquitectura*, no. 189, Jul 1998, pp. 8-21.

Dias Comas, Carlos. "Memorandum latinoamericano: la ejemplaridad arquitectónica de la marginal" in *2G*, no. 8: Arquitectura Latinoamericana, 1998, pp. 130-143.

Glusberg, Jorge; "Dibujos de arquitectos: La ciudad y su gente. Colección Alfa Romeo" in *Summa +*, no. 33, Oct-Nov 1998, pp. 102-109.

Massad, Fredy; Yeste, Alicia; "La arquitectura de Clorindo Testa", in *Experimenta*, no. 23, Nov 1998, pp. 50-56.

De Brea, Ana; Dagnino, Tomás, "Señores arquitectos... diálogos con Mario Roberto Álvarez y Clorindo Testa, Ed. *UBROC*, Buenos Aires, 1999.

Glusberg, Jorge; "Clorindo Testa" in *Interni*, no. 493, Sep 1999, pp. 72-73.

Barbero Sarzábal, Hernán; Castiglione, Sergio; "Con el debido respeto", in *Summa +*, no. 39, Oct-Nov 1999, pp. 110-115.

Testa, Clorindo. "El hombrecito del monobloque" in *Revista de Arquitectura*, no. 195, Dec 1999, pp. 40-41.

"Originalidad y profesionalismo. nuevo anexo del Colegio de Escribanos de la Capital Federal" *Arquinauta*, no. 2, Dec 1999, pp. 6-13.

"Clorindo Testa" in *Arquinauta*, no. 3, Feb 2000, pp. 34-39.

"Entrevista exclusiva a Clorindo Testa", in *Moradas*, no. 1, Apr-Jun 2000, pp. 16-21.

Corona Martínez, Alfonso; "Lugar de testimonios", in *Summa +*, no. 42, Apr-May, 2000, pp. 66-77.

"Premio Architector 1999-2000 Entrevistas a los ganadores" in *Architector*, no. 29, May 2000, pp. 8-42.

"Obra. Sede complementaria del Colegio de Escribanos de la Capital" in *Architector*, no. 34, Apr 2001, pp. 20-24.

Ravera, Rosa; Testa, Clorindo. "Conversaciones" in *Temas de la Academia, El sentido de la arquitectura*, 2002, pp. 169-177.

Liernur, Jorge Francisco; "La arquitectura in la Argentina, la modernidad y los mejores", in *rd2*, no. 47, Sep 2002, pp. 36-45.

Pampinella, Silvia; "Clorindo Testa in el Centro Cultural Recoleta. Coleccionismo infantil, o in el juego del orden", in *47 al Fondo*, no. 11, Jul 2003, pp. 28-32.

"Un encuentro con Clorindo Testa", in *47 al Fondo*, no. 11, Jul 2003, pp. 24-27.

Dellepiane, Sol; "Al estilo de Clorindo Testa" in *D&D*, no. 77, Sep 2003.

"Ciudad Cultural Konex. concurso nacional e internacional de idea y anteproyecto", in *47 al Fondo*, no. 10, Nov 2003, pp. 84-87.

Di Costa, Gustavo Daniel; "Ciudad Cultural Konex" in *Habitat*, no. 43, Jan 2004, pp. 24-28.

Jmelnitky, Ricardo; Arteca, Raúl; Pampinella, Silvia. "Un encuentro con Clorindo Testa in El Centro Cultural Recoleta. Coleccionismo infantil o el juego del orden" in *47 al Fondo*, no. 11, Jul 2004, pp. 24-32.

Garello, Mercedes; "CCEBA. cambio de imagen", in *90+10*, no. 1, Nov-Dec, 2004, pp. 32-33.

Liernur, Francisco; Aliata, Fernando; Biografías. - *Diccionario de Arquitectura in La Argentina*, vol. S-Z, Clarin Arquitectura, 2004, pp. 45-49, 108-114.

2 Bibliotecas, Clorindo Testa + OMA. 12 comentarios", in *Quaderns*, no. 244, Dec 2004, pp. 80-105.

"Ciudad Di Tella" in *Summa +*, no. 72, Apr 2005, pp. 76-81.

"Mesa redonda: Arquitectura de calidad in un contexto sustentable" in *Architector*, no. 41, 2005, pp. 6-20.

"Entrevista: Clorindo Testa" in *Architector*, no. 41, 2005, pp. 50-52.

Gonzalez Montaner, Berto (editor); *Vanguardias Argentinas. Obras y movimientos in el siglo XX.* 2005, no. 3: Arquitectura contemporánea I, pp. 102-113, 150-155.

Gonzalez Montaner, Berto (editor); *Vanguardias Argentinas. Obras y movimientos in el Siglo XX.* 2005, no. 5: Arquitectura reciente, pp. 30-33, 38-47, 148-155.

Diez, Fernando. "Vivir in una Testa" in *Barzón*, no. 7, Oct 2008, pp. 111-141.

Casanegra, Mercedes, "El humorista rebelde. Clorinda Testa" in *Barzón*, no. 7, Oct 2008, pp. 216-227.

"Testa, Clorindo; Bullrich, Francisco. Museo del Libro, Las Heras y Austria" in *Entreplanos*, no. 16, Nov-Dec 2008, pp. 12-15.

"Entrevista: Clorindo Testa. 60 años de arquitectura y plástica" in *Rd2*, no. 62, 2008, pp. 40-48.

Liernur, Francisco, Arquitectura in *La Argentina del siglo XX*. La construcción de la modernidad. Fondo Nacional de las Artes, Buenos Aires, 2008.

"Concurso nacional de anteproyectos para el frente ribereño de San Fernando y sus accesos inmediatos" in *Rd2*, no. 62, 2008, pp. 50-54.

Schere, Rolando H.; "10 concursos argentinos. propuestas de renovación", in *Summa +*, no. 100, Apr 2009, pp. 64-77.

"Fuentes, Oscar; Mele, Jorge S.; Fontana, Juan; Blanco, Ricardo; Clorindo Testa, *Hitos Urbanos*, Revista 1:100, no. 26, May 2010.

Project Credits and Chronology

Location:
Calle Reconquista 101, corner of Reconquista and Bartolomé Mitre, in the financial district of barrio de San Nicolás, Buenos Aires, Argentina
Length of the site on Reconquista: 75 m
Length of the site on Bartolomé Mitre: 45 m

Architectural Competition
Organizer of the competition and client: Banco de Londres y América del Sud, represented by Gerald W. Wakeham, architect, RIBA
Duration: January until the end of May 1960
Brief: Offices and banking hall for 1,500 employees, providing about 7 m^2 per employee

Construction
Demolition of former branch building: May 1961
Start of construction: 15 December 1962
Construction workers on site: average 600 to 700
Completion of construction: October 1966
Total area: 26 300 m^2

Credits
Architecture and project management: Sánchez Elía, Peralta Ramos y Agostini, arquitectos und Clorindo Testa, arquitecto
Structural engineers for the reinforced concrete frame: Ingenieros Consultores Fernández Long y Reggini
General contractor: Crivelli, Cuenya y Goicoa Construcciones S.A.I.C.F. e I.

Subcontractors
Demolition and excvation works: Agromartin, De Leo y Franchini
Scaffolding: Acrow Argentina S.A,
Paintwork: Alba S.A.
Safes: Bash S.A.
Floor finishes: Bozzi Hnos. S.A.
Marble: Carlos Campolonghi S.A.
HVAC: Carrier Lix Klett S.A.
Structure of the suspended floors: Compañía Británica de Construcciones de Acero Ltda.
Metal furniture: D'Alvia e Hijos
Suspended aluminum ceiling: Demayo Lonardi S.A.
Paint: Elaston S.A.I.C.
Glass: Er-po S.R.L., Panza Hnos. S.A.I.C.
Computers: English Electric S.R.L.
Telephones: Ericsson S.A.C.I.
Wall cladding: Glasiris S.A.
Furniture: Grupo Charcas S.R.L.
Cement: Loma Negra Argentina S.A.
Carpentry: Nordiska Kompaniet S.A.
Aluminum roof und sealants: Nutria
Elevators and escalators: Otis Elevator Co.
Electrical equipment and installations: Onecor S.R.L.
Substructure and framework: Sebastián Maronese e Hijos S.A.

Conversion
On the occasion of the change in ownership 1997-1999 to Banco Hipotecario
Architects: Clorindo Testa, Arquitecto, and Equipo de Arquitectura del Banco Hipotecario S.A.

Renovation
Restoration and color scheme in 2008-20010
Architects: Clorindo Testa as architect in charge and Equipo de Arquitectura del Banco Hipotecario S.A.

Biographies

SEPRA

SEPRA is an Argentinean architectural office founded in 1936 in Buenos Aires by Santiago Sánchez Elía, Federico Peralta Ramos y Alfredo Agostini. In this constellation it projected some of the most important buildings in Argentina until 1972, when Alfredo Agostini died; after the death of Santiago Sánchez Elía in 1976 and Federico Peralta Ramos in 1991 their sons continued their work. Among the most important buildings by SEPRA in Buenos Aires are the headquarters of the newspaper La Nación from 1955-1980, the República building of the Empresa Nacional de Telecomunicaciones ENTel finished in 1964, the Victoria building in front of the Plaza de Mayo from 1960, the Hotel Sheraton from 1968-1972; in 1961 SEPRA built the new Town Hall of the city of Córdoba. The most prominent work of the office was the headquarter of the Banco de Londres y América del Sud in Buenos Aires planned together with Clorindo Testa.

Santiago Sánchez Elía

The architect Santiago Sánchez Elía was born in Buenos Aires in 1911. He studied at the Escuela de Arquitectura of the Universidad de Buenos Aires, making his diploma in 1935. In 1936 he founded SEPRA together with Federico Peralta Ramos and Alfredo Agostini. Santiago Sánchez Elía died in 1976.

Federico Peralta Ramos

The architect Federico Peralta Ramos was born in Buenos Aires in 1914. He studied at the Escuela de Arquitectura of the Universidad de Buenos Aires. Immediately after graduating in 1936 he founded SEPRA together with Santiago Sánchez Elía and Alfredo Agostini. Federico Peralta Ramos died in 1991.

Alfredo Agostini

The architect Alfredo Agostini was born in Buenos Aires in 1908. He studied at the Escuela de Arquitectura of the Universidad de Buenos Aires. Immediately after graduating in 1936 he founded SEPRA together with Santiago Sánchez Elía and Federico Peralta Ramos. Alfredo Agostini died in 1972.

Clorindo Testa

Clorindo Manuel José Testa was born in Naples in 1923. He studied at the *Escuela de Arquitectura of the Universidad de Buenos Aires.* After graduating in 1948, he travelled through Italy, France and Spain. Back in 1951 he started a double career as architect and artist.

As an architect, his first work was the *Cámara Argentina de la Construcción* in Buenos Aires (with B. Dabinovic, A. Gaido and F. Rossi), followed by the *Centro Cívico de Santa Rosa de La Pampa.* The first work of international relevance was the *Banco de Londres y América del Sud planned with SEPRA.* In the next decades he realized the *Biblioteca Nacional* developed (with F. Bullrich and A. Cazzaniga), the *Hospital Naval Central de Buenos Aires* and the *Centro Cultural Recoleta* in Buenos Aires (with J. Bedel and L. Benedit), as well as the Guido Di Tella residence in Buenos Aires and the beach houses "Capotesta" in Pinamar and "La Tumbona" in Ostende.

As a painter, the first exhibition from 1952 was followed by many others on thematic series as "Habitar, Circular, Trabajar" or "La peste en Ceppaloni" from the 1970s, "Autorretratos" from the 1980s, and "El cerro de Potosí y las mulas del General Belgrano" and "La fiebre amarilla en Buenos Aires, 1871" from the 1990s.

Manuel Cuadra

Manuel Cuadra is professor for the History of Architecture / History of the Build Environment at the School of Architecture, Town Planning and Landscape Planning at the Universität Kassel.

Born in 1952, Cuadra studied architecture at the Universidad Nacional de Ingeniería in Lima and doctorate at the Technische Universität Darmstadt. His research work with Günter Behnisch in Darmstadt centered on the constructive fundaments of architectural design, teaching at the Städelschule in Frankfurt with Enric Miralles on the avant-garde tendencies of the moment. Other stages were the Kunsthistorisches Institut of the Universität Heidelberg and the schools of architecture of the Universidad de Belgrano in Buenos Aires and the Universidad de Talca (Chile).

The publications by Cuadra present and discuss architecture in an historical and cultural, urban and landscape context. Acknowledging his academic and critical work, as an author and curator, Manuel Cuadra was elected honorary member of the Bund Deutscher Architekten BDA and member of the International Committee of Architectural Critics CICA; since 2005 he is a member of the directors board of CICA, since 2008 its secretary general. Since 2005 he is a director of the "experimenta urbana" – formerly "documenta urbana" – in Kassel. In 2011 the Universidad Nacional de Ingeniería in Lima conferred upon him the title Doctor Honoris causa.

Jorge Francisco Liernur

Born in Buenos Aires (1946), Jorge Francisco Liernur graduated as an architect from the University of Buenos Aires, with postgraduate studies on art and architecture history with Manfredo Tafuri (Istituto Universitario di Architettura di Venezia) and Tillman Buddensieg (Kunsthistorisches Institut, Philosophische Fakultät, Universität Bonn).

He is currently Chairman of the Center of Studies on Contemporary Architecture at the Torcuato Di Tella University in Buenos Aires, and Researcher of the Argentine National Council for Research on Science and Technology. At the University of Buenos Aires he was director of the Instituto de Arte Americano e Investigaciones Estéticas, and founder and director of the "Juan O`Gorman" Latin-American Architecture Chair. He acted as visiting scholar and critic at several Universities in America and Europe inlcuding Harvard, Princeton, SCI Arc, Columbia New York, Navarra, Sevilla, Barcelona, Catholic University, Universidad Mayor (Chile), La Sapienza, Politecnico di Torino.

He is the author and editor of numerous books (*Architecture in XXth Century Argentina*, *Writings on XXth Century Architecture in Latin America*, *Architecture in Latin America, 1965–*

1985, The Threshold of the Metropolis, The Shadow of the Avant-Garde. Hannes Meyer in Mexico, etc.) and articles on modern architecture in Latin America and Argentina, published in journals in the Americas, Europe and Asia.

Wilfried Wang

Wilfried Wang is the O'Neil Ford Centennial Professor in Architecture at The University of Texas at Austin. Together with Barbara Hoidn, he is founder of the office of Hoidn Wang Partner, Berlin.

Wang studied architecture in London, where he was in partnership with John Southall. In 1979 he was founding co-editor of 9H magazine and co-director of the 9H Gallery from 1985 to 1990. From 1995 to 2000 he was the director of the German Architecture Museum.

He taught at the Polytechnic of North London, University College London, ETH Zurich, Harvard University and the University of Navarra.

Wang is the author and editor of various architectural publications. He has served on competition and award juries, is the chairman of the Schelling Architecture Foundation and a member of the design review board of Munich Airport. He is an honorary member of the Federation of German Architects and a foreign member of the Royal Swedish Academy of Arts. He holds an honorary doctorate from the Royal Institute of Technology, Stockholm and is a member of the Academy of the Arts Berlin.

Photo Credits

Cover: Wilfried Wang

Construcciones: pages 197 (right), 199 (right), 203 (right), 206, 224

Manuel Cuadra: pages 228, 230, 233, 234, 235, 236, 237, 280, 281

Carolina Kogan: pages 232

Banco Hipetecario Nacional: pages 216, 217, 219, 220, 223, 225

El Croquis: page 23

Nuestra Architecture: page 271

Gustavo Sosa Pinilla: pages 195, 202, 203 (left), 204, 206 (right), 211, 213, 217

Studio of Testa: pages 194, 196, 197 (left), 198, 199 (left), 200 (right), 201, 207, 209, 210, 212, 215, 218

Summa: pages 208 (left), 214

Wilfried Wang: pages 182, 185, 186, 187, 188, 189, 190, 191, 192, 193, 200 (left)